LONDON RECORD SOCIETY
PUBLICATIONS

VOLUME XXVI
FOR THE YEAR 1989

LONDON VIEWERS AND THEIR CERTIFICATES, 1508–1558

CERTIFICATES OF THE SWORN
VIEWERS OF THE CITY OF LONDON

EDITED BY
JANET SENDEROWITZ LOENGARD

LONDON RECORD SOCIETY
1989

The publication of this volume has been made possible by a grant from
the Corporation of London.

Phototypeset by
Wyvern Typesetting Ltd, Bristol
Printed and bound in Great Britain
at The Bath Press

CONTENTS

ACKNOWLEDGEMENTS

I have had help from so many people and institutions that I am reluctant to list them for fear of omitting someone who should not be omitted. While doing the research for this volume, I was fortunate to have been awarded, at different times, a Summer Stipend from the National Endowment for the Humanities and a grant from the Penrose Fund of the American Philosophical Society; I owe thanks to both organizations. I am especially grateful to the past and present staff of the Corporation of London Records Office: Miss Betty Masters, Mr. James R. Sewell, Miss Anne Sutton, Mrs. Juliet Bankes, Mr. Piers Cain, and Mrs. Vivienne Aldous; and Mr. James Pegram, who wheeled so many trollies of volumes and files to my reading table. I am indebted to the Mercers' Company and the Drapers' Company for their permission to print excerpts from their unpublished records and to the clerks and archivists of a number of livery companies, especially to Mr. Robert Brown, education officer of the Drapers' Company, Miss Jean Imray, the former archivist of the Mercers' Company, and Miss Sutton, the present archivist. The clerks and other personnel of the Skinners', Clothworkers', and Goldsmiths' Companies were also very helpful and I am grateful to them and to their Companies for allowing me to look at their records. Dr. Caroline Barron's notes on the early Journals cleared a path through unindexed records. Dr. Martha Carlin's reading of an early draft of the indexes caught several errors and pointed out omissions. Obviously, all remaining errors are entirely my own. The late Mr. A. R. B. Fuller, librarian of St. Paul's Cathedral, and Canon Philip Buckler, of the Minor Canons of the Cathedral, were generous with their time in allowing me to go through the records in their care. Special thanks are owing to Mr. William Kellaway, the general editor of the London Record Society from 1964 to 1983, who not only suggested this project but who answered questions and offered help throughout its slow path to completion. Finally, I owe a great many thanks to my daughter, Maranda, to whom this volume is dedicated, for her encouragement and for hours she spent in helping me read and reread, check and recheck, certificates and indexes.

ABBREVIATIONS

Beaven	Rev. A. B. Beaven, *The Aldermen of the City of London, temp Henry III – 1908* (1908), vol. 1
CLBA-L	*Calendar of Letter-Books of the City of London, A–L*, c. *1275–1497*, ed. R. R. Sharpe, 11 vols. (1899–1912)
Cal. P & M Rolls	*Calendar of Plea and Memoranda Rolls preserved at Guildhall, 1323–1437*, ed. A. H. Thomas; *1437–82*, ed. P. E. Jones, 6 vols. (1926–61)
Carpenters' Records	*Records of the Worshipful Company of Carpenters*, transcr. and ed. B. Marsh, 7 vols. (1913–68)
CLRO	Corporation of London Records Office
Ekwall	E. Ekwall, *Street-names of the City of London* (1954)
GL	Guildhall Library
Harben	H. A. Harben, *A Dictionary of London* (1918)
Journals	Journals of the Court of Common Council, CLRO
Keene and Harding	D. Keene and V. Harding, *Survey of documentary sources for property holding in London before the Great Fire* (LRS 22, 1985)
Knowles	D. Knowles, *The religious houses of medieval England* (1940)
Knowles and Hadcock	D. Knowles and R. N. Hadcock, *Medieval religious houses in England and Wales* (1953, repr. 1971)
LBA (–ZZ)	Letter-Book A (to ZZ), CLRO
Liber Albus	*Liber Albus: the White Book of the City of London*, ed. and trans. H. T. Riley (1861)
Liber Custumarum	*Liber Custumarum* in *Munimenta Gildhallae Londoniensis*, ed. H. T. Riley, 3 vols. in 4 (Rolls Series 12, 1859–62)
Liber de Antiquis Legibus	*De Antiquis Legibus Liber*, ed. T. Stapleton (Camden Society vol. 34, 1846)
LRS	London Record Society

Mercers' Company Acts of Court, 1453–1527	*Acts of Court of the Mercers' Company, 1453–1527*, ed. L. Lyell with F. D. Watney (1936)
Nuisance	*London Assize of Nuisance, 1301–1431*, ed. H. M. Chew and W. Kellaway (LRS 10, 1973)
Rep/s	Repertory/ies of the Court of Aldermen, CLRO
Stow, *Survey*	John Stow, *A Survey of London* (1603; ed. C. L. Kingsford, 2 vols., 1908, repr. 1971)

INTRODUCTION*

I.

Sixteenth-century London was busy, proud, prosperous, and – above all – expanding. But even a constant expansion in area could not match an ever growing population; London was also congested, noisy, and dirty. The certificates here calendared offer detailed, even official, evidence of the physical difficulties inherent in the cheek-by-jowl existence of Tudor Londoners. Many of the disputes which involved the viewers would be familiar to a modern city dweller: one man has built beyond his property line, another's chimney is about to fall down onto his neighbour's roof, a third has made a new house so close to one already standing that all access to light and air has been cut off to the old one, a fourth has directed the rainwater from his gutter onto the property next door. Other quarrels, of course, would not be so familiar because they arose from deplorable sanitary conditions long since improved, from a sudden influx of former church property into the real estate market, and from lingering medieval ideas of propriety – ideals which became more and more anachronistic as population swelled and subdivision of tenements became the norm.

For almost five hundred years, the City of London appointed master masons and carpenters, in the 16th century joined by tilers, to act in connection with these disputes; from the beginning, these men visited a site with or without other officials, examined the alleged encroachment or nuisance, and reported their findings back to the mayor and aldermen. The system was almost as old as the Mayoralty and was closely related to it.[1] The Assize of Buildings ascribed to Mayor Henry Fitz Ailwin and traditionally if improbably dated to 1189, included provisions for arranging the peaceful settlement of neighbours' quarrels. Certainly the text as it exists in later redactions speaks of many of the problems with which the 16th-century viewers would deal: noisome privies, spouting gutters, unprivileged windows. The dating of the Assize of Buildings and an evaluation of the authenticity of various texts have been dealt with extensively and authoritatively by William Kellaway and Helena M. Chew in their introduction to *London Assize of Nuisance 1301–1431*[2] and need not be discussed here. Suffice it to say that at least in part the Assize appears to date from the 13th century; that it is the basis for the medieval London assize of nuisance and to some extent for 16th-century legal treatment of nuisance in London; that it prescribes a view by the mayor

---

* The records of the Mercers', Drapers', Merchant Taylors', and Clothworkers' Companies are at their respective halls. All other manuscripts cited are in the Corporation of London Records Office unless otherwise stated.

1. The men do not seem to have been called 'viewers' until the second half of the fifteenth century. Early references are simply to sworn masons and carpenters, or to masters elected and sworn to perform specified acts set out in their oath; see for example *CLBG*, p. 267. An entry in the Journal for 1454 uses the term (Journal 5, f. 217 [new pagination]): 'Iste die Edwardus Stone & Johis Wise, carpenters, per dictos Maior & aldros elec' sunt lez viewers pro nocumentis amovend' in Civitate . . .' See p. xxii below.

2. LRS vol. 10 (1973), hereafter cited as *Nuisance*.

xi

and 12 elected men of land and tenements for which the assize of nuisance had been demanded; and, more specifically, that it deals with party and boundary walls, gutters, windows overlooking a neighbour's land, and cess-pits constructed after 1189 about which complaint had been made. The 12 elected men are not defined as aldermen in the earliest recension of the Assize of Buildings, that in the Liber de Antiquis Legibus,[3] but they are in later texts and it is likely that aldermen were meant. There is no reason to believe that the 12 were connected with the building trades, nor are sworn masons and carpenters mentioned in early texts: the Assize, the early 13th century Lex de Assisa which lists ten men – at least some of them known to be aldermen – as jurors 'for the assize of stone walls', and the contemporary regulations (drawn up for the better prevention of fire after a disastrous blaze in 1212) which call for a view of wooden houses by the mayor, sheriffs, and 'discreet men' of the City.[4] Yet there were problems in leaving the views to the aldermen. Not all 12 had to appear at a given assize and apparently it was common for six or even fewer to be present at one.[5] But even so, given the number and variety of situations which could arise, viewing must have been time-consuming work. More importantly, the aldermen were not particularly expert in the construction of cesspits and the condition of walls; how should they measure the depth of arches in a party wall or calculate the proper direction of a gutter? It is not surprising that sworn masons and carpenters, whose training and livelihood involved just such measuring and calculating, seem to have been associated with the assize of nuisance from at least the beginning of the 14th century and possibly as early as 1271.[6] None are mentioned in the City records, however, before a Liber Custumarum entry for the Monday before the Conversion of St. Paul, 29 Edward I (24 January 1301) noting that Richard de Wythe, mason, came before the mayor and aldermen and swore to give proper consideration to all men of the city and suburbs of London concerning ruinous, partible, and non-partible stone walls between neighbours and touching the other things pertaining to his office, as often as required to do so. On the same day Robert Osekyn and John de Britele, carpenters, were sworn in similar language to deal justly concerning boundary walls, ruined and partible walls, gutters, and other things touching their office.[7] Wythe and Osekyn were still acting as viewers almost three years later, when they found a stone wall likely to become ruinous, and they were joined by Reginald de Swafham, carpenter, sworn into office on 13 January 1310 'to do all things pertaining to assizes and divisions of tenements'.[8] But in

3. See the Appendix to the *Liber de Antiquis Legibus*, pp. 206–11.
4. The Lex de Assisa is printed in M. Weinbaum, *London unter Edward I und II* (Stuttgart, 1933), ii, 46–8. The regulations are in *Liber Custumarum*, i, 86–8.
5. *Nuisance*, p. xiii.
6. C. J. Eltringham suggests, without citation of sources, that the office dates to an action taken in 1271, during the mayoralty of Walter Hervey; see GL Fo. Pam. 281, p. 1, a brief abstract of his thesis 'Building Control and the Carpenters' Company of London, 1588–1600' (1954). His comment is quoted by B. W. Alford and T. C. Barker, *A History of the Carpenters Company* (1968), p. 13.
7. *Liber Custumarum*, i, 100. *CLBC*, p. 86, also records the appointment of the men, under the dates 25 January and 2 February 1301.
8. Misc. Roll DD, mem. 5, calendared *Nuisance*, 53; *CLBD*, p. 14.

Introduction

August of 1313, three men previously unmentioned – Robert Nor-
thampton, carpenter, and Simon de Pakenham and Alexander de Canterbury, masons, said to be 'sworn to make and supervise assizes and
partitions of tenements in the City' – went with the chamberlain to
partition a tenement.[9] Thereafter appointments appear periodically in
the records, as do references to the viewers' work and, occasionally,
copies of their reports; the City's Letter-Books, the Plea and Memoranda
Rolls, the Journals, and the three Miscellaneous Rolls DD, FF, and II,
record the selection and activities of the sworn masons and carpenters
throughout the 14th and 15th centuries.

Nor did the existence of sworn viewers end with the certificates here
calendared. Apart from copies of later reports found in livery company
records, there exist in the Corporation of London Records Office
originals and copies of later bills, among them a series (in poor condition)
for the period 1623–1636.[10] From these, it appears that the nature of the
viewers' activities remained largely unchanged from what it had been in
the earlier half of the 16th century, although it is hard to judge how
successfully the sworn masons and carpenters functioned or how useful
their efforts were; London was booming and four men, even if diligent
and experienced, could do only so much.[11] There is indeed some hint of
decline in the office. Either Stuart viewers were operating under a
narrowed mandate and greater supervision or they had lost the self-
confidence of their predecessors, for their certificates are more deferen-
tial in tone and show little willingness to venture beyond technical
comments based on professional expertise. But the Great Fire of 1666
was the event precipitating major change. There had been a proclamation
of 13 September 1666, ordering the City to produce a survey of the ruins
so that ownership of land could be determined;[12] the City duly appointed
several men, among them Edward Jerman, a carpenter and former
viewer and the builder of the Royal Exchange, to work on it with three
men appointed by the king himself, one of them Christopher Wren. The
Rebuilding Act of 8 February 1667 (An Act for Rebuilding the City of
London, 19 Charles II, c. 3) also called for the appointment of City
surveyors, and London chose four men the next month: three of them,
Robert Hooke, Peter Mills, and John Oliver, eventually took office.[13]
The institution of the City viewers was not abolished, but the work of
rebuilding London was not under their supervision; the surveyors and the
Fire Court set up under the Rebuilding Act were responsible for both

9. *CLBD*, p. 15.
10. Viewers' Presentments, 1623–1636 (1 box, location number 204A).
11. At least on the point of controlling building, see the comment by T. F. Reddaway:
    'There was nothing to admire in the records of the enforcement of the long series [of
    proclamations governing the construction of private houses in London] proclaimed in
    former years by the Crown. The Common Viewers were incapable of doing better . . .'
    The Rebuilding of London after the Great Fire (1940), p. 152.
12. Proclamation of 13 September 1666, 'To prohibit the Rebuilding of Houses after the
    Great Fire of London without conforming to the General Regulations therein
    premised': printed W. deG. Birch, *The Historical Charters and Constitutional Docu-
    ments of the City of London* (1897), pp. 224–30, esp. pp. 228–9.
13. Reddaway, op. cit. p. 108. Jerman, also appointed, declined.

settling disputes and policing compliance with the Act of 1667 and the Second Rebuilding Act (An Additional Act for the Rebuilding of the City of London, 22 Charles II, c. 11). A terse note in the Repertories in July 1668 reflects the new situation without comment: the first clerk of the Mayor's Court was in future to attend the surveyors when they viewed disputes and to draw up their presentments 'as hee useth to doe of the views of the common viewers of this Citty.'[14]

Viewers continued to be appointed and to function, however; the Repertories carry accounts of their admission to office and of their activities.[15] In the 1670s and even later, there seems to have been some division of labour between them and the surveyors, although its rationale is not entirely clear. Ordinarily, it appears that the surveyors handled matters concerning new construction alleged to be 'irregular' under the Building Acts while the viewers dealt with the complaints, made by private parties or on behalf of the City, resulting from such building – lights stopped up, encroachment – and with public nuisances such as stairs obstructed by rubbish. But the division was not consistent; on 7 August 1679, for example, an alderman, his deputy, the Surveyors of New Buildings, and the viewers were all told to view a house under construction in the Old Jewry 'and inform themselves whether the same be irregular or not'.[16] Nor is it clear how the viewers managed to perform their traditional functions since they were no longer necessarily experts in the construction trades. For reasons which are not stated in the Repertories entries, the mayor and aldermen admitted a glazier as viewer in December 1679 and, more startling still, a weaver in October 1685 and a glover in April 1695.[17] Choice of such men must have diminished the viewers' authority and in fact the Repertories entries give the impression that the post had become more or less a sinecure: in 1695, a new man was admitted to his place 'to have hold exercise & enjoy the said place with all fees proffitts And comodities thereunto due & of right belonging. So long as he shall well & honestly use and behave himself therein'.[18] There is no mention of duties or of oaths. The 1679 and 1685 entries use similar language.

Yet there are hundreds of reports existing in the CLRO archives for the period 1659–1704, and while many are by the surveyors and others by aldermen and their deputies, a substantial number were made by the common viewers.[19] Nor was 1704 the end of the viewers' existence. There

14. Rep 73, f. 225v. See comment by Reddaway, op. cit. p. 151.
15. E.g. Reps 85, f. 39; 90, f. 143; 99, p. 541 for admissions; and, for the activities of a single year (1679) chosen at random, Rep 84, ff. 129, 144, 151, 184v, 213v.
16. Rep 85, f. 184v.
17. Reps 85, f. 39; 90, f. 143; 99, p. 541.
18. Rep 99, p. 541.
19. Three volumes of reports exist: vol. 1 has those from 1668–70, vol. 2 those from 1674–84, and vol. 3 those from 1684–91; (all at location number 32C). Originals and copies of some of the reports entered in the three volumes are filed in a box, location number 41B. Additionally, originals and copies of still other reports for the period 1659–1704 are filed in Misc. MSS Boxes 92 and 93. Of certificates 101–20, filed separately in Misc. MSS Box 93 and dating in the main from between 1690 and 1704, 11 are by the surveyors, aldermen and their deputies, or other City officials while nine are by the viewers. The reports deal with light, a watercourse stopped up, a new timber building (contrary to the

are in the Corporation of London records at least five reports by surveyors and others made after that date, and the earliest (from 1718) is clearly a viewers' certificate.[20] I have not examined 18th-century Repertories, but Edward Basil Jupp, the editor of the Carpenters' Company records, wrote that the last person whose appointment he saw entered was a carpenter, John Norris, named in 1737.[21] In any event, certainly the Building Act of 1774 (An Act for the further and better Regulation of Buildings and Party Walls. . . within the Cities of London and Westminster . . ., 14 George III, c. 78), providing for the appointment of sworn district surveyors (s. 62), would seem to have left small reason for the old 'sworn masons and carpenters'.[22]

The institution had by then lasted almost 500 years. Its very antiquity may have been one reason why it was not abolished or transformed earlier; it was among the most venerable of civic arrangements. Another reason may have been inertia, of course, and a third probably lay with the livery companies themselves. Providing viewers had long been a source of prestige and power – and patronage – for the masons, carpenters, and tilers, for the office was not unimportant and it was not held by unimportant men. Master masons and carpenters were significant figures in late medieval London; their work affected the very growth and appearance of the City.[23] The addition of a master tiler to the group in 1550 followed by other appointments of tilers thereafter is itself a signal that London was changing its appearance; the tilers were closely related to the bricklayers – the two crafts amalgamated their organisations in 1568 – and in the 16th

Act of Parliament), encroachment, a jetty larger 'than the statute doth direct or by law they ought to have', irregular new buildings, and similar situations.

20. It appears unlikely that the later ones resulted from their activity. Two (in 1742 and 1762) are by George Dance the elder. One, dated 1785 and concerning a ruinous party wall, is by four named men but there is no salutation, no closing, no statement of who the men are or by reason of what office they have made the view. A fourth, dated 1796, is an evaluation of a building made by two named men, again with no statement of capacity. All are at CLRO Miscellaneous MSS 269.6. The last certificate which can certainly be attributed to the sworn viewers is dated 1718, in which 'the two elder and two younger' viewers report to the Court of Aldermen that they disagree on the quality of repairs made to a house in Ship Yard, Bartholomews Lane (CLRO Misc. MSS 23.21).

21. E. B. Jupp, *An Historical Account of the Worshipful Company of Carpenters of London* (2nd ed., 1887), pp. 192–3.

22. Because they were assigned to do much the same work, as is made clear in the oath before the Court of Aldermen to be taken by surveyors within the City, set out in the same section of the statute. None of these positions – the surveyors of the ruins in 1666, the Surveyors of New Buildings of 1667, the district surveyors of 1774 – seems to have been the direct ancestor of the present-day office of City Surveyor. Betty Masters has traced that office back to the 15th century post of Clerk of the City's Works; the title was changed to 'Architect and Surveyor' as of 20 January 1848 and in 1891, the office of City Surveyor was substituted. See Betty R. Masters, 'The City Surveyor, the City Engineer and the City Architect and Planning Officer', *Guildhall Miscellany* vol. 4, no. 4 (April, 1973), pp. 236–55.

23. Their significance is reflected in the amount of legislation they occasioned. There are repeated references in City records to the wages and hours of masons and carpenters as well as oaths to be taken by them concerning both their workmanship and compliance with City building regulations. See, for example, *Liber Custumarum*, i, 99, 100; *Liber Albus*, pp. 251, 410.

century, brick was becoming the building material of choice, replacing the stone favoured earlier by wealthy citizens.[24]

Throughout the two hundred years preceding the certificates here calendared the master masons and carpenters sworn to the City, the chosen representatives of the premier construction crafts, gradually gathered to themselves privilege and status. In 1371, they successfully petitioned to be discharged from payment of taxes, tenths, fifteenths and other subsidies due the king, as their predecessors in office had been – for the last hundred years, they alleged, taking the office of viewer back again to 1271.[25] In 1442 they petitioned, equally successfully, to be discharged from serving on juries, inquests and other offices because they were working on the great new project of Leadenhall.[26] Within the period covered by this volume, in 1522, they were voted a ray (striped) gown annually from the Chamber of London, provided that they 'geve their diligences & attendances' when called by an alderman to survey purprestures. They probably received no other salary from the City, for the grant of striped gown was conditioned on their attendance 'without enything takyng for their labors in that behalf.'[27] But there was a fee payable to them for every view they made not involving the City as a party – payable by the individuals and companies and religious bodies involved in the 'private' views here calendared – and a man's share in the 5s. commonly mentioned, multiplied by hundreds of views, must have added up nicely over the months and years.

For the 16th century, at least, it is clear that the viewers were men at the top of their profession. Of the carpenters, almost all were masters or wardens of their Company and well regarded outside their own ranks. Stephen Poncheon, viewer until his death in 1535, was a warden and, in 1533, master; he was also carpenter to the Drapers' Company in 1520.[28] John King (Kyng), viewer briefly in 31–32 Henry VIII (when he died), had been a warden and master, and was carpenter to the Mercers.[29] William Walker, Thomas Pecock, Thomas Smart, and Philip Coseyn (Cosyn) were all both wardens and masters, and so was John Russell, who was also the King's Carpenter from October 1532 until his own death in 1566.[30] The masons were hardly less distinguished. The Company's records show Thomas Newell, Henry Pesemede, Gilbert Burffame (Burfame), John Hilmer (Hylmer, Elmer), and John Humfrey as prominent members of the livery of the Freemasons, and Nicholas Ellys, viewer

24. See John Schofield, *The Building of London from the Conquest to the Great Fire* (1984), chs. 5 and 6, for comment on the changes in construction in late 15th and 16th century London.
25. *CLBG*, p. 444.
26. *CLBK*, p. 276.
27. LBM, f. 150; see also **348**.
28. *Carpenters' Records*, vol. 3, p. 211; The Worshipful Company of Drapers of London, Minutes and Records 1515–1552 (Rep. 7 + 130/1, + 130/2 and + 130/3), vol. 3, p. 58. The volumes are hereafter cited as Drapers' Company, Minutes and Records 1515–52.
29. *Carpenters' Records*, vol. 3, p. 211; *Mercers' Company Acts of Court, 1453–1527*, p. 764.
30. *Carpenters' Records*, vol. 3, pp. 210–12, 214. See also David R. Ransome, 'Artisan Dynasties in London and Westminster', *Guildhall Miscellany*, vol. 2, no. 6 (October, 1964), p. 243.

rom 1545 until he died in 1556, was the King's Mason.[31] The tilers, chosen viewers intermittently after 1550, are less easy to trace since their Court of Assistants' minutes start only in 1580.[32] But Walter Cowper, one of the two tiler viewers within the period of the existing certificates, was under contract to the Drapers in 1534, when he built them a cellar for £5.[33] Terms such as 'ancient', and 'sad' (in its 16th-century meaning of 'grave' or 'serious'), illustrate the qualities thought desirable in a viewer: he was to be mature, dignified, and of course both honest and competent.[34]

There is one puzzling exception, important for the light it throws on the entire selection process. William Coleyns (or Colyns, or Collins), carpenter, appears fairly often in the records of the Carpenters' Company, and not entirely favourably. Coleyns was chosen under warden of the Company in 1533. But in February 1534 two members of the Company 'founde a boye working on making of skrewys in a Seller' of Coleyns; he had worked two years as a carpenter but he was not an apprentice.[35] A further note on what appears to be the same incident suggests that Coleyns illegally employed two boys: the master and the upper warden had investigated on knowledge that there was a 'foryner' working on screws in a basement of Coleyns and had found the work going on; but the boy's name differs in the two reports.[36] Yet shortly after this incident, in October 1535, an entry in the Repertories notes that the names of Philip Coseyn, John King, and Richard Maddok (Madok), carpenters, were brought to the Court so that one of them might be chosen viewer in place of Stephen Poncheon, who had died; 'and by good deleberation by way of scrutynye ye sayd Wyllyam Colyns was chosen and namyd to be yn the seyd Rowme and sworne accordyngly'.[37] The carpenters reacted predictably. It was not 'ye said Wyllyam Colyns', of course; he had not been among the nominees of the Carpenters' Company. They came into the Court of Aldermen to demand that they have the nomination of a viewer 'and sayed that they by act of Parliament ought to have the same'; a day was given them to bring in their evidence.[38] Apparently their case was weak, for there is no further talk of Acts of Parliament. Instead, some four months later, in February 1536, ten carpenters – three of them viewers or future viewers – came into court and swore on oath to the truth

31. *Records of the Hole Crafte and Fellowship of Masons*, ed. Edward Conder, Jr. (1894), p. 100; on Nicholas Ellys, Rep 11, f. 460 [new pagination]. See also Ransome, op. cit., p. 241. Ellys was the nephew by marriage of John Russell; he married Russell's niece, Joan, in 1545 (ibid.)
32. The first tiler shown as a viewer in the certificates here calendared is John Cowper, the certificate (**281**) dating from 30 August 1550. He was succeeded sometime between 28 July 1554 and 9 March 1555 by another tiler, Walter Cowper; see **355** and **356**.
33. Drapers' Company, Minutes and Records 1515–52, vol. 2, p. 499.
34. As were candidates Nicholas Ellys and Gilbert Burffame in 1546; they were presented as 'beyng ii of the moste Ancyent and dyscrete persones of theyr felowship', Rep 11, f. 252v [new pagination].
35. *Carpenters' Records*, vol. 3, pp. 9–10.
36. Ibid., p. 16.
37. Rep 9, f. 130.
38. Ibid., f. 132. I have seen no Act to that effect, nor have I found any such provision in a charter granted to the City nor in any collection of the City's customs.

of a 'boke of Articles of Mysdemeanors obiectyd ageynst Wylliam Colyn Carpenter'. He had, they alleged, through friends had work in hand for the Mint in the Tower and in connection with it had been given a commission to carry wood from the king's wood at Enfield Chase; he had tried, by virtue of his commission, to compel men of Cambridgeshire to take the wood to London in their carts, knowing that they would pay him to escape the duty. He had been discovered by 'wise and discrete men' and sent to the Marshalsea. Moreover, they said, he had once told the Court of the Company under oath that Thomas Sherys – one of those testifying against him – owed him £30 whereas it was found that instead Coleyns owed Sherys five marks (£3 6s. 8d.). Finally, he had once refused payment for three loads of timber taken for the king's works and had later sworn that 20 loads were involved.[39] This scarifying recital did not, apparently, move the Court of Aldermen as strongly as the Carpenters had hoped; perhaps there was some question in more than one official mind as to why the Carpenters would elect such a scoundrel to high office in their Company. In any event, there is a laconic entry in the Repertories for 24 February 1536 to the effect that Coleyns' answer had been read 'and upon the submyssyon of the sayd Coleyns to Master & Company of Carpenters [they] shall remytt all theyre displeasures to the said Colyns & accept hym ageyn ynto their Company.' And later the same day was added the dignified, official note that the Carpenters of London had presented to the Court John Sampson and William Walker to be viewer in place of Stephen Poncheon and that Walker by way of scrutiny was elected and sworn. Coleyns was therefore discharged of the office by his own agreement and the record discharged.[40] But he had indeed assumed office and acted for as long as four months: by chance, one certificate (**115**) survives showing Coleyns as a viewer.

Despite the Carpenters' claims, the earliest records do not make clear who had the right of presentation of candidates for the viewers' positions; the Letter Book entries generally simply state that X and Y were elected and sworn. The one exception, in October 1383, suggests that the viewers did the nominating: Thomas Mallyng, Richard atte Churche, masons, and Stephen Warde, carpenter, the three surviving viewers, 'elected' (*elegerunt*) William Dudecote, carpenter, in place of Thomas Fant who had recently died, and presented him to the mayor who accepted him; Dudecote was sworn in on the same day.[41] However, in the first half of the 16th century – whether by right or otherwise – the Carpenters' and Masons' Companies apparently did ordinarily present candidates when a viewer's post became vacant and, with the one exception of William Coleyns, one of their nominees was elected and sworn. The Repertories for the period occasionally show four names of carpenters or masons, with two – presumably the unsuccessful nominees – crossed through.[42]

---

39. Ibid., ff. 154–155v.   40. Ibid., f. 156v.   41. *CLBH*, p. 216.
42. See, for example, Rep 2, f. 58v (1 February 28 Henry VII.) The entry on the election of Gilbert Burffame is explicit as to how the choice was made: the wardens of the freemasons 'accordyng to the ancyent custom of this Cytie' presented two men 'that the Court accordyng to the sayd Custome shulde electe one of theym': Rep 11, f. 252v [new pagination].

But the Companies' freedom of nomination could be circumscribed by the unwillingness of the Court of Aldermen to consider certain candidates and by the Court's concern for its own rights. When the Carpenters presented only one candidate in November of 1540, the Court noted that 'the Wardens of the Carpenters have presented to this Court one Richard Maddok, Carpenter, to be one of the vyewers ... whose admyssyon was respyted for that they presented not ii hable persones of theyr Company accordyng to the lawes & auncyent Customes of this Citye'; a month later, when the Carpenters brought in the name of John Russell in addition to Maddok's 'to the intent that this Court should elect & chuse the one of them', the Court 'dyd elect & chuse neyther butt dyd stay the same untyll the next Court day'. Another month later, the Carpenters named Maddok and John Arnold 'to the intent that this Court accordyng to an Auncyent Custome & lawe in that behalfe shulde electe & chuse one of theym'. The Court chose John Arnold; Maddok was never a viewer.[43] The refusal to choose between Russell and Maddok certainly suggests an objection to both men; yet when John Arnold died in 1546 and the Carpenters once again presented Russell as one of two candidates, he was elected. Apparently even the mayor and aldermen could yield to pressure; John Russell was the King's Carpenter. The suspicion of intervention by outside forces becomes a certainty in the election of Nicholas Ellys, the King's Mason; he was admitted to the liberty of the city in March 1546 and his fine remitted, and he was nominated as a candidate to be a viewer in early April of the same year. The Court chose instead Gilbert Burffame. The next opening occurred in July 1548 and the entry in the Repertories is blunt: the letter to the mayor from an unidentified 'Right Honorable greatt Maister' asking that Ellys be 'admytted to the same or lyke Romes [places] within this Cytie as John Hylmer, mason, lately deceased had' was read and for 'dyvers reasonable & greatt causes & consyderations movyng the Court lovingly accorded & agreyd that he the said Ellys' should have the office. Ellys was sworn forthwith.[44] The next election, that of Thomas Pecock, carpenter, in May 1553, was once again in the usual form and in November 1556 the Court agreed to be 'advysed of the Contents of the bill exhybyted here this day by the wardens of the fremasons' concerning election of a viewer to succeed Ellys, who had recently died; John Humfrey was elected.[45]

Whatever the basis for their claim in 1535, the Carpenters' right to choose members of their fellowship to be named viewers was not regularised until February 1607, when new ordinances – granted under the seals of the Lord Chancellor, Lord Treasurer, Lord Chief Justice, and Chief Judge of Common Pleas – set out that 'viewers carpenters' were to be elected and chosen by the Master and Wardens of the Fellowship, 'they to name such persons as shalbe hable aswell in cunnynge as otherwise' for the office.[46] The basis of the Masons' claim to choose a viewer is even less clear; they apparently did not consider their right as

43. Rep 10, ff. 179, 186, 189.   44. Rep 11, ff. 270, 275v, 276, 482.
45. Rep 13, No. 2, ff. 447, 449.
46. The provision is part of a set of bye-laws dated 10 November 5 James I (1607), set out in
    GL MS 4339, a bound volume headed 'Carpenters Company Charters and Bye-Laws',

secure as the Carpenters' since they asked the Court to 'be advised by their nominations. As for the Tylers – not yet amalgamated with the Bricklayers during the period covered by the certificates – there is no suggestion in surviving City records that they were consulted at all in July 1550 when 'for reasonable consideracions movyng the Court, John Cowper, tyler, was this day admytted and sworne one of the common viewers of this Citie in the place of Gylbert Burfame, freemason, lately deceased'.[47] Neither, apparently, were the Masons a party to the decision, though the admission of a tiler in place of Gilbert Burffame cut their representation on the panel of viewers in half. But the Carpenters' triumph of 1607 was of short duration; several post-Fire Repertorie entries simply report the admission of new viewers by the Court of Aldermen, suggesting that the three livery companies had lost whatever power of selection they had held. Indeed, they must have: none would have been likely to present a glazier, a weaver, or a glover as candidates.

At least by the middle of the 15th century and probably before that, appointment was for life or until advancing age or other physical incapacity made it impossible for a viewer to perform his duties, with termination earlier only for unexcused nonfeasance. On 2 April 1459, William Robert, carpenter, became a viewer for the purpose of removing nuisances of buildings between neighbours in the City '*quamdam se bene gessit etc.*': during good behaviour.[48] Entries in the Letter Books, Journals and Repertories concur. John de Totenham was discharged for age in 1369, on his own petition; he was, he said, old and his eyesight was failing. He had served since June 1325.[49] Thomas atte Barnet was discharged in 1377 because he neglected his duties; one entry mentions that he had been absent from London for a long time and that the Masons agreed to his replacement.[50] In 1553, within the period of the certificates here calendared, William Walker 'because of continual sickness' wished to surrender his place into the hands of the mayor and aldermen; the chamberlain was instructed to take his surrender and Thomas Pecock was chosen in his stead.[51] But generally a new viewer replaced one recently deceased. John de Totenham himself took the place of the dead Adam de Rothynge; in 1383 William Dudecote was elected for Thomas Fant, deceased; John Lovebond replaced the late John Burton in 1504.[52] During the first half of the 16th century, first William Coleyns and then William Walker were chosen in the stead of Stephen Poncheon, deceased.[53] Henry Pesemede replaced the dead Thomas Newell in 1539;

p. 101. The Carpenters' Company Court Book shows agreement to the proposed 'new ordenances' at a February 1607 meeting of the Court of Assistants and indicates that the ordinances, ratified by the named officials, were read out at another meeting held on 7 December 1607 (GL MS 4329/3, ff. 129, 148.)

47. Rep 12, No. 1, f. 251.
48. Journal 6, f. 153v; for persistence of the phrase (translated) see also Reps 85, f. 39, and 90, f. 143 (1679 and 1685).
49. *CLBG*, p. 223; *CLBE*, p. 207.
50. *CLBH*, p. 13.
51. Rep 13, No. 1, f. 53.
52. *CLBE*, p. 201; *CLBH*, p. 216; Journal 10, f. 317v.
53. Rep 9, ff. 130, 156v. The altercation over the first choice lasted from October 1535 to February 1536.

ohn Arnold replaced the late John King in 1541 and on his own death
✓as succeeded by John Russell.[54] Only days before, in April 1546, Gilbert
Burffame had been chosen to replace Henry Pesemede, deceased;
Burffame died in July 1550, and was succeeded by John Cowper.[55]
Nicholas Ellys' death in 1556 opened a place for John Humfrey,
reemason.[56] Viewers' terms thus varied greatly. John Hilmer was
already serving at the opening of the reign of Henry VIII, having been
appointed in February 1509;[57] he died, still a viewer, between July and
October 1548. Perhaps only John de Totenham's 44 year tenure exceeded
his record. John King, on the other hand, lasted only from 1539 to 1541,
and Gilbert Burffame from 1546 to 1550; even a guarantee of tenure
quamdam se bene gessit could not prevail over the limits imposed by
mortality.

II.

The Letter Books and Miscellaneous Rolls and later the Repertories and
Journals suggest a function essentially related to settlement of private
disputes between neighbours, albeit disputes which City courts might be
called upon to decide.[58] But there was a more public side to viewers'
duties; from early on, they were to report nuisances in which the City had
an interest.[59] The 16th-century records of views involving public nuisance
focus on purprestures and encroachments on the public streets and other
public lands – bay windows, porches, stairs, fences, cellar doors and those
constant problems, pentices and jetties, as well as entire new structures –
and require the sworn masons and carpenters to report their findings to
the chamberlain.[60] Nor was that main highway of London, the Thames, to
be ignored: the viewers were to note encroachments on the waterside or
into the river and report them to the aldermen.[61] The expectation was
that London would be under the watchful surveillance of its sworn
masons and carpenters, whether or not there had been a specific
complaint.

The viewers' oath over the years reflects the obligation to deal with
both public and private nuisance, with emphasis shifting gradually toward

---

54. As to Pesemede, see Rep 10, f. 111. The entry reads 'John Peseman, mason, was admytted one of the vyewers of thys Cytye in the stede of Thomas Newell, mason, deceassed ...' No 'John Peseman' was ever a viewer and the certificates show that Henry Pesemede succeeded Thomas Newell. As to John Arnold, see LBQ, f. 7; for John Russell's election, Rep 11, f. 164v [new pagination].
55. Rep 11, f. 252v [new pagination]; Rep 12, No. 1, f. 251.
56. Rep 13, No. 2, ff. 447, 449.
57. Rep 2, f. 58v.
58. *CLBC*, p. 86. When Reginald de Swafham was admitted to office in 1310, he swore 'to do all things pertaining to assizes and divisions of tenements in the City and suburb, so far as they belong to the trade of a carpenter, according to the custom of the City, where and whensoever he shall be required': *CLBD*, p. 14. Fifteen years after that, John de Totenham was required 'to keep the assizes in the City between neighbours, and adjudicate upon partition of houses, land etc. when called upon': *CLBE*, p. 201. In 1368, partition of 'lands, rents, and tenements' was mentioned:*CLBG*, p. 223.
59. *CLBH*, p. 13.
60. See, for example, LBN, ff. 70, 150.
61. LBP, f. 47v.

the first. An early 14th-century oath calls on the sworn carpenters an masons to 'trewly serche the Right be twene party and party' in a manner of nuisances, without showing favour, and to report to the mayo and aldermen 'aftir yowr witt and connyng so help yow god and holydon and by the book'. Squeezed in after 'book', in a different colour ink there is added 'and other edifying within this Citee of London that ye sha be charged of by the Maire . . . and trew Report therof make . . .'.[62] There are what appear to be paraphrases of an oath in the Liber Custumarun entries concerning the oaths of Richard de Wythe, Robert Osekyn, anc John de Britele.[63] Edward Stone, who took office in 1455, swore that he would well and faithfully oversee judicial investigation of nuisance between neighbours and do and carry out all and singular other things which pertained to his office, reporting to the mayor for the time being.[64] But a late 16th-century text in the 1586 Book of Othes appears to reflect the emphasis on public nuisance, an emphasis no doubt brought about by the unparalleled building and unstoppable expansion of Elizabethan London: 'Ye shall sweare that ye shall truely present from tyme to tyme to the Maior and Aldermen of this Cytye for the tyme beinge or to the Chamberleyne, All such buyldings and purprestures as ye shall fynde sett or made upon anye parte of the comon grounde of the saide Cytye And from henceforth ye shall not make nor suffer to your knowledge to be made any newe buyldinge in anye place within the libertye of this Cytye but ye shall the same shewe unto the said Maior and Aldermen or Chamberleyne for the tyme beinge, to the entent that reformation thereof maye be had. And allso ye shall truelye and indifferentlye searche all maner of noysaunces, buyldyngs, and edyfyenges betwene partye and partye, when ye shalbe charged by the Maior of the Cytye of London so to doe, without anye favor shewinge to anye partye, And true reporte make to the said Maior for the tyme beinge uppon the premisses. And thus ye shall doe. As God helpe you.'[65] Whether the emphases reflected in the oath were paralleled by the activities of the viewers is unclear since the great majority of the surviving certificates deal with private quarrels.[66] Moreover, most of the surviving records which deal with the background of litigation are also private: livery company records and churchwardens' accounts can be pieced together to provide a comprehensive (if often less than objective) picture of how the viewers fitted into the litigious activity

62. *CLBD*, p. 195; see LBD, f. 86.
63. *Liber Custumarum*, i, 100. See also *CLBC*, p. 86. *Liber Albus*, which contains (pp. 265–76) oaths for many city officials, has none for the City's 'sworn masons and carpenters' although there is a provision that all master masons and carpenters are to take an oath not to make purprestures nor to build contrary to the statutes of the City: p. 410.
64. Journal 5, f. 226.
65. Book of Othes (CLRO location number 37C), f. 30. There was an earlier book of oaths, apparently no longer extant; a reference in Rep 7, f. 27, says that in June of 1525 John Hilmer, Thomas Newell, Thomas Smart and Philip Coseyn were sworn viewers 'accordynge to the Tenor of the Othe in the Boke of Othes fol. 26'.
66. The problem of 'private' and 'public' views is discussed below at pp. xxviii–xxix. Kellaway and Chew suggest that in the 14th and 15th centuries, the Assize of Nuisance was never used extensively for public nuisances, since most were handled in wardmotes: *Nuisance*, pp. xxvi–xxviii.

of 16th-century Londoners and their multitude of religious and trade or craft associations.

As a result, it is possible sometimes to reconstruct the events leading to, and often much of the procedure of, a 'private' view while references in the Repertories and Journals provide a far less detailed outline of the viewers' activity when the City itself was a party. An individual, or the individuals in a corporate body, who felt wronged by a neighbour or who wanted certainty about the extent of land could and did 'call in the viewers' before taking other legal action. 'Agreed that the Master with the Wardens and with Mr Cremor and Mr Burton and Mr Carter shall doo call in the Vewers to vewe our house that Appleyard dwellyth in', says an entry in the Drapers' minutes, and again, concerning a gutter made by the Abbot of Stratford upon the Drapers' ground, 'that the Wardens at the Cost and Charge of thys house shall have the Vewers of the Cetye to vewe hyt and afterwards they shall by theyr advyse of lerned Counseyll folowe the extremyte of the lawe ageynst the sayd Abot hys officers and tennants excepte they reforme yt'.[67] The application seems to have been made in person, by appearance at Guildhall before the mayor himself. At least that is the suggestion in the Mercers' Company Acts of Court; one entry notes that the viewers 'by the commaundement of the Lord Maire upon a complaynt made unto hym by the prior of Seynt Mary Spitall' viewed a sewer, and another directs the Wardens to be at the Guildhall on the following Tuesday to 'requyre of my lorde Mayre that the Vewers like as is aforesaid may oversee and vewe' ground in dispute.[68]

Grant of a view appears to have been a matter of course; certainly I have seen no statement anywhere that a request was denied. Possibly there was a fee payable for the grant alone, but the evidence is unclear. Two certificates (**386, 394**) are endorsed '*debet pro impositione huius visus*', with no sum mentioned, and there is a note in the records of the St. Mary Magdalen Milk Street churchwardens' accounts to the effect that they paid 22d. to 'the Judge of the Mayor's Court for the allowance of the view'.[69] But both the *impositio* and the allowance could refer to a later stage in the proceedings and 22d. is an odd sum for a standard fee. In any event, the grant did not mean that the view was assured. One could specify that it be 'at once' or 'within this sennyght' as the Mercers and Drapers sometimes did, but sometimes the viewers did not come as expected. The Mercers' minutes note that a tenement 'hath ben ordeyned by severall actes of this Company to be vewed by the Vewers of this Citie and entered uppon, and not yet done', adding yet again that it be ordained that the view be taken 'in as short tyme as may be'.[70] That delay may have been due to the master and wardens, but there is no such possibility in another entry: the Grocers paid 12d. 'for wyne that was dronk when Mr Petit and others taryed for the vyewers and they came

67. Drapers' Company, Minutes and Records 1515–52, vol. 1, p. 213, vol. 2, p. 428.
68. Mercers' Company, Acts of Court, 1527–1560, f. 27v (1529); *Mercers' Company Acts of Court, 1453–1527*, p. 196 (1489).
69. GL MS 2596/1 (Cash Book, St. Mary Magdalen Milk Street: Churchwardens' Accounts 1518–1606), f. 52v.
70. Mercers' Company, Acts of Court, 1527–1560, f. 80v (1535).

nott'.[71] Perhaps they had not been 'warned' or 'brought'. The parish of St. Mary at Hill paid 10d. to 'the ofeser' who 'warneyd the vewars' in 1509, while 23 years later, in connection with a 1532 lawsuit, St. Mary Magdalen Milk Street paid double that to the 'Mayors offeser' who performed the service.[72] The fee paid by St. Mary at Hill was 12d. in 1535 and the money was paid to 'the servaunt'; that the 'servaunt' was in fact the mayor's serjeant becomes clear from entries in the Quarter and Renter Wardens Accounts of the Clothworkers' Company concerning 'Wefer the Mayres serjeant' who both warned and brought the viewers – twice, for a total of 16d.[73] The 'bringing' cost money, too. The Clothworkers on another occasion paid 'Wefer' 12d. for that service; the Drapers paid a total of 10s. to the viewers and William Nycolson, the mayor's serjeant who accompanied them, 'for their pains' in the dispute with the Abbot of Stratford; the Skinners paid one Broke, identified as 'the Mayor's Serjeant to them [the viewers] assined' 12d. 'for his Reward'; the parish of St. Mary at Hill paid an undefined person an undefined sum 'for bryngyng the vewers to Foster Lane'.[74] Once they had been warned and brought to the site, there was more money to be spent. The churchwardens of St. Margaret Pattens laid out 13d. at a tavern to entertain the viewers when they settled a quarrel concerning the church steeple; the wardens of St. Stephen Walbrook fed them breakfast at 'the Myter' for 9d.; St. Mary at Hill made a habit of spending small sums 'at the taveryn' on them.[75] The livery companies' records show similar payments.[76]

There were, of course, fees to be paid as well. There is no table of fees; recorded payments suggest that in a view not involving the City the amount was ordinarily either 5s. or 10s., the latter representing payments of 5s. by each party. In 1542 and 1546, a 5s. charge was mentioned in the

---

71. GL MS 11571/4 (Grocers' Company, Quires of Wardens' Accounts 1521–1533), f. 365.
72. GL MS 1239/1 (Churchwardens' Accounts, St. Mary at Hill), Pt. 2, f. 287; GL MS 2596/1, f. 52v.
73. GL MS 1239/1, Pt. 3, f. 652; Clothworkers' Company, Quarter and Renter Wardens Accounts 1520–1558, ff. 5v–6v. The mayor's serjeant had apparently performed similar duties as far back as the 14th century; see Betty R. Masters, 'The Mayor's Household before 1600' in *Studies in London History Presented to Philip Edmund Jones*, ed. A. E. J. Hollaender and William Kellaway (1969), p. 96. William Wefer or Wever became one of the serjeants in 1532. By the 1530s the title of serjeant carver had commonly replaced that of serjeant of the mayor (ibid., p. 98), but the livery company records consistently use the older form.
74. Clothworkers' Company, Quarter and Renter Wardens Accounts 1520–1528, ff. 5v, 6; Drapers' Company, Minutes and Records 1515–52, vol. 2, p. 437; Skinners' Company, Receipts and Payments 1510–1535 (Acct. Book, No. 2), unnumbered folio; GL MS 1239/1, Pt. 2, f. 495.
75. GL MS 4570/1 (St. Margaret Pattens, Church Wardens' Accounts 1506/7–1557), f. 70v; GL MS 593/1 (St. Stephen Walbrook, Churchwardens' Accounts 1474–1553), f. 4v (1537); GL MS 1239/1, Pt. 2, f. 287 (6d.), f. 365v (2d.), f. 495 (12d., including the cost of bringing the viewers).
76. See Clothworkers' Company, Quarter and Renter Wardens' Accounts 1520–1558, f. 6 (12d.); Skinners' Company, Court Book, No. 1, 1551–1617, unnumbered folio (5d.). The Grocers, who had already drunk wine in the tavern waiting for the viewers who never came, spent 6d. 'for the drynkyng of Master, Wardens and Mr Petyt and the vyewers and others' on an occasion when they did come (GL MS 11571/4, f. 365.)

.ertificates (**176, 200**). In 1524, the Grocers paid the mayor's serjeant 5s. for the one halff for the labarres and costes for the iiii vewers for there _abours for Mr Lamberdes house betwene Anthony Vivolde and my masters the grocers' and 6s. for another view with a copy of the verdict.[77] The Clothworkers paid 10s. for two views in 1534 and three years earlier, n 1531, the parish of St. Mary Magdalen Milk Street paid 5s. for a single view.[78] St. Margaret Pattens likewise paid 5s. for a view in 1549, as did St. Mary at Hill in 1509.[79] Sometimes higher sums of money paid clearly represent additional work done by the viewers or their clerk. The Skinners gave 20s. when the viewers also measured ground for them; the Grocers gave an additional shilling for a copy of the 'verdict'.[80] In fact, with or without his performing additional work the clerk who came with the viewers was also 'rewarded', and sometimes the payment is noted separately; for example, the Skinners gave an otherwise unidentifiable 'Symon Lorimer theyre [the viewers'] clerk' 4d.[81] Possibly some undifferentiated payments higher than 5s. include such payments to clerks and serjeants. But sometimes the additional payment is less easily explained. In their major quarrel with the Abbot of Stratford of 1532–1533, the Diapers paid the viewers and Nicolson, their serjeant, 10s.;[82] it is unlikely that the serjeant's portion alone accounts for a sum double the usual amount. In 1540, they paid 20s., again double the usual amount, for two views of houses in Aldermary and Mark Lane which were subjects of serious concern and, in one case, protracted litigation.[83]

Some payments to 'viewers' which appear to be much lower than the common 5s. fee result from performance of less than a standard view. Sometimes the view was apparently not official, although a sworn viewer was involved. Between May 1543 and June 1544 the Grocers paid 2s. to John Hilmer, a sworn viewer at the time, 'in reward to view the wyndowes and hall Roffe' at their hall; one of the City viewers joined a Company carpenter and tiler to measure ground which the Drapers were effectively subdividing; St. Stephen Walbrook paid 12d. to 'one of the vewers for his advise' about a brick wall in 1522.[84] Sometimes, indeed, the unofficial view may have been made by a team of carpenters and masons, sworn or otherwise, chosen by the party or parties; 'viewing' was a common method used to settle uncertainties about metes and bounds or other technical points and craftsmen, often employed on a retainer basis

77. GL MS 11571/4, ff. 81v, 365.
78. Clothworkers' Company, Quarter and Renter Wardens' Accounts 1520–1558, f. 6; GL MS 2596/1 ff. 48, 52v (apparently referring to the same view).
79. GL MS 4570/1, f. 101v; GL MS 1239/1, Pt. 2, f. 287.
80. Skinners' Company, Receipts and Payments 1510–1535 (Acct. Book No. 2), unnumbered folio; GL MS 11571/4, f. 365.
81. Skinners' Company, Receipts and Payments 1510–1535 (Acct. Book No. 2), unnumbered folio.
82. Drapers' Company, Minutes and Records 1515–52, vol. 2, p. 437.
83. Drapers' Company, Wardens' Accounts 1508–1546, f. 11.
84. GL MS 11571/5 (Grocers' Company, Quires of Wardens' Accounts 1534–1555), f. 203; Drapers' Company, Minutes and Records 1515–52, vol. 2, p. 689; GL MS 593/1, f. 3 (1522).

by organisations such as livery companies, frequently made such inspections.[85]

But payments did not end when the viewers and their entourage left the premises. Four certificates (**60, 152, 154, 160**) from the reign of Henry VIII state or imply that a fee was paid to a named common clerk apparently when a certificate was presented in court and presumably for that presentment: that is, probably, for its reception as an official document and its filing. Twenty others speak of a fee paid (or not paid) to 'the common clerk'; with few exceptions, the amount specified is 2s. Before 1533, endorsements read that the *billa* or *recordum* or *visus* '*insertatur*', '*certificatur*', '*infertur*' or '*importatur*', sometimes by one of various named officers; but the fee seems still have to have gone to the common clerk. Certainly William Paver, at least, felt able to dispose of 'his fee' as he chose; the endorsement to a 1524 certificate (**60**) recording a dispute involving the abbess and convent of Minoresses says '*Importat' in Cur' te' Baldry* 3.8. Mr. Paver hath gevyn the Abbesse his fee'.[86] During the tenure of William Blackwell – after 1540 – the connection is made even clearer. '*Infert' iste visus etc. ij.12 . . . tunc prox' etc. Hayward solutum feodum communis clerici*' (**153**), he writes, or '2s. *pro feod' meo pro presen' /.11 Ao 33 H8 super recepcione*. Blak'' (**154**) or '*r' 2s. 16.11 ao 33 h8 super recepcione istius visus hunc Curiam*. Blackwell' (**158**).

There were also fees for getting 'a copy' of what was often called the 'verdict'. The appearance here of two separate charges produces some uncertainty. Possibly one was for the common clerk's grant of permission to a party to have a copy and the other the fee for the actual physical writing of the report by another clerk. Thus St. Margaret Pattens' churchwardens paid 3s. to Master Gibbes, the mayor's clerk, 'for the copie of the vewers verdyt and the Engrossing thereof' and the Grocers paid 'Mr Towne Clerke' 2s. for a copy of the report and Rutland, his clerk, 12d. 'for writing thereof', which would come out to the same amount.[87] Similarly, the Drapers noted that the viewers 'gave up in wrytyng' their view and that they paid one of the clerks 16d. for the copy

---

85. This may explain, for example, why in 1523 the Grocers gave the odd sum of 2s. 8d. for a view of their weigh-house gate (GL MS 11571/4, f. 40v). Indeed, reading the court minutes and account books, it is sometimes difficult to be sure when the City viewers are being referred to, except where they are distinguished as 'the iiii vewers' or 'the sworn vewers', 'the City vewers', 'the comon vewers'. Sometimes expertise does not seem to have been required and the view was by men, usually not in the building trades, appointed by the Mayor on petition of the parties. More often still it was by members of the interested organisation. Most of the livery companies and parishes appear to have made periodic inspection of their premises, choosing members to accompany the Master and Wardens to do so. The Grocers, for example, appear to have had officers called viewers; periodically, three or four of them plus the Renter Wardens were named to view the lands and tenements of the company. See, for example, GL MS 11588/1 (Grocers' Company, Orders of the Court of Assistants 1556–1591), f. 14v (1557). Usually no payment was involved although there was sometimes provision for food or drink.

86. William Paver was Town Clerk between 1514 and 1533, when he died a suicide. See Betty Masters, 'The Town (Common) Clerk', *Guildhall Miscellany*, vol. 3, No. 1 (October, 1969), p. 61.

87. GL MS 4570/1, f. 102v; GL MS 11571/4, f. 81v.

of it and Mr. Pavyer, the Town Clerk, another 2s. 'for the allowance'.[88] In 1549–1550 the Skinners paid the standard 3s., presumably receiving a copy, and the Grocers paid 3s.4d. – as the Drapers had – to 'Master Blackwell's clerk' for the copy of yet another bill.[89] On the other hand the smaller fee, usually 12d., may have involved simply the formal copying of the report – presumably from notes taken by the clerk on site – for the official files.[90] The Mercers' records note that the viewers are to make a record of their view to the intent that it appear in the Mayor's Court and are to be recompensed as appropriate, and in 1543 the Goldsmiths paid Gibbs, a clerk of the Mayor's Court, 7s. for 'recording of divers views and serches for divers evidence'.[91] It is possible, then, that only such copying for the record was involved when the Clothworkers gave 'Pykeryng the mayors clerk' 12d. for a copy of 'the byll that the vewars delivered uppe' and the Drapers paid 12d. for the 'first copy of the award of the iiii vewers' in 1524/5.[92] Neither hypothesis explains the Drapers' entry noting payment of only 8d. for a copy of the viewers' award concerning a wall, or the Skinners' 1512 report that they had paid John Halle of the Mayor's Court 7d. for copying the verdict, or the Merchant Taylors' note that in 1549 or 1550 they paid 4d. for a copy of a view in the parish of Little St. Bartholomew.[93] All that can be said is that the explanation for such sums is not self-evident and is no longer traceable. There is no question of inflation; not only does the 4d. payment date from late in the period, but the Merchant Taylors paid the more standard amount shortly thereafter, in 1551/2, when they gave 12d. 'for the copie of a view'.[94] It is difficult to determine whether there was a fixed fee and harder to know what such a fee covered even in routine transactions. But it is almost impossible to understand exactly what was being paid for where the language is out of the ordinary or imprecise: what does it mean, for instance, that in 1541

88. Drapers' Company, Minutes and Records 1515–52, vol. 2, p. 437. 12d. seems to have been a fairly standard fee for a copy; the Merchant Taylors also paid that amount for a copy of the decree in the Court of Aldermen in their March 1551–2 case against the Clothworkers: Records of the Merchant Taylors' Company: Account Books vol. 4:1, 1545–1557, f. 260v; available in GL as microfilm 298(4).
89. Skinners' Company, Receipts and Payments 1510–1535 (Acct. Book No. 2), unnumbered folio; GL MS 11571/5, f. 390. See also the puzzling endorsement copied with its certificate into the Mercers' Company Book of Writings, vol. II, f. 196v.: 'Ista collatione concord' cum orig'. Blackwell'; could it explain the common clerk's fee?
90. Another possible meaning of the endorsement to the Mercers' Company certificate mentioned above; the reference would be to the formal copy of the view which has been checked against the clerk's earlier notes.
91. Mercers' Company, Acts of Court, 1527–1560, f. 287 (1556); Goldsmiths' Company, Wardens' Accounts and Court Minutes, vol. 6 (vol. G), p. 42.
92. Clothworkers' Company, Quarter and Renter Wardens' Accounts 1520–1558, f. 6v (1534); Drapers' Company, Wardens' Accounts 1508–1546, f. 2v (1521/2).
93. Drapers' Company, Wardens' Accounts 1508–1546, f. 2v (1521/2); Skinners' Company, Receipts and Payments 1510–1535 (Acct. Book No. 2), unnumbered folio; GL microfilm 298(4), f. 167. The Merchant Taylors' records do not specify that payment was made to the Town Clerk; possibly the copy was privately made. Yet the entry is headed 'A view taken upon our ground and one Ormeston, clothworker, in the parish of Lyttell Seint Barthylemew'; there are two parties, so it is not likely to have been an internal view.
94. GL Microfilm 298(4), f. 237.

the Drapers gave the Mayor's officer and the viewers 6s. 'at there Repor makyng of the vew in Aldermary parishe'?[95]

Performance of unusual services by the viewers meant payment to them of less usual 'rewards'. When three of the four came before the Drapers' Court of Assistants to affirm that they would abide by their view, they cannot have received a set fee.[96] Nor can they when they agreed to speak with both the Residencers of St. Paul's counsel and the Goldsmiths' counsel to gather evidence before giving a verdict.[97] Such activities may go far to explain some of the more mysterious 'rewards' and payments which rise up to puzzle and trouble. But these special services themselves – the informal advising, the affirmation of intent to maintain an opinion – together with the funds spent on drinking and eating; the retaining of the mayor's clerks at an annual fee, as the Clothworkers did, or of his serjeant, as the Skinners did;[98] and the selection of men already viewers or likely to be chosen to that office as Company carpenters on an annual retainer (a practice common to many of the livery companies), do not make for unbounded confidence in the system. The 16th century apparently found acceptable or at least tolerable what the 20th considers inappropriate conduct in its governmental officials.

One reason for the tolerance may have been that the public/private distinction was much less sharply defined. This becomes obvious in looking at the fewer than two dozen extant views which might be considered 'public'. It is clear from the Letter Books, the Journals and Repertories, and the certificates themselves that for various reasons the mayor and aldermen periodically ordered the viewers to look into a situation and to report their findings; hence the comments in Letter Books and Journals about remuneration for such work.[99] The aldermen, the chamberlain, the recorder, even – rarely – the mayor might go along.[100] Sometimes it is not certain how officials learned of the problem, although there were periodic surveys of their wards by aldermen for the purpose of bringing to light purprestures and encroachments and similar forays by viewers, while in other cases it appears that the viewers simply brought in information based on their own observations, or that another official or an aggrieved party introduced the matter.[101]

---

95. Drapers' Company, Wardens' Accounts 1508–1546, f. 5v.
96. Ibid., Minutes and Records 1515–52, vol. 2, p. 677.
97. Goldsmiths' Company, Wardens' Accounts and Court Minutes, vol. 5 (vols. E and F), p. 53 (1537).
98. Clothworkers' Company, Quarter and Renter Wardens' Accounts 1520–1558, ff. 6v, 8; Skinners' Company, Receipts and Payments 1510–1535 (Acct. Book No. 2), unnumbered folio, entry for 1526–7.
99. See LBN, f. 150; Journal 11, f. 330.
100. For examples chosen from within the period covered by the certificates here calendared: **144** (the chamberlain and the alderman of the ward involved); Rep 2, ff. 3v (five aldermen), 9v (two aldermen and the Bridge Masters) and 108v (five aldermen, the chamberlain, and five other named men identified only as grocer, goldsmith, salter, ironmonger, and draper); Rep 10, f. 296v (three aldermen, the recorder, and the chamberlain); Rep 12, No. 1, ff. 37(35) (the chamberlain) and 86(85) (two aldermen and the chamberlain).
101. See, for example, Journal 11, f. 330 (aldermen); LBP, f. 47v (viewers told to view all

But leaving aside questions of how a public view was commissioned or ꞁow it was carried out or even to whom and where it was reported – and ꞁot only the Repertories entries but the certificates themselves roughly ꞁutline what was done – the issue is in trying to understand what a public ꞁiew was. The fewer than two dozen extant certificates in which the City ꞁppears to have had an interest may be divided into three categories. ꞁirst, and clearly public, are the certificates which reflect the everyday ꞁssues of governance which preoccupied the mayor and aldermen: the ꞁontrol of public nuisance, public safety, sanitation, safeguarding of ꞁublic land, administrative decisions. A house encroaches on public ꞁround, a common way is stopped up or a ditch filled in, two wards ꞁuarrel over a boundary line (**4, 45, 87, 121, 144** and its duplicate, **145, 157, 174, 251, 348, 384**). Second are the matters in which the City appeared in a proprietary capacity, and the line begins to blur. The Masters of the Bridgehouse appeared very much like any private owners of property, as both plaintiffs and defendants, to protest about encroachments, to insist on repairs to houses, to explain why their own houses were in decay and causing injury to neighbouring buildings (**35, 164**). During the reigns of Edward VI and Mary, the Masters of the Hospital of St. Bartholomew, identified as 'aldermen and others', similarly represented the City's proprietary interests (**298, 393**). And the chamberlain very commonly represented such interests when he called for a view for the purpose of determining the metes and bounds of property adjoining ground owned by the Chamber of London (and leased to a third party), or acted against encroachment onto such property by a neighbouring building (**39, 42, 348**).[102] Third are the cases in which a dispute originally between two private parties suddenly took on a quasi-public aspect because of findings made by the viewers. When John Brugge complained of John Sabbe's wharf into the Thames, the City was not a party. But the viewers nonetheless found a public nuisance, which they ordered abated (**68, 71**). A discussion about cleaning and repairing a jakes took on public overtones when the viewers discovered that a shop of one party encroached on the king's highway and commented that it ought not of right to stand there and that the chamberlain should pull it down (**267**).

Other quarrels involved the City even more remotely; six tenants of properties owned by the Chamber refused to pay tithes on several small buildings erected by the Chamber on the grounds that they were outbuildings of existing tenements, not income producing units. Obviously a finding on the nature of the buildings would have some economic effect on the Chamber, but the viewers did not take specific note of its interest (**141**). Still other certificates are hard to pigeonhole because it is not clear whether named City officials are acting in a private or official capacity. Three aldermen and the common clerk moved against Thomas Bates, concerning the measurement of certain houses in Birchin Lane and

encroachments on the waterside of Thames); Journal 6, f. 74v, and LBO, f. 42v (a viewer and the City's plumber, Thomas Gonne, bring in a plat concerning the Moorditch); Rep 10, ff. 248, 255.
102. In the last, the chamberlain was specified to be acting 'in the right of the City' and a note adds that there is to be no fee 'quia pro Camerario'.

obligations of both parties concerning gutters (**314**). There is no sugges
tion at all that the City had an interest, and yet it is highly unlikely that th
plaintiffs would have been co-owners of a property in their privat
capacities. On the other hand, when the chamberlain in 1555 became
defendant because of a wall on his ground which overhung plaintiff'
ground, it seems likely that he owned the wall personally (**407**).[10]
Officials' constant shifting about from one role to another both within the
structure of government and between their official and personal lives
must have made it difficult for observers to be certain which of the City's
interests were involved and when. And, except in cases of blatant
misconduct, it must have been almost impossible to be certain when
various roles came into conflict.

Nevertheless, the wearing of many hats by relatively few men was built
into the structure of City government. City officials – most particularly
the mayor and aldermen – had no clear jurisdictional limits to the several
roles they played. The same men sat in more than one body. They dealt
with different problems in different rooms of the Guildhall on different
days, but they were the same men. The rather protean nature of their
functioning is well illustrated by the viewers' reports: the certificates are
directed to the mayor and aldermen, but what actually happened once the
viewers had dictated their findings? Where was a certificate deposited?
More significantly, how did it come to the attention of the men to whom it
was so elaborately addressed? Where were those men sitting when the
report – and often the viewers themselves – came to them? Written
evidence, much of it from casual statements made in other contexts, is
contradictory. The clear view of government at work afforded by
Journals and Letter Books, churchwardens' accounts and livery company
records, suddenly dims once the viewers have left a site. But it is not
impossible to follow the procedure a little further, in part by piecing
together the offhand remarks and making what seem to be warrantable
inferences, and in part because the certificates themselves offer a guide.
Evidence of what happened between the time of the view and the time
reports were brought to the mayor and aldermen, together with some
glimpse of court procedure in a matter in which there had been a view,
comes from the certificates' physical condition and from the subscriptions
and endorsements recorded on them. Thus – at the risk of appearing to
catalogue holes, tears, and dampstains – it is necessary to give some
description of the 400-odd pieces of vellum which make up the Corporation of London's collection of 16th century viewers' reports.

The certificates in the collection vary widely in size. The earliest, those
in an envelope marked 'Viewers' Certificates Circa 1508' in CLRO Misc.
MSS Box 91 (**1–5**), are on heavy vellum, carefully cut into long, narrow
rectangles ranging in length from $15\frac{1}{2}''$ to $22''$ (39.4 to 55.9 cm) and in width
from $2\frac{1}{4}''$ to $6''$ (5.7 to 15.2 cm). All are intact, with no tears at the margins
although there are holes at or near the centre folds of several, but they are
badly worn and damp-stained and portions of each are illegible. The
handwriting in all five is very small and careful and some ruled guidelines

103. There is no comment on his capacity and no note concerning waiver of the fee.

re still visible. Each certificate has two holes at the left margin except **4**, which has four; **1** also has a spindle slit in the centre.

The 200 certificates for the reign of Henry VIII (**6–205**), are now bound into a hardcover volume with the file name 'Viewers' Reports 1509–1546' CLRO MS Bound Volume 204A). Initially they are shaped more or less like those described above, but over the course of the reign the certificates become less long – some are only 10″ in length – and, necessarily, wider; the average is between 12″ and 14″ (30.5–35.6 cm) long and 5″ and 6″ (12.7–15.2 cm) in width. They are not as carefully cut, they are on lighter vellum, and the handwriting is larger than that of the five certificates filed as 'Circa 1508'. Handwriting does not vary greatly over the period, although it is possible to note where different clerks have been at work. For the years 1509–1541, almost all certificates appear to bear two holes at the left margin and a spindle slash in the center; for the period between 1541 and 1546, fewer than ten appear to have a slash. However, extensive repairs and rebacking may have obscured both holes and spindle marks in a number of cases.

A vellum frontispiece to the bound volume was once apparently a wrapper for a bundle of certificates. It is at its greatest length 19¼″ (48.9 cm), but is irregularly shaped and torn away at the edges. It is marked:

Vewes
de tempore regni Regis Henrici octavii
H8
vewes

Two holes at the lower left margin, 1″ (2·5 cm) apart, correspond to holes in the certificates which are usually at the upper left margin, suggesting that the vellum was a back, rather than a front, cover. The dorse of certificate **116** (irregularly shaped, between 16½″ and 17″ (41.9–43.2 cm) long and 3½″ and 4″ (8.9–10.2 cm) deep) is marked:

Visus de temporibus
H8 E6 P&M

Two holes at the left margin, 1″ (2.5 cm) apart, correspond to holes in the certificates and, from their placement, indicate that this certificate was also at one time used as back cover for a bundle, probably sometime after 1558.

The surviving certificates for the reigns of Edward VI and Philip and Mary (**206–404**), are loose in CLRO Misc. MSS Box 91. They vary greatly in size but overall are both smaller and more irregularly shaped than earlier certificates and they are on still-lighter vellum. Only two or three have been spindled in the centre, but all bear holes, some in pairs, at the left; two, three, four, even seven and eight holes and slashes exist in the margin. The handwriting is clear, although two certificates for 8 May 1554 are written in a sprawling, careless hand different from any before or following them. Many of the certificates for the reign of Philip and Mary are rotted and blackened at the margins, particularly those from 1554.

Fragments of 11 certificates (**405–15**) from the same reign are collected in an envelope marked 'Viewers' Certificates Circa 1554', also kept in CLRO Misc. MSS Box 91. They are held together by a string, apparently not contemporary, through a hole in the upper left corner of each; they

are not strung in chronological order. Each has at least one other hole an
most more than one. In most cases, at least half the certificate is missing
Those for which a date is legible in the text or endorsement in fact dat
not from 1554 but from 1555, suggesting that the 1554 and 1555 certif
cates were damaged at the same time and probably by the same agency
Later certificates for the reign are in better condition although sever:
from 1557 lack the upper right corner.

The size of the certificates and the placement of holes, in themselves c
less than compelling interest, are nevertheless of some importanc
because they suggest the way in which the certificates were handled. Th
earlier ones, at least, must have been brought into court individually
perhaps spindled at the time of their presentation, and then filed wit
many others on a thong or wire threaded through the two holes at the lef
so that they would lie flat on a shelf. An entry in Miscellaneous Roll F
explains that the viewers came to court to deliver their certificate which i
now '*in filac' inter billas assis' noc' de hoc anno*'.[104] The certificates for th
later years of Henry VIII, still bearing only two holes and with or withou
spindle marks, also seem to have been bundled only once and wer
probably handled the same way.[105] But the certificates for the reigns o
Edward VI and Philip and Mary, with their many holes and slashes at th
left margin and sometimes with tears from those holes to the vellum's lef
edge, as if the certificate had been ripped out of a bundle, may have been
brought into court already strung together and then rebundled and re-
strung through other holes at a later time. I have been unable to find any
correlation between the existence of an endorsement to a certificate –
showing that the certificate had been brought into court – and the number
and position of holes it bears. It is unlikely that all certificates came to the
court's attention; party views, for example, probably required no further
official action. But it is possible that an entire bundle was brought in and
that endorsements were then made to individual certificates without
removing them from the file or, in some cases, by tearing them out of it.

There is no definitive internal evidence to show by whom the certificates were handled or where they were kept once they had been set down
by the clerk to whom they must have been dictated, who was almost
certainly the First Clerk of the Mayor's Court. Certainly the senior clerk
of that court was the clerk of 'bails and views', and, as noted above, after
the Great Fire there is a reference to his drawing up and entering views
for the surveyors as he had formerly done of the views of the common
viewers.[106] Probably they were kept by that clerk, although possibly they
remained with the viewers, who were after all sworn officers of the City,
until such time as the court heard a report of the view. Certificates were
brought into court by a variety of officials including, for the reign of

104. CLRO Miscellaneous Roll FF, mem. 35v, calendared *Nuisance*, 604. A filacer was a
thread or wire on which writs or bills were strung.
105. A 'certificate of a noysaunce by the vewers' from 20 May 1510 explains that a wall
belonged to the Mercers 'as more plainly may appere by the viewers byll remaynyng
upon the file of billes of viewers [in] this Court of Record.' (Rep 2, f. 112v.)
106. See note 14 above. The senior clerk's function in the mid-seventeenth century is so
described in CLRO, Mayor's Court Original Bills, Lists of Schedules to Mayor's Court
Original Bills, p. i.

Henry VIII, the Serjeant at Mace (**65**); a clerk of the Mayor's Court (**37**, **88**); other unidentified serjeants (e.g. **29**, **30**);[107] the clerk of the Compter in the Poultry (**85**); one of the sheriff's clerks (e.g. **66**, **77–8**, **80**, **84**, **185**); once possibly a party to the action, although the wording is not entirely clear (**164**); and, particularly during the earlier years of the reign, the viewers themselves (**8**, **12**, **14**, **27**, **81–3**, **86**, **88**, **90–2**, **95–8**, **160**), for whom others are sometimes stated to be acting (**78**, **80**). Clearly, not everyone was authorised to 'bring in' a view; one notation comments that a certificate was brought to court by one 'Ru ... Spenfold...' but that the court had been unwilling to receive it by his hand and that afterwards John Hammond, one of the sheriff's clerks, had presented the view in the name of the viewers (**78**). Similar evidence for the reigns of Edward VI and Philip and Mary unfortunately does not exist; certificates from the middle of the 1540's to the end of the period – all during the tenure of William Blackwell as common clerk – either lack endorsements, or these are limited to brief notes that a certificate has been received and payment made (or not made) to the common clerk.

No matter who produced the certificates in court, endorsements were apparently made there by the common, or later town, clerk. There are references in the endorsements to the three common clerks of the period – William Paver (1514–1533), William Ryshton (1533–1540) and William Blackwell (1539/40–1570) – and even more references simply to the unnamed '*communis clericus*'. At least twelve endorsements are signed by the common clerk (**78**, **92**, **96**, **98**, **150–2**, **154–5**, **158–60**); occasionally a certificate appears to have been signed by him in two places, following the endorsement and elsewhere. It is probable that endorsements were at times made by the first clerk of the Mayor's Court, the common clerk's deputy in the Mayor's Court and secondary of that court.[108]

Physical custody of the certificates once in court probably rested with the clerks of the Mayor's Court, all of whom were among the clerks of the common clerk.[109] Thomas Hayes, William Hayward, William Dummer, William Pykering, and Robert Christopher, clerks of the Mayor's Court at one time or another between 1508 and 1558, are mentioned in six endorsements in varying capacities other than the one of bringing certificates to court. Hayes and Hayward are said to have been paid the common clerk's fees (**41**, **88**, **153**). Christopher apparently made a copy of a view for a party (**279**), and Dummer and Pykering were listed, in the margin of a certificate reproduced in a Journal entry, as being present in an official capacity: a certificate was delivered to the chamberlain of London '*in plena curia in presenc[ia] W Pykering et W Dummer clericorum et alii*' (**419**).[110]

Much of the evidence from the endorsements and elsewhere suggests that the court in which the certificates were presented, and any further

---

107. William Nicolson is described as the mayor's serjeant in Drapers' Company, Minutes and Records 1515–52, vol. 2, p. 437.
108. Mayor's Court Original Bills, Lists of Schedules, p. i.
109. Betty Masters, 'The Town (Common) Clerk', *Guildhall Miscellany*, vol. 3 No. 1 (October, 1969), p. 59.
110. Journal 14, f. 200.

action taken, was the Mayor's Court, held in the Outer Chamber at th Guildhall. The Assize of Buildings had specified that an assize of nuisanc was to be demanded in full Husting and assigned a day there; if the cou was not then sitting, as at harvest time or during various fairs, the assi₂ was to be granted at a congregation of the mayor and aldermen.[111] Base on the limited sittings of the Husting, on the rolls of the Husting (Common Pleas and Pleas of Land, and on the Plea and Memoranda Rol for the 14th and 15th centuries, Kellaway and Chew have concluded th; it was more common for pleas to originate in Congregation; particularl after 1448, they are noted only rarely in the Husting records.[112] By th 16th century, practice had apparently altered again; the court of Hustin still retained jurisdiction over nuisance using the procedure specified b the Assize of Buildings, but apparently few applied to it.[113] Nor is it likel that a congregation of the mayor, aldermen, sheriffs, and commonalt was taking up the overflow; by the 16th century, Congregation me almost solely to elect various civic officers. More fundamental still, th₆ assize of nuisance can no longer have met the needs of Londoners, if onl because it was limited to freeholders at a time when more and mor₆ citizens were tenants. Many cases of nuisance may have been handled b₇ the action of trespass on the case, commonly brought in the Mayor'. Court, so that the viewers' certificates would have been taken into tha court. There can be no certainty; for the period between Henry VI and Elizabeth, the Mayor's Court records are largely missing.[114] But there i₅ again internal evidence: fourteen endorsements specifically mention tha the certificates to which they were appended were taken into the Mayor's Court (**9–13**, **15–17**, **19**, **49**, **64–6**, **113**):[115] '*importatur ista billa in Curia[m Maioris*' is common, although a few say '*Certificatur in Curiam Maioris*' and one refers to the Lord Mayor: '*In curiam Domini Maioris*' (**66**). A number of endorsements begin with the name of the Mayor, as '*Tempore Spencer Maioris, in Curia his . . .*' (**77**). One, from 1519, adds '*Certificatur ad Curiam Domini Regis tent' xix die Marcii anno x Henrici VIII coram Maiore et Aldermanis*', which certainly was the style used at a later time for the Mayor's Court (**41**).[116] Moreover, one certificate (**416**) has been found among the surviving original bills of the Mayor's Court, where it did not belong, to be sure, but exactly where it might have been left by oversight if it had been brought into that court in connection with an action there. Additionally, an entry in the Mercers' Company Acts of Court in 1556 notes that the Company's court had agreed that the

111. *Liber Albus*, pp. 277–8.
112. *Nuisance*, p. xiii.
113. CLRO, Husting Book 2, 1506–1537, contains only two clear examples of the assize, one in 23 Henry VII (f. 18v) and the other in 10 Henry VIII (f. 168).
114. There is a composite file, consisting of some 48 entries, the majority for debt. But fragmentary original writ files exist for the Mayor's Court from 1587 and include an action of trespass on the case dealing with access to leased premises and one of *conventione fracta* concerning repair of leased premises.
115. Again, later endorsements, where present, tend to note only that a view was 'brought in' (*infertur*), without mentioning a court.
116. See Lewis E. Flyn and Frank S. Jackson, *The Mayor's Court Practice* (2nd ed., 1896), p. 1.

wardens would ask the mayor for a view by the sworn viewers, representatives of the Company to accompany them, 'to thentente a recorde thereof may be made to appere in the Mayors Courte.'[117] Similarly, as noted above in another context, the churchwardens of St. Mary Magdalen, Milk Street, paid 22d. 'to the Judge of the Mayor's Court for the allowance of the view' and those of St. Mary at Hill paid 4d. to 'Palmer, the Attorney in the Mayors Courte' in connection with their suit in that court against one John Banastre, in which there had been a view.[118]

Yet the constant references to views presented to the Lord Mayor, both in the certificates themselves and in other records,[119] provide certain problems. By the middle of the 16th century, the mayor no longer presided in the Mayor's Court; the recorder did. The mayor did preside, however, in another court: that of the Mayor and Aldermen sitting in the Inner Chamber, the later Court of Aldermen – basically an administrative rather than judicial body. It seems likely that a substantial percentage of certificates came before the aldermen in the Inner Chamber. By the 17th century, it is clear that the Court of Aldermen was receiving views and dealing with the issues they presented,[120] and certainly after the Great Fire it was responsible for supervision of surveyors. I have seen no viewers' certificate for the period 1508–58 copied into the Repertories, which, beginning with the first volume in 1495, contain the proceedings in the Inner Chamber. But the Repertories do contain snippets of evidence which, pieced together, suggest that the aldermen sitting there were exercising the same functions in the 16th century. The 1542 dispute between the Drapers and St. Mary Aldermary, in which there was a view (**159**), was brought to the Inner Chamber early on by the Drapers' petition and continued to claim the aldermen's attention as attempts were made at mediation.[121] The view of adjoining houses between Richard Felde and the Masters of the Bridgehouse (**164**) was ordered in the Inner Chamber and the viewers told 'to make report thereof to this Court'.[122] The variance between the parish of All Hallows the Great in Thames Street and the parish of St. Michael Crooked Lane was before the aldermen,[123] who must have seen the certificate made concerning it (**165**). The Merchant Taylors' account books show payments of 'Expenses in the Law in the Defense of the Mistery against the Wrongfull Suit made by the Company or the Mistery of Clothworkers'; one, for 12d., was for a copy 'of the decree of the Court of Aldermen in the Clothworkers' case'; there had been a view.[124] Moreover, a comment in the Repertories more than 30 years earlier, in 1510, suggests that the Court received such certificates

---

117. Mercers' Company, Acts of Court 1527–1560, f. 287 (22 March 1556).
118. GL MS 2596/1, f. 52v; GL MS 1239/1, Pt. 2, f. 351v.
119. E.g., Mercers' Company, Acts of Court 1527–1560, ff. 63, 118v.
120. See the reference in P. E. Jones and R. Smith, *A Guide to the Records at Guildhall in London* (1951), pp. 68–9, describing the 17th century certificates as 'reports made to the Court of Aldermen by the sworn viewers and by Mills, Hooke and Oliver, the three surveyors for rebuilding after the Great Fire . . .'
121. Rep 10, ff. 252, 275v, 289v.
122. Ibid., f. 248.
123. Ibid., f. 254v.
124. GL microfilm 298(4), ff. 237, 260.

as a general rule; a report by four wardens of the Carpenters' Compan
refers to 'the viewers byll remaynyng upon the file of billes of viewers [in
this Court of Record'.[125]

Only very hesitantly do I suggest that the viewers could have reporte
in yet a third forum: the Court of Common Council, which handle
legislative matters. The evidence here is sparse and uncertain, but i
exists. There are in fact six Henrician viewers' certificates (**416–21**
copied into the Journals, which from 1495 onward report mainly the wor
of the Court of Common Council. Moreover, a record in the Drapers
archives of the 1541/2 dispute between themselves and the parish of St
Mary Aldermary may mean that Common Council, as well as the
aldermen sitting in the Inner Chamber, was involved in settlement of the
quarrel, so that it, too, would have seen a view in that connection. The
Drapers' entry notes that a view was brought to the mayor and aldermen
and that the mayor offered the opinion that the parish would do well to
settle the matter. The Drapers straightaway sent their clerk to urge an
agreement, as advised by 'my lord the Mayre on Tuesday last in the
Counsell Chamber at the Yeld Hall'.[126] There is a similar entry in the
Merchant Taylors' records; the action against them by the Clothworkers
was decided in the Court of Aldermen, but their expenses for 1551 2
show a payment of 43s. 6d. 'for pleading before the Mayor and Aldermen
and Common Counsell'.[127] It is not clear why the mayor and aldermen
sitting in the Court of Common Council would have concerned themselves there with a private dispute between a livery company and a parish
or between two companies; Common Council was primarily a legislative
body. But it was, after all, related to Congregation, whose mandate to
hear the assizes of nuisance went back to the Assize of Buildings. And, as
A. H. Thomas noted for an earlier period,[128] and as was true in so many
other instances, in the first half of the 16th century there were no hard and
fast boundaries, no rigid demarcations of jurisdiction. Perhaps it is once
again a question of the mayor and aldermen conducting essentially
judicial activities when sitting in primarily legislative or administrative
bodies because the same men who sat as judges sat also as administrators
and legislators, albeit in a different room of Guildhall. But the key words
are 'possibly' and 'perhaps'; the evidence does not justify any unqualified
hypotheses, let alone conclusions.

III.

Leaving aside the City itself – and its various agencies such as the
Bridgehouse – almost all parties to views can be divided into three general
categories: religious bodies, livery companies, and individuals. The list of

125. Rep 2, f. 112v (20 May 1510). There is a marginal heading 'certificate of noysaunce by
 the vewers', but the reference is to an earlier report, not quoted, by the sworn viewers.
126. Drapers' Company, Minutes and Records 1515–52, vol. 2, p. 709. Foster has suggested
 that the 'counsell chamber' mentioned by John Stow in his *Survey* was doubtless for the
 Common Council, as the Inner Chamber was for the Court of Aldermen and the Outer
 Chamber for the Mayor's Court (F. F. Foster, *The Politics of Stability: A Portrait of the
 Rulers in Elizabethan London* (1977), p. 77); see Stow, *Survey*, vol. 1, p. 272.
127. GL microfilm 298(4), f. 237.
128. *Cal. P. & M. Rolls, 1323–1364*, pp. viii–x.

those who used the viewers' services ranges from the most wealthy and powerful members of London society to those who must have been close to the bottom of its marginally respectable layers. It should be said at the outset that any attempt to categorize parties to views is beset with problems innate in the data base. First, a total of 26 of the 415 certificates in the CLRO collection have been damaged so that the name or nature of one or even in a few cases both parties is illegible; of the 26, 16 are Marian and seven date from a period beginning sometime in 1554 and ending sometime in 1555. Probably more important, other certificates, particularly from the reign of Edward VI, do not identify one or both parties beyond giving their names, so that the occupation or status of 67 individuals is unknown.[129] Moreover, comparing litigants during the reign of Henry VIII with those during the reigns of his son and daughter means comparing 205 Henrician views stretching over a period of 40 years with 134 Edwardian views covering six and 76 views surviving from 1554–58. Either there were fewer views per annum during Henry's reign or many more of them have been lost, and there is no way of knowing which possibility is correct. Obviously, then, conclusions based on existing data must be subject to careful scrutiny and evaluated in the light of other records and related evidence.

Keeping in mind this caveat, one can still see fairly clear patterns in the nature of litigants emerge and shift, and can draw conclusions about what the shift meant for London government and society. Above all, Henry VIII's Reformation, the violent re-shaping of the English church, is mirrored in the lists of plaintiffs and defendants. Of the 205 certificates from his reign surviving in the Corporation records, 70 have a religious body as a plaintiff, 62 as a defendant. Parishes, a bishop, religious confraternities, St. Paul's cathedral and its component entities, chantry priests, religious foundations centred outside London but with holdings in the City, and above all the great London religious foundations, litigated endlessly. The priory of St. Bartholomew West Smithfield; the house or hospital of St. Thomas of Acre; the Minoresses of the convent of St. Clare without Aldgate; the Hospital of St. Thomas the Martyr in Southwark; the Charterhouse; the priory of St. Mary Overy, also in Southwark; Elsing Spital; Austin Friars; the convent of Haliwell; St. Mary Spital; the priory of St. Helen's; St. Mary Graces, the 'new abbey on Tower Hill'; the priory of Holy Trinity Aldgate: all are there, together with their not-far-distant neighbour, the Free Chapel of St. Stephen, Westminster, attacking and defending property rights with considerable zest. The prior of St. Bartholomew was the moving party in four views and the defending party in three; no other religious figure quite matched that, although the master of St. Thomas of Acre ran a close second with involvement in six views. Religious bodies acted against each other – 29 views record their quarrels – and to a lesser extent against livery companies, with nine views. In 32 instances, the defendant was an

---

129. The information can sometimes be gleaned from other sources such as livery company or parish minutes, the Repertories and Journals, or non-City records. For example, defendant Lewes Stokkett (**222**) may well have been the Lewes Stocket who was later Surveyor of the Works to Queen Elizabeth.

individual and individuals returned the interest: 22 views record their complaints against various parishes, St. Paul's cathedral, and the occasional priory or hospital.

But the picture changes abruptly during the last decade of Henry's reign, and of the 134 certificates surviving for the reign of Edward VI only four involve religious bodies – all parishes – as plaintiffs while five show a variety of religious groups as defendants (**241, 280, 266, 213, 331**). Religious bodies had disappeared from the certificates as a meaningful presence. Priories and convents had been dissolved, brotherhoods and chantries followed soon after. Only the parish churches and St Paul's cathedral survived, and these had lost much of their property. They had little inclination to embark on litigation; surviving churchwardens accounts and vestry books show parishes struggling to keep pace with government-mandated changes in practice and in fabric, demolishing altars and accounting for plate. They cannot have wished to draw further attention to their remaining possessions and rights. Nor did the picture change during the reign of Mary, suggesting the permanency of the alteration. The sample is small, but out of 76 certificates for the years 1554–8, only two involve clergymen or religious bodies as plaintiffs and two as defendants. Yet, again, the certificates provide an accurate mirror of political life: while three of the Marian views involve parishes and individuals, the fourth shows the abbot of a briefly-revived Westminster Abbey, John Feckenham, disputing with the bishop of London, Edmund Bonner, over sanctuary ground (**397**).

The change in parties to certificates over the 50 year period here under discussion reflects more than religious upheaval, however. It could be characterised as a shift from corporate to individual litigants. None of the limitations inherent in the evidence vitiates the suggestion that the livery companies, the second great group of corporate litigants, were – like religious bodies – less active participants in views at midcentury than they had been earlier. The difference is not so evident in the number of views they sought; the companies, particularly the great companies, were plaintiffs in 25 of 205 certificates from the reign of Henry VIII and in 13 of 134 from the reign of his son (although the 76 certificates from the years of Mary – too few to be relied on – offer a very different picture with only three companies appearing as plaintiff).[130] But the companies disappear as defendants. They were defendants in 23 extant Henrician views, in two from Edward's reign, in none from the Marian period.[131] The loss of

130. What is more, only nine of the 25 Henrician certificates show a complaint against individuals while ten are against a religious body and five against another livery company (one, certificate **75**, was against the King's College of Eton, which does not fit neatly into any of the other categories). For the next reign, one certificate shows a dispute with a religious body and the other 12 reflect quarrels with individuals. For 1554–58, two of the three views requested by livery companies were against individuals, while the identity of the defendant in the third is uncertain.

131. The plaintiffs were individuals in either six or seven of the 23 Henrician certificates in which companies were defendants while in nine or ten they were religious bodies (the nature of the plaintiff in **73** is not entirely clear). In five they were other livery companies; in two they were the City itself. In the two certificates extant from Edward's reign showing livery companies as defendants, both plaintiffs were individuals, a grocer and a merchant taylor.

ertificates for all three reigns would have had to be very selective to roduce those figures if in fact there was no shift in parties. The meaning f the change is another matter, by no means as obvious as the meaning of ae decline in litigation involving the church. The position of the livery ompanies was not static between the beginning and end of the 16th entury. Keene and Harding, in their *Survey of Documentary Sources for Property Holding in London before the Great Fire*, point out that many ompanies lost property which they had held for chantry purposes in 548, when chantries were finally dissolved, or else found it necessary to ell some holdings to raise money to redeem the chantry charges on the est.[132] Other sales may have been made in order to consolidate holdings n one area. Are either or both of these circumstances reflected in the ertificates? Did the companies, like the churches, for a time move less aggressively against their neighbours than they once had, thereby prompting less litigation? Or, on the other hand, had they solidified their ioldings in a way which provoked fewer challenges? Did the decrease in itigation mirror a decrease in other company activity? Or had some itigants simply turned to other methods of settling some disputes?

In any event, it is individuals who make up the majority of litigants after 1547. In 97 of the Edwardian certificates, both parties are individuals; three have individuals acting against religious bodies; two have individuals against livery companies. Individuals were defendants in three views requested by parishes, in 12 asked for by livery companies. For the reign of Mary, 58 certificates show plaintiffs as individuals while 59 show them as defendants; the number might be still higher if several damaged Marian certificates were more legible.

What sort of person 'called in the viewers' or faced them? Almost anyone of fixed abode and regular income. Except as already noted, the certificates commonly identify parties by company membership, occupation or status: mercer, grocer, gentleman, widow, alderman, mariner, latener, innholder. Noblemen were scarce as parties; two appear during the reign of Henry VIII – both as defendants – and only one thereafter, also a defendant. Knights (and their ladies) were more often parties: apart from knights who were also aldermen, of whom there are five named, seven are plaintiffs, six defendants.[133] Gentlemen were present frequently in views throughout the period and became more so towards midcentury: 14 plaintiffs and 15 defendants during Henry's reign, seven plaintiffs (but eight certificates: one figures in two views) and four defendants during Edward's, and a surprising six plaintiffs and seven defendants during Mary's. They are joined by a handful of squires – eight over the 50 years covered, half plaintiffs, half defendants. Almost one-fifth of the views, then, concern men and women who neither belonged to livery companies nor, apparently, practised any gainful occupation within London. Others identified by status probably did; ten certificates show aldermen acting in a private capacity, and all those men necessarily

132. Derek Keene and Vanessa Harding, *A Survey of Documentary Sources for Property Holding in London before the Great Fire*, LRS vol. 22 (1985), p. 12.
133. But two certificates, **68** and **71**, deal with the same plaintiff, who is also identified as an alderman in each case.

belonged to a livery company. It is very likely that the landlords, tenant: and executors mentioned without further identification did also.[1] Widows probaby did not. Twenty-four women who appear in the certif cates acting alone are specified to be widows – and they appear ovei whelmingly as defendants. Of the nine who were parties to views from th reign of Henry VIII, three were not defendants; of the 11 from 154 through 1553, two were not. Only the Marian certificates show a reversa of the pattern; among five widows mentioned, four were plaintiffs Women identified as 'lady' or 'dame' or 'mistress', but not as 'widow' did better overall; during the period 1508–47, one was a defendant an⊷ one a plaintiff while during 1547–53 two were plaintiffs, one later being ⅎ defendant against the same party. Between 1554–8, one lady was ⅎ plaintiff, one a defendant.[135] One does not wish to draw extensivⅇ conclusions from scanty data, but it is hard to avoid the impression that ⅎ woman of modest circumstances and alone perhaps presented her morⅇ litigious neighbours with the prospect of easy advancement of theiⅈ property interests; simply calling in the viewers might have been enougⅠ to force a compromise. But the prospect might well have grown dimmeⅉ when the woman in question was My Lady Damice (**106**) or the Worship‑ ful Lady Dame Johanna Morgan (**391**), whatever her marital status!

Widows may have had neither recognized occupation nor membershiⲣ in a company; clergy at least had the former. Identified variously aꜱ clerks, priests, clerics, and parsons, they did not often appear as individu‑ als rather than as representatives of a parish or other religious body; I have counted ten acting for themselves in the reign of Henry VIII, divided evenly between plaintiffs and defendants, and two for the reign of Edward VI, also equally divided.[136]

People who might be characterised as royal officials or courtiers form another discrete group of potential litigants who were not entirely fitted into the structure of London society: William Cheynes, gentleman, acting 'as in right of the King'; Richmond Herald; Garter King of Arms; the Lord Chief Justice; Somerset Herald; Edward VI's secretary; the King's fletcher; the yeoman of the Queen's larder are found, three times as defendants and five times as plaintiffs. William Cheynes, alone of the group, seems to have been acting in the King's behalf rather than as a private person (**76**). As already noted, the same question of role arises with those litigants identified as municipal officials – the Mayor and Aldermen, the Common Clerk, the Chamberlain, the Master of the Bridgehouse. It is a question which seems to have escaped the 16th century clerks who wrote up the certificates, because the desire to draw such lines escaped both the officials who called for views and the craftsmen who made them.

But gentlemen and widows, royal and municipal officials, clerics and tenants, all together account for only a minority of individual parties to

---

134. Four certificates involve men identified only as executors; several of them, however, are shown elsewhere as sheriffs, aldermen, and members of great companies.
135. Ten women are shown in the certificates as parties together with their husbands, while the status of one woman is unknown owing to the illegibility of the certificate.
136. Three were at issue with their own churchwardens.

certificates. The majority of individual litigants were identified by their companies. The twelve great companies are well, but unevenly, represented: for example, during the reign of Henry VIII, members of the Goldsmiths', Skinners', Salters', Ironmongers', Vintners', and Clothworkers' companies litigated infrequently and Haberdashers not at all, while Merchant Taylors were party to a total of 16 views and Drapers to 15. Mercers, Grocers, and Fishmongers came in the middle with eight, nine, and six appearances respectively. Nor did the general pattern change over the course of the next reign.

One would expect to find members of the great companies in the certificates, just as one would expect to find gentlemen and aldermen and priests. Views were concerned with real property and rights in it; property owners, leaseholders for terms of years, and others with an interest worth defending tended to be men of substance. Moreover, views and the whole procedure they involved were not cheap; the 5s. fee alone must have deterred more than one individual who thought he had been put upon by his neighbour. It would be harder to predict the extent to which the lesser people of London were involved in the procedure and the capacities in which they were: were they present at all in significant numbers? Did they actively seek views, were they plaintiffs? Or did they appear primarily as defendants? If the latter, were their appearances related to their occupations? The certificates offer at least tentative answers to such questions. In fact, men from a range of trades and crafts and professions of varying profitability and respectability appear in a substantial minority of certificates. For the entire period 1508–58, 113 parties to views are identified as members of one or another of the minor companies and associations. There is at least one armourer, baker, barber-surgeon, blacksmith (blacksmith spurrier), bowyer, brewer, butcher, carpenter, cook, cooper, cordwainer, currier, cutler, dyer, embroiderer, fruiterer, girdler, glazier, innholder, joiner, lorimer, painter stainer, pewterer, plumber, poulterer, saddler, scrivener, shearman, stockfishmonger (the last two not yet amalgamated into the Clothworkers' and Fishmongers' Companies), tallowchandler, tiler, waxchandler, weaver, and woodmonger. Another 22 men are identified as members of professions, trades, or other groups which were not represented by a livery company, although several – like lawyers, physicians, cobblers, and at least some of the otherwise-unidentified 'merchant strangers' – enjoyed organisation, and were indeed regulated as a body. Others, like the men identified simply as 'yeoman', did not and were not; still others, like waterbearers (not watermen) and sandmen, tailors (not Merchant Taylors) and crossbowmakers, lateners and mariners, are difficult to fit into the companies as their membership then stood.[137]

The fact of these men's appearance, of course, is less significant than the capacity in which they appeared: however unwilling to participate one might be, he had no choice in whether to be a defendant. Forty-six such people were plaintiffs, 89 defendants. What produced the disparity? At

137. For information on the membership and nature of the companies, I have used W. Carew Hazlitt, *The Livery Companies of the City of London* (1892; repr. New York, 1969), pp. vi–viii.

the start, one might hypothesize that some trades might by their very nature be likely to involve their practitioners in litigation. Did, for example, practising butchers, brewers, dyers, and curriers appear frequently simply because of the nature of their work, which created unpleasant odours or other offences to their neighbours? Clearly, butchers' scalding houses and their disposal of entrails had presented a serious nuisance since at least the beginning of the 14th century and probably before that; early records mention actions brought against those who threw animal blood and filth into the highways and ditches.[138] At first sight, butchers appear to conform to the expectation. Men identified as 'butcher' were defendants in six of the nine extant views to which a butcher was a party in the reigns of Henry VIII and Edward VI, but none of the causes shown appears to have any relation to the defendant's trade. Moreover, men belonging to other potentially offensive trades were actually as often plaintiffs as defendants; and like the butchers, none of the quarrels involving dyers or curriers seems to have been connected with premises used in a defendant's practice of his metier: they concern measurements, encroachments, repairs, and other common causes of action. As for the brewers, while the premises involved in several certificates are identified as brewhouses, only one view (**85**) stemmed from defendant's use of those premises in his trade. It is true that by the 16th century company affiliation did not necessarily indicate one's actual trade or occupation, so that possibly some defendants did not practise the craft or trade by which they were identified. But someone must have been a practising butcher, brewer, dyer, currier – and his work gave rise to no complaints which necessitated a view.

The same lack of connection between occupation and dispute exists with regard to views brought by or against members of the two other crafts most frequently found in the certificates, bakers and carpenters. Bakers' ovens often encroached, but neither ovens, encroachment, nor heat were at issue in the five appearances that men shown as bakers made as defendants, and indeed only one (**88**) involved a structure identified as a bakehouse; nor is a bakehouse or oven mentioned in the two instances in which such men were plaintiffs. Similarly, work done by carpenters themselves does not play a prominent part in the six certificates in which they were defendants and their craft is not involved in the four in which they were plaintiffs.

Always bearing in mind the possibility that great numbers of relevant certificates are missing, it still seems fair to conclude that use of one's premises in connection with one's occupation was not a significant factor in determining the frequency with which one would meet the viewers, even though that use created heat, stench, or noise. The conclusion receives support from the work of Kellaway and Chew, who found a 'strikingly small' number of 14th and 15th century nuisance actions arising from practice of a craft.[139] A comparison of two 16th-century

---

138. See Ernest L. Sabine, 'Butchering in Mediaeval London', *Speculum*, vol. 8 (July, 1933), pp. 335–53.
139. *Nuisance*, p. xxxi. They suggest that such problems were probably handled in the wardmote.

groups engaged in noisome occupations points in the same direction and, additionally, offers evidence of what factor might be significant: for the period 1508–58, members of the Curriers' Company (a minor company engaged in dressing leather) were parties to four views, in three cases as plaintiffs. Members of the Skinners' Company, a major company whose avowed trade was not much more pleasant than the curriers', were involved in ten views, with four skinners as plaintiffs and six defendants. But no case involving a skinner was based on practice of that occupation, and in fact, by the 16th century many members of the Company probably did not practise the skinning trade.

Looking beyond occupation, one might hypothesize that 'lesser men' appearing as defendants in views did so primarily in connection with violations of the terms of their leases – particularly concerning repairs – since they must have frequently been tenants. The certificates do not bear out that assumption. Only a total of nine of 89 such defendants – or at most 11, as two certificates are ambiguous – were the objects of complaints by lessors about the condition of leased premises.[140] Moreover, complaints about tenants were not directed only at one group. At least six gentlemen and members of the great companies were defendants in similar matters, more if some quarrels about repairs were actually based on a lease as they appear (but are not stated) to be. Tenancy and the stringent obligation to repair under which most tenants held their leases cannot account for the disparity of participation in views between 'greater' and 'lesser' men or even for incidence of defendants among one group as opposed to the other. In fact, a careful reading of the certificates indicates that the issues most commonly leading to a view do not vary greatly according to the circumstances of the parties or their position in society: gutters, encroachment, party walls and the like concerned every element of the population.

Given that fact, a comparison of the 199 members of the great companies plus the 94 noblemen, knights, ladies and gentlemen, squires, courtiers, royal officials, and aldermen present in the certificates with the 135 parties who were members of lesser companies or unofficial organisations or of no organisation at all suggests strongly that the most significant factor bearing on whether one would meet the viewers was social status, often reflected in official status. Small as the numbers are, the comparison above between skinners and curriers is a striking demonstration of the point. Still more convincing evidence is the overlap between parties and London officialdom. Among others, Robert Fenrother, Michael Dormer, William Roche, John Lowen, Andrew Judde, Humfrey Baskerfeld (or Baskervile; here 'Berskerdfeld'), Thomas Kytson, William Butler, Christopher Ascue, Christopher Draper, Thomas Whyte or White,

---

140. Eight certificates dealing wholly or partly with repairs to be made under a lease either do not identify the defendant as anything other than 'tenant' or are partially illegible so that it is not possible to learn the defendant's occupation. If all or a substantial percentage of these defendants were in fact men of the lesser companies or otherwise of lower status, obviously the result would be different. But there is no reason to believe that they were since among the tenant defendants whose occupations were shown in similar cases were a fishmonger, a mercer, a salter, a vintner, a merchant taylor, and a haberdasher.

Thomas Curtes, Henry Dacres, Richard Rede, John Brugge or Bruge, Robert Trappes, Richard Dobbys or Dobbes, William Locke – each was a party to at least one private view and each was at one point in his career an alderman; some also held the mayoralty.[141] Moreover, they were most often plaintiffs and when they were not, their opponents were of stature equal to their own. Thus the executors of a late Lord Mayor asked for a view in an altercation with William Roche, a merchant taylor asked for one against John Lowen, the Merchant Taylors against Humfrey Baskerfeld, the abbot of Rowley against Thomas Kytson, another alderman against Christopher Ascue, the Fishmongers against Thomas Curtes (**28, 297, 308, 104, 89, 236**). The only exception seems to have been when Thomas Whyte found himself opposing one Peter Baker, 'citizen and scriver', whom the viewers in fact found to be in the right (**398**). 'Lesser men' did not casually take on officialdom.

But they were disproportionately often defendants. To equal the plaintiff/defendant ratio of members of the great companies, the 135 'lesser men' would have had to produce 99 plaintiffs instead of the 46 they actually did; to equal that of the noblemen/knight group, they would have had to produce 101. Moreover, the only significant factor I have found which can account for the disparity is socio-economic status.[142]

It is not necessary to conclude that the well-born or well-to-do made a habit of attacking their less able or well-off neighbours through the mechanism of the view. They may have, indeed, but it is also possible that the disparity is not so much in numbers of defendants as in numbers of plaintiffs. That is, the less wealthy and powerful may simply have preferred to settle differences without calling in officials of the City; they may have been reluctant to appear before the mayor even to request a view, hesitant to set in motion an expensive proceeding which might embroil them further with a government they preferred to keep their distance from whenever possible.

In any event, the pattern is no surprise. Sixteenth-century London was not run by or for its fruiterers and blacksmiths and scriveners and the remarkable thing is that they and others like them appear as often as they do, not only as defendants but to challenge their neighbours and even their betters in defence of their watercourses and walls.

IV.

Despite the formal humility of the certificates, it is clear from early in their history that the viewers were doing more than simply reporting fact. They were applying law, law in the form of binding custom. In September 1373, in a dispute over fixtures removed from a leased tenement, they listed the fixtures which should not have been removed 'following the usage of the City'. Likewise in January 1408, in a matter between a widow and her son or stepson, they examined utensils and household goods to

141. See Beaven for an almost complete listing of aldermen of the period.
142. But it should be noted that if the aldermanic knights are left out, as they probably should be for these purposes, the plaintiff/defendant ratio within the nobleman/knight group drops precipitously to 43/42, meaning that the 135 'lesser men' should have produced 91 plaintiffs in order to maintain the ratio.

determine which were removable and which not under City custom. In March 1409 they declared that John Crosseby had built a stone wall 'against law and reason and against the custom of the said City'.[143] There are, however, no specific recommendations for action to be taken, only the occasional formulaic 'through which may it please you to ordain a remedy', which, by the early 15th century, had evolved into the cautious 'On which may it please you to ordain a remedy if it be that neither of the said parties is able to show any evidence or specialty to the contrary.' There are not enough certificates extant from the 15th century to trace either the growing self-confidence of the viewers or the gradual expansion of their activities. Certainly there is no authorisation for either development in the Letter Books, the Plea and Memoranda Rolls, or the Journals. Yet the certificates in the CLRO collection show that by the 16th century viewers were both unafraid to tackle questions going well beyond simple craft expertise and confident of their ability to apply legal rules to the facts they found. Nor, apparently, did they regard their reports as simply informational. It is worth noting that the prayer for remedy had disappeared; the viewers simply stated their conclusions as to what should be done, adding 'unless there be any evidence or specialty to be shewed to the contrary.' By 1508, in fact, their decision was enough to settle many disputes out of court. This was, of course, more likely when two parties were trying to resolve a dispute arising from uncertainty about boundaries or obligations, but it happened also when there were true adversary proceedings. The Mercers' records show the procedure at work: a view made at the request of the prior of St. Mary Spital had declared that a sewer should run through the Mercers' gardens and that the Mercers should keep it in repair (**87**). 'Wherefore,' says an entry in the Mercers' Court Book for 1529, 'it is ordained that the said watercourse or sewer shall be made at the costs charges and expense of this Fellowship according to the view and report before expressed'.[144] There had been a transformation of a group of expert witnesses into something like an administrative tribunal.

Decisions carrying this kind of authority were arrived at in a variety of ways. Certainly the viewers and their retinue went out and measured boundaries and poked mortar and stared out of windows and watched water pour from gutters. They relied not only on their instruments and the established measuring units of the day: feet, inches, and, less commonly, ells – '. . . 6 ells and 3/4 ell by the standard of the ell that is now used', says a 1538 certificate (**130**) – but on their own practised hands and eyes: 'the iiii viewers say in the judgement and sight of a man's ie [the garden ground] belongeth to the said plaintifes', explains a 1542 view (**167**). But they were not limited to on-site evidence. They could and did examine and interpret documents: leases, deeds, earlier views, 'other writings', even the Husting Rolls (**29**). When they were puzzled by evidence or lack of it and when no documents were shown them, the viewers gathered information in other ways, apparently without first seeking the guidance of any court. Sometimes they called the parties to

143. *Nuisance*, 583, 646, 661.
144. Mercers' Company, Acts of Court 1527–1560, f. 27v.

xlv

them; sometimes they interviewed witnesses, particularly 'ancient men' with a recollection of earlier roads and boundaries (**233**). In August 1536, in a dispute between two London wards, the certificate records that 'they have viewed and seen' and have acted 'upon their diligent search, inquisition, and deliberate examination of the oldest men and longest dwellers within the said wards now living' as well as on 'good and substantial other evidence and proof' (**121**). In April, 1543, they 'herd, examined, and well considered the depositions, evidence, and testymony of iiii old inhabitantes and dwellers thereby ... being sworne as afore a judge to give true evidence unto the said viewers in that behalf' (**179**). No statement of theory could better reflect their actual status and function. Sometimes despite all they might do there was uncertainty, and then there was resort to talk about experience and to vague hints about good and sufficient proof, or to remarks about conscience.[145] But their decision was frankly part guesswork: they drew a line between Henry Mynge and John Howe, who did not know the limits of their properties, bounding the ground 'that ys most Doubtfull that belongeth to the said Henry Mynge' (**386**) – by which they apparently meant that it was most likely to be his.

Occasionally, the evidence necessitated a decision which the viewers regretted In such instances, there is a recognition of their own limitations, but the language still sounds magisterial: in August 1549 for example, they discovered a door from a defendant's house into a plaintiff's garden and a right of way from there into a neighbouring alley. 'The which dore we cannot denie hym,' they acknowledged mournfully, 'but we thinke that there may evyll inconveniences growe by yt if that dore do stonde there. Unto all this we the said viewers ar agreed' (**257**). One remembers that John Stow, in the *Survey of London*, remarks that Empson and Dudley, Henry VII's notorious henchmen, met secretly via just such a door to further their schemes.[146]

In only two instances in the CLRO collection did the viewers find themselves unable – or unwilling – to come to a conclusion. One was when six tenants of the Chamber of London refused to pay a tithe to the parson of All Hallows Staining for six little buildings recently erected by the Chamberlain and occupied by them. Although the reasoning is not spelled out, the tithe apparently depended on whether the buildings were houses or sheds. The viewers determined 'that they be houses, and no sheddes, and that also the said Tenantes do not lete oute the said houses nor any of theyme to ferme', but they would go no further: 'As touching the said tithes or parsons dutye the said viewers sayen that it ys no parte of their charge nor nothyng appurteynyng unto theym to discusse or medle with' (**141**). They would not become involved in ecclesiastical matters. (The certificate also provides an unintentional glimpse at Tudor domestic attitudes: the new buildings are 'made for houses of easement & necessary Rowmes for withdraughtes, for lodgyng of servantes, & to ley in wood & coles or any other thing ...'). The second occurred when Christopher Ascue took down certain entries and rooms of easement belonging to Richard Dobbys (Dobbes) in July 1530. The viewers were willing but

145. See for example **287**, involving an attempt to determine the original location of a fire.
146. Stow, *Survey*, i, 224.

unable to say how much space Dobbys had had 'for as moche as every thing is taken downe there that myght lede them to any further knowlege in that behalf'. Therefore, they said on their consciences, Dobbys should have what he could prove that he had had before 'by triall and witnesse of neighbors and other that have seen and knowen the same . . .' (**89**). But the 'triall' did not take place in court; Letter-Book O contains an entry marked 'Viewers Award' and dated October of the same year, showing that the parties had asked the four men to act as arbitrators in the matter. How they arrived at their decision is unclear – they speak of 'right good knowlege and profe' of the existence of a cistern for a withdraught – but the viewers ordered the construction by Ascue of a new cistern and vault and a new entry, all of specified sizes and materials. They were not recommending; the language is 'awarde, iuge & ordeyn' and 'awarde ordeyne & deme' and they set their seals to the award, expecting it to end the matter, as it did.[147]

But they were careful to note that they did so as arbitrators; acting simply as the common viewers, however confident and competent, they could not have so foreclosed review of their decision by the mayor and aldermen. The form of the certificates leaves open the possibility that City officials will overrule the findings set out and the viewers' conclusions must have been subject to review, although neither the procedure nor the forum are ever set out. I have seen only two examples of anything like a challenge to their decisions. In the first, in May 1510, the wardens of the Carpenters' Company came before the Court of Aldermen. There had been a dispute between the Mercers and the Abbess and Convent of the Minoresses; the viewers had found that a wall belonged to the Mercers and had presented their bill to that effect.[148] Then at some later time, 'for the more perfet knowleage of the trouth of the premises' the wardens of the Carpenters were charged and commanded by the Court of Aldermen 'to serche and examyn the trouth in that behalf'. The wardens saw the wall and reported back only 'that the presentment of the said viewers ys true, as ys aforesaid in their said bill'.[149] The matter apparently ended there.

The second group who attempted to challenge the viewers' findings were dealt with less gently. In the celebrated quarrel between the Drapers and St. Mary Aldermary (**159** reflects only one stage of it) the Drapers complained of encroachments and nuisances done in the building of a new house by the parish. The Drapers' records give the story in detail, with some relish: on 25 September 1542, the wardens of the Company went to the mayor and asked that he send for the parson and churchwardens of Aldermary to hear their answer to the complaint. The next day, all went before the mayor and aldermen and both the plaintiffs' 'bill' and the viewers' report were read. The churchwardens acknowledged that they had no writing to support their position, but 'sayd that xxxii masons Carpenters and bricklayers had sene and vewed theyr sayd new tenement and that they had found and could prove that our [the

147. LBO, f. 202. See **418** for a transcript of the Award.
148. It is not in the CLRO collection.
149. Rep 2, f. 112v.

Drapers'] tenement there ys incroached uppon theyr grounde.' To which the mayor replied – and the rhetoric of the Book of Job comes irresistibly to mind – 'Who appointed or gave any commandement to the sayd xxxii persons so to do, or before whom were they sworen? For suche bysnes my brethern and I have appointed iiii master vewers whiche be sworen in all suche matters to be indyfferent and we must geve credence unto theym and not unto suche as you have appoynted thereunto.' And then, in a broad hint as to how any decision would go, recorded with some satisfaction by the Drapers' clerk, the mayor concluded, 'Wherefor I wold advyse you, (sayd my lord), to commune with the drapers and aggree with theym.'[150]

It must have been a gratifying moment for the four master masons and carpenters, who had, after all, appeared before the Drapers' Court of Assistants only a few months earlier, in November 1541, to affirm that they would abide by the view they had presented to the mayor and aldermen in August of the same year. It was an unusual performance and suggests that both the Drapers and the viewers expected a challenge.[151]

Even if reversal, or at least review, by municipal authorities was a less than likely occurrence, there were still other constraints on the viewers' freedom to make decisions; they were not free to work a kind of rough equity based on their perception of simple right. The custom of London, altered at times by statute, ordinarily formed the basis for their decisions. Sometimes, though, even revered custom had to give way to extra-legal considerations. By the fourth decade of the sixteenth century, social and political events disrupted the even tenor of the certificates; here is a point at which social, political, and legal history not only intersect but collide with the intrusion of the Reformation. Some 21 certificates attest, in one way or another, to the religious upheaval taking place; 18 specifically mention that property in dispute between two individuals had once been church land. Following the dissolution of the monasteries and chantries and the subsequent influx of lands onto the real estate market, many purchasers of former church properties apparently did not know what they held. They were sometimes uncertain of the existence of rights of way or other easements, unclear about what was in the leases of people who were now their tenants. But alleging a right in oneself derogating from one's adversary's enjoyment of his property, or alleging anything which might look like a defect in his title, was a touchy thing: purchases had been made 'of the king's grace'. Moreover, the king was essentially the guarantor of the buyer's title, since the present owner's right was, as the viewers declared solemnly, 'in as ample manner and forme as the same and every parte therof to our said soveraign lorde the kinge dyd come and belonge by Acte of parliament' (**239**). The trick was to do justice without giving offence, all the harder when the purchasers were persons of standing, like the Lord Chief Justice of England (**324**) or Sir Robert Chester, who bought the Parish Clerks' Hall (**375**).

Fortunately, Henry's and Edward's activities did not touch the bases for decision of a majority of disputes in which the viewers were involved.

150. Drapers' Company, Minutes and Records 1515–52, vol. 2, p. 708.
151. Ibid., p. 677.

But change came from other sources. London was growing and becoming ever more crowded; the mayor and aldermen railed against it, monarch after monarch issued proclamations to try and stop it, but London went on expanding. The certificates, again, reflect that development. For the first 25 years of the reign of Henry VIII, from 1508 to the mid-1530s, the viewers were most frequently active settling boundary disputes, acting essentially as surveyors. During the reign of Henry VIII as a whole, 75 variances were concerned with the boundaries of either void ground or land with a structure on it; 32 involved measurement of a wall, often a party wall which may or may not have been a house wall. Thirty-five dealt specifically with encroachments and another 24 with overhang – early Tudor walls seem to have leaned rather dramatically.[152] Thirty-one had to do with fences or pales, made or to be made. Obviously, drawing boundaries of neighbouring properties was important; doing so, in one form or another, involved almost three-quarters of the 205 extant certificates.[153] But of the 210 certificates extant in the CLRO collection for the period 1547–58, 45 were concerned with boundaries of void ground or land with a structure; 28 measured a wall, often a party wall; 13 dealt with encroachments and only one specifically with overhang. Thirty-eight had to do with fences or pales. Given that some views dealt with more than one variance or used several descriptions of the same variance, the total adds up to fewer than half of the extant certificates.[154] In other words, a high percentage of disputes for the later period do not deal with the boundaries of neighbouring gardens nor even with neighbouring houses taken as entire units. A new kind of measurement was becoming important: the lateral division of a tenement. During the entire reign of Henry VIII, only ten certificates appear to concern a single property divided among several tenants; for the next 11 years, the number is 25. Defendant claims a warehouse and loft over plaintiff's kitchen (**231**); plaintiff must maintain the lower part of a house while defendant must tile and cover the upper part and keep it windtight and watertight (**262**); a warehouse under plaintiff's house is rightfully held by defendant and he is to have access to it (**217**); defendant is not to alter the stairs, floor, and chamber of a house during plaintiff's lease of a room in it nor refuse him a right of way to his chamber (**385**); most telling of all, landlord is not to evict a tenant holding two houses under a lease with years yet to run in order to be able to divide those houses into smaller units for more profit (**277**). London's growth was producing more tenants and smaller units, and disputes changed accordingly, not by fiat but because of demography. The viewers' contribution was an attempt to sort out the ensuing confusion and to protect at least those who could provide evidence of their property interests.

Where they could, the viewers clung to what they liked to call 'the

152. Several certificates indicate the somewhat casual construction of buildings and of attempts to keep them standing; see e.g. **164, 178, 181**.
153. Because some certificates include more than one variance between the parties concerning property measurement, or state the same variance in more than one way, only a total of 149 certificates is actually involved.
154. A total of 97 certificates is involved.

honorable custom of this ancient City' or what they referred to as its constitutions; the two at base were often intertwined, since much of the custom applied by the viewers actually derived from, or was reflected in, early legislation. The certificates, then, provide a glimpse of custom in action in the 16th century; a glimpse, not a carefully-drawn picture. Sometimes the viewers state both the custom and their application of it. But in other instances, the existence of a custom remains unspoken, clearly there in the viewers' thinking and the basis for their decision, but never articulated. And sometimes the word has its common late medieval meaning: not 'the way things are done in London with regard to this generalised issue' but 'the way things have always been done in this particular case'. Half a dozen customs of London figure in the certificates. One, obviously significant at the time, was on latrines – an unending source of litigation. The Assize of Buildings had provided that one could demand a nuisance action for any offending cesspit made after 1189.[155] Pits were to be lined, not simply dug in the ground, and they were to be a given distance from a neighbour's land: one lined with stone could be as close as $2\frac{1}{2}$ ft (76 cm), one lined with brick or other material $3\frac{1}{2}$ ft (1.07 m).[156] But in 1546, a stone wall dividing two latrines was to be 2 ft (61 cm) thick (**202**) and in 1537, when one Ambrose Wolley's withdraught had no wall 'but only plaintiff's stone wall', the viewers declared that defendant should have one of brick or stone 18 inches (45 cm) thick. Contiguous latrines on adjoining properties, at least, were obviously no longer subject to the older rule (**128**). In any event, a pit with no wall at all was 'unlawfully done and ought not to be suffered', said the viewers in 1542 (**171**). That would seem to require little more than measuring, but the problem was that neighbours very often shared pits and then there was debate about who was responsible for repairs and cleansing, and when. There was an eminently sensible custom on the point: one counted up the number of tunnels into the vault and divided the costs proportionately. Men 'cleansed their jakes according to their falls by even portion, according to the custom of the City of London' (**272**).[157] But there was still the question of which family would suffer the inconvenience and worse of a vault being broken open and ordure being carted to the street, sometimes through the house itself. The viewers' ingenuity was taxed to its utmost to devise equitable solutions. When Henry Dolfyn and John Dymok, both well-to-do drapers, could not arrange matters, the viewers noted that Dolfyn had only one stool while Dymok had three, but ordered that the wall of the withdraught be broken within Dolfyn's warehouse and 'clensed and conveyed through his house'. Recognising that Dolfyn had had 'all the noyaunce and trouble . . . and the said Dymok none at all', the viewers, relying – as they declared – on their consciences as their guide, ordered that Dymok pay all the charges for both the

155. *Liber de Antiquis Legibus*, p. 208. For discussion of sanitary arrangements in the 14th and 15th centuries, see E. L. Sabine, 'Latrines and Cesspools of Mediaeval London', *Speculum*, vol. 9 (July, 1934), pp. 303–20.
156. *Liber de Antiquis Legibus*, p. 208.
157. The custom is not always mentioned, but it is the basis for the viewers' comments in a number of cases. See, e.g., **209**, **263**, **323**.

cleansing and the remaking of the vault wall, a total of 56s. 8d. (**170**). Many Londoners would have considered him to have had the better part of the bargain. But there is no record of a challenge to the decision; it was a party view and the viewers, calling the parties before them, had received in advance a promise from both 'to abyde and stand to the jugement of the said viewers'. Nor was there a saving clause at the end of the certificate; no evidence or specialty would be accepted to support a contrary decision. Here again, the line between recommendation to the mayor and aldermen and binding arbitration, between expert witnesses and administrative tribunal, becomes too fine for the 20th century eye to see.

The Assize of Buildings also dealt with party walls, gutters, pavements, and light, and, except for pavements, which are not the subject of a variance in any of the certificates in the CLRO collection,[158] all gave rise to disputes. The Assize had specified that stone party walls were to be 3 ft (91 cm) thick and 16 ft (4.88 m) high and the cost of their building was to be shared; if one party did not wish to join in building the wall, he was to give 3 ft (91 cm) of his land and his neighbour was to build it alone.[159] Judging from measurements given in the certificates, the three-foot thick rule seems not to have been uniformly followed in the 16th century and it is clear that usually more than half a wall was built on one party's land. In any event, construction of new party walls, stone or otherwise, seems to have been less important than use and alteration of them. One co-owner could neither alter nor destroy a wall without consent of the other party. Since a party wall was often part of the foundation of a building, or even formed one side of the building, this raised problems when one party wished to alter or tear down a tenement. Owners argued proportions of ownership, complained of encroachments on the wall, demanded the right to build on it, moved to prevent its destruction. The viewers duly measured and apportioned. Their decisions appear to assume a body of underlying standards, settled understandings, but the basis is never stated: there is no reference in the certificates to either custom or the Assize.

It was otherwise with water. Concern with the removal of water, both clean and dirty, from one's property is present in most of the certificates. Londoners did not ask the viewers to deal with their neighbours' activities which affected the availability or purity of the water they drank or washed in; no certificate in the CLRO collection specifically deals with that issue. But they argued interminably about the flow of water from eaves and kitchens, about watercourses and ditches and gutters: who should make them and how, who should repair them and when, who had damaged or removed or filled them in. From the viewers' comments, it appears that water was supposed to run from gutters or through watercourses into ditches and from there into a network of common sewers – or from sewer

---

158. For discussion of how pavements could create nuisance and disputes, see E. L. Sabine, 'City Cleaning in Mediaeval London', *Speculum*, vol. 12 (January, 1937), pp. 19–43, esp. p. 22.
159. *Liber de Antiquis Legibus*, p. 207. *Nuisance* has a discussion of party walls and ruinous walls, pp. xx–xxii.

to ditch, since at least one common sewer emptied into a ditch leading to the Moorditch (**87**). But when a ditch was stopped up, deliberately or otherwise, the system failed and water backed up onto the street. The viewers said that they relied on custom to support their orders that sewers and ditches be cleansed and re-opened: a watercourse had been used since time out of mind and water should pass as it had before (**78**). Water was to have 'his course & currant... as it hath of old tyme ben used & accustomed' (**87**). There was particular trouble in the parish of St. Botolph without Bishopsgate: in 1528, the parson and wardens of St. Michael Cornhill complained of Robert Clerke, who had filled in a ditch which ran along the ground of both plaintiffs and St. Mary Spital (**78**); in 1550, defendants John Rowseley and his tenant of ground in the parish lately belonging to St. Mary Spital were told that a 6 ft-wide (1.83 m) ditch – possibly the same one – ought to run the length of the plaintiffs' property to a common sewer 'as it has been used of old custom' (**268**). Here the custom invoked is surely less a specific substantive right available generally under certain given circumstances, a 'custom of London', than a matter of a particular protected usage; we might say of a right gained by prescription. Watercourses are less clearly defined than ditches. Sometimes the term was used to describe an ordinary gutter, but generally it meant water collected from one point and conveyed some distance across the property of another to another point. The means of conveyance could be a pipe, a closed gutter, or a natural channel, depending on location. When the viewers said that Thomas Blunte ought to have his watercourses, one through the chamber of Rychard Smythe – for clean water only – and a second through Smythe's stable and yard, presumably the first would be enclosed while the second might or might not be (**293**). Likewise, Thomas Whytelocke's watercourses ran from his own premises through one man's kitchen and another man's shop, into a party gutter between the two men's houses, and finally onto the ground behind them. These watercourses and gutters were for not only rain but waste water from plaintiff's houses, since the viewers ordered him not to use the courses for water from those houses made since his purchase 'excepting only rain water' (**351**). The wording of some certificates leaves the basis for the right vague; again, there appears to be a kind of easement by prescription. The watercourse in question had existed 'in time past' (**395**), or 'of long time' (**351**) or 'time out of mind' (**398**). A more specific measuring period is the date of purchase of premises by plaintiff, defendant, or both; it is mentioned in four certificates (**286**, **293**, **351**, **376**), including one which first spoke of 'long time' usage, thus suggesting the thinking behind the more general term (**351**): plaintiff had the right to a watercourse as it was when he bought, defendant was obliged to continue to tolerate the situation which existed when he took title. That was their 'custom'.

No certificate contains wording suggesting that a right to a watercourse through another's premises was based on the custom of London. In fact, the custom decreed the contrary: every man was to bear the water from his own house onto his own ground. Again the basis was the Assize of Buildings, which contained provisions for party gutters, the right to discharge roof water and the obligation to receive it.[160] But time and circumstances had embroidered on those provisions, filling in gaps not covered by the terse language, and by the 16th century the Assize was never cited. The first certificate in the collection to mention the custom (but not the first to follow it) dates from 1529, with an order that fillet gutters be made 'according to the custom of the City' (**81**).[161] But it is not until twenty years thereafter, beginning with a variance concerning 'certain houses and gutters' (**236**), that certificates start commonly to repeat the formula, 'Either party to bear his own water in his own ground after the manner and custom of the City of London' or a variant of it. The provision appears in some 48 certificates between 1549 and 1558, often when the variance did not appear directly to involve water.[162] Neighbours could, of course, agree not to be bound by the custom; one could give another the right to run his waste water through a house or yard and the arrangement would bind subsequent purchasers, as we have seen. More commonly, neighbours could agree to make a party gutter at both their charges;[163] occasionally they were told or advised to do so, particularly when the view was a party view and lacking an adversary nature (**92, 212**). But often they could not agree. Londoners argued interminably about gutters: who should make them and how, of what they should be made, how they should be repaired and by whom, who had damaged or removed them.[164] Tenants or even neighbours took away gutters; men stole them for the lead.[165] More than sixty certificates deal with gutters as a cause of dispute, because gutters had considerable practical importance. Londoners had not yet widely employed the downpipe; ordinarily, gutters simply collected water and spewed it out.[166] Thus in houses with party walls, or those adjacent even without a party wall, rain from one roof was likely to spill down onto the roof and wall of the neighbouring structure, rotting timbers and loosening roof tiles (**8**). Rain from a misdirected gutter emptying into a neighbour's yard either swept away soil or else stood stagnant. And not only rain runoff was involved; the certificates' insistence that a party allow only rainwater into a gutter suggests that household waste was too often poured from doors and windows to be carried off – or, more often, not carried off (**351**). The custom of London was firm; the only question was whether one party had a right to direct his water onto another's land, based on specific agreement between neighbours, prescription – again, condition of the premises

160. *Liber de Antiquis Legibus*, p. 208. See the discussion of gutters and watercourses in late medieval London in *Nuisance*, pp. xxii–xxiv.
161. Earlier certificates merely mention that parties ought to bear their own water all the length of their houses or on their own grounds; see **12** (1510), **34** (1517); also **53** (30 December 1522), **74** (1527), **84** (1529).
162. E.g. **249** (measurement of house and grounds); **285** (damage to plaintiff's house done by defendant in building his own); **298** (measurement of house under construction); **325** (use of new house).
163. **319** explicitly recognises this alternative.
164. In the case of party gutters, very often costs were split: **182, 200, 201, 288, 332**. While ordinarily each party was responsible for his own gutters, there were exceptions when damage had been done by another: e.g. **176**.
165. **156, 301, 366**; also **236**.
166. For exceptions, though, see **77, 200**, and probably **314**.

at the time of purchase by the parties was significant (**279, 316, 325, 333**) – or sometimes prior condition of the land, as when property formerly under one ownership had been subdivided or a physical feature altered.[167] Without such a right, the offending party could expect to be told to construct a gutter to divert the water onto his own premises.

While boundaries and party walls and gutters were the most common causes of discord, and perhaps most useful to a researcher trying to trace patterns of land ownership, two other topics less often encountered offer more interesting questions. One is the landlord and tenant relationship. Viewers' pronouncements on landlord and tenant obligations, as reflected in the certificates, seem to have been founded not so much on recognised City custom as on practices which had grown up based on what the market would bear and had found their way into leases. One source of landlord-tenant conflict was repairs. Naturally enough, a tenant was responsible for repair of damage he had caused to the leasehold.[168] But tenants' obligations went far beyond the remedying of their own negligence or abuse. No certificate states that either constitution or custom demanded the practice, but frequently the viewers declared that a tenant was responsible for major repairs to a leased property, even when those repairs were occasioned by normal wear and tear.

Sometimes, a lease was clearly the basis for the decision: the viewers commented that they had seen it, or paraphrased its terms. 'An indenture for term of years' obligated Margaret Williamson, whose husband had held at least four tenements from the king until Henry VIII sold them to plaintiff, to do tiling, roofing, carpentry, brickwork, daubing, and replacement of timber at an estimated cost of £80! (**189**). The tenant of the 'great tenement brewhouse called the Skomer' and two other properties was luckier: his premises needed plating, replacement of a rafter and gutter, pointing, tiling and daubing, all his responsibility under his lease and all to be done within the next two weeks, but costing an estimated £6 8s. 4d. (**204**). John Garrett, salter, was told in December 1553 that repairs to premises he leased would cost £23 13s. 4d. and that they ought to be made within the time limited to him by his lease or 'at the farthest' by the following July (**344**). Evered Shepperd was not even a party to the view in which it was declared that he was bound by his lease to put in plates and a principal post and repair a well (**214**). What is more, none of the four certificates has a saving clause: apparently the lease was thought to be conclusive on the issue of liability and the viewers may indeed have been called in only as experts in assessing the extent of repair needed.[169] On the other hand, when repairs were at issue between two parties who were not landlord and tenant – that is, usually, between neighbours – the viewers tended to be less specific both on the nature of necessary repairs and on

---

167. On prescription: sometimes there is a clear sense that the viewers assessed the fairness or at least the utility of what looks like a prescriptive arrangement: **119, 326**.

168. Several certificates specify that the tenant has caused the injury complained of: **211, 329, 380**. **329** states the rule prospectively.

169. But when a house was said to be 'well and sufficiently repaired according to the words of the [lease] that plaintiff holds of defendant', there was a saving clause – perhaps because repairs were not the central issue; six tenements were measured (**206**).

the estimate of cost, and there was often, though not always, a saving clause.[170] It was apparently common for leases to specify a time within which repairs were to be made; sometimes there was also a clause providing for termination of the tenancy if there was default. 'For we say accordyng to the tenor of the lease which geveth a quarter of a yeris warnyng yt may be made tenantable. And yf it be not made tennantable within the said terme after warnyng geven, that then the same lease is voyd', says a 1551 certificate (**292**; see also **344**).

Leases could, of course, apportion repairs or even provide that they be made by the landlord, and those provisions, too, bound the viewers. More than one purchaser of ecclesiastical real estate may have been surprised to learn, as was Christopher Jackson in 1551, that under the terms of a lease from the religious body which was the original owner of premises he now held 'it appears that the lords having the fee simple of the house are bound to repair the same ... and to maintain the same as often as need shall be' (**301**). More commonly, a lease bound the landlord to make repairs 'to the principals', leaving all others to the tenant.[171] But where there was no such provision, there were few limits on a tenant's liability. The unfortunate Margaret Williamson, who had to 'rip' tenements and new frame roofs to the extent of £80, offers an example; so does John Garrett, who had to rip, tile, rafter, plate, daub, plumb and 'set upright' a stable, a mill house, and a shed. Yet perhaps neither faced the expense that awaited William and Martin Pery, lessees of a large 'garret or hay loft' so decayed that – the viewers found – it could not be repaired but required taking down, together with the tenements under it. In one of those lateral divisions so common at the time (1548), the tenements between the ground and the garret belonged to another party – the plaintiff in the view – who may well have held the fee of the garret as well; he was to rebuild the 'nether part' of the structure. But the garret was to be taken down and newly made by the Perys, at their cost, 'because [they] are bound by their lease to all manner of repairs' (**219**). And all manner of repairs was deemed to include construction *de novo*.

The issue of responsibility for maintenance becomes more difficult to understand when the parties to a view are identified as landlord and tenant but the provisions of a lease are not mentioned as the basis for the viewers' decision. Is the omission simply an oversight? Is the finding nonetheless based on the specific provisions of a written indenture, read but not recited? Or is there – in the absence of a document – some other basis for apportioning repairs? What was the authority relied on when the viewers simply declared that the lord and owner of the tenement was 'bound to repair and maintain all principals of the tenement' and that the tenant was 'bound to all other repairs', including stone walls, bricks, tiling, carpentry, gutters, windows and keeping the tenement 'from wind

170. See **114**, **310**, **362**; **290** includes an estimate that repairs would cost £7.
171. In **206**, John Vandernott, 'being Owner and Landlord oweth of right to make newe the plates' of two houses, together with chimneys which had sunk as a result of the decayed plates; the repairs are characterised as 'reparacions for the principalles'. His tenants were responsible for a long list of other repairs, but the terms of the leases are not spelled out.

and rain, wind tight and water tight' (**207**)? Again, why did the variance between Rychard Westram and William Broke involve 'all and singular repairs except principals' of the house in which Broke dwelt; Broke was to lathe, daub, tile, and defend the house against wind and rain – effectively making him responsible for the roof – but he was not to touch the essential wood structure (**310**). And why, in a variance 'for certain principals and principal posts' in the house inhabited by defendant, did the viewers find that plaintiffs – almost certainly the property owners, given the situation – ought to maintain the 'principals' at their own costs (**389**)? Specific agreement lacking, was there an understanding of what was included in 'principals' and what fell under repair and maintenance of a tenement? The certificates do not offer a hint, but medieval leases suggest that liability was then commonly divided along these lines, while practice was changing (to greater overall tenant liability) in the 16th century.[172]

The other principal cause of dispute between landlord and tenant, removal of fixtures at the end of a term, was clearly governed by the custom of London. What improvements could a departing tenant take away with him? The City custom on the point was not unlike the rule in New York City today: in modern terms, anything annexed to the freehold by a tenant became part of the realty and could not be moved. Sixteenth century London put it more particularly: 'asmoche of the ... other necessaryes as have ben made in tyme past withyn the said tenement by tenantes of the same for their own ease whiche is not fastened or nayled unto any part of the frame of the said tenement with any manner of nayles or pynnes of iron or tymber may be lawfully taken away. And all suche of the premisses as be fastened or nayled with any nayle or pyn as is aforesaid may not be removed nor taken awey without speciall licence of the said landlord. Except there be any covenant or promise made to the contrary' (**172**). The lists of what could and could not be taken away says something about 16th century ideas of comfort and utility – and about building practices. Ceilings of wainscot, shelves, and wareboards had been installed by John Butler, the ceiling some 89 yards square. As much of it as had not been fastened or nailed to the frame of the tenement could be removed (**172**); what that meant in practice is unclear. Jane Jewett's executors wanted to remove seats, benches, doors, locks and keys, glass, lattices and windows. The viewers disagreed; the named improvements were 'implements and standards' and ought to remain in place as such, 'according to the ancient custom of the city of London' (**226**). And William Froke – whose apparent attempts at renovation, together with his failure to repair, had in the viewers' eyes done damage to the great capital messuage he leased – was told that he ought not to take away the 'selinges of waynscott, glasse, flores of bordes', which presumably he had put in, 'by the Custome of the citie of London' (**380**). The custom was significant enough to appear in records of the livery companies. The Mercers' Company Book of Ordinances includes a list of things 'not to be removed or takyn away without lycens of the landlord', including all things made fast with iron or timber pins, such as pentices, glass, locks,

---

172. See *CLBA*, pp. 154, 168–9; compare P. E. Jones, *The Fire Court*, I (1966), p. vi.

keys, screens, and benches; anything fastened with 'stone chalk or mortar', such as furnaces, chimneys, corbels, and pavements; and anything planted in the earth, such as vines, trees, and herbage.[173] The Will and Charter Book of the Ironmongers has an entry[174] headed '*De fixis non amovendis*' and continuing '*consuetudo de fixis non amovend' in angliis verbis in civitate Londini, usitata et approbata uti patet in Libro K f. 221 in Latinis verbis. Dunethorne Lond''*, referring to the custom's appearance in City documents. It goes on to translate the relevant provision in Letter-Book K: there was 'a matter of doubt' about the custom in the 23rd year of Henry VI (1444–5) and 'the old books, many records and old processes and judgments' were searched, as a result of which the mayor and aldermen at the time declared 'for an old prescribed Custome of the Citty that it should not be lawfull for any such tenant for terme of life or for terme of years within the said Citty at thend of his terme or at any other time to Cast downe take away or pull upp in any wise any easement to the house or in the grounds of the said tenure by him nayled fastened or affixed with nayle Iron or of Timber . . .'[175] Even a cursory look at the old books and records would have shown the mayor and aldermen that the custom was truly far older than Henry VI; it is originally stated in the 1365 '*Ordinacio de appenticiis et aliis asiamentis factis in tenementis*' found in Letter-Book G,[176] and as early as 1373, the sworn masons and carpenters viewed a tenement and various fixtures, including a malt bin nailed to the frame, and declared that they could not be removed according to the custom of the City.[177]

The final custom which substantially affected the viewers' deliberations – and the shaping of London itself – deals with the mutually contradictory rights to light and to privacy. The idea that there is or is not a right to sunlight, and the related concept of ancient lights, deserves an introduction all to itself.[178] Suffice it to say here that 38 certificates touch on light in one way or another. But 'the custom of London' is rarely mentioned as such; in fact, the viewers refer to it explicitly only once, in a certificate, largely illegible, dating from sometime late in the reign of Edward VI. 'The viewers say that the variance is for certain lights there cast out . . . a great glazed window there set forth which ought of right . . . a clerestory right with the same house . . . set up to the soil of the same window and also . . . cast forth on that side of the house of the said party . . . the air after the ancient custom of London . . . at charges of defendant. And further . . . part of the house on the West side of . . . annoy the plaintiff' (**336**).

Nonetheless, the existence and gravamen of a custom on the right to light is no secret. Like that on water-bearing, it is based on a provision in the Assize of Buildings.[179] It is the subject of the first case in Sir Henry

173. Mercers' Company, Book of Ordinances (Rebound 1777), ff. 221v.
174. GL MS 17003 (Ironmongers' Company, Will and Charter Book), unnumbered folio.
175. LBK, f. 221 (*CLBK*, p. 298).
176. LBG, f. 174 (*CLBG*, p. 205); *Liber Albus*, p. 371.
177. *Nuisance*, 583; see also ibid., 646.
178. The entire question of the right to light and the right to privacy in late medieval England is one on which I hope to write in some detail in the near future.
179. *Liber de Antiquis Legibus*, p. 208; *Liber Albus*, p. 280.

Calthrop, *Reports of Special Cases touching several Customes and Liberties of the City of London*; and it remained the basis of litigation by Londoners into the modern period.[180] In London (and this was not the custom of several other major cities, most notably York) a landowner had the right to build upright on his own frame even though he thereby blocked the light of his neighbour. At least four certificates specifically comment that 'every owner may lawfully build upon his own ground line right and plumb' (**210, 260, 317, 326**) and it is clear that the language is designed to negate a right to light; certificate **260**, an instance of a dispute about windows, adds that the construction which would 'take the light' from a neighbouring trunk window must not be done in point of malice, and certificate **317**, reciting the right to build, adds that it may be done 'in front of any light there.' There were some instances in which light was protected, a few mentioned in the treatises or the handful of relevant cases, others set out elliptically in the certificates. One had the right to an unobstructed window overlooking a public way even if later that way came into private hands (**98, 251**); one could reserve one's light when dividing premises and retaining only part of them in one's own hands; one could make an agreement with one's neighbour and it would bind subsequent purchasers of the property (**6, 183**). But one could not prescribe for a light in London, could not claim a right by long user. There is language in the certificates which seems to suggest the contrary; windows are protected because they were in place 'before the time of their purchase' (**279**) or 'as it hath been in long time past before their purchases' (**272**) or 'as they have been used of old custom' (**222**). But in fact the viewers are thinking of something quite different, another custom of London also related to windows, one not set out in the treatises but underlying perhaps a dozen certificates: the right not to be 'overlooked' by a neighbour. What is really being said in those certificates is not that no one may build in front of a given window because of its long use, but that the window as it stands is lawful because of its long use.[181] Building of windows was apparently a source of dispute more often than their blockage. In 1528, the viewers looked at Maude Russell's window and declared that it ought to stand and continue as ordered and devised by themselves without interruption of the neighbouring parish church (**77**). Blockage of Maude's light was not the issue; she was the defendant. The explanation must be that the parson and churchwardens had complained of her window. In 1533, in a suit between the Drapers and the Abbot of Stratford (**98**), the viewers announced that they had found windows which ought to be permitted in the future as they had been in the past since they were lawfully and conveniently made, so long as they were not

---

180. Henry Calthrop, *Reports of Special Cases touching several Customes and Liberties of the City of London* (1670, repr. 1872), p. 1. The case is *Hughes v. Keeme*, spelled variously as Keame, Keane, Keen, Keyme or Keyne, heard in King's Bench in Trinity term 7 James I and reported, among other places, at Godbolt 183, Yelverton 215, and 1 Bulstrode 155. Stat. 2 & 3 William IV c. 71 s. 3 abrogated the custom in general, but it was apparently not immediately clear whether London was affected. See Alexander Pulling, *The Laws, Customs, Usages and Regulations of the City and Port of London* (2nd ed., no date but listed in the British Library catalogue as 1842), p. 268.
181. See, for example, **278**.

'noysance nor displeasant to the said plaintiff'. One way windows could be 'displeasant', of course, was by having filth thrown from them and a number of certificates specify that the openings are to be barred or glassed 'so no filth be cast out of them' or so they do not offer convenient but wrongful access to a neighbouring gutter (**119, 347**). Another problem was that windows in a party wall could weaken it; this could be the reasoning behind the statement in a 1555 certificate permitting a defendant to build his house on a stone wall existing at the boundary of his ground but 'making no light hole or window' through it (**357**). But most often the simple existence of the window was the displeasure, the nuisance. For Londoners, the right to privacy was a right to physical privacy. In 1538, Johanna Thorpe, whose four-light window overlooked the garden of the Master of the Temple 'whereby she may so oversee the said garden', was told to 'set in' a screen 'that there be no sight thereby into the said garden. Or else [the window] to be stopped up, forasmuch as the said defendant may have sufficient light both back and front partes of her house' (**129**). Clearly, it was a balancing act: light v. privacy, and the balance was achieved in ingenious ways. Early in the 14th century, the mayor and aldermen ruled that a defendant could have no windows facing his neighbour's land except at a height of 16 ft or greater; by 1340, complaints specified that windows were less than 16 ft from the ground, suggesting that 16 ft had become the accepted norm.[182] Unfortunately, there is no reference to that rule in the existing certificates, except possibly the tantalising reference to a clerestory window in the fragmentary certificate from the reign of Edward VI (**336**). But lower windows could be rendered harmless in other ways: apart from Johanna Thorpe's screen, a 'loupe light' could be set in (**103**) or a 'trunk light' erected (**260**), 'cutting the view' but admitting some light – unless a neighbour exercised his right to build to the property line.[183] The customs of London on light held their own inner contradictions, but taken together they would have made for little enough sun and air in most rooms – and no view, for a 'prospect' was never protected. By 1600, when London was bursting at the seams with new population and the dreaded construction of cheap new buildings, most properties must have been dark indeed.[184] One must wonder what would have happened had there been no Great Fire and subsequent building regulations!

It is right to end this introduction with the Great Fire, for the Fire, more than any other circumstance – more than all the Tudor and Stuart

182. *Nuisance*, 230; see also pp. xxv–xxvi and no. 359.
183. The screen is not described. The 'trunk light' consisted of boards or planks set closely together and nailed at an angle, against the wall at the bottom of the window, a foot and a half away from the wall at the top of it. The 'loupe light' was a louvre set several feet outside the window itself, rather like an outside Venetian blind.
184. A number of articles and books discuss the expansion of London in the late 16th and 17th centuries. Among them are E. Jeffries Davis, 'The Transformation of London' in *Tudor Studies*, ed. R. W. Seton Watson (1924), Norman G. Brett-James, *The Growth of Stuart London* (1935), and A. L. Beier and Roger Finlay, eds., *London 1500–1700: The Making of the Metropolis* (1986). C. C. Knowles and P. H. Pitt, *History of Building Regulation in London, 1189–1972* (1972), ch. II, also discusses the problem and some early royal proclamations.

proclamations, more than the fulminations of mayors and aldermen, more than the plague itself – spelled the end of medieval London as the viewers and their contemporaries knew it. And with the end of the old City, with its warren of crooked alleys crowded with subdivided tenements and leaning walls, came the end of the viewers as they had historically functioned. The new London was not to have the 'irregular' buildings that the masons and carpenters had measured so carefully, not to have the leaseholds and even freeholds which ranged across neighbouring houses on varying floors, the leaning walls and the 'fled out posts'. The surveyors were to assure that it did not. Whether or not they could carry out that function is not here a concern; certainly the viewers could not. London, even had there not been a fire, had grown too large, too populous for four men, no matter how expert and diligent, to act effectively as building inspectors, arbitrators of private quarrels, surveyors, protectors of the integrity of public streets and ways and the like. Even had there been no fire, sooner or later the institution of the sworn viewers must have fallen of its own weight. With the coming of the surveyors, the office of viewer became vestigial, perhaps even a sinecure, no longer really a necessary part of the daily functioning of municipal government – unlike the position of the true Renaissance men of 1508–58 who moved with confidence and zest among the tangled affairs and tight-packed dwellings of their litigious neighbours.

Note on the Certificates
All the viewers' certificates in the Corporation of London Records Office for the period 1508–58 are in English, although earlier reports were in law French; the change of language occurred during the 15th century. To a considerable extent, the style of the report was established at least by the middle of the 14th century; Miscellaneous Roll FF includes a report from 1365, the first one set out in full in those rolls, which begins with the familiar salutation to the honourable lords and 'droitals' the Mayor and Aldermen, identifies the view as made by carpenters and masons ordained to survey nuisances and sources of disquiet between neighbours, and proceeds to identify parish, parties, and problem, ending with a finding of fact and the rote statement that the aforesaid things have been well and faithfully shown and addressed between the parties 'come nostre serement voet et demande'.[185] Based on Latin summaries of earlier certificates in Miscellaneous Rolls DD and FF, there is no reason to believe that the language was new in 1365. By early in the 1400s, it had evolved into virtually the form used in the 16th century; a certificate in the archives of St. Paul's Cathedral, on internal evidence dating from before 1410,[186] begins 'Le honourable Sir the Maire and Aldermen de la Citie de Londres, monstrent . . . masons and carpenters de Citie que comme . . . ils feurent charges per vostre comandments de surveier un noisance de certein tenements', followed by the parish and the parties and findings of fact and ending with the saving clause 'Sil ne fait quascune des ditz parties

185. Miscellaneous Roll FF, m. 15v, calendared *Nuisance*, 527.
186. The St. Paul's Cathedral archives are now in the Guildhall Library: the document is now GL MS 25121/1220.

faet monstre ascun evidence or especial' a la contrarie.' The transition to English entailed only the addition of a few adjectives, as is clear from one of the earliest examples in that language, a certificate copied into the Journals.[187]

During the 16th century, there were minor alterations in form but no change appears to have had any obvious effect on substance. Early certificates bear no date and hence have no reference to either calendar or regnal year; beginning in 1514, the year of the reign of the king is included. Beginning in 1523, there is intermittent reference to 'the reign of King Henry the VIII, king by the grace of God'; 'by the grace of God' disappears in 1528 and Henry becomes 'Our Sovereign Lord King Henry the VIII'. It is, of course, tempting to see political or theological undertones in the change but there is no intrinsic evidence for either and the style does not in fact reflect that used in charters, writs and other documents of the same periods.[188] For the reign of Edward VI, the certificates continue to refer to the king simply as 'Our Sovereign Lord', with the single exception of a fragmentary report at the very end of the reign (**336**). It is during the reign of Mary and later Philip and Mary that the certificates tend to reflect the style which the monarchs used in other documents and hence also reflect both political and religious considerations. Early certificates speak only of 'the reign of Our Sovereign Lady Quene Mary', a clear continuance of the Edwardian language. But, although there is no change in handwriting, a certificate (**353**) of 21 June 1554 reads, 'In the fyrst yere of the Reigne of Our Soveraigne lady Marie by grace of god Quene of England, Fraunce and Ireland, defendor of the Fayth and in earthe of the Churche of England and also of Ireland the Supreame Head.' It was in fact a form that Mary used on official documents at the time but it appears only once among the certificates; succeeding reports return to the older and simpler usage. Upon Mary's marriage in July 1554 the form expanded to include Philip. But a totally new form was introduced in a certificate (**357**) of 8 August 1555: '. . . the Reignes of our sovereigne lorde and lady Philippe and Marie by the grace of god Kinge and Quene of England, France, Neapells, Jerusalem and Ireland, Defendors of the Fayth, Princes of Spayne and Sicilie, Archdukes of Austria, Dukes of Myllayne, Burgoyne and Brabant, Comtes of Haspurge, Flanders, and Tirolle'. Why the form was suddenly appropriated for the certificates is unclear but where it came from is not; again, it was the style commonly used in public documents between 25 July 1554 and August 1556[189] and again, it was not followed consistently in the certificates. Following the abdication of Emperor Charles V in August, 1556, at least one certificate (**398**) reads 'Philippe and Mary, by the grace of god king and quene of England, Spayne, Fraunce, both Ciciles, Jerusalem and Ireland, Defenders of the Fayth, Archdukes of Austridge,

---

187. Journal 3, f. 2 (?1436).
188. Henry used 'Dei gratia Rex Anglie et Francie et Dominus Hibernie' from his accession until 1521, when he added 'Fidei Defensor'. The form changed over the course of the reign, but Henry used 'Dei gratia' consistently until his death. See John Eyre Winstanley Wallis, *English Regnal Years and Titles* (1921), pp. 58–9.
189. Ibid., p. 59.

Dukes of Burgundy, Myllayne and Brabant, Counties of Hespurge, Flanders and Tyroll'; once more it was a translation of the style used in public documents for the same period. Copies of two certificates dating from 9 May 1558[190] are the first I have seen to date a certificate by the calendar rather than regnal year; as unofficial copies they cannot, of course, prove that such a style was actually in use.

No early report that I have seen refers to the masons and carpenters as viewers; the first use of the word in a certificate (**26**) in the CLRO collection dates from March 1514, with the phrase 'which ground and brewhouse the said vewers have measured . . .' The permanent form was established in 13 March 1517 (**34**): '. . . the iiii masters of freemasons and carpenters, viewers indifferent sworn to the said Citie. . .' Perhaps significantly, the certificate is in a new hand.

The final clause in the certificate, the saving clause, leaves the door open to further proof to be introduced in future by one or another party. 'Without there can be shewed any other evidence or specialtie unto the contrary', say a certificate of uncertain date (**5**) and one from 1 Henry VIII (**6**), and that phrasing, sometimes with the omission of 'or specialtie', became the standard phrase for the rest of the reign, with some infrequent variation. Only one saving clause appears to have substantial meaning specific to the matter it concludes: **172**, dated 18 August 1542 and involving a dispute between landlord and tenant concerning removal of improvements made by tenant, concludes 'Except there be any covenant or promise made to the contrary.' The predominant phrase during the reign of Edward VI is 'Except there be any [writing] evidence or specialty to the contrary to be shewed' or 'to shew the contrary' but there is less uniformity and the clause occasionally appears to reflect the circumstances of the individual case. There are exceptions for 'the words of the lease to the contrary' (**227**), for 'writing, evidence, specialty or covenants' (**233**), for a charter (**279**), for 'evidence or record they have not had' (**287**), or for 'writing, evidence, specialty or [other] view to the contrary'.[191] During the reign of Philip and Mary, however, any attempt to make the saving clause reflect the facts of the certificate was apparently abandoned and the standard phrase became 'Except there be any writing, evidence, or other specialty to the contrary to be shewed', with minor variations (e.g. **376**, **398**). Apart from fragments, 28 certificates have no saving clause at all; most of them involve findings of fact about costs of repairs, damage to buildings or walls, and the necessity of taking down or rebuilding ruinous structures. Again, the omission may reflect the circumstances of a case since it is unlikely that any writing or evidence could negate a conclusion on damage or the need to tear down a dangerous structure.

Note on Editorial Method

Because this is a calendar with more than 400 certificates to be included,

190. Mercers' Company. Register of Writings, vol. II, f. 197r–v.
191. The last form is likely to be an individual clerk's choice of style rather than a statement of circumstances; it appears in five certificates all dated between 14 May and 3 June 1549 and nowhere else: **242–3**, **246–7**, and **251**.

common form has been omitted so far as possible in most cases. For each reign, however, a number of certificates have been printed in full, with original spelling and, to some extent, capitalisation; capitalisation in the originals is both haphazard and uncertain, as some letters appear identical in upper and lower case forms. In all cases punctuation, largely missing in the originals, has been supplied. The certificates printed verbatim fall into three categories: they are the earliest ones for a reign, or they contain material of unusual interest, or they are simply in such poor condition that no abstract is possible.

All dates set out in the text of certificates in the Corporation of London Records Office collection are in terms of the regnal year. I have substituted the calendar year. Where no date is given within the certificate, or the date has become illegible, but an endorsement exists, the certificate has been headed with the endorsement date. In all cases, I have reckoned the calendar year from 1 January, not 25 March. However, the endorsements to the certificates almost always give the day and month of the year in numerals: 13.5. The reference is to neither the calendar year nor the regnal year but the mayoral year, beginning on November 1; this was the practice of the Mayor's Court (see Corporation of London Records Office Bound MS Volume Mayor's Court Original Bills, p. vi). Occasionally the regnal year is not even mentioned, the term of the current mayor being used instead: Tempore Baldry maioris Civitatis London 3.8.

Several conventions have been adopted in calendaring those certificates not printed verbatim. Family names and names of specific buildings except parish churches have been given in their original spelling and style. Common Christian names have been given their modern spelling; unusual Christian names have been transcribed as they stand. Occupations have been put into modern form and spelling, followed by the original in round brackets in the case of some less-common trades: Hugh Davy, currier (corryer). Names of parishes and other religious institutions have been retained in their original style; where a variant name of a parish was used, the more familiar name has followed in square brackets if required for clarity: St. Toulles [Olave]. Names of streets and other geographic reference points have been used in their original style, but spelling has been modernised with the original spelling following in round brackets where it is significantly different. Where a street name has changed substantially from that used in the certificate, the newer name is given in a footnote. Original spellings have been retained where a street or other location cannot be positively identified at the present day. Identification of streets, parishes, buildings and other locations within the City has been made using H. A. Harben, *A Dictionary of London* and Eilert Ekwall, *Street-Names of the City of London*. Identification of religious houses outside London has been made using Dom David Knowles, *The Religious Houses of Medieval England*, and David Knowles and R. Neville Hadcock, *Medieval Religious Houses in England and Wales*. John Stow's *Survey of London* has been useful for miscellaneous information.

Significant variations on the usual formulae have been included, such as statements that the viewers heard witnesses or saw a lease or that they acted at the request of both parties. When in common form, the saving clause at the end of most certificates has ordinarily been abbreviated: Without *etc.*, Except *etc.* Original spellings or forms of other words within the body of the certificates have occasionally been given where they differ substantially from the modern form; they follow the modern spelling in round brackets.

'Plaintiff' and 'defendant', never abbreviated in the originals, are here consistently abbreviated. Where there is no identification of a party as a plaintiff or defendant, as in a view by consent or with reference to third parties, the full names are given at their first appearance and thereafter only last names are used. The designation of persons and institutions as 'of London' does not appear consistently in the originals. Where given, it has been retained for institutions but omitted for persons except where required for clarity. Livery companies have not been given their full honorific titles but are referred to simply by craft or trade: the Skinners, the Goldsmiths, the Mercers.

Directions of the compass, written out in the originals, are here abbreviated: N, S, E, W *but* northward, southward etc. All numbers, whether in dates or measurements, have been put into Arabic numerals although in the text of the certificates they are uniformly either written out or shown in Roman numerals. Endorsements and subscriptions, generally abbreviated and in Latin, have been expanded where possible, the supplied material being enclosed in square brackets, but not translated.

Where there is a gap due to missing or illegible words, the omission is marked by three ellipsis points. In the calendared certificates, words which are wholly or partly illegible, although the context makes their meaning clear, or which have been inserted for clarification, are enclosed in square brackets. In certificates quoted verbatim, where the reading of a word or words is by itself uncertain owing to illegibility or loss of letters but the gap has been explained by another reference within the certificate or the writing has been recovered under ultraviolet light, the word or words are enclosed in square brackets; where the uncertainty persists, the word has been enclosed in square brackets but preceded by a question mark. Where a word has been inserted either for clarification or to give missing information gleaned from another source, it is both italicised and enclosed in square brackets: It [*the land*] stretches westward. Editorial comments concerning the body of the certificate or the endorsement have likewise been put into italics: *Same viewers, signed, endorsed.*

The calendar is numbered consecutively from **1** to **433**. Numbers assigned by the Corporation of London Records Office to a series of bound certificates from the reign of Henry VIII (here **6–205**) are shown as given in CLRO file 'Viewers' Reports 1509–1546' (Bound Volume 204A), but are preceded by the letter 'B' and enclosed in square brackets: **144** [B.139]. No other certificates in the Corporation's archive have been bound or numbered. Therefore, in addition to its sequential number I have identified each such certificate in square brackets by the file in which it is found and in chronological order within that file as follows: I have ssigned the letter 'A' to the file of earliest certificates in the CLRO collection (**1–5**), those dating from an undetermined period very early in the 16th century, which exist in a separate envelope in CLRO Misc. MSS Box 91. I have assigned the letter 'C' to the certificates for the reigns of Edward VI and Mary filed loose in Misc. MSS Box 91 (**206–404**); and I have assigned 'D' to a series of fragments apparently dating from between 1554 and 1556, found in a separate envelope in Misc. MSS Box 91 (**405–416**). Certificates not in these files but found in the Journals or in livery company records (**417–433**) have simply been ordered by provenance and numbered consecutively.

In the index, it has not always been possible to distinguish between several persons of the same name nor to identify positively two entries as referring to the same person, particularly when one entry gives an individual's trade or other information and the second does not. Where there are several instances of the same name with the same or no information given, there is one index entry. Where one reference includes additional information and a second does not, or where the additional information is not identical, there is one entry but the differing references are noted. Where a name is spelled variously in several certificates but clearly refers to the same individual, there is one entry with the variant spelling noted. Names of monarchs and viewers, found in every certificate, do not appear in the index.

Also in the index, a street or other geographic location referred to in a certificate by a name different from its more common or modern usage is listed under both names; variants are shown in cross-references or round brackets as necessary. Parish churches are ordinarily listed under the name most commonly used in the certificates, with variants in round brackets; cross references have been used where necessary. In all cases, I have attempted to give sufficient information, either in round brackets or by cross reference, to permit certain identification.

LIST OF LONDON VIEWERS, 1509–1558

Before 12 November 1509–5 November 1513: Thomas Wade, Thoma Smart, John Hilmer, Philip Coseyn
– March 1514–10 January 1530: Thomas Smart, John Hilmer, Phili Coseyn, Thomas Newell
– February 1530–19 June 1535; John Hilmer, Philip Coseyn, Thoma Newell, Stephen Poncheon
10 December 1535–February 1536: John Hilmer, Philip Coseyn, Thomas Newell, William Coleyns
14 March 1536–17 March 1539: John Hilmer, Philip Coseyn, Thomas Newell, William Walker
17 July 1539–9 March 1541: John Hilmer, William Walker, Henry Pesemede, John King
10 June 1541–30 January 1545: John Hilmer, William Walker, Henry Pesemede, John Arnold
26 June 1545–8 March 1546: John Hilmer, William Walker, Henry Pesemede, John Russell
4 May 1546–18 July 1548: John Hilmer, William Walker, John Russell, Gilbert Burffame
24 October 1548–10 July 1550: William Walker, John Russell, Gilbert Burffame, Nicholas Ellys
30 August 1550–16 May 1553 or later: William Walker, John Russell, Nicholas Ellys, John Cowper
22 September 1553–28 July 1554: John Russell, Nicholas Ellys, John Cowper, Thomas Peacock
9 March 1555–14 July 1556: John Russell, Nicholas Ellys, Thomas Peacock, Walter Cowper
17 November 1556: John Russell, Thomas Peacock, Walter Cowper.
3 February 1557–2 August 1558: John Russell, Thomas Peacock, Walter Cowper, John Humfrey

This list is based on viewers named in extant certificates, together with information from Journals and Repertories. The dates are, for the most part, those of the first and last certificates showing a given set of viewers. There are obvious gaps, because there are periods for which no views have survived. There are also inconsistencies: the election of John Arnold would, according to the certificates, have taken place between 9 March and 10 June 1541, but an entry in the Repertories dates it at 20 February 1541. No record has been found of the election of Stephen Poncheon, although there is a note of his death in connection with the choice of his successor, and no record has been found of the election of Walter Cowper.

VIEWERS' CERTIFICATES

CORPORATION OF LONDON RECORDS OFFICE MISC. MSS BOX 91 [A]

(Envelope marked 'Viewers' Certificates circa 1508')

The envelope contains five certificates. All are undated and only one (**3**) has a visible endorsement: 21 June 1 Henry VIII (1509). It is impossible to know their exact chronological order, although a rough order can be imposed based on the names of the viewers and other internal evidence.

1. [A.1; undated; between 22 October 1479 and 6 December 1500][1] To the right honourable lord and worshipfull sovereynes the Mayer and Aldermen of the Noble Citee of London
Shewen unto your honourable lordship and discrete Wisedomes Thomas Wade John Burton Robert Crosby and Thomas Mauncell, the fower maysters of Fremasons and carpenters sworn to the said Citee, That where they were late charged by your honourable comaundement to oversee a Noysaunce of a Wall of stone & breeke beyng part therof under the plates of the side of a ten[emen]t now pertaynyng to Robt Tate of London, Alderman, sett & beyng in the parissh of Seynt Mighell Pater Noster beside the Vyntree in London and [another] parte of the said Wall beyng sett and fixed in the void grounde hereafore beyng ten[emen]tes next adioynyng thereto, now beyng perteynyng to the Wardeyns and [Fellowship] of the Craft of Vyntners of the Citee of London. And the said wall is in variance betwene the same Robt Tate on the oon partie and the said Wardeyns and Felaship of Vyntners on the other partie, Which Noysaunce the same iiii maisters by oon assent will and agrement of the said parties have serched seen and ripely examyned by all their discrecions. And thereupon they say that they fynde the same Wall New made to thentent behove and ease aswele of the same tenement perteynyng to the same Robt Tate As of the same voide grounde ... ten[emen]ts perteynyng to the said Wardeyns and Felaship. Also the said iiii maisters say that they fynde by all their discrecions as all manner Lightes there owe to be contynewed reserved ... kept ... as of old tyme have been accustomed and used unto the ease profit and Wele of both the parties on lesse than ther can be shewed any evidence or specialtie unto the contrary. Also they fynde by their discrecions that the said Wall conteyneth in length by measure in the Este there stretchyng by the side of the grete ten[emen]t there of ... Robt Tate now in the tenure of the Felaship of Inneholders from a principall post in a part of the ten[emen]t Brewhouse next adioynyng to the said Wall set & beyng in the parish of

Alhalowes the More beside Dowgate in Theamstrete of London, unto th
comon lande there called the Bowe lane in the West, xxxv fote ix ynche
and an half of assyse. Also they fynde by measure the said voide groun
stretchyng on the Est side thereof from the north to the South to a corne
post there perteynyng to a ten[emen]t belongyng to the Abbot an
Covent of the [place] of Our Lady of Grace beside the Tower Hill xlvi fot
& iii ynches of assise. Also they fynde by measure the same voide ground
stretchyng by the Southsyde from the Este to the West to the said lan
called Bowe Lane xlvii fote vi ynches. And an half of assise. And also the
fynde the same voide grounde by measure strechyng in the same Bow
Lane from the South to the North xlvi fote x ynches and an half of assise.

> 1. The certificate must date from between 22 October 1479, the date on which Rober
> Tate was elected Alderman of Queenhithe ward, and 6 December 1500, the date of his
> death: Beaven, 190.

2. [A.2; undated]
To the full noble lord and Right Worshipfull Soverains the Mare an
Aldermen of the Citee of London
Shewen unto your good lordship and maisterships Thomas Wade John
Burton Robert Crosby and William Chacom, the four maisters of Masons
and Carpenters sworn to the seid Citee [that where they were late]
charged by your honorable comaundement to oversee a noysaunce in the
parish of Seint Sepulcre without Newgate of london betwene Robert
Laverok, John Goldyngton, Sadiller, William Heyward ... Baker,
wardeyns of the Fraternite of our lady and seint John Baptist founded in
the parissh Churche of Seint Sepulcre aforesaid, plaintifs on that oon
partie, and John Walden, Gentilman, defendant on the other partie,
Whiche noysaunce the seid iiii maisters have serched sene and ripely
examined by their alther discrecions And thereupon they say that they
fynde there how the seid defendant hath buryed a Foreyn ... a Siege, in
the West part of his Gardyn abuttyng upon a Stonewall belonging to the
seid plaintifs. And the seid iiii maisters seyen also by their alther
discrecions that the seid Foreyn hath a ... wall and caused it to go down
and so it hath put the housyng of the seid plaintifs stondyng upon their
seid stone wall in iepde [jeopardy] of fallyng down contrary to the
constitucions of this honorable Citee... Furthermore that the seid
defendant by their discrecions owed not to have buryed his seid Foreyn
ageynst the seid stonewall without he had made a lawfull defence upon
hym self to defende the seid ... of lesse thanne he have or can shewe any
evidence or specialte unto the contrarie.

3. [A.3][1] 21 June 1509
To the full honourable lord and right wise sovereignes the maire of [*sic*]
Aldermen of the Citie of London
Shewen unto your good lordship and wise discretions Thomas Wade
Thomas Smart John Hilmer and Philip Cosyn the iiii Maisters of
Fremasons & Carpenters sworne to the [said City that whereas they were]
late charged by your honorable commaundement to oversee a gate hows
with certayn grounde therto perteyning set & being in the parisshe of
seynt Andrew Undershaft ... belonging to Henry Hichecok of London,

2

Baker, partie playntif, being in variance betwene the same Henry on that
on partie and Robert Fenrother of london, Goldsmith ... Pasteler,
defendauntes on that other partie. Whiche gate hows and grounde the
same iiii maisters have seen serched and examyned by all their discretions
nd ... Gatehows ys in brede Est and West by the kynges high wey there
ii fote ii ynches of assise perteynyng and belongyng all the same ... to
the same party [plaintiff] ... poste there the grounde stretching in length
Northward xxxii^{ti} fote & vii ynches of assise. Also they say from a south
Est poste there the grounde ... lengeth ... ynches of assise. And they say
at the ende of the saide length upon bothe sides of the same grounde there
t is in brede xi fote & x ynches belonging to the ... that the same xxxii^{ti}
ote & vii ynches of lengith Northwarde the said grounde stretcheth in
lengith upon the bothe sides of the same grounde xx^{ti} fote & fyve ynches
.. north part of the same grounde xi fote & ii ynches and a half of assise
belonging to the same partie playntif. All the length and bredeth afore
rehersed line right and plombe ... or specialties shewed unto the
contrary.
Endorsed: Importat[ur] ista bill[a] xxi Junii A[nn]o r[egni] r[egis]
Henr[ici] VIII primo

1. The right third of the certificate is illegible: it has been damp and is blurred.

4. [A.4; undated]
To the right honourable lord maire of this Citee of London and to his
Bretheryn Aldermen of the same Citee
In right humble wyse shewen unto your good lordship and wyse discrecions Thomas Wade Thomas Smart John Helmer and Philip Cosyn, the
iiii maisters of Fremasons and Carpenters sworn to the said Citie that
whereas they ... comaunded by your honourable comaundment to
oversee a variance now beyng between Maist[er] Nicholas Mattok,
Chamberleyn of the Citie of London, and the comonaltie of the Warde of
Dowgate in London in the ... right ... and Comons of the said Citie,
playntyfes on the oon partie, And the Wardeyns and Felaship of the Craft
of Dyers of the said Citie of London, defendauntes on the other partie,
touchyng to a certeyn ground ... the edificacion upon the same, late ...
[Robert] Tate, Alderman, now perteyning to the same Craft and Felaship
of Dyers in the parish of Alhallowes the Little in Theamstreet of London
within the Warde of Dowgate aforesaid being next adioining to the
comon hall of the said Craft and [Felaship of Dyers] on the Est parte, and
the landes and ten[emen]ts perteyning to Roger Lee, Gentilman, on the
West partie. The which grounde the same iiii maisters have seen
examyned and serched by all their discretions. And thereupon they say
that the said ... the Theames side upon the South partie xxxviii^{ti} fote and i
ynches of assyse and so stretchyng in length Northwest lix^{ti} fote fyve
ynches of assise. And the said ground ... xxx^{ti} fote ... and strechyng ...
in length strechyng Northward viii^{xx} and ix fote of assise. And the said
grounde is in brede East and West xix fote iiii ynches of assise and ys from
the said ... strechyng in length ... Thamestrete hundredth and six fote of
assyse. And the said grounde is in brede East and West xviii fote Which
forsaid grounde so beyng in variance ... belongyth to the foresaid Craft

3

or Felaship of Dyers Without there can be any other evydence o
specialtie shewed to the contrary.

5. [A.5; undated]
To the full honourable lord the Mayre and Aldermen of the Citie o
London
Shewen unto your good Lordship and discrete wysedomes Thomas Wade
Thomas Smart John Helmer and Philip Cosyn the iiii maisters of the
Fremasons and Carpenters [sworne to the said Citie that where] as they
were late charged by your honourable comaundement to oversee a . . . in
the parish of Alhalows the . . . of London in the . . . variance bitwene
Thomas Bulstrode, Gentilman, and William Grene . . . defendant on the
other partie, Which stonewalle the said iiii maisters have . . . by all their
discretions . . . that the said stone wall is . . . defendant strechyng in length
from the Kynges highwey there Eastward . . . to the place called the . . .
Stywards [?Inn] . . . the said stone wall as it is nowe builded and edefied
from the Northside of the said [?stonewall] . . . all the said length in
thyknes xxiiii ynches of assyse. Also they say that plaintiff oweth to
withdraw his wall from the Southside of the aforesaid stonewall perteyning to the partie defendant all the said length of xxvii [?fote] . . . defendant
may make his said stone Wall all the said lengith, lyne right and plome.
Also the said iiii maisters say that . . . to bere his own house withoute
there can be any other evydence or specialtie shewed to the contrary.

CORPORATION OF LONDON RECORDS OFFICE FILE 'VIEWERS' REPORTS 1509–1546' [B]

(Bound Volume 204A)

. [B.1] Between 22 April 1509 and 21 April 1510.

To the fulle honourable lord the Mayre and his bretheren the Aldermen of the Citie

Shewen unto your good lordship and maistershippes Thomas Wade, Thomas Smart, John Hylmer and Philip Cosyn, the iiii maisters of Fremasons and Carpenters sworne to the said Cytie [that whereas] they were late charged by your honourable commaundement to oversee a certeyn voide grounde and housyng sett and beyng in the parissh of Seynt John Zakerys of London [now being in variance] betwene the parson churchwardeyns and parisshioners of the same parissh, playntiff, on the oon partie, and the maister, wardeyns and felaship of the Craft of Waxchaundlers [of London, defendants of the other] partie. Which voide grounde and housyng the said iiii maisters have seen serched and ripely examyned by all theire discretions. And thereupon they say that they fynde there a certeyn [void ground] conteynyng in length xvii fote and viii ynches of assise and in brede vii fote and iii ynches of assise, Which hath been of old tyme out of mynde reserved unbilded for the light of both the forsaid parties, the playntif and defendaunt, and so they say by all ther discrecions hit shall so contynew withoute there can be shewed any evidence or specialtie to the contrary. Also they say that they fynde ther two Jeties oon over another of the housyng perteynyng to the said partie playntif which two Jeties they say that they owe to be occupied . . . of the said . . . alle the length as they appier ther with alle the lightes belongyng to the said housyng as it is now divided and occupied, withoute ther can be shewed any evidence [to the contrary] . . . Also they [say that] they fynd ther a litle house withoute the forsaid Jeties in brede north and south Fyve fote and an half of assise and in lengeth est and west vii fote and an half of assise belonging to the [party plaintiff]. Also they say that they fynde there a litle voide grounde in the south part of the forsaid voide grounde bitwene the litle house and a gardyn grounde ther belongyng to the partie playntiff. Which [void] grounde in the south part is In length Est and West ix fote of assise and in brede v fote and an half of assise north and south. Which belongeth to the said partie defendaunt [without there] be shewed any evidence to the contrary. Also they say that they fynde there a stone walle perteynyng to the said partie playntiff on the Est side of the grounde of the said partie [defendant, which] wall is in lengith from the Southest post of the new housyng belongyng to the said partie defendaunt stetchyng Southwarde xxxvi fote of assise. Which wall [they say oweth to

go] lyne righte and plome all the said lengith at the costes and charge o▪
the said partie playntiff and at the ende of the said Walle the same parti▪
playntiff shall make a defence betwene . . . ther said houses ther, lyn◄
right and plome. Also they say ther aswele the said partie playntiff an◄
the same partie defendaunt shall kepe of the water indifferently. Withou▪
shewing evidence or specialty to the contrary.
Endorsed: . . . importat[ur] ista billa in Cur[iam] r[egni] r[egis] Henric◄
VIII primo

See also **183** below.

7. [B.2] 22 November 1509.
Parish of St. Leonards in Foster Lane. Variance between the parson an◄
churchwardens of the parish church of St. Mary at Hill and Rober▪
Nayler, gentleman, concerning a stone wall with a house thereto pertain◄
ing to the parish church of St. Mary at Hill. The view is by common assen▪
of both parties. The viewers find that the wall pertains to both parties▪
stretching from the SW post of the house belonging to St. Mary at Hill 21▪
ft. 9 in. eastward to the SE post of the said house. The said SE post ought▪
to be moved 22½ in. northward from the S side of the wall pertaining to▪
Nayler to the SW post of the house of St. Mary at Hill, line right and▪
plumb. Without *etc.*
Endorsed: . . . xxii die Nov[embris] anno 1 Henrici VIII

8. [B.3] 28 January 1510.
Parish of St. Faith under St. Paul's. Variance between John Copeland,
gentleman, pl., and the dean and chapter of the Cathedral Church of St.
Paul, defs., concerning a lead gutter set over a tenement pertaining to
defs. The viewers find that the gutter contains 22 ft. 1 in. in length from S
to N, all of which length from a NW corner post of a tenement of pl.
northward defs. ought to make and repair as their own land, without *etc.*
They find by all their discretions that defs. ought at their costs and charges
to make and repair again all such tiling and hurt they have done to the
tenement of pl. by changing the current of the gutter.
Endorsed: Importat[ur] ista billa per Johann[em] Helmer unum superins-
cript[i] oper[?arii] infra Civitate xxviii die Januarii a[nno] p[rimo]
H[enrici] VIII

9. [B.4][1] 24 February 1510
Parish of All Hallows in Honey Lane. Variance between the [master,
wardens and] fellowship of the Drapers in London and the master,
wardens and fellowship of the Skinners in London, concerning a void
ground now unbuilt in Westcheap. The view is by assent of both parties.
The viewers say that the said void ground pertains to the Drapers and
their successors. It is in breadth by the king's highway . . . to Mistress
Rygby on the E and the tenement of the Skinners on the W 20 ft. 5 in. [and
the ground is] in length from the S on the W side stretching northward to a
principal post of the Skinners 15 ft. and at the said . . . is in breadth from
W to E 18 ft. 10 in. It is 13 ft. 2 in. in length from the said post stretching
[further] northward to the cont. . . . of the void ground to a post pertain-

ing to the Drapers. At the end of the length, the ground is 18 ft. 3 in. in length on the E side from the N to the [?S at the king's] highway; it ought to be line right and plumb at the ground. All the measure on the W part of the ground lies line right and plumb from principal to principal. Without *etc.*

Endorsed: Importat[ur] ista billa in curiam Maioris xxiiii die Febr[uarii] a[nno] Regis Henr[ici] VIII primo

1. The certificate is in very bad condition, with the right third of it illegible.

10. [B.5] 27 February [1510].
Parish of St. Lawrence in the Old Jewry. Variance between Thomas Crisp, mercer, pl., and the prior and convent of the house of Our Lady of Elsing within Cripplegate of London, defs., concerning a nuisance of two chimneys in housing pertaining to defs. The viewers find that one chimney is on the ground of pl. in the parish of St. Martin in Ironmonger Lane; it is 6 ft. 9 in. in breadth from N to S. On the N side it is 2 ft. [?1] in. in depth and on the S side it is 2 ft. 2 in. in depth. They find there another chimney in a chamber pertaining to a tenement of defs. which chimney is thrust over the ground of pl. It is 3 ft. 3 in in breadth and 1 ft. 11 in. in depth. The two chimneys ought of right to be taken away and withdrawn from the ground of pl.
Without *etc.*

Endorsed: Importat[ur] ista billa in Cur[iam] Maioris xxvii die Febr[uarii] anno r[egni] r[egis] H[enrici] VIII primo

11. [B.6][1] 12 March [?1510].
Parish of St. Katharine Creechurch within Aldgate. Variance between John Atkynson, baker, and the master, wardens and fellowship of the Vintners in the City of London, concerning a certain ground pertaining to Atkynson. The view is by assent and consent of both parties. [The viewers find that] the ground is in breadth by the king's highway in the N between the tenement of ... fellowship upon the E part of the ground and the tenement pertaining to the prior and convent of [Creechurch] on the W 17 ft. 1½ in. ... the W ... to a principal post belonging to the prior and convent 17 ft. [4] in. ... and from the said post to another principal post of the prior and convent the ground stretching southward in length ... breadth from E to W at the said length 16 ft. Also the ground is in length from the highway stretching southward upon the ... and from the said angle stretching more southward to a corner post belonging to the Vintners 20 ft. .... Also the ground is in length more southward to the end of the said ground, to a brick wall belonging to William ... E and W 15 ft. 9 in. All the said ground measured from place to place ... Without *etc.*
Endorsed: Importat[ur] ista billa in Cur[iam] [?Maioris] xii die Marcii a[nno] R[egis] Henr[ici] VIII ...

1. The certificate is in very bad condition, with the right third illegible.

12. [B.7] 7 October 1510.
Parish of St. Benet Fink. Variance between the prior and convent of the house of Austin Friars in London, pls. and the master, warden and

fellowship of the Merchant Taylors, defs., concerning a nuisance in a stone wall behind a brewhouse called 'the Cok' in Fynke Lane. The viewers say that there is a stone wall belonging to defs.; it is 71 ft. 9 in. in length from a brick wall pertaining to the parish church of St. Michael in Cornhill stretching northward. In the wall they find a truss of stone 10 ft. in length, set to bear a chimney. It ought to be withdrawn and taken away at the costs and charges of defs., line right and plumb the whole length. Defs. ought to bear their own water all the length. Without *etc.*

Endorsed: Importat[ur] ista bill[a] in Cur[iam] Maioris etc. per infranominat[em] Thomam Wade, vii die Oct[obris] anno r[egni] r[egis] Henr[ici] VIII secundo

13. [B.9] 11 November 1510.
Parish of Our Lady Aldermary in the lane called Hosier Lane. Variance between the wardens of the brotherhood of Our Lady founded in the parish of St. Margaret at Westminster, pls., and the parson and church-wardens of St. Mary Aldermary, defs., concerning a wall of timber. The viewers say that the wall pertains to def. and contains 36 ft. 1½ in. in length from E to W. Pls. have set up two principal posts from the S side of the said principal posts [*sic*]. Defs. ought to withdraw all the length of the timber wall at their charge so pls. may build their house line right and plumb. Without *etc.*

Endorsed: Importat[ur] ista bill[a] usque in Cur[iam] M[aioris] xi die Nov[embris] anno R[egni] R[egis] Henr[ici] VIII s[e]c[un]do

14. [B.8] 14 March 1511.
Parish of St. Olave beside the street called Mark Lane. Variance between John Brown, citizen and mercer, pl., and Oliver Claymont, citizen and shearman, def., concerning a nuisance of certain walls and a chimney in a tenement of def. next adjoining the N side of a void ground pertaining to pl. The viewers find a wall of timber and loam belonging to def. stretching eastward 15 ft. 9 in. There stands a principal post of def. which must be withdrawn and set plumb upright. [In the wall] there is an angle stretching northward 3 ft. 8 in. and from the angle eastward 22 ft. 8 in. line right and plumb. And stretching eastward 30 ft. 3 in. line right and plumb to a corner post in the SE of def.'s tenement, there must be a stanchion set. Pl.'s void ground is 32 ft. 6½ in. in breadth by Mark Lane between the tenement of def. on the N and the tenement of John Genkynson, citizen and haberdasher, on the S. Eastward along Genkynson's house 15 ft. 9 in. from Mark Lane, the void ground must be 31 ft. 7½ in. in breadth between the tenements of def. and Genkynson. So they say the housing and wall of Genkynson must be withdrawn all the length line right and plumb. Without *etc.*

Endorsed: Importat[ur] ista billa per lez vewers Civit[atis] London xiiii die Marcii anno regni Regis Henrici VIII s[e]c[un]do

15. [B.10] 30 May 1511.
Parish of St. Michael in Cornhill. Variance between the prioress and convent of the monastery of St. Helen within Bishopsgate, pls., and the

parson, churchwardens and parishioners of the parish church of St. Michael in Cornhill, defs., concerning a nuisance of a stone wall and timber [*sic*]. The viewers find that the wall is 30 ft. 7½ in. in length from a corner post of defs. standing by the king's highway and stretching northward to defs.' principal post on the E side of the ground of pls. It ought to be withdrawn line right and plumb all its length. They also say that the ground there pertaining to pls. is 39 ft. 2 in. in breadth by the king's highway named Cornhill, between the tenement pertaining to defs. on the E and the tenement of late pertaining to Master Charleton on the W. It is 38 ft. in breadth E and W on the N side of the tenements rehearsed.

Endorsed: Importat[ur] ista billa usque in Cur[iam] Maioris die Veneris penult[imo] die Maii anno r[egni] r[egis] Henr[ici] VIII tercio

16. [B.11] 5 December 1511.
Parish of St. Sepulchre without Newgate of London. Variance between Margaret Down, widow of Thomas Down, blacksmith, pl., and George Langley, brewer, def., concerning a nuisance of a ground and cellar. The viewers find that the ground and cellar adjoin the N and W side of the tenement of def. They contain [?on the S] side thereof 9 ft. 8 in. from E to W. On the N side they contain 8 ft. 10 in. in length from E to W and . . . on the E side they contain 5 ft. 9 in. in breadth from N to S. On the W side the ground and cellar contain 7 ft. 5 in. from N to S. [The ground] and cellar and all the remnant of the tenement with appurtenances held by pl., and the tenement with appurtenances held by def., were lately owned by one Piers Short, who divided and reserved ground for a common siege for the easement of both parties. So it has been continued and used for a long time, as it appears. The ground and cellar ought to be built, covered and continued as a siege for easement of both parties. Def. at his costs and charges ought to make a brick or stone wall 9 ft. 8 in. in length on the S side of the cellar, up to the rasen of his house. On the N side outside the wall he ought to bring up a brick pipe for a siege. Either party at equal costs ought to make a stool, with sufficient partition between them, and so to be continued forever. Repair and cleansing of the ground and cellar over the siege and cleansing it and taking away ordure as often and when need shall require are to be done at equal cost of the parties. There is a gutter on the N side of def. and the S side of pl. which was made by the late owner of the whole ground for the common ease of the tenements. Therefore the gutter ought to be made and maintained by both parties at their common cost indifferently and at their like cost covered over sufficiently with planks. Def. ought to make a grate at his kitchen at the E end of the gutter so that nothing passes through but such matter as is lawful to pass through. 'The which view the said iiii maisters thynk by theyr alther discretions to be good and trew in all degrees as they have made it. And so oweth to be taken by the said parties. Of lesse thanne ther can be shewed any evidence or specialtie unto the contrary.'

Endorsed: Importat[ur] ista bill[a] in Cur[iam] Maioris quinto die Decembris anno r[egni] r[egis] Henr[ici] VIII iii

9

17. [B.12] 5 December 1511.

Parish of St. Michael in Huggin Lane [Wood Street]. Variance between Gilbert Egleston, goldsmith, pl., and John Joskyn, gentleman, def., concerning a nuisance of a wall of timber and loam. The viewers find a NE corner post pertaining to def. which ought to be set upright and plumb. From the post stretching W 18 ft. 8 in. there is another principal post of def. which must be withdrawn 9 in. at its foot. From that post stretching westward 21 ft. 10 in. there is another NW corner post of def. which ought to be set upright and plumb. All the wall between the said three posts ought to be line right and plumb. Without *etc.*

Endorsed: Importat[ur] ista bill[a] in Cur[iam] Maioris quinto die Decembris anno R[egni] R[egis] Henrici VIII tercio

18. [B.13] 15 June 1512.

Parish of St. Magnus in Bridge Street. Variance between William Ramsey, citizen and fishmonger, pl., and the master, wardens and post in fellowship of the Goldsmiths in the City of London, defs., concerning a nuisance of the side of a house pertaining to defs. The viewers find that the side of the house overhangs the ground of pl. $4\frac{1}{2}$ in. at the NW corner post in the upper story; stretching eastward to the NE corner post, that post overhangs $2\frac{1}{2}$ in. The house side ought to be withdrawn line right and plumb all its length at costs and charges of defs. 'On less thann the said partie defendant can shew any other evydence or specialtie to the contrary.'

Endorsed: xv° die Junii anno r[egni] r[egis] Henr[ici] VIII iiiii[to] ista bill[a] importat[ur]

19. [B.14] 19 June 1512.

Parish of All Hallows [Bread Street]. Variance between Aleyne Hobard, citizen and merchant taylor, pl., and the master, wardens and fellowship of the Salters in the City of London, defs., concerning a nuisance of the S end of a new house of defs. in Watling Street. The viewers find the SE end of the new house of defs. at the rasen is plumb down with the plate of the old corner house of pl. stretching N and S, overhanging the old corner house 12 in. The SE end of the new house ought to be withdrawn 12 in. line right and plumb at costs and charges of defs. Unless than *etc.*

Endorsed: Importat[ur] ista bill[a] huc in Cur[iam] Maioris xix die Junii a[nno] iiii[to] Henr[ici] VIII

20. [B.15] [?25] October 1512.

Parish of Our Lady called Aldermary Church in Watling Street. Variance between the master, wardens and fellowship of the Skinners of London, pls., and Ralph (Rauf) Wylson, citizen and blacksmith, def., concerning the measurement of certain ground in Basing Lane. The viewers find that the ground pertaining to pls. is 95 ft. in length from the king's street called Cordwainer Street on the E stretching westward along Basing Lane to the tenement of def. The ground pertaining to pls. is 47 ft. 11 in. on the E part from Basing Lane northward along Cordwainer Street, adjoining the tenement in the tenure of John Breteyn, merchant taylor, pertaining to Thomas Birnell, mercer, late [of] Master Richard Chawry, sometime mayor and alderman of London. The N part of the ground of pls. stretches 76 ft. westward along by a tenement in the tenure of Breteyne [*sic*]. There the ground is 49 ft. 9 in. in breadth from Basing Lane northward. The ground stretches from the tenement of Breteyne westward along the tenement belonging to the Salters 14 ft. 6 in. to a corner post belonging to the tenement of def. and there it is 52 ft. in breadth. The ground of pls. is 4 ft. 7 in. from the corner post of def. stretching westward to an angle. From Basing Lane northward by the tenement of def. to the said angle, the ground of pls. is 43 ft. 8 in. All the ground pertaining to pls. within these bounds ought to be line right and plumb from place to place. Without *etc.*

Endorsed: Importat[ur] ista bill[a] in Cur[iam] hic [?25] die Oct[obris] anno r[egni] r[egis] Henr[ici] VIII iiii^{to}

21. [B.16] 30 December 1512.
Parishes of St. Stephen in Walbrook and St. Mary Woolchurch of London. Variance between the master, wardens and fellowship of the Drapers, pls., and the parson, churchwardens and parishioners of St. Stephen, defs., concerning a stone wall set in both parishes. The viewers say that the wall is partible between the parties. It stands upon the N side of St. Stephen's churchyard and is 39 ft. 6 in. in length from a SW corner post of a house pertaining to pls. stretching westward. The viewers by their discretions say that pls. ought to have 6 in. of the wall from the N side southward all its length of 39 ft. 6 in., to be allowed at the ground, line right and plumb. Without *etc.*

Endorsed: Istud Record[um] intrat[ur] penultim[o] die mensis Decembris anno R[egni] R[egis] Henrici Octavi quarto

22. [B.17] 4 January 1513.
Parish of St. Botolph in Thames Street. Variance between the parson, churchwardens and parishioners of St. Leonard in Eastcheap, pls., and the parson, churchwardens and parishioners of St. Botolph, defs., concerning a stone wall. The viewers understand that the wall is partible. They find that pls. ought of right to have ground 20 ft. 5 in. in breadth by the king's highway between the tenement pertaining to the Goldsmiths on the E stretching westward to the tenement pertaining to defs.; stretching northward 20 ft. from the king's highway, there the ground is 19 ft. 9 in. in breadth. Also stretching [further] northward from the king's highway 40 ft. the said ground is 19 ft. 7 in. in breadth. All the ground there of pls. is 91 ft. in length and 15 ft. 7 in. in breadth, from place to place line right and plumb. Without *etc.*

Endorsed: Istud Recordu[m] intrat[ur] iiii^{to} Die Januarii anno regno Regis Henrici Octavi quarto

23. [B.20] 10 May 1513.
Parish of St. Sepulchre without Newgate. Variance between the prioress and convent of the house of Holywell beside London, pls., and the abbot and convent of Leicester and Robert Brykyt of London, brewer, their tenant and fermor, defs., concerning certain ground where a new pale is

11

to be made between the ground of pls. and ground pertaining to the tenement 'Sarsyn's Hede' belonging to the abbot and convent, of which Brykyt is charged with repairs. The viewers find that Brykyt ought at his costs and charges to make a new pale on the ground pertaining to the abbot and convent, stretching southward 30 ft. line right and plumb from the corner of a stone wall of the abbot. The corner post at the end of the pale ought to be 25 ft. 10 in. from the SE post of the corner of a little house there pertaining to pls. Unless *etc.*

Endorsed: Importat[ur] ista bill[a] in ista Cur[iam] x° die Mai[i] a[nno] v^to h[enrici] VIII

24. [B.19] 5 November 1513.
Parish of St. Martin within Ludgate. Variance between the chantry priests of St. Peter's College belonging to the Cathedral Church of St. Paul in London, pls., and the lord master and his brethren of the hospital of St. Thomas of Acon, otherwise called St. Thomas of Acres, in Cheapside beside the great conduit (condith), defs., concerning a stone wall and a timber wall. The viewers say that the stone wall is partible 7½ ft. in length; 7 in. in the thickness all the said length pertains to dets. The remnant pertains to pls. They find a new house built by defs. and set on the stone wall, 10 ft. in length, which overhangs towards pls. 3 in. at the SE corner and 4 in. at the NE corner. At the NE corner stands a corner post pertaining to defs. adjoining the house, which overhangs pls. 10 in. From the post [the ground] stretching northward 19 ft. 7 in. to a jetty (gety) belongs to pls.; the timber wall there ought to be set line right and plumb all its length by defs. Without *etc.*

Endorsed: Importat[ur] ista bill[a] in Cur[iam] v die Nov[embris] a[nno] quinto h[enrici] VIII

25. [B.21] 31 March 1514.
Parish of St. Margaret in Bridge Street. Variance between Master Geoffrey Wren, parson of the church, and his deputy and attorney, Richard Hun, merchant taylor,[1] pls., and the churchwardens and parishioners of the said parish church, defs., concerning the church stone wall on the S side of the parish church. The viewers say that the wall contains 47 ft. in length from a quoin at the SW corner of the church stretching eastward to a [buttery corner]. It is 22 ft. in height from the ground to the upper side of the rasen and it is 2 ft. 2 in. in thickness. It overhangs into the churchyard W and E 3 in. at both ends and 4 in. in the middle. Also they say the wall 'is rent and crakkyd in dyverse places of the same and old and febyll'.

1. Possibly this is the famous Richard Hunne, merchant taylor of this parish, who refused to pay a mortuary for the burial of his infant child, was accused of heresy, and died mysteriously in the bishop of London's prison on 14 December, 1514, only nine months after this view. If so, the fact that Hun/Hunne is here acting for his parish priest may have some bearing on the dispute over whether he had been considered suspect before the quarrel about the payment.

26. [B.18] March [no day given] 1514.
Thomas Smart, John Hylmer, Philip Cosyn and Thomas Newell, freemasons and carpenters, viewers.

Parish of St. Alphage within Cripplegate. No variance stated. The viewers have been charged to measure a ground and brewhouse thereon named 'the Rose' pertaining to Richard Harry Yonge, coiner. They say that the ground and tenement is 30 ft. in breadth by the king's highway on the N between the tenement named 'the Son' pertaining to the fraternity of Our Lady and St. Giles in the church of St. Giles without Cripplegate on the W and the tenement pertaining to John Sterne, currier, on the E. On its E side, the ground and brewhouse extend 72 ft. 8 in. in length from the king's highway [on the N] to the tenement of John Thomas on the S. On the W side of the tenement, it is 13 ft. 7 in. in length from the king's highway stretching southward to an angle. The ground and tenement is 37 ft. in breadth between 'the Son' on the W and the tenement of Sterne on the E. Stretching southward from the angle to the tenement of Thomas and to the S end of the same brewhouse the ground is 23 ft. in breadth. The viewers also find a gutter between 'the Rose' and 'the Son' which they say is a partible gutter and ought to be repaired at the indifferent charges and costs of Yonge and the brotherhood of Our Lady and St. Giles. All the ground ought to remain line right and plumb to Yonge 'if ther can be noone other evydence or specialtie shewed to the contrary.'
Endorsed: [?1559]
Subscribed: Importat[a] f[uit] ista bill[a] in [?mensem] Marche a[nno] v^{to} h[enrici] VIII

27. [B.22] 31 May 1514.
Parish of St. Peter in Broad Street of London. Variance between the prior and convent of the house of Austin Friars (Freer Austyns) in London, pls., and Master Richard Nicollas, clerk and parson of St. Peter's, def., concerning certain ground. The viewers find that the ground is 77 ft. in length between the tenement pertaining to pls. on the S and stretching northward to a brick wall also of pls. Pls. may build housing 14 in. from the post of a shed of the parson into their own ground. They may also build housing at the N end of the ground 14 in. from a quoin of a brick wall belonging to them there. 'Alle which ground and beeldyngs have been assented and fully agreed betwene bothe the forsaid parties in manner and forme above rehersed to be made lyne right and plom, alle the length afore shewed as it is measured by the forsaid vewers. If there can be noone other evidence or specialtie shewed to the contrary.'
Endorsed: Import[ata] f[uit] ista bill[a] per lez vewers xv° die Junii a[nno] v^{to} Henr[ici] VIII

28. [B.23]^1 28 March 1515.
Parish of St. Dunstan in the East. Variance between the executors of the Right Worshipful Thomas Knesworth, deceased, late mayor of London, pls., and William Roche, citizen and draper, def., concerning certain grounds, lands, tenements and edifications which [blank] Norys, woodmonger, holds and occupies. The viewers find that def. has encroached and built $2\frac{1}{2}$ in. upon ground pertaining to pls. all the length of his [def's.] new house. They find that at the NW corner post of the house of pl., 41 ft. 10 in. from the king's highway southward [pertains to pls.] Pls. ought to

have a space 4 ft. 9¾ in. without the said corner post westward and stretching southward 76 ft. 7 in. to the SW corner of pls.' house there. Pls. ought to have a space of 3 ft. 'withoute the coyne of the foundation of the said corner westward, and so from the said corner down unto the campshide ende of the same William Roche as it is now kytt. And so from the king's highway afore rehersed down southward to the water of Theamese from place to place as it is aforespecified, lyne right and plome'. Without *etc.*

Endorsed: ... this bill ... the iiii[to] day of April which is Tenebre Wednesday a[nno] vi[to] h[enrici] VIII[to]

1. This certificate is copied in Journal 11, f. 222.

29. [B.24] 11 June 1515.
Parish of St. Andrew in Holborn. Variance between Harry West, dyer, pl., and John Pasmar, merchant taylor, def., concerning certain ground, lands, tenements and rents of pl. next adjoining the great tenement called 'Barnardes Inne' on the E and the tenement pertaining to def. on the W. The viewers find sufficient evidence and writing enrolled in the Hustings in London to appear that pl. ought to have ground 4 yds. in breadth by the king's highway and 5 yds. in breadth in the middle of the edifications. He ought to have 'v yards a quarter and one half of assise' in breadth at the inner part of the housing and tenements. Also the ground pertaining to pl. there should be 10 yds. in breadth at the middle part, as the aforesaid writing shows. At the inner part, the grounds should be 12½ yds. in breadth. The ground, lands and tenements pertaining to pl. have been diminished and withdrawn in part by def., contrary to the writing and evidence of pl. Def. ought of right to restore all such parcel of the ground withdrawn by him to pl. and his assigns. Without *etc.*

Endorsed: Monoux maior per Gravely servien[tem]

30. [B.25] 20 July 1515.
Parish of St. Pulcres without Newgate. Variance between the prior of the monastery of St. Bartholomew in West Smithfield and the convent of the same, pls., and [?John] Pynner, tallowchandler, def., concerning a certain ground. The viewers say that it is 45 ft. 6 in. in length from a NW corner post of a house of pls. stretching [?northward] line right to a mark made by the viewers upon an old plate there on the N part of the said ground. The parties ought of right to make and be charged to make the defence indifferently between them for the defence of the said ground. Without *etc.*

Endorsed: ... xxiii die Juliii a[nno] vii h[enrici] VIII tempore Monoux M[aioris] per William Nicolson servien[tem]

31. [B.27] 12 December 1515.
Parish of St. Leonard beside Eastcheap. Variance between the parson and churchwardens of St. Dunstan in the East, pls., and the prior and convent of St. Bartholomew in Smithfield, defs., concerning a certain void ground, which ground of old time was built for a pastry house pertaining to pls. The viewers find that the ground contains 18 ft. in length

om a SE corner post of a shed belonging to pls. and from a mark of a
ross with a nail driven into a wall of the tenement that John Palmer,
ilor, now dwells in, stretching eastward to ground pertaining to defs.
he ground is 8 ft. in breadth between the tenement that Palmer dwells in
nd the middle of a stone wall on the N part of the ground. The stone wall
; partible. The void ground in the aforesaid length and breadth pertains
o pls. Unless than *etc.*
Endorsed: . . . ista bill[a] insert[atur] per Lorymer ix die Decembr[is] . . .

32. [B.28] 3 July 1516.
'arish of St. Dunstan in the West. Variance between the master and
wardens of the fraternity and brotherhood of St. Dunstan's, pls., and the
lean and his brethren of the Free Chapel of St. Stephen's at Westminster,
lefs., concerning a certain ground with edification upon the same. The
viewers find the ground with edification thereupon by the king's street is
2 ft. 10 in. in breadth, and from the street northward underneath a stair
here of the pls. it is 22 ft. in length. The ground and edification ought of
right to belong to the said fraternity of St. Dunstan, line right and plumb
all the said measure. Without *etc.*
Endorsed. . . . Julii [anno octavo regni] r[egis] h[enrici] 8 . . .
Subscribed: . . . x die Julii a[nno] [octavo] R[egni] R[egis] II[enrici] 8
import[atur] ista bill[a] etc. . . .

33. [B.26] 8 July 1516.
Parish of St. Pulcres without Newgate. Variance between John [Tynny],
salter, pl., and Giles Polyver, gentleman, def., concerning a nuisance of a
channel (cannell) for the conveyance of water. The viewers find a well
which is partible between the parties. The well water and the water from
def.'s house and kitchen now have a course through the grounds of pl.
Def. ought of right to withdraw the watercourse or else come to an
agreement about it with pl. There is a shed over the well which stands and
overhangs upon the grounds of pl. from the middle of the well southward;
def. ought to withdraw it. Without *etc.*
Endorsed: Tynny and Polyver. viii die Julii anno r[egni] r[egis] [Henrici]
octavi viii certificat[ur] et importat[ur] cor[am] Will[elm]o Butler Maire
. . . etc.
Subscribed: [?viii] die Julii A[nn]o viii R[egni] R[egis] Henr[ici] VIII . . .
certificat[ur] et importat[ur] coram Will[elm]o Butler milite et Maior[e]
etc.

34. [B.29][1] 13 March 1517.
Parish of St. Giles without Cripplegate. Variance between Oliver
Moryell, crossbowmaker, pl., and the parson and churchwardens of the
parish church of All Hallows Bread Street, defs., concerning a certain
ground for a defence to be made and set between two gardens and for a
nuisance of a side of a house. The viewers find that pl. ought to make the
defence from a SE corner post of his house stretching eastward to the
common Moor ditch by the S side of five marstones there set in the ground
by the viewers, line right by all the length of the ground. They find the N

side of a house 50 ft. in length belonging to defs. whose water falls on th
ground of pl. Defs. should of right bear the water on their own ground
'All whiche premyses and noysaunces aforsaid owen to be reformed an
amended in manner and forme as afore is rehersed.' Without *etc.*

1. The certificate is in a hand different from that of preceding certificates.

35. [B.30] 27 April 1517.
Parish of St. Botolph without Aldgate. Variance between the masters c
the Bridgehouse of London and John Hygent, butcher, concerning
certain nuisance of and for the building and setting up of a new house an
parcel [*sic*] of an old house belonging to the Bridgehouse of the City. Th
view is by common assent of both parties. The viewers say that the N
corner post of the new house by the king's highway ought to be withdraw
southward 4 in. from the house of Hygent. From the same corner post th
new house stretches eastward 19 ft. 2 in. to its NE corner post, which pos
ought likewise to be withdrawn 2 in. From post to post the new hous
should be line right and plumb. Also a gable end of an old house stretche
eastward 14 ft. 1 in. from the said NE corner post to an old corner pos
pertaining to the Bridgehouse. The gable end is partible and ought to b
repaired and supported at the parties' equal charges. From the old pos
stretching eastward 9 ft. 1 in. to the S side of a principal post of Hygen
there is a daubed wall, which wall line right and plumb belongs to the
Bridgehouse. Hygent ought to bear all his own water all the length of his
house. All which premises and nuisances *etc.* Without *etc.*
Endorsed: Betwene the Master of the Brigehouse and John Higent . . . 29
die Aprilis

36. [B.31] 13 June 1517.
Parish of St. Vedast. Variance between the parson and churchwardens of
the parish, pls., and the master, wardens and fellowship of the Saddlers,
defs., concerning a nuisance. The viewers have been commanded first to
oversee a stone wall belonging to defs. on the S side of the church, which
wall they find is 14 ft. 4 in. in length from the W side of another stone wall
of defs. against the E end of the church stretching westward to a brick or
angle on the wall. The length ought to be line right and plumb from the
first stone of the jamb of a door there as is marked on the timber work by
the viewers and from the foresaid brick or angle stretching westward 28 ft.
by the N side of the wall to the NW side of a corner post of defs., line right
and plumb as the wall appears and as the viewers have marked on the end
of a stone wall there of pls. A timber wall and a brick wall on the N side of
the church, in the tenure of William York, embroiderer (browtherer),
stretches westward 17 ft. 8 in. from the stone wall of defs. [at the E end of
the church], where there is an angle. From the angle it stretches westward
13 ft. 1 in. to a stanchion of the brick wall there in the tenure of William
Clerke, carpenter. At the stanchion, the brick wall and the house built on
it overhang the ground of pls. $4\frac{1}{2}$ in. The SW corner of the jetty of the
same house overhangs the ground 8 in. From the stanchion stretching
westward 11 ft. the brick wall, the timber wall, and the stone wall ought to
go line right and plumb from place to place and be reformed, without *etc.*

urthermore, whereas the viewers were desired by pls. to view the
uilding of the church from its choir (quyre) door eastward [to say]
whether it is of one building or has been lengthened or added to, the
iewers say that all is one building, built at one season.
Endorsed: A view concerning Seynt Fosters

37. [B.32] 1 October 1517.
Parish of St. Augustine beside Paul's Gate. Variance between Henry
Polsted, merchant taylor, pl., and Christopher Nicolson, merchant
aylor, def., concerning a certain void ground. The viewers find that the
ground is 40 ft. 5 in. from the E side of the N post of the frame of a partible
wall stretching northward to the E side of a SE corner post of a shed.
From the same E side of the two posts westward to a tenement of the
Petty Canons of [St.] Paul's and a tenement pertaining to the College of
Windsor, line right and plumb, the void ground belongs to pl. Further, pl.
ought to make a sufficient defence between his ground and def.'s. All
which premises *etc*. Without *etc*.
Endorsed: . . . H 8
Subscribed: . . . per Hayes Certificatur ad Cur[iam] . . . sexto die
[N]ovembris a[nno] ix° r[egni] r[egis] H[enrici] VIII

38. [B.33] 26 January 1518.
To the right honorable lord and worshipfull Soveraignes the Mayre and
Aldermen of the Citee of London
Shewen unto your good lordship and discrete wisedoms the xxvi daye of
January in the ix^th yere of the Reigne of Kyng Henry the VIIIth Thomas
Smart, John Hylmar, Philip Cosyn and Thomas Newell, the iiii maisters
of Fremasons and Carpenters, viewers indifferent sworne to the said
Citte, that where as they were late charged by your honorable com-
maundement to oversee a certayn Ten[emen]t wherin Richard Wolstone,
Bocher, now dwelleth, sette and beyng in Estchepe in the paryssh of Saint
Clement beside Candilewykestrete of london, now beyng in variance
betwene the said Richard of that one partie and the parson and wardeyns
of the parisshe Churche of Saint Clement aforesaid of that other partie.
Forasmoche as the said Richard holdeth the said Ten[emen]t of the
forsaid parson and wardeyns by leas indented for terme of yeres in whiche
leas amonges other things it ys conteyned thus, Provyded alwey that yf at
any tyme within the said terme it fortune the said Ten[emen]t with
thappurtenances to be of newe bylded, Than the said parson and
wardeyns for theym & their Successours wole & graunte by these presents
that the said Richard Wolstone, his excecutors & assignes, shall have and
hold the said Ten[emen]t to thende of the said xxi yeres for suche yerely
Rent as shalbe then rated & assessed by the iiii comen viewers of london
for the tyme beyng without fraude or malengyne As in the said leas
indented playnly it doth appere. The whiche Ten[emen]t with all the
rowmes, necessaryes and easements of the same now beyng newe bylded
the said iiii viewers by all their discrecions have serched seen and rypely
understond And therupon they sey adiuge & deme the said Ten[emen]t
to be better & more worth by xiii s. iiii d. by yere then it was before the
newe bylding therof and that the said Richard ought so to pay for the

17

same Ten[emen]t. Without ther can be any other evidence or specialti
shewed to the contrary.
Endorsed: A[nno] ix° H 8

39. [B.34] 14 May 1518.
Ward of Aldgate. Variance between the Chamberlain of the City o
London and Thomas Turbervyle, gentleman, concerning a defence to b
made and renewed where an old timber wall now stands between th
garden of the tenement called the 'Stywards Inne', belonging to th
Chamber of London and now in tenure of William Tull, tiler, on the E
and the garden belonging to the abbot of Evesham, now in tenure o
Thomas Turbervyle, on the W. The viewers find that the old wall contain
60 ft. 4 in. in length from the S end of a brick wall belonging to the prior o
Christ Church in London to the N end of another brick wall belonging to
the abbot of Westminster. The defence or wall ought to be made
supported and kept at the costs and charges of the abbot of Evesham o
his assignees. Without *etc*.
Endorsed: . . . x° H 8
Subscribed: Infer[tur] ad Cur[iam] tent[am] xx die Maii a[nno] x^to r[egis
h[enrici] 8

40. [B.35] 26 June 1518.
Parish of St. Brigit in Fleet Street. Variance between the wardens and
fellowship of the Vintners, pls., and the abbot of the New Abbey at
Tower Hill, def., concerning a nuisance of and for the building and setting
up of a new house for pls. The viewers find that the ground belonging to
pls. northward on the king's highway of Fleet Street contains 19 ft. 8½ in.
in breadth between a tenement of def. on the E and a tenement of the
Bishop of Sare [Salisbury] on the W. The NW corner post of the tenement
of def. and the rasen upon the same post overhang the ground of pls. by 1
in. The same ground from the king's highway of Fleet Street stretching
eastward to a SE corner post of the house of def. contains 26 ft. 3½ in. in
length and there the rasen of the house overhangs the ground of pl. by 2
in. It ought of right to be withdrawn and set up right by def. or else pls. to
have liberty to enter their frame into the timber of def.'s house where
need requires, line right and plumb between the said two posts. Pls. have
made their frame 1 in. too large by the street side from the height of the
first story there upward, which ought to be withdrawn by them. All of
which premises and nuisances *etc*. Without *etc*.

41. [B.36] 17 March 1519.
Parish of St. Dionis Backchurch. Variance between Edward Boughton,
gentleman, pl., and the dean and chapter of the Cathedral Church of St.
Paul, defs., concerning a certain old house end. The viewers by all their
discretions have viewed, seen and searched by good advisement and ripe
deliberation. They find that the old house end adjoining the E end of a
new house lately built there contains 12 ft. 5 in. in wideness from N to S
and 11 ft. 2 in. from E to W. The W part of the old house, which lately
stood where the new house now is set, being then one house and one

:ame, was cut away from the said E end of the same old house. As far as ne viewers can perceive and find, the old house end now there stands on he ground and within the bounds of pl. Without *etc.*

Endorsed: A viewe brought yn to this Court the xix day of March a[nno] *mo* h[enrici] VIII

Subscribed: [M]yrfyn mayor. Certificatur ad Cur[iam] Dom[ini] Regis ent[am] xix die Marcii anno x*mo* Henr[ici] VIII Coram Maiore et Ald[e]r[man]is.

Sol[utum] feod[um] ii s. per Hayes

42. [B.37] 1 February 1520.

Parish of St. Botolph in the Ward of Billingsgate. There is a void ground belonging to the Goldsmiths, 'somewhat in variance' between the Right Worshipful the Chamberlain of the City of London and the master and wardens of the Goldsmiths. The view is with the assent, will and agreement of both parties. The viewers find that the void ground contains 20 ft. 2½ in. in breadth by the king's highway of Thames Street, from a tenement belonging to the Chamber of London on the E to a tenement belonging to the parson and churchwardens of the parish church of St. Leonard in Eastcheap on the W. Stretching northward 31 ft. 2 in. from Thames Street on the E side of the ground, the ground is 20 ft. 7 in. in breadth from E to W. Stretching further northward 16 ft. 8 in. on the E side, which is at the end of the stone wall of a vault belonging to the Chamber, the void ground is 20 ft. 4 in. in breadth. There is another stone wall stretching northward from the stone wall of the vault 16 ft. 3 in. in length. It stands against the gable end of a house belonging to John Myldenale, grocer; it is 22 in. in thickness at its S end and 2 ft. 4 in. in thickness at its N end and it belongs to the Goldsmiths in its entirety. From the NW end of that wall stretching 19 ft. 10 in. northward to a NW corner post of a gable end of another house of Myldenale, the void ground is 17 ft. in breadth. At the same corner post is an angle 2 ft. deep eastward and from that corner post stretching 7 ft. northward to the N side of another stone wall belonging to the Goldsmiths, the void ground is 19 ft. in breadth from E to W. There also ends the length of the void ground from N to S. The ground ought of right to have its course line right and plumb from place to place as is afore limited and expressed. All which premises *etc.* Without *etc.*

43. [B.38] 5 March 1520.

Parish of St. Giles without Cripplegate. Variance between the master and wardens of the Goldsmiths, pls., and the prior of Barnwell in the county of Cambridge, def., concerning a certain garden belonging to pls. and a defence to be made to the same ground. The viewers find that from the NW corner of a post of a wall of timber and loam belonging to pls. stretching southward 59 ft. 6 in. on the W side of the ground to the S side of a stake set in the ground by the viewers, and from there further southward 40 ft. 8 in. to the N side of a pale [?stretching westward], where the viewers have set another stake, the ground, line right and plumb from mark to mark to the W side of the said 2 stakes, is the ground of pls. The

19

pale stands between ground of Robert Smyth, brewer, and a garden of chantry founded in Pardon Churchyard by Master Thomas More sometime dean of [St.] Paul's. At the pale and stake there is an angle 3 ft deep eastward to the NE corner of a pale post and from there the groun of pls. stretches further southward 30 ft. 9 in. line right and plumb to th W end of a wall adjoining a house belonging to the chantry. And th viewers say that pls. ought to make the defence to their ground from th NW corner of the ground to the pale, following the marks and bound aforelimited and set out by the viewers. All which premises *etc.* Withou *etc.*

44. [B.39] 12 June 1520.
Parish of St. Michael at Querne. Variance between the Right Worshipfu Sir William Butler, knight, Alderman of the City of London, pl., and William Seintpier of London, merchant taylor, def., concerning a nuisance. The viewers find a vault (vawt) in the parish which contains 5 ft. 2 in. in length and 21 ft. 8 in. in breadth from the outside of the walls of the vault. They also find a stone door 4 ft. wide and 7 ft. high on the E side of the vault adjoining a little cellar of def., which was mured up with stone and mortar and lately broken open by def. The vault belongs wholly to pl., as does the door 'as far as the said vewers can perceyve and have any understonding or knolage in that behalve.' Without *etc.*
Endorsed: Infertur xxii° die Junii anno r[egni] r[egis] hen[rici] VIII xii°

45. [B.40] 19 September 1520.
Parish of St. Andrew beside Paul's Wharf [by the Wardrobe]. Measurement, by commandment of the Mayor and Aldermen, of the length and breadth of a tenement or house belonging to the brotherhood of Priests of Papey in London. The viewers have meten and measured the house. They say that it contains 24 ft. 6 in. in length on the N side from a tenement on the E belonging to the abbot of Reading to the NW corner post. It contains 19 ft. 6 in. in breadth in the W end from the NW corner post to the SW corner post, which abuts on a tenement belonging to the Charterhouse. On the S, the house contains in length 22 ft. between the tenement of the abbot of Reading on the E and the common lane called the Newsteyre on the W. It contains 22 ft. 6 in. in breadth on the E between the tenement belonging to the Charterhouse on the S and the king's highway of Thames Street on the N. The viewers say that of time past, the ground of the Brotherhood extended further N 11 ft., a little more or less, where Thames Street now lies. The priests have as much ground for it [now] to the S, on land which had been common ground and on which the S side of their house now stands. The viewers have also measured a little yard of the Brotherhood containing 36 ft. 10 in. in length on the E and W from N to S and 19 ft. 5 in. in breadth in the N from E to W by the Charterhouse ground and 17 ft. 10 in. in breadth in the S abutting the common ground.

46. [B.41] 11 December 1520.
Parishes of St. Benedict beside Paul's Wharf and St. Mary Magdalen in

20

Old Fish Street. Variance between the parson and wardens of the church of St. Benedict, pls., and the master of St. Bartholomew's Hospital in West Smithfield, def., concerning a stone wall in both parishes. The viewers find that the wall is 24 ft. 6 in. in length from a tenement at the E end belonging to the House of Saint Eleyn in London stretching westward. There is a break in the wall and it then stretches further westward 1 ft. 4 in. to the E end of a house belonging to def., in which house William Gybson, tailor, dwells. The stone wall ought to be partible; either party ought to have like much in the thickness of the wall all its length. The defence that shall be made there between the houses of the parties ought to be made at the equal charges of the parties. Without *etc.*

47. [B.42] 28 January 1521.
Parish of St. Mary Colechurch. Variance between John Wanell, prior of the house of Our Lady of Elsing Spital in London, pl., and the master and wardens of the Mercers, defs., concerning a nuisance at the W end of the new work and building of defs. in the ward of Cheap. The viewers find that the SW quoin of the new building of defs. overhangs the ground of pl. 2 in. westward at the height of 15 ft. above the ground. Stretching northward 14 ft., they find a break in the wall of the new work, and there the wall overhangs 2 in. at 20 ft. above the ground. Stretching more northward from the break 5 ft. 6 in., the wall overhangs 2½ in. at 26 ft. above the ground; 17 ft. still further N, the new wall overhangs 2½ in. at 22 ft. above the ground. Stretching 5 ft. 8 in. N to a quoin of brick, the quoin and wall overhang 5 in. The new wall ought to be reformed or withdrawn from the SW quoin to the break aforesaid line right and plumb, and from the break line right and plumb by all the length of 27 ft. 2 in. northward in form aforesaid, without *etc.*

48. [B.43] 5 June 1521.
Parish of St. Mary Colechurch. Variance between the master and wardens of the Mercers, pls., and the prior of the house of Our Lady of Elsing Spital in London, def., concerning a nuisance in the ward of Cheap. The viewers find a new brick wall set on the E side of the ground of def. adjoining the W end of the new building of pls. At the S side of it, by the king's highway of Cheap, from W to E the wall is, and ought to be, 10 in. in thickness at a height of 11 ft. 6 in. from the upper side (upsyd) of the shop floor of def. Stretching northward from the S side 14 ft., there is a break in the W end of the new building of pls. 4 in. deep out of the line right. There the brick wall of def. is 14 in. in thickness at a height of 11 ft. 6 in. Stretching more northward from the break 30 ft. 8 in. to its N end, the wall is 9 in. in thickness at the same height. The wall ought to lie line right and plumb from place to place as aforerehearsed. Also, def. has broken into the wall of pls. at the W end of the [pls.'] building, from the N end of the wall of def. stretching southward 15 ft., in the deepest place 3 in. and at diverse other places 2 in. and 1 in. All of which premises and nuisances *etc.* Without *etc.*
Endorsed: a[nno] xiii° Henr[ici] VIII ... Importat[ur] tempore ... soll[utum] ... ii s.

21

49. [B.44] 9 July 1521.
Parish of St. Lawrence in the Jewry. Variance between the vicar an churchwardens of St. Lawrence, pls., and John Kynnersley, squire, def concerning a tenement with appurtenances thereto belonging i Cateaton (Catte) Street. The viewers have indifferently measured a follows: the tenement contains 14 ft. 1½ in. in breadth from E to W by th king's highway of Cateaton Street between a tenement belonging to th church of St. Lawrence on the W and the land of John Weston, mercer on the E. Stretching northward 28 ft. 3 in. on the E side of the tenement t a NE corner post, the house is 14 ft. 4 in. in breadth. Stretching mor northward 14 ft. 8 in., it is 21 ft. 10 in. in breadth. There is an angle stretching eastward 2 ft. 3 in.; stretching northward from the angle 25 ft. in. to another NE corner post, the tenement contains 23 ft. 2½ in. in breadth from E to W to a stone wall of 'the Sarysons Hede'. There is an angle of the ground and housing of 'the Sarysons Hede' approaching eastward 7 ft. 4 in. There they find a void ground with a shed lately set up which ground and shed contain 15 ft. 10 in. in breadth from the angle to the NE corner post E to W, and 61 ft. 8 in. in length on the W side of the angle stretching northward to a stone wall belonging to Bakewell Hall and 15 ft. 6 in. in breadth from a wall of timber and loam on the same W side stretching eastward by the said stone wall; and 65 ft. in length on the E side from the NE corner post to the stone wall of Bakewell Hall at the same breadth. 'The whiche tenement and grounde aforemeasured by all that the said iiii vewers can perceyve and knowe aswell by their owne reasons and discrecions as also by good and substanciall evidence in writyng to them shewed and redde, ought of right to belonge unto the said churche of Saint Lawrence lyneright and plumb from place to place all the length and brede of the same as is afore rehersed.' Without *etc.*
Endorsed: ... Importatur [Curiam Maioris] ...

50. [B.45] 13 August 1521.
Parish of St. Dunstan in the West. Variance between Henry Dacres, merchant taylor, pl., and Nicholas Whyte, skinner, def., concerning a nuisance. The viewers find certain houses built on ground which def. holds by lease of the prior and brethren of the house of St. John of Jerusalem in England, which houses contain 67 ft. in length on their E side from the N end of a brick wall standing betwixt the gardens of pl. and def., stretching northward to a NE corner post of the same houses. The viewers say that def. ought to bear all the water of the said houses all their length and to convey that water to his own ground. The which nuisance *etc.* Without *etc.*

51. [B.46] 21 July 1522.
Parish of St. Katharine Christchurch. Variance between the wardens and fellowship of the Haberdashers, pls., and the prior and convent of Christ Church in London, defs., concerning certain nuisances. The viewers find the S end of a kitchen belonging to pls. with a stone foundation containing 14 ft. in breadth from the ground of defs. on the E to an entry of pls. on the W; the foundation ought to be line right and plumb all the length.

Also the entry is 8 ft. 4 in. in breadth between the SW corner post of the kitchen and the E side of pls.' house on the W side of the entry; stretching southward from the corner post 20 ft. the entry is 8 ft. 5 in. in breadth. [At the length of 20 ft.] is the outer (utter) part of the foundation of defs.' brewhouse. The entry on the E side there ought to be line right and plumb. Also, in the garden of a tenement belonging to pls. the viewers find the S side of a house belonging to defs. containing 46 ft. in length from E to W, which ought to bear its (his) own water with a fillet gutter by all the length aforesaid at costs and charges of the defs. Without *etc.*

Subscribed: Certificat[ur] xxiiii[to] die Julii a[nno] r[egni] r[egis] Henr[ici] VIII xiiii° T[empore] Milburn M[aioris]. Sol[utum] feod[um] ii s.

52. [B.47] 7 November 1522.
Parish of St. Dunstan in the West. Variance between the master and wardens of the Brotherhood of Our Blessed Lady and St. Dunstan in the West of London and the parson and churchwardens of the parish church of St. James at Garlickhithe concerning a nuisance in Fleet Street. The view is by assent of both parties. The viewers find that at the height of the rasen the W side of a house belonging to the church of St. James overhangs the ground of the Brotherhood 5½ in. at the NE corner post of a house belonging to the Brotherhood by the king's highway of Fleet Street. Stretching southward 28 ft. from the street, the W side of the house overhangs the ground of the Brotherhood 5 in. at the height of the rasen and stretching more southward 21 ft. 2 in. by the W side of the house, the W side of the house so overhanging ought of right to be withdrawn line right and plumb from place to place all the length at the costs and charges of the parson and churchwardens. Without *etc.*

Endorsed: A view brought . . . 8.1 a[nno] xiiii h[enrici] VIII

53. [B.48] 30 December 1522.
Parish of St. Mary Woolchurch. Variance between the parson [and churchwardens] of the parish church, pls., and the prior and convent of Christ Church within Aldgate of London, defs., concerning a nuisance of two chimneys in Bearbinder (Berebynder) Lane. [The viewers find] the ground there belonging to pls. . . . lane stretching southward 20 ft. to a principal post at a break of the tenement there belonging to defs. on the E [?and further stretching] more southward 31 ft. 8 in. to a wall of brick and stone. The ground contains 29 ft. 10 in. in breadth by the said lane between the [tenement of] the prioress and convent of Haliwell on the E and the said tenement of defs. on the W. And [?stretching along] the said lane by the W side of the plates of the said tenement of the prioress and convent of Haliwell to an angle under the . . . assise and there the ground of pls. contains 35 ft. 9 in. in breadth. And stretching more southward [?26] ft. . . . assise there the ground is 36 ft. 11 in. in breadth with the thickness of the chimney, which chimney is set standing on the . . . pls. without the house of defs. 2 ft. 11 in. by all the breadth of the chimneys. And the viewers say that either of the parties ought to bear his [*sic*] own water between the ground aforesaid. All which premises and nuisances *etc.* Without *etc.*

23

54. [B.49] 30 December 1522.
Parish of St. Mary Woolchurch. Variance between the prioress and convent of Haliwell and the parson and churchwardens of the said parish church concerning nuisances of old buildings in Bearbinder (Berebynder) Lane. The view is by assent and agreement of both parties. The viewers say that the gable end of the tenement there belonging to the prioress and convent over the NW corner post by the lane overhangs the ground of the parson and churchwardens 6 in. westward at the height of the rasen; stretching southward by the plates of the house 12 ft. 9 in. to a brick in the house, it overhangs 3 in. Stretching more S 13 ft. 5 in. to a SW corner post under a jetty which sails southward 2 ft. 5 in. without the plates of the house, the jetty by all its length and breadth from the nether part of the joists (giosts) thereof belongs plumb upright to the prioress and convent. From the nether part of the jetty all the ground without the plates of the tenement of the prioress and convent belongs to the parson and church-wardens; the tenement overhanging as aforesaid ought to be withdrawn line right and plumb from place to place. Either party ought to bear their own water. All which premises and nuisances *etc.* Without *etc.*

55. [B.50] 1? March 1523.
Parish of St. Botolph without Aldgate in the suburbs of London. Variance between the abbess and convent of the House of Minoresses without Aldgate and Christopher Raynwyk, draper, concerning certain ground for a defence to be made and set upon [*sic*]. The view is with assent and agreement of both parties. The viewers say that the defence ought to be made and set from a SE corner post of a house called 'the Welhouse' pertaining to the tenement belonging to the abbess and convent, where John de Boyne, tiler, dwells, stretching eastward to the S side of a stake standing beside an ash in the middle of the ground from E to W, and so stretching to the E end of the same ground to a mark drawn by the viewers on the boards of the defence between Cornwales' grounds and those of the abbess and convent, line right and plumb, as limited. The defence should be made at the costs and charges of the abbess and convent, without *etc.*

56. [B.51] 12 May 1523.
[Parish of St. Mary le Bow]. Variance between the parson and church-wardens of the church of Our Blessed Lady of Bow, pls., and the prior of Christ Church, Canterbury, def., concerning certain vaults under the parish church. The viewers say that the W end of the church is 77 ft. 8 in. in breadth from the NW quoin to the SW quoin. The S side of the church is 75 ft. 8 in. from the SE quoin to the SW quoin. The E end of the church is 73 ft. 8 in. in breadth between the NE quoin adjoining the parsonage there and the SE quoin of the church. The length of the church from the NW corner of a buttress of the steeple there above the first skew of the buttress stretching eastward by the N side of the church is 53 ft. 1½ in. to the W end of the parsonage and there is an angle of 2 ft. 9 in. from the church wall to the NW corner of the parsonage (under which angle all the water of the gutter of the S side of the roof of 'the King's Head' comes

through the parsonage into the church gutter), and stretching eastward from the NW quoin and angle of the parsonage 33 ft. 10 in. to the lane called Bow Lane, which is the length of the parsonage. The parsonage is 14 ft. 6 in. in breadth at the E end thereof, between the tenement of St. Bartholomew's Hospital and the NE quoin of the church wall. All the ground underneath the church and parsonage, as well the vaults as main ground, within and by all the length and breadth of the same line right and plumb from place to place as aforelimited, belongs to Bow. Without *etc.*

57. [B.52] 30 July 15 1523.
Parish of St. Giles without Cripplegate. Variance between Thomas Wrythesley, alias Garter King of Arms, pl., and the prior and convent of the New Hospital of Our Lady without Bishopsgate of London, defs., concerning a nuisance. The viewers say that the SW corner post of a brick wall belonging to pl. (Master Garter) by the king's highway called Barbican, adjoins the SE corner post of a tenement there of defs.; stretching northward 12 ft. 9 in. to the middle of a principal post of the same house, there is a break (breke) out of the line right and the post overhangs the ground of pl. $5\frac{1}{2}$ in. eastward at the height of the rasen. Stretching more northward 12 ft. $4\frac{1}{2}$ in. to the NE corner post of the house, that post overhangs the ground of pl. 3 in. eastward at the same height. The two posts ought to be withdrawn line right and plumb by defs. Stretching more northward 92 ft. along by the W side of the brick wall of pl. to a garden ground belonging to Lord Willoughby, the wall stands all on pl.'s ground. All of which nuisances and premises *etc.*, without *etc.*

58. [B.53] 30 October 1523.
Parish of St. Bartholomew the Little in the Ward of Broad Street. Variance between the abbess and convent of the house of Minoresses without Aldgate of London and John Benet, merchant taylor, concerning a certain ground for a defence to be made. The view is with assent of both parties. The viewers say that the garden ground there belonging to the abbess and convent is 27 ft. 1 in. in breadth between the E side of a stone wall of James Wylford, merchant taylor, stretching eastward by the N side of a brick wall of the abbess and convent to a mark made on that wall by the viewers; then stretching northward from the mark 130 (vi^{xx}x) ft., which is the length of the ground, to a stake driven in the ground in the hedge in the NE corner, the ground is 36 ft. in breadth between the stake and the E side of a brick wall of James Wilford. The ground ought to be line right and plumb by all its length and breadth and the defence ought to be made by the abbess and convent. A shed there of Benet ought to be withdrawn as is marked on it by the viewers. All which premises *etc.*, without *etc.*

59. [B.54] 23 April 1524.
Parish of St. Botolph without Aldrichgate. Variance between John Blanerhasset, gentleman, pl., and Thomas Tamworth, gentleman, def., concerning certain defences between certain gardens. The viewers find a timber and loam wall standing on a foundation of brick and covered with

tile, between pl.'s garden on the W and def.'s garden on the E. The wall from the NE corner post adjoining a mud wall there, stretching southward 42 ft. 6 in., belongs to pl. and ought to be made and repaired at his costs and charges. At the end of that wall and length there is another wall, adjoining the same wall and also stretching southward 18 ft. 4 in. to a SE corner post and from thence westward to another post in an angle of 10 ft., which belongs to def. and ought to be repaired and maintained at his costs and charges. From the same angle stretching more southward 47 ft. 4 in. to a SE corner post adjoining another mud wall, the wall ought to be repaired at costs and charges of def. All such lengths as def. has or shall have in his said garden adjoining the defence and wall of pl. ought to be made lower than the plates of pl.'s wall because they shall not rot the plates. All which premises *etc.*, without *etc.*

Endorsed: Certificat[ur] xxviiii° die Aprilis anno r[egni] r[egis] Henr[ici] VIII xvi te[mpore] Thomas Baldry M[aioris] sol[utum] feod[um] ii s.

60. [B.55] 30 May 1524.
Parish of St. Michael in Wood Street. Variance between the abbess and convent of the Minoresses without Aldgate of London, pls., and the parson and churchwardens of the said parish church, defs., concerning a nuisance of a house. The viewers find the SW corner post of the house there belonging to defs., where one [blank] Banks dwells, overhangs the ground of pls. 9 in. at the height of the rasen of the house by the street side. Stretching eastward from the street 20 ft. to a principal post of the house, that post overhangs the ground of pls. 11½ in. at the same height. Stretching more eastward 18 ft. 6 in. to another post of the house, that post overhangs the ground of pls. 13 in. at the same height. The house ought to be withdrawn by defs. line right and plumb from place to place all its length. Which nuisance aforesaid *etc.*, without *etc.*

Endorsed: Importat[ur] in Cur[iam] te[mpore] [B]aldry 3.8 Mr Paver hath gevyn the Abbesse his fee. Te[mpor]e Baldry maioris Civitatis London' 3.8

61. [B.56] 4 July 1524.
Parish of St. Mildred in the Poultry. Variance between the wardens and fellowship of the Skinners, pls., and the wardens and fellowship of the Barbers, defs., concerning a nuisance of a house set and being within Coneyhope Lane. The viewers say that the SE corner post of the house of defs. overhangs the ground of pls. eastward 6½ in. and southward 1½ in. at the height of the rasen. Stretching northward 13 ft. to a NE corner post of the house, that post overhangs the ground of pls. 6 in. at the same height; and stretching westward from the SE corner post 23 ft. to a SW corner post of the house of defs., that post overhangs the ground of pls. 7½ in. southward at the height of the rasen. The house ought to be withdrawn by defs. line right and plumb from place to place by all the length. Without *etc.*

Endorsed: [5].9 import[atur] . . . Cur[iam] 2 s.

62. [B.57] 17 September 1524.
Parish of St. Albans in Wood Street. Variance between the master and

wardens of the Shearmen (Shermen), pls., and John A'Parke, mercer, def., concerning certain nuisances of building. The viewers say that the SW corner post of a new house of def. stands 1 in. on the ground and stone wall of pls. Stretching eastward 9 ft. to a SE corner post of the new house, that post stands 6 in. on pls.' ground and stone wall. More eastward 4 ft. 4 in. to the middle of a principal post belonging to pls., which post has fled out at the foot 2 in. onto the ground of def., and then stretching more eastward 6 ft. $6\frac{1}{2}$ in. to the SW corner post of another new house of def., that post stands upright and truly on ground of def. Def. ought to withdraw his two posts standing on the wall and ground of pls. Pls. ought to withdraw their post which has fled out so that it is line right and plumb from place to place all the length. Which nuisance aforesaid *etc.*, without *etc.*

Subscribed: Certificatur xx° die Septembris anno r[egni] r[egis] Henrici VIII xvi Te[mpore] Thome Baldry M[aioris] Sol[utum] feod[um] ii s.

63. [B.58] 22 October 1524.
Parish of St. Giles without Cripplegate. There is a ground for a defence to be made, now 'somewhat in variance' between Piers Duffe, sandman, of one party and John Aleyn, armourer, and Margaret Whaplyngton, widow, of the other party. The view is by assent of the parties and at the charge of Duffe. The viewers say that the ground of Duffe, which lies and bounds upon the ground of Aleyn in part and the ground of Margaret Whaplyngton in part on the S and the ground of the Company of [Parish] Clerks of London on the E, contains 42 yds. 2 ft. in length from a SE corner post of an house there belonging to Duffe, stretching eastward to the SE corner of a stake of oak there driven into the ground by the viewers. The stake and three other stakes there likewise driven into the ground by the viewers stand upon the ground of Duffe, on which ground he may and ought to set and make his defence line right and plumb from stake to stake all the length. Without *etc.*

64. [B.59][1] 10 April 1525.
Parish of St. Mildred in Bread Street. Variance between the parson and churchwardens of the parish church and Thomas Browne, citizen and cordwainer (cordoner), concerning a certain stone wall with a door in it set and being in the parish, to wit at the E end of the churchyard. The view is by common assent of both parties. The viewers say that the stone wall is 21 in. in thickness and contains 8 ft. 11 in. in length between another stone wall belonging to the house of Browne on the S and the vestry of the church on the N. They say that $8\frac{1}{2}$ in. in thickness on the W side of the wall belongs to the parson and churchwardens and the residue, $12\frac{1}{2}$ in., belongs to the house of Browne. 'All which premises the said viewers afferme to be true in forme aforsaid', without *etc.*

Endorsed: ... 31.7 ...

Subscribed: Certificat[ur] in Cur[iam] Maioris ult[imo] die Maie a[nn]o xvii° R[egni] R[egis] H[enrici] VIII Te[mpore] Bayly Maioris

---

1. This certificate is copied in Journal 12, f. 333v, and in Letter Book N, f. 284v.

65. [B.60] 27 June 1525.
Parish of All Hallows in Honey Lane. Variance between the warden and
fellowship of the Drapers, pls., and the parson and churchwardens of the
parish church of St. Mary Magdalen in Milk Street, defs., concerning a
certain jetty of a house and a little void ground under the same jetty. The
viewers say that the jetty and void ground are 4 ft. 7 in. in breadth at the
NW corner post of a draught house belonging to pls. Stretching northward from the corner post 17 ft. by the W side of the house to the N end of
the jetty, the jetty and ground are 4 ft. in breadth. The jetty and ground
belong to pls. Without *etc.*
Subscribed: Infert[ur] in Cur[iam] Maioris per Joh[ann]em Edmay
servien[tem] ad clava[m][1] ix.9 a[nn]o 17 R[egni] R[egis] Henr[ici] VIII

    1. Serjeant at mace in the Mayor's Court.

66. [B.61] 12 August 1525.
[Parish of St. Mary at Axe]. Variance between Master Richard Mabot,
parson of the parish of St. Mary at Axe, pl., and the prioress and convent
of the House of Saint Elene in London [the priory of St. Helen's], defs.,
concerning a certain parcel or part of the parsonage of St. Mary at Axe, to
wit on the N side of the parsonage. The viewers say that the parcel or part
contains 7 ft. 5 in. in breadth from the ground which pl. has in possession
on the S side of it to the N side adjoining a tenement of defs. The ground is
14 ft. 6 in. in length between the king's highway on the E and the ground
of defs. on the W. The building and ground line right and plumb belong to
pl. all the length and breadth. Moreover, the viewers say that the
parsonage wholly (hooly) ought of right to contain 20 ft. 7 in. in length by the
king's highway from the church on the S to the tenement of defs. on the N
and 14 ft. 6 in. in breadth from the king's highway on the E to the ground and
building of defs. on the W. Furthermore, they say there is a little gallery or
tresance on the W part of the parsonage adjoining the churchyard there
southward, 17 ft. in length and 3 ft. 6 in. in breadth at the E end adjoining the
parsonage and 4 ft. in breadth at the W end adjoining the tenement of defs.
The gallery or tresance belongs to pl. and the parsonage line right and plumb
all its length and breadth. All which premises *etc.*, without *etc.*
Subscribed: Infert[ur] in Cur[iam] Dom[ini] Maioris 17.10 per Joh[an-
n]em Hamond anno R[egni] R[egis] Henr[ici] octavi decimoseptis . . .
sol[utum] feod[um]

67. [B.62] 27 April 1526.
Parish of All Hallows Staining. Variance between Roger Whaplode,
draper, pl., and William Birche, gentleman, def., concerning certain
buildings. The viewers find a chamber over a coalhouse with a withdraught in it. The coalhouse, as it is framed, contains 11 ft. 8 in. in length
from the E stretching westward to a little yard of pl. and 7 ft. 8 in. in
breadth from the N part adjoining the house of def. stretching southward
to the middle of a principal post between the coalhouse and another little
house of def. on the S. Also they find a gallery going over the ground of pl.
which is 4 ft. 1½ in. in breadth from the N side of posts that bear the gallery
and 33 ft. 6 in. in length from the chamber over the coalhouse on the E

stretching westward to another house and chamber belonging to pl. Into which gallery def. has a door which ought to be dampered (dampred) and stopped up. Further they find a cellar vaulted with stone under the house of pl. and in part under the tenement belonging to def., which vault is 10 ft. 6 in. in breadth within the walls from the street on the W stretching eastward. The viewers say that the gallery and chamber, cellar and vault, line right and plumb by all the length and breadth aforelimited and expressed, appertains and belongs to pl. Without *etc.*
Subscribed: John Aleyn M[aior] . . . Cur[iam] henr[ici] VIII . . . Paver . . . ii s. per co[mmun]e[m] . . . et feod[um]

68. [B.63] 17 May 1526.
Parish of St. Dunstan in the East. Variance between John Bruges (Brugges), knight and Alderman of London, pl., and the Orphans or Heirs of John Sabbe, defs., concerning a nuisance of a frame of timber with a stair made into the Thames. The viewers say that the said frame is set out southward from Sabbe's Wharf so that the first post thereof next to the wharf stands 2 in. before the wharf of pl.; stretching southward 24 ft. into the Thames to a post at the head of the stair, that post stands $3\frac{1}{2}$ in. before the said wharf of pl. The stair going down to the water is 19 ft. in length southward and 8 ft. in breadth. The frame and stair ought to be withdrawn the 2 in. in one place and $3\frac{1}{2}$ in. in the other, line right and plumb from place to place by all the length thereof aforerehearsed. Without *etc.*

See also **71** below.

69. [B.64] 18 May 1526.
Parish of St. Michael in Crooked Lane. Variance between Thomas Cremor, draper, and Walter Palley, stockfishmonger, concerning a certain old stone wall set, lying, and being in Thames Street. The view is by assent and agreement of both parties. The viewers say that at the N end of the wall Cremor ought of right to have 14 in. of the thickness of the wall from the W side eastward; the residue of the thickness belongs to Palley. Stretching southward 36 ft., Cremor ought to have 20 in. of the thickness from the W side eastward and Palley the residue. And so Cremor may make his wall line right and plumb from place to place all the length aforesaid. Without *etc.*
Endorsed: . . . Johannes 28.7
Im[portatur] in Cur[iam]

70. [B.65] 24 July 1526.
Parish of St. Sepulchre. Variance between Robert Moldyng, brewer, and Mary, his wife, pls., and Richard Morys, one of the tenants of the lands there sometime of the Earl of Warwick, def., concerning a tenement brewhouse called 'the Cok upon the Hope' with two shops annexed; set and being within Newgate. The viewers say that the said tenement and shops contain together 36 ft. in breadth by the king's high street from the tenement belonging to the brotherhood of Our Lady and St. Stephen in the church of St. Sepulchre on the E to a tenement sometime of the Earl

of Warwick on the W. The tenement and shops contain 25 ft. 2 in. in length from the said street on the N stretching southward to a SW corner post of the said brewhouse. At that corner post there is an angle stretching eastward 4 ft. 9 in. From that angle stretching more southward 50 ft. 4 in. to the lands lately of the Earl of Warwick, there the tenement brewhouse contains 27 ft. in breadth from the lands of the Earl of Warwick on the W to the lands of the Brotherhood on the E. And so pls. ought of right to have their tenement brewhouse line right and plumb from place to place by all the length and breadth thereof aforesaid. Without *etc.*

71. [B.66] 5 September 1526.
Parish of St. Dunstan in the East. Variance between John Brugges, knight and Alderman of London, pl., and the Orphans or Heirs of John Sabbe, defs., concerning a nuisance of a frame and bridge of timber with a stair made into the Thames. The viewers say that the frame and bridge is set out southward from Sabbe's Wharf so that its first post next to the wharf stands 2 in. before the wharf of pl. Stretching southward 24 ft. into the Thames to a post at the head of the said stair, that post stands $3\frac{1}{2}$ in. before the wharf of pl. The frame is 12 ft. in length above the ground and the stair going down to the water is 19 ft. in length southward and 8 ft. in breadth. And over that, there are four spurs set into the E side of the bridge before the wharf of pl., of which the first spur next to the wharf is 2 ft. 3 in. in breadth eastward and 9 in. in thickness. The second spur is 2 ft. 6 in. in breadth and 1 ft. in thickness. The third spur is 2 ft. 6 in. in breadth and 11 in. in thickness. The fourth spur is 3 ft. 6 in. in breadth and 6 in. in thickness. The viewers say that not only the said posts and spurs of the frame ought to be withdrawn from before the wharf of pl. line right and plumb from place to place by all the length aforerehearsed, but also all the said frame, bridge, and stairs ought to be removed and taken away because it [*sic*] stands upon the common ground of the City, to the great nuisance and hindrance and common [?hurt] as well of the king's subjects as of all manner of ships, crayers and boats repairing to this City for the common wealth of the same. Without *etc.*

See also **68** above. For the dispute over Sabbe's Wharf, see *Calendar of the Letters and Papers foreign and domestic of the Reign of Henry VIII*, Vol. II, Part I (1515–1516), p. 642.

72. [B.67] 8 March 1527.
Parish of St. Sepulchre in the Ward of Farringdon Without. Variance between the prior and convent of the Charterhouse beside London, pls., and the abbot and convent of Thame in the county of Oxford, defs., concerning a certain nuisance nigh Seacoal Lane. The viewers find a brick wall and a stable built on the N end of the same wall belonging to pls. as of the gift (as they say) of Sir Robert Rede, knight, late Chief Justice of the Common Bench. The wall is 54 ft. in length, stretching southward from a brick wall on the N belonging to the parish church of St. Dunstan in the West. The wall overhangs westward 15 in. in the middle thereof by reason of the oppression and great weight of the earth and ground of a garden

elonging to defs. there lately laid, whereby not only the wall and stable
ut also another brick wall upon which the W side of the same stable
tands are likely shortly to decay and fall down as well, to the great hurt
nd damage of pls. and also to the great danger and peril of all the king's
ubjects going and coming through Seacoal Lane. The nuisance ought to
e reformed at the costs and charges of defs. Without *etc.*
Endorsed: In[fertur] in Cur[iam] 21.5 per Hamond cler[icum] Te[mpore]
Seymour Maior[is]

73. [B.68] 13 March 1527.
To the Right honorable Lorde the Mayre of the Citie of London and his
worshipfull brethern Thaldermen of the same.
Shewen unto your said Lordship and discrete wisedoms the xiii[th] daye of
Marche in the xviii[th] yere of the Reigne of Kyng Henry the VIIIth Thomas
Smarte, John Hilmar, Philip Cosyn, & Thomas Newell, the iiii Maisters
of Fremasons and Carpenters, viewers indifferent sworne to the said
Citie, That where as they were late charged by your honorable commaundement to viewe and oversee a certain brykwall sette and beyng in
the parisshe of Saint Gabriell Fanchurche in Langbourne Warde of
london, by thassent and agreement of William Birche, Gent, owner of the
said wall, as Tenant to the Prioresse and Convent of Halywell in the
Countie of Middlesex on that one partie, And the maister, wardens, and
feliship of the Crafte of Carpenters of london on that other partie;
Whiche wall the iiii viewers by all their discrecions have viewed, seen, and
rypely understond And thereupon they sey that the wall is in lenght [*sic*],
from the gardeyn grounde there belonging to the Feliship of Fissh-
mongers of london on thest parte stretching westward to thest syde of a
brykwall of the Churcheyard of Fanchurche aforesaid, viii fote of assese
And that the Northwest corner of the said wall belonging to the said
William Birche stondeth without the said Churcheyard wall Northward
into the groundes of the said Feliship of Carpenters ix ynches et di. of
assise. Whiche the said viewers fynden to be don by thassent, will,
consent, and agreement of the said maister, wardens and feliship of
Carpenters.
Endorsed: Import[atur] in Cur[iam] … 5 … per J Hamond …
Te[mpore] Seymer Maior[is]

74. [B.69] 8 May 1527.
Parish of All Hallows in Bread Street. Variance between the master and
wardens of the fellowship of the Merchant Taylors and the wardens and
fellowship of the Salters, concerning a stone wall. The view is by assent
and agreement of both parties. The viewers say that the wall contains 34
ft. 4 in. in length from the king's highway of Bread Street stretching
eastward to a break in the same and then more eastward 34 ft. Further
they say that the wall is partible. The Merchant Taylors ought to have as
much of the wall as is without the N side of the plate of the Salters' house
there, line right and plumb from place to place all the length. Either of the
parties ought to bear their own water without agreement to the contrary.
All which premises *etc.*, without *etc.*

75. [B.70] 8 May 1527.
Parish of All Hallows Bread Street. Variance between the master and wardens of the Merchant Taylors, pls., and the provost of the King' College of Eton in the county of Buckingham, def., concerning a certain stone wall. The viewers say that the wall contains 40 ft. 6 in. in length from the king's highway of Bread Street eastward to another stone wall belonging to pls. The ground of pls. there contains 31 ft. 5 in. in breadth at the W end by the street, between the ground of def. on the N and the Salters' ground on the S. At the E end it is 36 ft. 6½ in. in breadth between those grounds, line right and plumb all the length of the wall aforelimited. Without *etc.*

76. [B.71] 13 September 1527.
Parish of St. Michael at Queenhithe. Variance between William Cheynes, gentleman, as in right of our sovereign lord the king, pl., and the prior of the monastery of St. Bartholomew in West Smithfield in the suburbs of London, def., concerning a stone wall and other edifications. The viewers find that from the S end of an old plate lying in the ground by the water of Thames stretching northward 15 ft. 8 in. line right by the E side of the same plate to the S end of a pale there lately set up by pl. (which pale is in length 20 ft. to the S end of def.'s shed), a pale ought to be made by def. with the N end to be set 6 in. westward. The SW corner of the shed stands 4 in. on the ground of the king and ought to be withdrawn by def. Stretching northward 26 ft. from the SW corner post of the shed to its N end, there the king ought to have 8 in. eastward of the stone wall that the shed stands on. Stretching more northward 27 ft. to a break in the wall, the king ought also to have 8 in. of the wall. The shed ought to be withdrawn eastward 3 in. by def. Stretching 20 ft. 8 in. more northward to the back of def.'s chimney, that chimney is 6 ft. in breadth from N to S and stands 8 in. on the king's ground. Stretching more northward 8 ft. to a S corner of a wall bearing the king's house, the king ought to have 8 in. of the wall eastward, line right and plumb from place to place as limited. Also there is a chimney belonging to def. standing on another stone wall of the king by the E side of a garden in the tenure of Thomas Grey; that chimney is 3 ft. in thickness and 10 ft. in breadth and stands entirely on the king's ground. It ought to be withdrawn by def. The wall from the chimney . . . S end of the wall belongs wholly to the king. All which premises *etc.*, without *etc.*
Endorsed: . . . In . . . 12.2 R[egni] . . . Hamond . . . te[mpore] Sp[encer] Maioris

77. [B.72] 9 March 1528.
Parish of St. Mary at Hill. Variance between Maude Russell, widow, and the parson and churchwardens of St. Michael Cornhill concerning a certain window of a tenement wherein Maude Russell dwells. The view is by assent of both parties. The viewers say that the window ought to stand and continue as it is now made, ordered, and devised by the viewers without interruption, let, or contradiction of the parson and church-wardens or their successors or assigns at any time. Over that, they say that Maude ought to make a fillet gutter on the eaves of her house from a door

at the W side stretching southward 23 ft. or thereabout to the SW corner of the house, there to go down with a close pipe of lead to convey the water of the eaves of the house so that it does not fall upon and annoy the tenement there of the parson and churchwardens. Furthermore, the rafter of Maude's house must be cut shorter at the SW corner by one half foot in order so to be made line right and 'of at nought' at the N end of the fillet gutter. All which premises *etc.*, without *etc.*

Endorsed: 26.5 Te[mpore] Spencer M[aioris] Im[portatur] in Cur[iam] his per J Hamond

78. [B.73] 9 March 1528.
Parish of St. Botolph without Bishopsgate. Variance between the parson and churchwardens of the parish church of St. Michael in Cornhill, pls., and Robert Clerke, baker, def., concerning a ditch. The viewers say that the ditch is 41 ft. in length from the N side of the ground of pls. stretching southward all the length of the ground to a post belonging to the prior of St. Mary Spital and stretching 22 ft. more S against the W end of the prior's garden ground now in the tenure of John Newton, poulterer (pulter). Def. has filled the ditch with earth and wood and stopped the water course and the way of all water running from the tenement of pls. called 'the Half-mone' and diverse other tenements there; the water course has been had and used there since time out of mind. The viewers say that def. ought of right to cleanse and [re-]make the ditch he stopped up so that pls. and others may have their water pass that way as they had before (aforetyme). And pls. and all others having any gutter into the ditch ought to make a grate at their gutters' ends to keep out all things as would fill up and stop the ditch. Over that, the viewers say that the residue of the ditch ought to be made clean by all such persons as have any garden ground there lying, every man his own ground. All which premises *etc.*, without *etc.*

Endorsed: Im[portatur] in Cur[iam] 19.5 die Maii a[nno] xx [Henrici] VIII per Ru ... Spenfold ... Cur[ia] non vult recipere ... ad dict[um] Spenfold per man[u] eius etc. ... Et postea xxiiii^{to} die November a[nn]o R[egni] R[egis] Henr[ici] VIII xx Import[atur] in Cur[iam] per Joh[ann]em Hammond un[um] clericorum vic[ecomiti] London in nominibus infrascript[orum] vis[uum] voc[atorum] viewers etc.

Subscribed: Certificat[ur] Cur[iae] 24 No[vembris] a[nno] R[egni] R[egis] Henr[ici] VIII xx^{mo} prout [postquam] in dorso etc. Paver. Et sol[utum] feod[um] ... pro co[mmun]i cl[eric]o.

79. [B.74] 16 June 1528.
Parish of St. Dunstan in the West. Variance between the master and wardens of the brotherhood of Our Lady and St. Dunstan, pls., and the dean and chapter of St. Stephen's at Westminster, defs., concerning certain ground to be newly built on. The viewers say that the whole breadth of the ground of pls., where the houses and old buildings [have been taken] down, on the street side contains 61 ft. E to W with the little ground that the cook there, tenant to defs., has lately occupied, which is parcel of the whole and is 2 ft. 7 in. in breadth and 15 ft. in length from the

street stretching northward. The viewers say that the ovens there of the cook ought to be withdrawn 2 ft. 7 in. eastward by defs. and all the ground, line right and plumb, belongs to pls. Without *etc.*
Endorsed: Import[atur] in Cur[iam] 21.8 te[mpore] Spencer Maioris

80. [B.75] 20 November 1528.
Parish of St. Michael at Queenhithe. Variance between the parson and churchwardens of the parish church of St. James at Garlickhithe, pls., and Thomas Grey, ironmonger, def., concerning certain buildings and housing. The viewers find a house belonging to the church of St. James which sometime was a brewhouse and which contains 56 ft. 3 in. in length at the S side from the SW corner post stretching eastward to the SE corner post and 17 ft. 11 in. in breadth from the same SE corner post northward to a stone wall which is the partition between the house and shops there by the street. From the SW corner post northward 32 ft. 5 in. to a NW corner post of the house and from the same NW corner post eastward 30 ft. 10 in. by the king's highway of Thames Street to the E side of the entry into the said house, the viewers say that all the house and ground with all manner of housing built thereupon belongs to pls. by all the length and breadth thereof, line right and plumb. Without *etc.*
Endorsed: Te[mpore] Rudston M[aioris] 24.1 Import[atur] in Cur[iam] per Ham[mond] un[um] clericorum vic[ecomiti] London in no[min]ibus infrascript[orum] vis[uum] voc[atorum] viewers

81. [B.76] 2 January 1529.
Parish of Aldermanbury. Variance between the prior of Elsing Spital in London, pl., and the parson and churchwardens of St. Alban in Wood Street, defs., concerning buildings and housing. The viewers say that pl. ought to have a stone wall on the S side of his ground adjoining the garden of a great tenement belonging to defs. and now in tenure of Henry White, gentleman. The wall contains 46 ft. in length from the E side of a new stone and brick wall lately made there by defs. stretching eastward against the said garden; it is 20 in. in thickness. On the wall at its W end there is a chimney which ought of right to be withdrawn and taken away all its breadth and thickness. Also, the viewers say, defs. ought of right to bear the water of all their houses adjoining pl.'s ground, with fillet gutters, according to the custom of the city. Furthermore, there is a corner of a stone wall of defs. standing in the SW corner of pl.'s ground; it is 2 ft. in breadth and stands 4 in. on pl.'s ground and it ought to be withdrawn 4 in. All which premises *etc.* Without *etc.*
Endorsed: 14.3 Te[mpore] Rudston Mayoris Import[atur] in Cur[iam] [per] Thome Newell un[um] de viewers de Civ[itatis].
Paver.
Subscribed: Certificat[ur] in dorso

82. [B.77] 20 January 1529.
[No parish given] Variance between the prior and convent of the monastery of Ely, pls., and Henry Mathison, poulterer, concerning the side of a house in Gracechurch Street which Robert Wright, poulterer,

nolds of the prior and convent. The viewers say that the house is 18 ft. 4½ in. in length at the N side from the NW corner post of a house there belonging to the Charterhouse stretching westward to the NE corner post of the house of Agnes Goldesburgh, widow, where def. dwells. From the same N side [the house extends] 10 ft. 4 in. southward to an angle of a wall of timber and loam which wall stands 8 in. within pls.' grounds and ought to be withdrawn all its length by 8 in., line right and plumb without *etc.*

Endorsed: Im[portatur] in Cur[iam] [per Philipum] Cosyn un[um] viewer infrascript[um] xxiii [die] Januarii a[nno] R[egni] R[egis] Henr[ici] VIII xx

83. [B.78][1] 24 February 1529.
Parish of St. Michael in Cornhill. Variance between the prior and convent of St. Mary Overy in Southwark in the county of Surrey, pls., and the parson and churchwardens of the parish church of St. Mary Woolnoth in Lombard Street and the parson and churchwardens of St. Mary Woolchurch, defs., concerning a certain old house and other buildings with a void ground. The viewers say that the house belonging to pls. contains 25 ft. 7 in. in breadth by the ground on the N side by the king's highway of Cornhill, between the tenement that William Game, draper, lately dwelt in on the E and a common alley leading from Cornhill into Lombard Street through the tavern called 'the Cardinalls Hatte' on the W. It contains 40 ft. 3 in. in length on the E from Cornhill stretching southward to a tenement of the said tavern belonging to the church of St. Mary Woolnoth, part of which tenement stands on the ground of pls. and which part is 17 ft. 11 in. in length from the NE corner post stretching westward to the NW corner post, and 5 ft. ½ in. in breadth at the E end and 4 ft. 1½ in. in breadth at the W end. It ought to be withdrawn line right and plumb. The ground of pls. is also 31 ft. 2 in. in length on the W from Cornhill stretching southward by the alley to a void ground enclosed with a pale, also belonging to pls. There the ground is 26 ft. 5 in. in breadth between Game's house on the E and the alley on the W. The viewers say that the alley ought to be 4 ft. 2 in. in wideness against the void ground and of the same breadth against Cornhill. The void ground and pale ought to be 11 ft. 6½ in. in length from its corner stretching southward by the alley and 8 ft. in breadth from the alley eastward. The tenement belonging to the tavern has there encroached and made less (mynyshed) 8½ in. and ought to be withdrawn by the parson and churchwardens of St. Mary Woolnoth, line right and plumb. Also, it shall be lawful to pls. to build their new house there on the said al[ley] ... the same alley abutting to the tenement there belonging to the parson and churchwardens of Woolchurch, line right and plumb ... jetty upward. All which premises *etc.* without *etc.*

Endorsed: viii die Martii a[nno] xx h[enrici] VIII Import[atur] in Cur[iam] per Joh[ann]em Hilmer mason un[um] de iiii viewers de Civ[itatis] Lond[on] etc.

1. A portion of the certificate is missing; there is a section torn out of the middle.

84. [B.79] 16 April 1529.
Parish of St. Faith the Virgin. Variance between the prior and convent of the house or priory of St. Bartholomew in West Smithfield, and Christopher Barker, otherwise called Richmond Herald at Arms, concerning certain houses in Pater Noster Row. The view is by assent of both parties. The viewers find a little house closed in with a stone wall. It was once a withdraught to the place sometime belonging to Lord Lovell but now in the tenure of Christopher Richmond [*sic*]. The house is set on the N side of that place; it is 9 ft. in breadth at its E end without the great wall of the place and 15 ft. in length stretching westward from the NE corner of the little house to the NW quoin or corner. In the W end it is 5 ft. 11 in. in breadth from the NW quoin southward to a stone buttress standing at the back of a chimney. The buttress is 3 ft. 2 in. in thickness on the N side and 3 ft. 9 in. in breadth on the W side. The house, stone wall, and buttress belong wholly to the great place now in tenure of Richmond; and whereas the building and houses of the prior and convent in some places are set into the walls or overhang them or the buttress, they ought to be withdrawn line right and plumb from place to place. Each party ought to bear his own water from his own houses according to the custom of the city. All which premises *etc.*, without *etc.*

Subscribed· Importat[ur] prout postquam in dorso ... et sol[utum] feod[um] ii s. per M[agistrum] Richmond [infrascriptum]

85. [B.80] 10 May 1529.
To the Right honorable Lorde the Mayre of the Citie of London And his worshipfull Brethern Thaldermen of the same
Shewen unto your good lordshipp and maisterships the xth daye of Maye in the xxi^th yere of the Reigne of King Henry the VIIIth Thomas Smart, John Hilmar, Philip Cosyn and Thomas Newell, the iiii maisters of Fremasons and Carpenters, viewers indifferent sworne to the said Citie That where as they were late charged by your honorable commaundement to viewe and se a certain noysaunce of a bruehouse at the signe of the Smyte in the parish of [Saint] Leonard in Estchepe of London, now beyng in variance betwene Maister Richard Eden, Clerke, and John Hedge, Bruer, plaintyfes of the one partie, and Robert Revell, owner of the said bruehouse, and John Cokke, Tenant of the same, defendauntes of the other partie, whiche noysaunce the said iiii viewers by all their discrecions have viewed & seen and therupon they sey that for default & lack of a sufficient wall which shuld be made betwene the said bruehouse and the Ten[emen]t there belonging to the said M[aster] Eden wherin the said John Hedge dwelleth, the same Ten[emen]t is sore anoyed with the hete and smoke of the fyre & lycour of the said bruehouse Whiche is not oonly to the grete noyance and displeasure of the said Hedge and all his houshold but also to the grete hurt, ruyn and decaye of the same Ten[emen]t lyke to fall downe by reason of the same and also grete jeopardy and perill of fyre for lak of the said wall to defende the same, Whiche wall must be in lenght xxiiii fote of assise and in height equall with the height of the said bruehouse and the said viewers sayen that the same wall ought to be made of bryk or stone substancially for the suretie of the said fyre, at the costes and charges of the said Revell & Cokke or of one of

hem. Without ther can be any any [*sic*] other evidence shewed to the
ontrary.
'igned on recto, lower right corner: Paver
Endorsed: 24.7 te[mpore] . . . M[aioris] . . . Computer in le Puultry etc.
. . dict[?orum] viewers
Subscribed: sol[utum] feod[um] 2 s.

86. [B.81] 21 May 1529.
Parish of St. Thomas the Apostle. Variance between the master of the
house of St. Thomas of Acres in London and Master Lye of Stockwell,
gentleman, concerning certain grounds and buildings. The view is with
assent of both parties. The viewers say that the ground of Master Lye
extends from the NE corner post of his house southward 20 ft. 6 in. to a
break; from there the ground stretches further southward 15 ft. 3 in. to
another break and then further southward 13 ft. 3 in. to the SE corner
post. All the length belongs to Master Lye, line right and plumb. Each
party ought to bear the water of all their own houses. Without *etc.*
Endorsed: 25.7 te[mpore] Rudstone M[aioris]. Import[atur] per
Thomam . . . per mandat[um] Hamond un[um] clerici comput[er] in le
Poultry

87. [B.82][1] [?19] February 1538.
[Much of salutation lost].
Shewen unto your said lordship and discrete wisdomes the [?xix] day of
February in the xxii yere of the reign of [King Henry the VIII], John
Hylmar, Philip Cosyn, Thomas Newell and Stephen Poncheon, the iiii
maisters of Fremasons and Carpenters [viewers] indifferent sworne to the
said Citie, That Where as they were late charged by your honorable
commaundement [to view and] serche for a comon sewer of the water that
falleth in the kynges highwey without Bisshoppesgate in the warde of
Bishoppesgate of London, that is to wete bitwene the Newe Hospitall of
oure blessed lady there, called saint Mary Spittell, on the North parte and
the hospitall of our Lady of Bethlehem on the south parte as the currant
therof bothe wayes doth fall. And therupon the said iiii viewers saye that
they fynd a hed of a sluce there made with hard stone & bryk on the west
syde of the kynges highwey aforsaid whiche appereth that one tyme ther
were iii grates to the said sluce, that is, to wete, one on the North syde
therof an other on the south syde and the third in the mowthe of the same
sluce, whiche was made to convey the water fallyng on the west syde of
the said highwey and cawsey westward undre the house or Ten[emen]t
there belonging to the maister & Wardeyns of the worshipfull Feliship of
Mercers of London, late in the tenure of Richard Gregory, gardener, by
whom the said sluce was stopped as it appereth by the same sluce which is
there redy made and undre the same house and wont of old tyme to have
his course from the same house stretchyng Westward thurgh the gardens
and grounde of the said maister and Wardeins in lenght xl Roddes of
assise unto a diche bitwene the grounde of the same maister and Wardens
and the grounde belonging to the Charterhouse, whiche diche is there
made to convey the said water into the morediche. And forasmoche as

the said Gregory then beyng tenaunt there stopped and fylled up the
diches in the said gardens wherby the said watercourse from the said sluc
was stopped, the said viewers saye that all the same diches so fylled &
stopped owen of right to be digged & made open that the said water ma
have his course & currant undre the said house and thurgh the said
grounde as it hath of old tyme ben used & accustomed, at the costes and
charges of the said maister and wardeins or of their tenantes there. Also
they say that the Aldermen and inhabitantes of the said Warde at their
propre costes and charges shall make and cover the forsaid sluce & hee
with stone bryk and with grates of Iron as it hath ben aforetyme asmoche
as is in the strete bitwene the said highwey and the said Ten[emen]t And
furthermore they say that the water fallyng on the est syde of the said
Cawsey & highwey oweth of right to have his course & currant estward
into the lane there called Berwards Lane beyng the grounde of the priour
of Saint Mary Spittell. All which premysses aforesaid owen to be
reformed and amended in manner and forme as is above rehersed
Without there can be any other evidence shewed to the contrary.
Endorsed: A view Import[?atus] in Cur[iam] 12.5 a[nno] R[egni] R[egis]
Hen[rici] viii per Philippum Cosyn un[um] iiii viewers Civit[atis] London
Subscribed: . , , 5 . Dodmer M[aioris] sol[utum] feod[um]

1. This certificate is copied in Mercers' Company Acts of Court, 1527–1560, f. 27v.

88. [B.83][1] 6 May 1530.
Parish of St. Leonard in Eastcheap in the Bridge Ward of London.
Variance between the parson and churchwardens of the parish church of
St. Dunstan in the East, pls., and Thomas Stephenson, their tenant for
term of years, def., concerning reparations needful in and upon a
tenement bakehouse with its appurtenances. The viewers find these
defaults: as touching the carpentry work of the roof next the street, the
rasens are perished and fled southward and northward and the gutters are
sunken and broken. With other carpentry work in diverse places, it will
cost at least 46s. 8d. to be done substantially. Also they find reparation of
tiling needed in diverse places; the cost will be at least 26s. 8d. for tile,
lath, nails, lime, sand, and workmanship. Repair of daubing of walls and
loaming of floors in diverse chambers will cost 20s. for stuff and workmanship. Repair of plumbery for lead and gutters will cost 30s. Cleansing
the well will cost 6s. 8d. Repair of pavement in the street and within
where needed will cost 6s. 8d. 'All which defaults afore rehersed owen to
be amended.'
Endorsed: Iste view importat[ur] ... cur[iam] per Ph[ilippum]
Cosyn Carp[enter] un[um] iiii viewers dict[i] Civit[atis] etc.
28.8 te[mpore] Dodmer maioris
Subscribed: ... Dodmer dom[ini] milit[is] [m]aioris ... [im]port[atur] et
soll ... per Hayes

1. The certificate is torn.

89. [B.84] 25 July 1530.
Parish of St. John the Evangelist. Variance between Richard Dobbys,
pl., and Christopher Ascue, alderman in the parish, def., concerning

certain old houses in the parish taken down by def. Pl. complains and says that def. has taken down entries and rooms of easement which were always appurtenant and belonging to pl.'s house (as he says). The viewers find a cistern of a withdraught there which it appears served both for pl.'s house and for the house taken down. They perceive by certain doors on the E side of pl.'s house that 'there hath ben goyng furth that wey in ii places.' But as to how far or how much room pl. had that way, 'the trouthe and certayntie thereof cannot appere unto the said viewers for asmoche as every thing is taken downe there that myght lede them to any further knowlege in that behalf. Wherefore the said iiii viewers upon their consciences sayen that the said playntif oweth of right to have ageyn asmoche Rowme and lyke easement there as he can prove that he had before, by triall and witnesse of neighbors and other that have seen and knowen the same afore it was taken downe. Without ...' *etc.*

Endorsed: 29 July import[atur] per Phil[ippum] ...

90. [B.85][1] 6 February 1531.
Parish of St. Alban in Wood Street, ward of Cripplegate of London. The viewers have been charged to view and oversee a wall between the ground of John Reve, citizen and scrivener, on the S and the ground of the Clothworkers on the N. They say that the wall is timber and loam and contains 29 ft. 3 in. in length from the ground of the abbot of Notley on the E stretching to the ground of ... [Mistress] Fenrother, widow, on the W. The wall by all its length stands on the ground of Reve and he ought of right to make, repair, and maintain it as often as need shall require. Further, the water of the S side of a house, 9 ft. in length, of the abbot of Notley, falls on the ground of Reve, as does [the water of] the E side of another house, 30 ft. in length, of Mistress Fenrother. The abbot and Mistress Fenrother ought of right to make fillet gutters, each for his [*sic*] own house, to bear the water. All which premises *etc.*, without *etc.*

Endorsed: 26.4 te[mpore] Parget[er] Maior[is] Recordum fuit ... certificat ... in cur[iam] per Stephen[um] Pun[cheon] unum viewers infrascript[orum]

1. The right margin of the certificate is badly dampstained and several words are lost on each line.

91. [B.86] 22 March 1531.
Parish of St. Botolph without Aldersgate of London. Variance between the prior of the Charterhouse next London and the wardens of the brotherhood of the Holy Trinity in the parish church of St. Botolph, concerning a wall or defence. The view is with assent of both parties. The viewers say that the defence or wall when made shall contain 68 ft. in length from the SW corner of a brick wall belonging to the monastery of St. Alban in the County of Hertford stretching southward to the NW corner post of a tenement set on the N side of Long Lane. The defence now there and that to be made ought to be made and repaired when needed at equal charges of the parties. Without *etc.*

Endorsed: Import[atur] in Cur[iam] ... 17.6 ... Pargeter M[aioris]

92. [B.87] 24 April 1531.
Parish of St. Margaret Pattens. Variance between the master of the Hospital of St. Thomas the Martyr in Southwark and the parson and churchwardens of the parish church of St. Margaret Pattens concerning a tenement. The view is by assent of both parties. The viewers say that from the NW corner post of the tenement which belongs to the Hospital stretching southward 20 ft., the parson and churchwardens may lawfully edify and build just to the W side of the plate of the tenement, line right and plumb for all 20 ft., and may cut and break the eaves of the house for the raising of the new building if need be; they at their costs and charges to repair and remake all tiling as shall happen to be broken for the building. They shall also make a gutter between their new building and the house to convey the water of the house northward into the Hospital grounds. It shall be lawful at all times when it shall please them for the parson and church-wardens to edify and build on their ground as far as it extends southward just to the W side of the plate of the tenement, line right and plumb from place to place as the plates now lie. All which premises *etc.* Without *etc.*
Endorsed: : Importatur per Johannem Hylmer, un[um] de lez viewers de Civitatis London xxv die Aprilis anno regis Henrici VIII xxiii Temp[ore] Thom[e] Pargeter milit[is] Maioris
Signed on recto and verso: Paver

93. [B.88] 5 October 1531.
Parish of St. Giles without Cripplegate. Variance between Master Ralph Waren, alderman, and the master and wardens of the gild or fraternity of Our Blessed Lady of Berking in London, concerning certain ground for a defence to be made. The view is by assent of both parties. The viewers say that the defence ought to be made and set there at the costs and charges of the Gild from the outer (utter) part of the NE corner post of an house belonging to the brotherhood of St. Giles called 'Kyng Aley' stretching eastward line right and plumb to a new brick wall on the W side of the Moorfield, the E end of the said defence to be set within the N end of the said brick wall southward 2 ft. line right and plumb from the said post. Without *etc.*
Endorsed: Viewe
Subscribed: Importat[ur] 12.12 feod[um] non sol[utum]

94. [B.89] 20 November 1531.
Parish of St. Sepulchre in the Ward of Farringdon Without. Variance between the prior and convent of the priory or house of St. Bartholomew in West Smithfield of London and William Colyns, carpenter, their tenant, pls., and the dean and chapter of Chichester and John Clamperd, haberdasher, their tenant, defs., concerning ground for a defence or pale to be made. The viewers say that the defence or pale ought to be made at the costs and charges of pls. from the SW corner of a post of a house belonging to defs. stretching westward 39 ft. 4 in. to the SE corner of an old stone wall with a house standing thereon. It shall be lawful for pls. to set their defence or pale within the S end of the stone wall 10 in. northward line right and plumb from place to place all the length. Without *etc.*

95. [B.90] 27 May 1532.
Parish of St. Pancras. Variance between the prior of Marten [Merton] in the county of Surrey, pl., and the parson and churchwardens of St. Stephen in Walbrook, defs., concerning a certain building and ground. The viewers say that the wall belonging to defs., which adjoins the parsonage of St. Pancras on the S, is plumb. Stretching northward 13 ft. 6 in. to a stone quoin which overhangs the ground of pl. 9 in. and stretching further northward 19 ft. to a brick wall belonging to St. Thomas of Acres, there is a beam of the tenement of defs. From the E side of the beam line right and plumb to the ground belongs to pls. Without *etc.*
Endorsed: 7.8 Impor[tatur] per Philippum Cosyn etc.

96. [B.91] 27 May 1532.
Parishes of St. Magnus and St. Botolph nigh Billingsgate. Variance between the parson and churchwardens of St. Magnus, pls., and the Butchers of Eastcheap of London, defs., concerning a certain wall of stone and brick on the W side of a lane called Birchin Lane (Berchereslane). The viewers say that from the king's highway of Thames Street stretching southward 36 yds. 2 ft., the lane ought of right to be 2¼ yds.in breadth between the plates and principal posts of the housing there belonging to the abbot of the New Abbey at Tower Hill on the E and the said stone and brick wall which belongs to pls. on the W. From thence to the water of the Thames, the lane ought to be the same breadth between the said limits and the wall ought to be withdrawn by pls. as much by measure as the lane lacks of that breadth, which has been encroached by the making of the wall. Without *etc.*
Endorsed: ... per Philippum Cosyn
Signed on verso: Paver

97. [B.92] 22 February 1533.
Parish of St. Margaret Pattens. Variance between the master of the Hospital of St. Thomas in Southwark and the master and Wardens of the Merchant Taylors, concerning certain nuisances. The view is with assent of both parties. The viewers say that they find the S side of a shed belonging to the Hospital which is 17 ft. 8 in. in length stretching westward from the NW corner post of a house there of the Merchant Taylors to the middle of a principal post of the shed. There is a break out of the line right as the plate of the shed now lies. The plate lies truly and ought not to be removed, but the viewers find that the principal post of the shed at the highest end overhangs its own plate southward 12 in. toward the ground of the Merchant Taylors and ought to be withdrawn and set upright by the master of the Hospital. And stretching more westward 8 ft. from the middle of the post to the NE corner of a post of another house there belonging to the Merchant Taylors, the S side of the shed from the plate upward as it now lies ought to be made line right and plumb from place to place by the master of the Hospital. 'And these be all the noysances and defaults that the said viewers can finde there, the which owen to be reformed and amended in manner and forme as is aforesaid.' Without *etc.*

41

Subscribed: Importat[ur] in Cur[iam] prim[o] die Marcii a[nno] Regis Henrici VIII xxiiii per Joh[anne]m Hilmer etc. in presence Maioris Co[mmun]is Clerici etc.

98. [B.93] 4 March 1533.
Parish of St. Clement. Variance between the master and wardens of the Drapers, pls., and the abbot and convent of the Grey Abbey at Stratford, defs., concerning a nuisance in St. Clement's Lane nigh Candlewick Street. The viewers find a gate and an alley on the N side of a house of defs. called 'Abbottes Inne' in the lane, which lead to a cartway out of the lane on the W stretching eastward to a great tenement now in tenure of Sir John Milborne, knight and alderman of London, and to another great tenement at the end of the alley where certain foreign merchants (merchaunts estraunges) inhabit. The gate, alley and great tenements belong to pls. They find at the end of the alley a nuisance of a lead gutter bearing water of defs.' house, which water falls northward into the alley and at the gate of one of pls.' tenements. The gutter ought of right to be taken away and the current turned southward into land of defs. at their costs and charges. They find on the N side of the 'Abbottes Inne' certain lights and windows into the alley which ought to be permitted and suffered as they have been in time past, being lawfully and conveniently made so that they are not a nuisance or displeasing (displeasant) to pls. or to their tenements. All which premises and nuisances *etc.* without *etc.*
Endorsed: 21.4 a[nn]o R[egni] Regis Henr[ici] VIII xxiiii Impo[rtatur] in Cur[iam] per Helmer un[um] iiii viewers Civ[itatis] London
Subscribed: 13.5 a[nn]o R[egni] R[egis] Hen[rici] VIII 24
Signed on recto: Paver

See also **185** below.

99. [B.94] 28 April 1533.
Parish of St. Sepulchre without Newgate. Variance between Thomas Compton, gentleman, landlord, and Thomas Whyte, gentleman, his tenant, pls., and the prior and convent of Thame, owners, and William Colyns, carpenter, their tenant, defs., concerning a defence to be made. The viewers find on the S side of the ground of defs. a stone wall and a timber wall 25 ft. 4 in. in length from a NE corner post of pls. stretching eastward to a NW corner post of pls., which walls of old time were the defence between grounds of the parties. The defence by all its length ought of right to be made and set upon pls.' ground between the said two posts line right and plumb at defs.' costs and charges. Without *etc.*
Endorsed: Importat[ur] [?xiv] die Maii anno R[egni] Regis Henrici VIII xxv Feod[um] non sol[utum]
Signed on verso but signature illegible.

100. [B.95] 28 April 1533.
Parish of St. Sepulchre without Newgate. Variance between Charles Bulkley, gentleman, owner of a garden in the said parish, and Alan Ryse, his tenant, pls., and the parson and churchwardens of the said parish church, defs., concerning the garden. The viewers find on the N side of

the garden a tenement of defs. which is 35 ft. in length from a tenement of the prior of Oseney on the E to a tenement of the prior of St. Bartholomew in West Smithfield on the W. All the ground from the S side of the principal posts of the tenement of defs. for all its length, line right and plumb, belongs to pls. It is lawful to pls. to build and set up, break down, and make any manner of building upon the said ground hard to the S side of the same tenement. Without *etc.*

101. [B.96] 6 June 1533.
Parish of St. Mildred in Bread Street. Variance between the master of St. Thomas of Acres in London, pl., and the wardens of the Salters, defs., concerning certain houses and buildings in Basing Lane. The viewers find on the N side of the lane three tenements belonging to pl. One is 21 ft. 7 in. in breadth from the ground of defs. on the E stretching westward and 26 ft. 6 in. in length from the king's highway of Basing Lane on the S stretching northward. The other two together contain 20 ft. 8 in. in length from the grounds of def. on the W stretching eastward and 9 ft. 6 in. in breadth from the lane stretching northward, line right and plumb from place to place. The ground of defs. contains 8 ft. 5 in. in breadth from E to W between the same tenements. Without *etc.*

102. [B.97] 9 June 1533.
Parish of St. Bride in Fleet Street in the suburbs of London. Variance between the master and wardens of the Brewers, pls., and the dean and chapter of St. Stephen's at Westminster, defs., concerning certain nuisances of buildings. The viewers say that the NE corner post of a house of defs. overhangs the binding joist (byndyng giost) of the new frame of pls. eastward 3 in. at the height of the rasen (reisin). And the SE corner post likewise overhangs the binding joist of the new frame eastward $3\frac{1}{2}$ in. at the rasen. And the middle part of the house overhangs the new building eastward $7\frac{1}{2}$ in. at the rasen (resyn). It ought of right to be withdrawn line right and plumb from place to place at defs.' costs and charges. Without *etc.*

103. [B.98] 9 December 1533.
Parish of St. Dionis Backchurch. Variance between John Antony de Negro and Peter Nodale, merchants of Venice, who hold a house there by lease of William Estrich, haberdasher, and John Dymok, draper and tenant to the said William Estrich, concerning a light or window. The view is by assent of both parties. The viewers say that the window takes its light from the N against the house and court of the merchants and gives the light into the warehouse of John Dymok. The window ought to be made with a loup (lowpe) light to be set 2 ft. without the old window northward and to be 2 ft. 9 in. in width and 2 ft. 6 in. in height, and to be made so that it does not shadow the light of the warehouse of the merchants. It is to be made with bars of iron 'for goyng in or out' and so that neither Dymok nor anyone in his household has any looking or sight into the house or court of the merchants; they are only to receive the light into Dymok's warehouse. The light and window are to be made at the costs and charges of Dymok. Without *etc.*

43

104. [B.99] 15 January 1534.
Parish of St. Stephen Coleman Street. Variance between the abbot and convent of Rewley (Rowley) and Robert Deane, grocer, their tenant, pls., and Sir Thomas Kytson, knight, and Thomas Adyngton, skinner, his tenant, defs., concerning a defence to be made between their grounds. The viewers say that the defence contains 138 (vi^{xx}xviii) ft. 9 in. in length from the ground of Antony Vyvald, merchant, on the E, stretching westward from the SE corner of an end of a mud wall upon the ground of Kytson to the S side of a principal post of a pale there on Kytson's grounds. The defence ought to be made and repaired at defs.' costs and charges line right and plumb. Without *etc.*

105. [B.100] 15 January 1534.
Parish of St. Leonard in Foster Lane. Variance between the prior and convent of St. Bartholomew in West Smithfield, owner of a tenement in the parish, pls., and Richard Chambre, their tenant, def., concerning reparations needing to be done on the tenement. The viewers say that the foundation with the stone vault, principal posts of timber, and other timber work are decayed and ought to be repaired and amended at costs and charges of pls. After the repairs are made, def. at his costs and charges ought to repair and make the tenement wind and water tight, that is to say in tiling, daubing, and lead gutters. And furthermore they say that by their estimation the tenement so repaired will stand and be tenantable for 13 or 14 years to come at the least. 'All which reparations owen to be done, repaired and amended in manner and form aforesaid, without' *etc.*

106. [B.101][1] Dated *temp.* Henry VIII, but date mostly lost.
Parish of St. Benedict Fink. Variance between My Lady Damice and the parson and churchwardens of St. Clement Eastcheap concerning certain tenements in Fynke Lane. The view is by assent of both parties. The viewers say that the chamber and the buttery and pantry of the great mansion of Lady Damice, now in tenure of Andrew Wodcok, grocer, is parcel of a tenement there belonging to the parson and churchwardens, the which tenement and chamber was divided and given to the parson and churchwardens by one Thomas Duglas. Furthermore, whereas a gutter of the kitchen of a tenement there belonging to Lady Damice now runs into the tenement of the parson and churchwardens, the viewers say that the parties ought of right to bear their own water and neither of them to annoy the other. All which premises *etc.*, without *etc.*

1. The certificate is in very bad condition, much blackened by damp. The approximate dates of this and the following certificate have been established by the names of the viewers.

107. [B.102][1] Dated *temp.* Henry VIII, but date mostly lost.
Parish of St. Dunstan in the East. ... Variance between the ... Clothworkers, ... pls., and Dame Katharine (Katreyn) Joiner, widow, def., concerning a nuisance. The viewers find the N side of a foundation of a house made of brick adjoining the ground of [pls.]; at the NE corner of the house it overhangs the ground of pls. 6 in. Stretching westward 20 ft.

to another corner post of the house, the foundation there overhangs the ground of pls. 4 in. It ought of right to be withdrawn and set upright line right and plumb from place to place. Also the water of the N side of the said house . . . of the E side of a high gabled end of another house and a dormaund gutter of the other house falls on the . . . [?ground] of pls., which water ought of right to be withdrawn and conveyed some other way from pls.' ground at def.'s costs and charges. All which *etc.*, without *etc.*

1. The certificate is in very bad condition, with entire lines illegible.

108. [B.103][1] 26 June 1534.
Parish of St. Benedict nigh Paul's Wharf. Variance between the parson and churchwardens of the said parish church and William Cowper, gentleman, their tenant, pls., and the abbot and convent of the mona[stery] . . . County of [?Hertford], defs., concerning certain nuisances. The viewers find three houses belonging to defs. which . . . from a stone wall belonging to the Lord . . . belonging to pls. 62 ft. by all which length the water of the said three houses . . . falls on the ground of pls., which water ought of right to be conveyed from the ground [?of defs.] with fillet gutters of timber and [?lead all the] length aforesaid at cost and charges of defs. Also, three little windows in the house of defs. ought not to be there without [?licence] of pls. All which premises and nuisances ought to be reformed and amended in manner and form aforerehearsed, without *etc.*

1. The certificate is in very bad condition, with many words illegible. The monastery could be St. Albans: Keene and Harding, 213.

109. [B.104][1] 4 July 1534.
Parish of St. Magnus. Variance between William Bronnsop, son and heir of Agnes Bronnsop, pl., and Richard Austen, late of London, mercer, def., concerning reparations to certain tenements and shops which late were Agnes Bronsoppe's, widow, [that is] the Bell Tavern in Fish Street now in tenure of Roger Dele, draper, and two shops adjoining together on the N side of the tenement in the same street now in tenure of Alex Bell, fishmonger, with two shops adjoining in the S side of the same street and two tenements . . . in the tenure of Thomas Turnbull, fishmonger, and another on the E side of the lane going into St. Magnus Churchyard in Thames Street, now in tenure of the said Alex Bell. The viewers say that 'the Bell' ought to be repaired in the kitchen, hall, and chamber in boarding of floors, amending of walls as well in timberwork as in daubing and tiling, amending of chimneys, and also stone work in the vault of the house. The other tenement in the same street ought to be repaired as well in tiling as in daubing; and a floor that a chimney stands on is sunken and must be amended. The two tenements in Thames Street which Thomas Turnbull holds must be repaired in the withdraught and tiling and daubing. The other tenement beside St. Magnus Churchyard is so ruinous and decayed it must be taken down and rebuilt. Furthermore, the four shops adjoining the tenements in Fish Street are parcel of pl.'s tenements. Without *etc.*

1. The certificate is in very bad condition, with many words illegible.

45

110. [B.105][1] 12 October 1534.
Parish of St. Michael in the Ryall. Variance between Elizabeth Corag[?eouse], widow, pl., and Robert Hamond, woodmonger, def., concerning an old stone wall. The viewers say that the wall is 55 ft. 8 in. in length from Bowyer Lane [*sic*] on the E stretching westward to the E end of a tenement of Whittington College. It is at its height 2 ft. 2in. in thickness. By all its length it is partible, to each 13 in. at the height of the wall. Furthermore, def. has encroached and set a brick wall on the stone wall from the W end thereof stretching eastward to the E end of the shaft of a chimney standing within the wall; the brick wall and chimney ought to be withdrawn 8 in. by def. line right and plumb from place to place, without *etc.*

1. The certificate is worn and somewhat stained.

111. [B.106] 15 February 1535.
Parish of St. Stephen Coleman Street. Variance between John Marchaunt, merchant taylor, pl., and William Fylloll thelder, gentleman, def., concerning a certain wall or defence to be made or set up between two gardens in the parish. The viewers say that the defence is 23 ft. 8 in. in length from the tenement of pl. on the N stretching southward to the tenements belonging to the church of St. Stephen. The new defence, be it wall or pale, ought to be set and stand line right and plumb upon the ground where the old defence now stands between the aforesaid limits. The defence belongs wholly to pl. and pl. may lawfully re-edify and set upon the wall by him to be made a house with a jetty sailing over the wall 22 in. toward the ground of def., as it was built of old time, as well appears there. Without *etc.*

112. [B.107] 9 April 1535.
Parish of St. Giles without Cripplegate. Variance between the wardens of the brotherhood of Our Lady and St. Giles, pls., and William Benet, fermor of the prebend of the Moor, def., concerning a certain ground for a defence to be made in the parish. The viewers say that the ground is 244 ft. in length from a great elm there standing in the N end of Moor Lane between the garden gate there [?of . . .] pl. on the W side of the tree and the gate there of the prebend on the E side of the tree, stretching northward to the NE corner of another old elm tree, by all of which length the defence ought to be made line right and plumb at costs and charges of pls., and all the elms and trees standing and growing in the place of the defence belong to pls. Furthermore, the viewers find a shed built and standing in a garden belonging to the prebend, now in tenure of one Walter Thomas, which is 13 ft. in length N and S and which encroaches westward upon pls.' ground 2 ft. . . . all its length. It ought of right to be withdrawn by def. All which premises *etc.* without *etc.*

113. [B.108] 14 May 1535.
Parish of St. George in Pudding Lane. Variance between the wardens of the Salters, pls., and Thomas Serle, butcher, def., concerning a partible stonewall. The viewers say that a principal post stands on the wall at the

46

;E corner of def.'s house. It has fled southward 3 in. onto the ground of
ɔls. Stretching from the SE corner 12 ft. westward, another principal post
.tands in def.'s plate on def.'s ground; it overhangs southward toward
ɔls.' ground 2½ in. Stretching more westward 12 ft. is the furthest end of
lef.'s ground. The S side of the house of def. ought to be withdrawn and
;et upright at costs and charges of def. line right and plumb all the length.
Without *etc.* Furthermore, they find on the S side of the ground of pls. a
NE corner post of a new house belonging to the Mercers, which
encroaches upon the ground of pls. 7 in. and ought to be withdrawn by the
wardens of the Mercers. Without *etc.*
Endorsed: 26/7 A[nno] r[egni] r[egis] Henr[ici] VIII xxvii import' [?fuit]
Cur[iam] M[aioris]

114. [B.109]¹ 19 June 1535.
Parish of St. Lawrence in the Jewry. Variance between the warden of the
guild or fraternity called the Rood Brotherhood founded in the chantry of
St. Lawrence, pl., and Robert Machon, merchant taylor, def., concerning certain defaults and [reparations] to be done and amended. The
viewers find a kitchen with an entry and a cabin (caben) partly under the
floor of the kitchen belonging to the tenement of pl. which John Malyn,
grocer, dwells in. The cabin is wrongfully taken and held from that
tenement. Further, the frame of def.'s house under the cabin, kitchen,
and entry lacks a groundsill to keep it upright and from sinking. Also, def.
ought of right to make sufficient trestles (trestyles) and other sufficient
timber between the first floor of his tenements called the three shops
[and] the floor of the kitchen; the groundsill and walls of the tenements
are in great ruin and decay and sink to the great hurt of the whole frame of
pl.'s tenement. They ought to be repaired and amended in manner and
form aboverehearsed, without *etc.*

> 1. The certificate is in bad condition, worn and darkened, with many lines in part
> illegible.

115. [B.110]¹ 13 December 1535.
To the Right honorable Lorde the Mayre of the City of London and his
worshipfull Brethern the Aldermen of the same.
Shewen unto your good lordship and discrete wisedoms the xiii[th] daye of
december in the xxvii[th] yere of the Reigne of Kyng Henry the VIII, John
Hilmer, [Philip Cosyn, Thomas] Newell and William Colyns, the iiii
maisters of Fremasons & Carpenters, Viewers indifferent sworne to the
said Citie, that whereas [they were late charged by your] honorable
commaundement to viewe and overse certain edificacions & buyldynges
with a wharf therto belonging called Marowes Key in the parish of [St.
Mary at Hill] of London nowe beyng in variance for default & lak of
reparacions to be don & made in & upon the same betwene Thomas
Marowe, gent, plaintif [of the one partie], and Antony Elderton of
London, Stokfishmonger, defendant, of the other partie, Whiche edificacions and other premysses the said iiii viewers by all their discrecions have
viewed, serched and seen And thereupon they saye that the Reparacions
nedefull & required to be don in & upon the premisses wole coste and

amount unto by their estimate ... the particular sommes herafte: folowing it shall appere, that is to saye: first Carpentry Worke for the wharf and amending of the framework of the same toward the thamys xl*s* Item for wetherbordyng and daubing of walls of the Celers & garnars and for a newe resyn within the same rowme ... of the wyndows iii *li*. vi*s*. viii*d*. Item for amendyng of the gate to the streteward and the Dores and Wyndows of shoppes & Celers and the Inner gate there ... is and amending of the stares goyng up into the hall xl*s*. Item for amending of the pavement in the strete and within the gate, xiii*s*. iiii*d*. Item for repayryng the rofe over the hall, the rofe on thest syde of the Courte, [*and*] the rofe over the colehouse, to make two newe resyns and the rofe over the parlor and toward the strete in carpentry worke, to all the same for stuf & workmanship, iiii *li*. Item for newe ryppyng, tylyng and poyntyng work about all the place where nede is, for lathe, nayles, tyles, lyme, sand and workmanship, viii *li*. Item for sowderyng and newe castyng of gutters & other lead work in dyvers places about the court ... other places iii *li*. vi*s*. viii*d*. Item in playstering work toward the strete and about the Courte and other places where nede is ... for lome, lath, nayles and work xl*s*. Item for a newe somer under the great ketchyn and newe payvyng the same ketchyn and for amending of the tymber worke bitwenc the said ketchyn ... pastry and beryng in of a new reysen for the same – iii *li*. vi*s*. viii*d*. Item for new pavyng of a ketchyn with stone whiche is paved with bryk and ... the tymbre work undre it, xl*s*. Item for repairyng of glasse wyndowes in the hall & other places where nede ys, x*s*. All whiche reparacions aboverehersed owen to be don, made & amended in forme aforesaid atte the costes and charges of the said defendant. Without there can be any other evidence shewed to the contrary.

1. The certificate is in bad condition and some words are illegible. This is the only extant certificate listing William Colyns, carpenter, as a viewer.

116. [B.111]¹ 13 March 1536.
John Hilmar, Philip Cosyn, Thomas Newell and William Walker, viewers.
Parish of St. Mary Colechurch. No variance stated. The viewers have been charged to view and measure certain grounds with edifications and buildings belonging to the Mercers of the City of London. The view is by the consent, assent and agreement of the Mercers and the master of St. Thomas of Acon of the same city. The viewers say that the chapel now being built in West Cheap is 12 ft. in width in the E end against 'the Myter' and 55 ft. in length from the ... There the chapel ground is 26 ft. 8 in. in width between the street and the SW corner of the church of St. Thomas. Stretching more westward along West Cheap 39 ft. 10 in. to the SW corner post of the new building ... quoin and corner stretching northward 26 ft. 8 in. there the ground is in width between the ... and the said ... a tenement belonging to the prior of Elsing in London 40 ft. Stretching more northward 60 ft. ... between the NW quoin and corner of the said church and a tenement belonging to the master of St. Thomas on the W side of the ground ... 2 in. And stretching more northward 37 ft. 7 in. to the S side of a house of the said Master [now in] the tenure of

Henry Fitzherbert, there the ground of the Mercers is in width . . . upon the W part and the NW corner post of a little house of the master of St. Thomas. . . and standing southward from the said corner post of the little house by the W side of the same house . . . to the NW corner of the church there the said ground is 45 ft. 6 in. in wideness between the W end of the said . . . of the master of St. Thomas on the W part[2] . . .

Endorsed: VISUS de temporibus H8 E6 P&M

1. The certificate is in very bad condition and has been backed with a sheet of paper, not contemporary, on which is printed: Vintners Victuallers & Innholders/Names, Companies, Signs, Residences.
2. Certificate **421** below, from the Mercers' Company Register of Benefactors' Wills, vol. I, f. cxvii, apparently refers to the same view but with additional material and significant discrepancies in measurement.

117. [B.112][1] 16 March 1536.
Parish of St. Lawrence in the Jewry. Variance between the master and wardens of the Mercers, pls., and the abbot and convent of the monastery of St. Peter of Westminster and Margaret Parke, widow, late the wife of John A Parke, mercer, deceased, tenant by lease for the term of years to the abbot and convent, defs., concerning certain new housing built in Milk Street. The viewers find an old house of pls. on the E part of the new house, 18 ft. 8 in. in breadth from an alley on the S side stretching northward to a garden ground of pls. At the SW corner of the old house, John A Parke when he set up the new house encroached, took and cut away 6 ft. 4 in. of the old house; stretching more northward 36 ft. 9 in. from the N side of the old house to the S side of another house of pls., now in tenure of Walter Marshe, mercer, A Parke encroached eastward 3 ft. 7 in. into pls.' garden ground. Defs.' new house contains [?54] ft. 3 in. in length by the king's highway of Milk Street from the alley stretching northward to a house of pls.; on the back side it is 52 ft. 2 in. It is 20 ft. 8 in. in breadth at the N end between the street on the W and the ground of pls. on the E and at the S end the breadth is 17 ft. 4½ in. It ought of right to be no more; the residue, which is encroached, ought of right to be withdrawn line right and plumb from place to place as aforelimited, without *etc.*

1. This certificate is copied in Mercers' Company, Register of Benefactors' Wills, vol. I, f. cxix.

118. [B.113] 7 May 1536.
Parish of All Hallows Barking. Variance between William Burngyll, citizen and draper, pl., and Master Rud, clerk, one of the chantry priests of All Hallows Barking, def., concerning a certain old stone wall. The viewers say that the wall contains 28 ft. 1½ in. in length E and W. The wall belongs to def. and is in great decay, likely to fall into the grounds of pl. It ought to be well and sufficiently repaired, line right and plumb, by all its length at the cost and charges of def. Without *etc.*

119. [B.114][1] 24 July 1536.
Parish of St. Michael at Querne. Variance between the master and brethren of Pappey, pls., and the parson and churchwardens of St. Michael, defs., concerning certain buildings and houses in Pater Noster

Row. The viewers find a door into an entry going out of Pater Noster Row to pls.' tenement. The entry contains 11 ft. 7½ in. in length N and S and 3½ ft. in breadth between the shops of defs. The door and entry stand within the frame of defs.' building. That notwithstanding, pls. ought of right to have and enjoy the door and entry as they have had time out of mind without interruption or contradiction of defs. In consideration thereof, the viewers say that whereas on the N side of defs.' tenements there, 40 ft. 11 in. in length E and W, all the water of the roof falls on pls.' houses, pls. shall bear the water as they have done. Saving that defs. shall bear one half of the charges of reparations of the gutters and other plumbery work for conveyance of the water from time to time when need shall be. If defs. will have any windows on the N side of their houses, as they have had in time past, then they ought to make iron bars to the windows, and glaze them, and so keep them continually close, so that there be no water nor filth cast out into the gutter of pls. All which premises *etc.*, without *etc.*

1. This certificate is copied in Journal 14, f. 12v.

120. [B.115] 24 July 1536.
Parish of St. Lawrence in the Jewry. Variance between Master Dormer, alderman, pl., and Richard Adams, brewer; John Boughan, brewer; and Thomas Mountpierson of the county of Wiltshire, gentleman, defs., concerning an old house belonging to pl. whereof William Clerk, mercer, now holds one part. The other part, the E part, is in the tenure of Adams, who dwells in the brewhouse called 'the VII Fanes' as tenant to Bowghan [*sic*] who holds the brewhouse by lease for term of years from Mountpierson, [who holds] in the right of the heir of one Clevedon late of the said county, gentleman, deceased. The viewers find the E part of the old house, which Adams holds and occupies, adjoins the kitchen of the tenement brewhouse. It stretches westward 10 ft. 6 in. from the NE corner post of the old house to the E part of the same house, which William Clerk holds. The E part contains 16 ft. 6 in. from N to S against the house [in the tenure of Clerk]. The E part of the old house in the tenure of Adams ought of right to belong to pl. by all the length and breadth of 10 ft. 6 in. E and W and 16 ft. 6 in. N and S, as it appears by the part of the house in the tenure of Clerk. Without *etc.*

121. [B.116] 14 August 1536.
Parish of St. Thomas the Apostle. Variance between the inhabitants and tenants of the Ward of Cordwainer Street of London, pls., and the inhabitants of the Ward of the Vintry of London, defs., concerning a certain house and garden set in Turnbaston Lane[1] in which house John Benglosse, clothworker, dwells. The viewers have viewed and seen and upon their diligent search, inquisition, and deliberate examination of the oldest men and longest dwellers within the said wards now living, and also by good and substantial other evidence and proof showed to them, they say that from the NE corner of the house 'ayenst the tonnes in the ryall belonging to Saint Thomas of Acres' stretching southward 70 ft. from Turnbaston Lane to the S side of a house where William Maye now dwells, is within the ward of Cordwainer Street. Stretching westward

from the said NE corner to the little lane that leads southward from Turnbaston Lane [and then going] toward St. Thomas the Apostle church 60 ft. to the SW corner of the parsonage belonging to and adjoining the church, [the area] also belongs to the Ward of Cordwainer Street. Stretching more westward from the little lane to the house where Benglosse dwells, which house stretches southward from Turnbaston Lane 56 ft. to an old brick wall on the S part of the said house, the house and garden are in the ward of Cordwainer Street. And stretching yet more westward [along Turnbaston Lane] to the NW corner of a stone house against the way and lane leading southward from Turnbaston Lane toward Garlickhythe 56 ft. to the house that John Russell, tailor, dwells in, [all the area] with all the bounds aforerehearsed from place to place is within and belongs to the Ward of Cordwainer Street. Without *etc.*

1. Turnbase Lane.

122. [B.117] 30 August 1536.
Parish of St. Swithin. Variance between Thomas Pope, gentleman, pl., and the Rt. Hon. Sir John Veer, Earl of Oxford, def., concerning a certain stone wall. The viewers say that the wall is 17 in. in thickness and 27 ft. 6 in. in length from the S side of the chapel of pl. stretching southward. By all its length and breadth it is line right and plumb and belongs to pl., without *etc.*

123. [B.118] 25 September 1536.
Parish of St. Christopher. Variance between John Jakes, merchant taylor, tenant by lease to Robert Trappes, goldsmith, and [blank] Covert of the county of Sussex, gentleman, pls., and the dean and chapter of Paul's, defs., concerning a stone wall. The viewers say that the wall, standing on the E part of the ground of pls., is a partible wall from the king's highway there called Broad Street on the N, stretching southward 50 ft. By all the length, there belongs to pls. 16 in. from the W side eastward; the residue belongs to defs. Without *etc.*

124. [B.119] 28 October 1536.
Parish of St. Vedast. Variance between Thomas Typlady, embroiderer (browderer), pl. and Richard Calard, painter stainer, def., which both parties are tenants by lease to the wardens and fellowship of Saddlers, concerning a cellar or warehouse, a chamber, and a garret. The viewers say that the cellar to the stone wall there against the N belongs wholly to pl. and the door broken into the wall ought to be stopped and closed up. The warehouse belonging to def. ought to be 27 ft. 6 in. in length from the court against the N stretching southward, and there the partition between the parties ought of right to be made under the principal somer at costs and charges of def. Four windows there, barred with iron, belong to def. The chamber over the warehouse as it now stands belongs to def.; the partition of it stands upon the principal somer that the partition of the warehouse should stand under. The partition of the garret chamber ought to be made and set on the second somer southward from the breast somer against the court of def. on the N, which chamber has a way up to it from a

51

stair going up to a chamber against the W part. And the garret chamber
from N to S is 9 ft. 6 in. and belongs to def. Without *etc.*

125. [B.120] 17 April 1537.
Parish of St. Stephen in Coleman Street. Variance between Thomas
Ofley, merchant taylor, pl., and the Master of St. Thomas of Acon in
London and Edmund Hurlok, currier (coryer), defs., concerning
grounds for a defence to be made. The viewers say that from the SW
corner post of a draught house made shedwise belonging to the Master,
stretching eastward 5 ft. 6 in. to the SE corner post of the same shed, and
stretching more eastward from the SE corner post 23 ft. 7 in. to the SW
corner post of another shed there belonging to Hurlok; and from the
same SW post stretching more eastward 28 ft. 10½ in. to the SW corner of a
brick wall of Hurlok: for all that length the defence ought to be made, line
right and plumb from place to place as is aforelimited, at costs and
charges of defs. or either of them for his own grounds. Without *etc.*
Endorsed: . . . 5 a[nno] regis . . . vi . . . etur de record.

126. [B.121] 30 April 1537.
Parish of St. Pancras. Variance between the master and brethren of St.
Thomas of Acon in London and William Wakefeld, waxchandler, concerning a certain ground in Soper Lane whereupon old ruinous housing
now stands. The view is by assent and consent of both parties. The
viewers say that the ground belonging to the master and brethren is 8 ft. 2½
in. in breadth against Soper Lane on the W, from a NW corner post of a
house there of the master and brethren stretching northward to the
ground of Wakefeld. The same ground is 8 ft. 2½ in. in breadth on the E
between a NE corner post of the house of the master and brethren on the
S and the ground of Wakefeld on the N. The ground and old house there
of Wakefeld is 7 ft. 1 in. in breadth against Soper Lane on the W between
the ground of the master and brethren on the S and the middle of a
partible post of an old house where John Nevyll dwells on the N. The
ground and house of Wakefeld is 13 ft. in length from Soper Lane on the
W stretching eastward to the foundation of another house there of the
master and brethren. Wakefield's grounds are 7 ft. 1 in. in breadth on the
E between the ground of the master and brethren on the S and John
Nevyll's house on the N. All which premises be true in manner and form
as is aforerehearsed. Without *etc.*

127. [B.122] 13 June 1537.
Parishes of Our Lady of Abchurch and St. Martin Orgar. Variance
between Henry Heyward, chantry priest of Simon Wynchecomer
founded in the Church of Our Lady of Abchurch and the churchwardens
of that church, pls., and Richard Baxter, clothworker, def., concerning
ground on which lately stood a stone wall. The viewers say that the wall
was 25 ft. 10 in. in length between an old post of a house of pls. there on
the N and an old stone wall standing on the S, and it was 20 in. in breadth,
by their estimation. The wall was partible. Whereas def. has taken down
all the same wall without pls.' assent, the viewers say he has done wrong.

Half the wall, on the W side, belonged to pls.; that is to wit 10 in. in thickness by all the length of the wall. Without *etc.*
Endorsed: xvi Junii a[nno]r[egis] h[enrici] 8
Heywood & Baxter

128. [B.123] 15 November 1537.
Parish of St. Dunstan in the East. Variance between Thomas Marowe, gentleman, pl., and the parson and churchwardens of the parish, defs., concerning a certain nuisance. The viewers say that from the SW corner post of the house of pl. stretching northward 20 ft. 2½ in. to another upright principal post of pl., the length belongs to pl. line right and plumb on the W side of the posts. Also there is a lead gutter between the parties' houses on the W side of pl., which is and ought to be partible all the length of the houses. Also there is a withdraught on the E side of pl. belonging to the house now in tenure of Ambrose Wolley, grocer; it has no wall of brick or stone but only pl.'s stone wall, whereas it ought of right to have a wall of brick or stone 18 in. in thickness on def.'s own grounds. Furthermore there is a shed built on a wharf in tenancy of Ambrose Wolley against the E side of pl.'s house, which shed is fastened, bolted and dogged with iron onto pl.'s house, which is a great hurt to the house and which ought not so to be used without pl.'s licence and agreement. All which premises and nuisances aforesaid *etc.*, without *etc.*

129. [B.124][1] 29 March 1538.
Parish of St. Dunstan in the West in the suburbs of London. Variance between Mr. William Ermystede, clerk, master of the Temple, pl., and Johanna Thorpe, widow, def., concerning a new house which def. has lately built on the backside of her garden against the S part of it. The viewers say that the house contains 19 ft. 6 in. in length from E to W. By all its length it stands southward 12 in. on a stone wall which belongs to and closes in the garden ground of pl. Def. also has set a chimney 6 ft. 6 in. in breadth E to W which stands on pl.'s wall 19 in. to the S. The house and chimney ought of right to be set on def.'s own ground and not on pl.'s wall without his license. All the water that falls from the S side of the house falls into the garden ground of pl.; def. ought to make a fillet gutter of lead to convey the water onto her own ground and not annoy pl. Moreover, def. has a window of four lights toward pl.'s garden whereby she may oversee the garden; the lights ought to be set in with a loupe so that there can be no sight into the garden, or else clean stopped up forasmuch as def. may have sufficient light both [?W] and E for her said house. All which premises *etc.*, without *etc.*

1. Much of the certificate is illegible.

130. [B.125] 29 May 1538.
Parish of St. Bride in Fleet Street in the suburbs of London. Variance between the abbot of Cirencester (Cicetor)[1] and William Pople, gentleman, and Alex Hudson, brewer, attorneys in that behalf for the abbot, and Thomas White, merchant taylor, concerning certain tenantrys and houses set and being in an alley called the Popinjay (Popyngay) Alley,

that is to say against the king's highway of Fleet Street on the S and between the tenement there belonging to the heirs of [blank] Peksall gentleman, late deceased, on the W and a tenement and land belonging to Thomas White on the E. The view is with assent and consent and agreement of both parties. The viewers say that the abbot ought of right to have in measure by the king's highway between the said limits E and W 6 ells and $\frac{3}{4}$ ell in breadth by the standard of the ell that now is used. All the residue of the tenantrys and ground now in tenure of the abbot and his tenants, which is 20$\frac{1}{4}$ in. stretching eastward, belongs to Thomas White line right and plumb from the ground upward to the whole height thereof. Furthermore, the water of the E side of the abbot's house falls on the house and gutter of Thomas Whyte [*sic*]. The abbot's house ought of right to bear its own water with a fillet gutter. All which premises aforesaid *etc.* without *etc.*

Endorsed: . . . Junii a[nno] 30 h[enrici] 8 . . .

1. See Keene and Harding, 142.

131. [B.126] 15 May 1538.
Parish of St. Giles without Cripplegate. Variance between the parson and churchwardens of the parish church of St. Peter next Paul's Wharf, pls., and Robert Ivy, citizen and tiler, def., concerning certain ground for a pale or defence to be made. The viewers say that the ground is 70 ft. 8$\frac{1}{2}$ in. in length from the NW corner post there of pls. against the S stretching northward to the SE corner post of a little house of the abbot of Westminster, now in the tenure of John Powle, joiner. The pale or defence ought to be made and set up betwixt the said limits line right and plumb all the said length at cost of def. Without *etc.*

132. [B.127] 4 September 1538.
Parish of St. Margaret Moses in Friday Street. Variance between the parson and churchwardens of the parish and Cutbert Bocher, draper, concerning a certain old wall made of stone and brick belonging to the parson and churchwardens. The view is by assent and agreement of both parties. The viewers say that from the SW corner of an old principal post of the house or tenement of Bocher stretching westward 19 ft. 4 in. against the N side of the old wall, the wall overhangs northward 2$\frac{1}{2}$ in. at the NW corner. In the middle the wall overhangs northward 7 in. toward the ground of Bocher. All the wall overhanging ought of right to be withdrawn line right and plumb from place to place as aforelimited, by the parson and churchwardens, or else at their costs and charges [Bocher may] break the wall in all such places as need shall be for the carpenters to enter their timber into the wall. Without *etc.*

133. [B.128] 26 September 1538.
Parish of All Hallows the Little in Thames Street. Variance between the master and wardens of the Dyers, pls., and William Forde, fishmonger, def., concerning certain ground for a pale or some other lawful defence to be made and set up. The viewers say that from the NE corner of a principal post of a house of pls. stretching northward 37 ft. 6 in. to the S

end of a brick wall a brick and a half thick, the brick of length belongs to pls. and the half brick belongs to def., as is marked and set out by the viewers on the wall. And furthermore the pale or defence ought of right to be made all the length line right and plumb from place to place at cost and charges of def. Without *etc.*

134. [B.129] 26 February 1539.
Parish of St. Giles without Cripplegate. Variance between the master and wardens of the Mercers and Walter Yong, merchant taylor, concerning certain grounds and buildings. The view is with assent and consent of both parties. The viewers say that the ground and building of the Mercers from Moor Lane against the W stretches eastward 16 ft. 1 in. to the NW corner post of a house belonging to Yong. And from the corner post [it stretches] more eastward 17 ft. 6 in. to the NW corner of a brick wall of Yong, which wall at the corner stands 2 in. on the ground of the Mercers. And the water of the N side of the house falls on the ground of the Mercers. Stretching from the NW corner of the brick wall 20 ft. to the NE corner of the wall, there the wall stands 6 in. on the Mercers' ground and the water of the N side of a house that stands on the brick wall, belonging to Yong, falls on their ground. Stretching more eastward 49 ft. 8 in. from the NE corner of the wall against a pale there belonging to the Mercers (and by them to be made and kept) to the NW corner post of another house of Yong, and from the said post 13 ft. 6 in. to the NE corner post of the same house, there is an angle of 6 ft. 6 in. southward. Stretching from the angle eastward, the N side of Yong's ground [runs] 48 ft. 6 in. And the water of Yong's house falls on the ground of the Mercers. From the NE corner post of the house stretching eastward to the Moor Field there is a pale and a hedge of the Mercers 266 ft. 10 in. to a mark made by the viewers on the rail of another pale of the Mercers. The pale and hedge ought to be made and repaired by the Mercers at their costs and charges. Yong ought of right to bear the water of all his houses with fillet gutters at his own cost and charge. Either party ought to have his own ground by all its length line right and plumb from place to place as aforelimited. All which premises *etc.*, without *etc.*
Endorsed on verso: 14.7 . . .

135. [B.130] 27 February 1539.
Parish of St. Michael in Cornhill. Variance between Robert Dimkyn, merchant taylor, pl., and Richard Traves, merchant taylor, def., concerning a certain warehouse. The viewers say that two tenements there, which pl. holds by lease, and the said warehouse at their first building were framed and built all jointly together; the warehouse is parcel of the two tenements and ought of right to appertain wholly to them. The two tenements are 54 ft. 9 in. in length from the king's highway of Cornhill against the S stretching northward to a garden there, and 39 ft. in breadth E and W. And the two tenements belong wholly to pl. all their length and breadth, line right and plumb from the ground to their highest part. Without *etc.*

55

136. [B.131] 17 March 1539.
Parish of St. Botolph without Aldgate. [No variance stated]. The viewers
have been charged to view and oversee a certain pale or fence between
the gardens and grounds of John Kedyrmyster, draper, and [Antony]
Antony, beer brewer (beirbruer). The view is with assent and consent of
both parties. The viewers say that the pale or fence on the S side of the
garden ground of Kedyrmyster, from the common highway entering into
his ground against the W stretching eastward to the ground belonging to
Antony, ought of right to be repaired at cost and charge of Kedyrmyster.
The pale or fence at the E end of Kedyrmyster's garden ground from the S
to the N against the ditch there ought to be made and repaired at cost and
charge of Antony. Either party to set the posts and rails of his pale toward
his own ground. All which premises *etc.*, without *etc.*
Endorsed: 29.5 . . . a[nno] Regis . . .
See also **153** below.

137. [B.132] 17 July 1539.
John Hylmer, William Walker, John Kyng, and Henry Pesemede,
freemasons and carpenters, viewers.
Parish of St. Andrew in Holborn in the suburbs of London. Variance
between Richard Hunt, gentleman, pl., and the prior and convent of
St. Mary Spital, defs., concerning certain ground. The viewers say that
the ground belonging to pl. is [?40] ft. in length from a mark or strike
made on a brick wall there belonging to the Bishop of Ely against the N,
stretching southward to the NW corner of a post there of pl., line right
and plumb. And the ground is [?27] ft. 1 in. in breadth against the brick
wall from the strike or mark on the W stretching eastward to the E side of
the pale of pl. And [the ground] stretches southward from the brick wall
to the NE corner post of the house there of pl., line right and plumb
against the grounds of Thomas Bowland. All which ground within the
limits aforerehearsed ought of right to belong to pl., without *etc.*
Endorsed: 24.9 . . . a[nno] reg[is] h[enrici] 8 . . .

138. [B.133] 17 July 1539.
Parish of St. Bride in Fleet Street. Variance between Frances Waserer,
tenant to the prior of Rochester, pl., and Thomas Cosyn, tenant in 'the
Bel Savage', belonging to [blank] Wyndham, Esquire, def., concerning a
certain brick wall. The viewers say that the brick wall is 19 ft. in length
from the N side of the back of a chimney of pl. stretching northward to the
S side of the plate of a house of def. The wall is 13½ in. in thickness. By all
its length and breadth the wall belongs to pl. Also the viewers find two
posts standing on the W side of the gatehouse of 'the Bel Savage', which
bear two somers and which stand on the entertise (enterteyse) and house
belonging to pl.; they ought to be withdrawn line right and plumb by def.
Pl. ought to bear his own water of all his houses with fillet gutters or
otherwise. All which premises *etc.* without *etc.*
Endorsed: . . . Julii a[nno] 31 . . .
[?9.2] h 8

139. [B.134] 19 August 1539.
Parish of St. Botolph without Aldgate. Variance between William Myles, grocer, pl., and Awdry Rookes, gentleman, owner of the great messuage or tenement there called 'the Crosse Keys', and Edward Rowesley, tenant of the same, defs., concerning certain housing and buildings. The viewers have viewed a shed, millhouse, and stable, built and set on the W side of 'the Crosse Keys'. The shed is 7 ft. 6 in. in breadth [without] the SW corner post of 'the Crosse Keys' stretching westward against the king's highway. Stretching from the king's highway northward 98 ft. 6 in. to the S side of a house called the millhouse, the shed is 10 ft. 7 in. in breadth without the said house of 'the Crosse Keys'. Stretching more northward 15 ft. . . . in. from the S side of the millhouse to the N side thereof, the millhouse is 15 ft. 7 in. in depth W without the wall of the house of 'the Crosse Keys'. And stretching more northward from the millhouse to the NW corner of a stable there, the stable is 26 ft. 11 in. in length and 10 ft. 3 in. in breadth at both ends without the W side of the tenement of 'the Crosse Keys'. There is a lead gutter lying on the W side of the tenement of 'the Crosse Keys' between the tenement and the shed, which belongs to 'the Crosse Keys'. Either party ought of right to bear the water of his own house. All the said shed, millhouse, and stable, by all their length and breadth as much as they stand without the W side of the tenement called 'the Crosse Keys', belong wholly to pl.; he may lawfully take down all the stable, millhouse, and shed or any part thereof to his own use and profit at his pleasure. All which premises *etc.*, without *etc.*

140. [B.135] 9 October 1539.
Parish of St. Martin [within Ludgate]. Variance between the parson and churchwardens of the church and Richard Aleyn, their tenant, of the one party, and the prior and convent of St. Mary Spital without Bishopsgate and Richard Cawod, their tenant by lease, of the other party, concerning certain lands and tenements without Ludgate. The view is with assent, will, and agreement of both parties. The viewers say that as the said lands and tenements belonging to the parties, with all manner of rooms, easements, and commodities to the same in any wise appertaining, have of long time hitherto been divided, used, and occupied, so they ought of right to continue and either party to keep and enjoy his own part and repair, uphold, emend, and maintain the same with reparations and buildings at all times when need be from time to time. Without *etc.*
Endorsed: 11.12 . . .

141. [B.16] 18 October 1539.
To the Right honorable lorde the Mayre of the Citie of London and to his worshipfull Brethern the Aldermen of the same.
Shewen unto your good lordship & discrete wisedoms the xviii[th] daye of October in the xxxi[th] yere of the Reigne of King Henry the VIII[th], John Hylmer, Will[ia]m Walker, John Kyng, & Henry Pesemede, the iiii maisters of Fremasons and Carpenters, viewers indifferent sworne to the said Citie, That whereas a variance is depending bitwene Long John, Richard Garlade, Arnold Lothebery, John Payne, Gyles Mas and

George Bysborowe, Tenauntes unto the Chamber of london at Blaunch-appelton in the parish of All halowes stanynges of london, playntiffes oi the one partie, and the parson of the said parysshe, defendant of the othei partie, for certain tithes & duties whiche the said parson claymeth and demandeth of the said tenantes of & for vi litle newe houses there lately buylded by the Chamberlayn of london nowe in the tenure and occupyng of the said tenantes. Whereupon the said iiii viewers were late charged by your honorable commaundement to viewe & overse the said vi litle newe houses, whether they be houses or sheddes. Whiche the said viewers by all their discrecions have viewed & seen, And thereupon they saye that the said newe houses ben buylded & sette upon the baksydes of the houses or Ten[*emen*]ts wherin the said vi Tenantes nowe dwell and inhabite, ordeyned & made for houses of easement & necessary Rowmes for withdraughts, for lodgyng of servantes, & to ley in wood & coles or any other thing at the pleasures of the said Tenantes for ther eases. And that they be houses, and no sheddes, and that also the said Tenantes do not lete out the said houses nor any of theym to ferme but do kepe theym in their own handes for their owne easement and uses as far as the said viewers can perceyve or knowe. And as touching the said tithes or parsons dutye the said viewers sayen that it ys no parte of their charge nor nothyng appurteynyng unto theym to discusse or medle with.
Signed: Ryshton
Subscribed: 20.1 a[nn]o 31 copia dd fuit partibus quer[entibus]

142. [B.137] 19 December 1539.
Parish of St. Elen. Variance between Alan Hawte, gentleman, and Guy Craford, gentleman,[1] of and for a new porch and countinghouse to be made and set up before the N side of the house of Hawte, set out 4 ft. 4 in. northward without the old frame of Hawte's house and 19 ft. 1 in. in length from the W side of a draught house of Hawte stretching eastward line right and plumb. The viewers say that the porch and countinghouse may lawfully be made within the same length, provided that no light be made to it except 'furthright northward'. And whereas Hawte has a draught there which is a nuisance to the house of Craford 'for Infection of evill and contagious ayre', Hawte ought of right to close up the wall of the draught with brick and mortar and make a vent to the same so that no air thereof shall come into the house of Craford. All which premises aforerehearsed *etc.*, without *etc.*
Endorsed: 19.3 A[nn]o 31 ...

1. There is no statement that the view is by assent of the parties, but they are not referred to as plaintiff and defendant.

143. [B.138][1] 31 January 1540.
Parish of St. Katharine Christchurch. Variance between Lawrence Maxwell and Ellys Dyall, citizens and tilers, pls., and Thomas Cutberd, barbersurgeon, def., concerning a certain old pale. The viewers say that the pale is 86 ft. 11 in. in length between the SW corner of a post of a house there of def. and the NW corner of a post of another house there, also of def. The pale ought to be made and set line right all that length,

)etween the W side of the two posts, at costs and charges of def. Without
tc.
Endorsed: 4.4 a[nno] 31 Hollys
Subscribed: 17 Feb[ruarii] a[nno] 31 H[enrici] 8

1. For more on Thomas Cutberd, see the entry in Journal 15, f. 129, for 29 November 36
Henry VIII (1544); he had not made repairs to his tenement in St. Katharine Creechurch
parish according to the terms of his lease from a religious foundation and Mistress
Cornwales, who had meanwhile bought the property from the king, re-entered and took
possession of the premises. Cutberd allegedly then fraudulently sold his forefeited lease
to one Mundes.

144. [B.139] 24 March 1540.
To the Right honorable Lorde the Mayre of the Citie of London and to his
worshipfull brethern the Aldermen of the same.
Shewen unto your good lordship and discrete wisedoms the xxiiii[th] day of
March in the xxxi[th] yere of the Reigne of our soveraigne lorde Kyng
Henry the VIIIth, John Hylmer, William Walker, John Kyng, & Henry
Pesemede, the iiii maisters of Fremasons and Carpenters, viewers indifferent [sworn] to the said Citie, that where as they were late charged by
your honorable commaundement [to view and] overse a certain lane
against the South syde of the parysshe Churche of Saint Martyn [in the
Vintry] of London The whiche lane the said iiii viewers by all their
discrecions have [viewed] In the presence & sight of the Right worshipfull
maister Dormer, Alderman of the same [Ward] and [Master George]
Medley, Chamberleyn of the said Citie, and dyvers other Inhabitantes . . .
present, And thereupon the said iiii viewers saye that the said lane . . .
therof v fote iii Inches of assise and hath ben used and accustomed tyme
[out of mind] to be a common wey from the high strete of the vyntry
downe to the Wharf there and specially . . . half of the lane from the said
high strete to the turning before the Celere there whiche hath ben moste
used and there the said lane ys in wydenes v fote of assise. And the other
half of the said lane ys stopped up by the assent & agreement of the
maister and wardeyns of the Merchanttailllors, owners of bothe sydes of
the said lane, Edward Burlace, mercer, beyng tenant on the West syde &
John Chamber, vyntner, being tenant on the Estsyde thurghout all that ys
stopped up of the said lane. And at the end of the said lane abuttyng to the
Wharf there the said lane was in wydnes but iiii fote & di. of assise and
there sometyme was a grate and iii high steppes to mount upon the said
Wharf. And they say that the said lane was but a fowle blynde lane & did
litle good, and that it may be well spared and foreborne, notwithstonding
that it hath ben of olde tyme accustomed to be a comon way as aforesaid.
Endorsed: 19.6 a[nn]o 31

See **145** below.

145. [B.140] 24 March 1540.
To the Right honorable lorde the Mayre of the Citie of London and to his
worshipfull brethern the Aldermen of the same.
Shewen unto your good lordship and discrete wisedoms the xxiiii[th] daye
of Marche in the xxxi[th] yere of the Reigne of our soveraign lord Kyng
Henry the VIIIth, John Hylmer, William Walker, John Kyng, & Henry

Pesmede, the iiii maisters of Fremasons and Carpenters, Viewers indifferent sworne to the said Citie, That where as they were late charged by
your honorable commaundement to view and overse a certain lane
against the south syde of the parysshe Churche of saint Martyn in the
Vyntry of London, the whiche lane hath ben used & accustomed over
tyme oute of mynde to be a comen wey from the Vyntry down to the
watersyde of Thamyse till nowe of late that same lane ys stopped & closed
up by Edward Burlace, mercer, who hath a leasse of the maister &
wardeins of merchaunttailors aswell of certain Celers or Warehouses on
the Este syde of the said lane as also of a gardeyn grounde on the West
syde of the same lane. By reason whereof the said Edward hath taken into
his said gardeyn the bredeth of the said lane by all the lenght of the same
gardeyn. The whiche lane the said iiii viewers by all their discrecions have
viewed & seen in the presence & sight of the Right Worshipfull maister
Dormer, Alderman of the warde there; Maister Medley, Chamberleyn of
the said Citie, and divers other Inhabitantes of the said warde beyng
present, And therupon the said viewers saye that the said lane was but
narowe & a fowle blynd lane and did litle good and that it may be well
spared and foreborne, Notwithstonding that it hath ben of olde tyme
accustomed to be a comon wey as is abovesaid.
Endorsed: (*at left*) 10 Aprilis a[nn]o 31 h[enrici] 8
(*at right*) 5 April a[nn]° 31 . . .

146. [B.141] 30 July 1540.
Parish of St. Pancras. Variance between the parson and churchwardens
of the parish of St. Christopher and Bartholomew Barnes, mercer,
concerning a certain stone wall standing on the E side of the ground of
Barnes adjoining against the tenement belonging to the parson and
churchwardens. The view is with assent and consent of the parties. The
viewers say that the ground of Barnes, with the thickness of the stone wall
also belonging to him, is 30 ft. 7 in. in breadth at the N end between the W
side of the tenement of the parson and churchwardens stretching westward to the little lane there called Pupkyrtell Lane. And stretching
[southward] from the [NW] corner post of the said tenement of St.
Christopher's 45 ft. to the SW corner post of the tenement, Barnes'
ground and wall is 26 ft. 4 in. in breadth stretching westward to the little
lane. All which premises aforerehearsed the viewers affirm to be true.
Without *etc.*

147. [B.142][1] Parish of St. Pancras. Variance between the parson and
churchwardens of St. Christopher and Bartholomew Barnes, mercer,
concerning a certain tenement with a shop. The view is with assent and
consent of both parties. The viewers say that the shop is 8 ft. 1 in. in
breadth against the street E and W and in length from the street
southward 12 ft. 10 in. There it is 8 ft. 10 in. in breadth and it is 9 ft. in
height. The shop is line right and plumb and belongs to the parson and
churchwardens in length, breadth, and heighth. All over the shop at . . .
belongs to Barnes. The tenement at the S end of the shop is 42 ft. 2 in. in
length from the same . . . And it is 21 ft. 9 in. in breadth at both ends

between the ground of Barnes [on the W] and the little alley there on the E. By all the length ... thereof line right and plumb it belongs to the parson and churchwardens. 'All which premises in manner and form aforerehearsed the said iiii viewers affirm to be true'. Without *etc.*

> 1. Both this view and the one immediately preceding it were apparently taken for the purpose of ascertaining the dimensions of premises Barnes was about to lease from the parson and churchwardens. The lease, dated 9 August 1540, recites the fact of the view and the dimensions given in this certificate. See *Wills, Leases and Memoranda in the Book of Records, Parish of St. Christopher le Stocks*, ed. Edwin Freshfield (1895), p. 13. See reference to the lease in **163** below.

148. [B.143] 4 August 1540.
Parish of St. Magnus. Variance between William Frestone, grocer, pl., and Robert Doket, grocer, def., concerning a certain entry. The viewers say that the entry is 4 ft. in breadth against the king's highway and 29 ft. in length from the street stretching westward; there [at the W end] it is 3 ft. 9½ in. in breadth or wideness. By all its length and breadth it is under the frame and building of the house and tenement there in the tenure and holding of pl., as it plainly appears. Without *etc.*

149. [B.144] 4 August 1540.
Parish of St. Thomas the Apostle. Variance between John Abbot, carpenter, pl., and Thomas Howe, merchant taylor, def., concerning a certain stone wall standing in the Ryall. The viewers say that from the S side of the stone tower there called 'the Tower in the Ryall', belonging to def., stretching eastward to a SE corner post also belonging to def., all the stone wall standing from the lineright [*sic*] southward line right and plumb between the S side of the tower and the S side of the corner post, belongs wholly to pl. Without *etc.*

150. [B.145] 13 September 1540.
Parish of St. Andrew nigh Baynards Castle. Variance between the parson and churchwardens of the church, pls., and Robert Hamond, wood-monger, def., concerning a certain lane called Rest Lane leading down to the common stair at the Thames side called the 'Newe Steyre'. The viewers say that the lane ought of right to be 9 ft. in wideness at the N end, between the tenement of pl. on the W and the ground, also of pl. and now unbuilt, on the E. The lane ought of right to be a common way for all the king's subjects to go and resort to the stair and water. There ought to be a post set in the middle of the N end of the lane at costs and charges of pls., so that no manner of cart nor 'carre' shall have any recourse or way through the lane, for fear of damage and peril to the king's liege people forasmuch as the lane is so narrow and strait that no man can pass by any cart or 'carre' there without great nuisance and peril. The def. as well as all other persons having or keeping any wharf there and keeping or occupying any cart or 'carre' ought of right to make ways for the same through their own grounds into the king's high street and not to come within the said lane for annoyance of the king's liege people, as is aforesaid. And furthermore, the said ground of pl., now to be built upon, is 24 ft. 8 in. in breadth between an old tenement there late belonging to

the Charterhouse next London on the E and the common lane on the W. All which premises *etc.*, without *etc.*
Endorsed: 16.11 A[nn]o 32 H[enrici] 8   Blackwell

151. [B.146]¹ 9 March 1541.
Parish of St. Botolph nigh Billingsgate. Variance between the parson and churchwardens of the parish, pls., and John Brown of Writtle (Wretyll) in the county of Essex, gentleman, def., concerning a certain wall of stone and brick set and being in Botolph Lane, for certain buildings which pls. intend to make and erect upon their own ground at the E end of the churchyard. The viewers find that the wall is a partible wall between the churchyard and the W end of a house and garden belonging to def. and now in tenure of George Thompson. From the NE corner post of a house there belonging to pls., pls. ought of right to have the stone wall to a thickness of 16½ in. eastward. From that corner post stretching northward 35 ft. 9½ in., pls. ought to have 8 in. of the thickness of the wall. By all the length, pls. may lawfully build on the party wall line right and plumb from place to place as aforelimited, without *etc.*
Endorsed: . . . Blakwell . . .

> 1. This certificate is copied in Journal 14, f. 249v.

152. [B.147] 10 June 1541.
John Hylmer, William Walker, Henry Pesemede, and John Arnold, masons and carpenters, viewers.
Parish of St. Peter night Paul's Wharf. Variance between Sir Gilbert Talbot, knight, and Sir Anthony Lee, knight, concerning ground where an old brick wall has fallen down and a new wall is to be made in the same place where the old wall stood. The view is with assent of both parties. The viewers say that the old wall stood between a post on the S stretching northward 25 ft. 10 in. to another post on the N. The two posts stand on the W part, and belong wholly to the house of Sir Anthony. Forasmuch as the old wall stood between the two posts on his ground, the new wall ought of right to be made thereof brick or timber at the costs and charges of Sir Anthony. And the house of Sir Gylbert stands on the E side. The new wall ought to be made as aforesaid, without *etc.*
Endorsed: 12.8 A[nno] 33 H[enrici] 8 seq[ui]t[u]r iste visus et sol[utum] feod[um] co[mmun]is clerici   Blakwell

153. [B.148] 11 June 1541.
To the Right honorable lorde the Mayre of the Citie of London and his worshipfull brethern the Aldermen of the same.
Shewen unto your good lordship & discrete wisedoms the xi^th daye of Juyn in the xxxiii^th yere of the Reigne of our Soveraigne lorde Kyng Henry the VIIIth, John Hylmer, William Walker, Henry Pesemede & John Arnold, the iiii maisters of Fremasons & Carpenters, Viewers indifferent sworne to the said Citie, That where as they were late charged by your honorable commaundement to viewe & oversee a certain grounde for a defence to be made & set upon the parysshe of Saint Botolf without Algate in the suburbes of London, nowe beyng in variance bitwene

Antony Antony, Bierbruer, playntyf of the one partie, and John Kedyrmyster, draper, of the other partie, Whiche grounde the said iiii iewers by all their discrecions have viewed & seen and therupon they aye that they fynd there an old pale post at the southend of a brykwall here belonging to the said playntyf ayenst the East And stretching from he said old post westward against the kynges highwey to a southwest orner post belonging to the said defendant the lenght wherof bitwene the aid ii postes ys Clxxiii fote x inches of assise. The whiche defence oweth of right to be made by all the said lenght lyneright & plombe bitwene the aid postes at the costes and charges of the said defendant. Without there can be any other evidence shewed to the contrary.
Endorsed: 12.8 A[nn]o 33 H[enrici] 8 infert[ur] iste visus etc. ij. 12 . . . unc prox[imum] etc. Hayward sol[uit] feod[um] co[mmun]is clerici etc.

154. [B.149] 12 July 1541.
Parish of St. Martin in the Vintry. Variance between Roger Tirry, alias Trerice, cooper (cowper), pl., and the master and wardens of the Merchant Taylors, defs., concerning a nuisance of a wall. The viewers find the E side of defs.' house there, stretching 30 ft. from the N to the E end. All the water of the E side all that length falls on the ground of pl. Defs. ought of right to make a fillet gutter to bear and convey all the water into their own ground according to the custom of the City, so that it does not fall onto the ground of pl. Also, there is brickwork set out without defs.' stone wall for conveyance of a withdraught out of defs.' house eastward to the common sewer. The brickwork is 5 ft. 6 in. in length from N to S and 12 in. in breadth at the N end outside the stone wall and 11 in. at the S end; it ought of right to be taken away by pl. forasmuch as it is a great nuisance. Also there is another withdraught there, conveyed with brickwork out of the house that William Lacy dwells in. It is 4 ft. 6 in. in length and it stands without the stone wall 16 in. at the E end. It is also a great nuisance and ought of right to be taken away and stopped up by pl. All which premises and nuisances *etc.*, without *etc.*
Endorsed: Rec[eptus] 2 s. pro feod[o] meo pro presen[?tacione] 7.11 A[nn]o 33 H[enrici] 8 super recepcione   Blak[well]

155. [B.150] 12 July 1541.
Parish of St. Michael Pater Noster. Variance between Roger Kydman, pl., and the Lord Marquis Dorset, owner, and Thomas Donne, his tenant by lease, defs., concerning an old stone wall. The viewers say that the wall is 52 ft. 6 in. in length from N to S and 2 ft. 4 in. in thickness. It is partible all its length. Pl. ought of right to have for his part 19 in. of thickness and defs. the residue, 9 in. Also, a partible lead gutter lies on the wall to bear and convey the water of both houses. All which premises *etc.*, without *etc.*
Endorsed: . . . rec 2 s. 15.9 a[nn]o 33 H[enrici] 8 te[mpore] recepcionis p[re]sent[u]m etc.   <u>Blakwell</u>

156. [B.151] 12 July 1541.
Parish of St. Olave [Hart Street]. Variance between Richard Eton, pl., and John Jenkynson, owner, and Eleanor Smarte, widow, his tenant by

lease, defs., concerning certain nuisances in Mart Lane. The viewers sa
that the S end of the house of defs. is 31 ft. in length from the gable en
against the E stretching westward. All the water of the S side for all tha
length falls on pl.'s house and ground. Defs. ought of right to make a fille
gutter of lead on the side of their house to bear and convey the water int
the street so that it does not annoy pl. Also, one John Pratt has taker
away a gutter of lead between the two old houses by reason of the buildin
of the house he dwells in, which he holds by lease of the king's highnes
and which adjoins the S end of pl.'s house. The gutter conveyed the wate
of the gutters of both pl.'s and defs.' houses from the gutters of the back
side of the houses into the street side; it was 18 ft. in length from the old
gutters to the street. Pratt ought of right to make a new lead gutter
between his new house and pl.'s house to convey the water of both
tenements into the street, at his own costs and charges. Also, a new post
at the NE corner of the new house is set within the house of pl. by 7 in.; it
ought to be withdrawn and set back. Also the viewers by all their
discretions say that, as the said two tenements of old time were divided as
they now are in possession of their owners now being and those that
hereafter shall be, so they ought to continue forever. All which premises
and nuisances *etc.*, without *etc.*

Endorsed: Rec[eptus] 7.11 a[nn]o 33 h[enrici] 8

157. [B.152] 25 July 1541.
Parish of St. Peter nigh Paul's Wharf. Variance between John Good,
dyer, tenant to the master and wardens of Dyers, pl., and Master George
Medley, Chamberlain of the City of London, def., concerning a putgaley
set and being in Boss Lane, otherwise called King's Lane. The viewers
say that the frame of timberwork that the putgaley stands on is 16 ft. in
length from the waterside of Thames against the S stretching northward.
There the said lane is 4 ft. 8 in. in breadth from E to W. The putgaley
stands on the W side of the lane on common ground of the City and so
ought of right to continue. Further, there is an oven standing on the E side
of the lane which is set out into the lane 2 ft. and is 5 ft. 6 in. in length; it
stands on common ground and ought of right to be withdrawn and taken
away by the owner of the same. All which premises *etc.*, without *etc.*

158. [B.153][1] 1 August 1541.
Parish of All Hallows Barking. Variance between the master and
wardens of the Drapers, pls., and John Asshton, gentleman, def.,
concerning certain nuisances in Mart Lane. The viewers find the back of a
chimney of def. edified and set 3 ft. 9 in. within and upon ground of pls.
They also find the back side of an oven standing 6 ft. 9 in. southward into
pls.' tenement; it is 7 ft. in length from E to W. The chimney and oven
ought by all their length and breadth to be withdrawn and taken away by
def. or else pls. may lawfully take away as much as stands on their ground.
Furthermore, the S side of a house lately built and in tenancy of def.
encroaches and is built on ground of pls. 8 ft. 5 in. at the E end from N to S
and stretching westward 21 ft. 9 in. from the W side of an old stone wall of
pl. to the E side of a brick wall of the Mercers. By all that length and

ɔreadth the building stands on pls.' garden ground and ought of right to ɔe withdrawn by def. line right and plumb from place to place as ɑforelimited. All which nuisances *etc.*, without *etc.*
Endorsed: r[eceptus] 2 s. 16.11 a[nn]o 33 h[enrici] 8 super recepcione ɪstius visus [?hunc] Cur[iam] illat' <u>Blackwell</u>

> 1. A copy of this certificate is bound into Drapers' Company Rep. 7 (Minutes and Records, 1515–53), p. 1107.

159. [B.154][1] 1 August 1541.
Parish of Our Blessed Lady of Aldermary. Variance between the master and wardens of the Drapers, pls., and the parson and churchwardens of Aldermary, defs., concerning certain nuisances. The viewers find a new tenement belonging to defs. with certain new buildings at the back of it westward. The new building at its SW corner post is set and encroaches southward 1 in. on pls.' ground; stretching eastward along the S side of the new buildings 16 ft. 6 in. from the SW corner post to another principal post of the tenement, that post is set and encroaches 6 in. southward on pls.' ground. The SE corner post and S side of the upper storey of the new tenement on the side toward the street encroach and are set 5 in. southward upon pls.' ground. All which encroachments ought of right to be withdrawn by all their length and breadth line right and plumb from place to place as aforelimited at defs.' costs and charges. Further, all the water of the gutters of the S side of the new buildings is conveyed so that it falls into pls.' grounds. Defs. ought of right to bear their own water with fillet gutters and convey it into their own ground or else into the street. All which premises *etc.*, without *etc.*
Endorsed: rec[eptus] 2 s. 16.11 a[nno] 33 h[enrici] 8 super recepcione presens' <u>Blackwell</u>

> 1. A copy of this certificate is bound into Drapers' Company Rep. 7 (Minutes and Records, 1515–53), p. 1109.

160. [B.155] 9 November 1541.
Parish of St. Mary Magdalen in Old Fish Street. Variance between William Holyngworth, fishmonger, pl., and the parson and church-wardens of the parish church, defs., concerning a new frame of timber work with a fore storey toward the street side in Knightrider Street, lately made by pl. by virtue of a lease of a chamber made to him by defs. The frame is 19 ft. 9 in. in length from E to W. 'The whiche newe frame the said iiii viewers by all their discretions have viewed and seen and therupon they saye that the said playntif oweth of right to sett or ley the nethersyde of his plate of his frame equall with the upper parte of the flore of the said Chambre, the whiche ys in height from the said flore to the nether syde of the gyeste abovehed x fote iiii inches of assise. And further the said viewers sayen that the said plate of the said story shalbe cut in two peces, that is to say, to every syde of the celer dore under the said Chamber, and ii posts of xii inches of height shalbe sett upon the said plate with a transom of tymber upon the heddes of the same postes to reserve a commonyon of wey down into the said Celer. And so the said playntif to enjoy the said Chamber with thappurtenances by all the said

lengt and height accordyng to the tenor and effect of his said lease. Without *etc.*

Endorsed: xi die Novembris Anno infrascript[o] infert[ur] istam per infranominat[um] Hcnr[icum] Pesemede et eodem die copia inde deliberat[a] fuit Henr[ico] Pemerton uni gardian p[ar]ochie infrascript[e]. Et eodem xi die Novembris idem Gardian sol[uit] feod[um] co[mmun]is Clerici v s. <u>Blakwell</u>

161. [B.156] 24 November 1541.
Parish of St. Michael at Queenhithe. Variance between Richard Broke, salter, and John Hyll, concerning a certain woodhouse or storehouse by the ground now in tenure of Broke and a chamber over the same house now in tenure of Hyll, being all one frame. The view is by assent and agreement of both parties. The viewers say that the woodhouse or storehouse and chamber built on it are 16 ft. 6 in. in length E and W and 13 ft. 4 in. in breadth N and S. Forasmuch as the woodhouse or storehouse has been in the tenure and holding of Broke and his predecessors of long time, it ought so to continue and be repaired or built from the ground up to the floor of the chamber as often as need be at costs and charges of Broke and his successors. And the chamber from the nether side of the floor upward, as it has of long time belonged to Hyll and his predecessors, ought to continue and to be repaired and built as often as need shall require from the floor upward as aforesaid at costs and charges of Hyll and his successors. And so both parties to continue and enjoy, either of them, his own part of the premises as is aforedeclared and as it has been used of long continuance. Without *etc.*

162. [B.157] 1 March 1542.
Parishes of All Hallows [Bread Street] and St. Mildred in Bread Street. Variance between the dean and chapter of the cathedral church of St. Paul's and the master and wardens of the Salters, concerning a certain old stone wall with certain old buildings set upon it. The view is with assent and consent of both parties. The viewers say the wall is partible. From the N side of the NW corner principal post of the tenement of the dean and chapter standing on the wall against the king's highway of Bread Street and stretching eastward 37 ft. 2 in., the dean and chapter ought of right to have $6\frac{1}{2}$ in. of the thickness of the wall from the S side northward, line right and plumb. At the end of that length there is an angle against another NW corner principal post of the tenement of the dean and chapter; from that post stretching eastward 21 ft. 9 in. (the whole length of the grounds of the dean and chapter), the [part of] the wall of the dean and chapter is 15 in. in thickness from the S side northward, line right and plumb all the length. All the residue of the thickness northward, line right and plumb from place to place, belongs to the Salters. Without *etc.*
Endorsed: . . . [?3] Marcii a[nno] 33 h[enrici] 8 infert[ur] iste visus etc. et [?ii] s. sol[utum] feod[um] co[mmun]is clerici etc.

163. [B.158] 4 March 1542.
Parish of Our Blessed Lady of Bow. [No variance stated]. The viewers

have been charged to view at the request and desire of the parson and churchwardens of the parish church and by the assent and consent of the parson and churchwardens of St. Christopher, for the purpose of viewing and measuring all the ground belonging to the parson and churchwardens of Bow and new and old buildings set in the parishes of Our Lady of Colechurch and St. Pancras. The viewers say that the great new house lately built by Bartholomew Barnes, mercer, who holds the ground in lease from the parson and churchwardens of Bow, is 28 ft. 8 in. in breadth from the NW corner principal post of the house stretching eastward by the king's highway of Westcheap to the NE corner principal post. And the house with its appurtenances is 116 ft. 10 in. in length on the W side from the said NW corner post stretching southward along by Tupkyrtell Lane[1] to St. Pancras church. And it is 110 ft. in length on the E side from the NE principal corner post stretching southward to the church of St. Pancras. And the ground with the old house of the parson and church-wardens of Bow, now being taken down, is 16 ft. $4\frac{1}{2}$ in. in length from the said NE corner post of the new house stretching eastward, and there the ground and old housing is [?10] ft. 8 in. in breadth from Westcheap stretching southward to the ground there of the parson and church-wardens of St. Christopher's. Stretching 8 ft. 4 in. more eastward [from the 16 ft. $4\frac{1}{2}$ in.] by the street side to a lane called Byrd Alley,[2] that measure of 8 ft. 4 in. E and W belongs to the parson and churchwardens of St. Christopher's. And the ground is 12 ft. in depth from the NE corner post of an old house on the same ground stretching southward by the lane. And the first storey of the old house is 10 ft. in height from the ground and pavement of the street to the upper part of the joists of the first floor, which first storey by all the 10 ft. in height, 8 ft. 4 in. E and W, and 12 ft. N and S, line right and plumb, belongs wholly to the parson and church-wardens of St. Christopher's. And from the first storey and floor above the said 10 ft. height by all the measure of 8 ft. 4 in. E and W and 12 ft. N and S, upright line right and plumb, belongs wholly to the parson and churchwardens of Bow. All which premises the iiii viewers affirm to be true. Without *etc.*

1. Popkirtle Lane.
2. Bordhaw Alley.

164. [B.159][1] 10 March 1542.
Parish of St. Magnus. [No variance stated.][2] The viewers have been charged to view and see two old houses, one belonging to [the Master of the Bridge]house and the other to Richard Felde, draper. The view is [by assent] of both parties. The viewers say that the house of Richard Felde is 8 ft. in breadth on the E [between the] N and S stretching northward from the SE corner post. It is 13 ft. $2\frac{1}{2}$ in. in length on the S side from the SE corner post stretching westward. It is 14 ft. 9 in. in length on the N side [from the NE corner post] stretching westward. It is 8 ft. $1\frac{1}{2}$ in. in breadth on the W side N and S stretching [from the SW corner post] to the NW corner post. The house belonging to the Bridgemaster . . . the said Bridge Street toward the E from the SE corner post of the house stretching northward to the NE corner post. It is 14 ft. 9 in. in length on the S side

toward Felde's house from the SE corner post northward to the SW [corner post]. It is 15 ft. 9 in. in length on the N side from the NE corne post stretching westward [to the NW corner post]. The two old houses ar both decayed for lack of reparations. The foundations are sunken towarc the S, by reason whereof both houses overhang southwards. Either part ought of right to repair and build his own house and set it upright so tha 'either house may stand upon hymself' and so that 'neither of the house: do lene nor overhang [the] other. Nor to be tyed togeder with boltes anc dogges of iron [as it hath been] in tymes past, the which tying togeder anc lak of good foundations hath ben the cause of the synking and decaye o' the said houses.' All which *etc.*, without *etc.*

Endorsed: 21.[?8] A[nno] 33 H[enrici]8. Infert[ur] iste visus et ... sol[utam] mediat[atem] feod[i] co[mmun]is clerici per infranominat[um] Ric[ardu]m Felde.

1. The certificate is in poor condition, with the right end illegible.
2. Rep 10, f. 248, makes it clear that the view was taken because Richard Felde complained that the house belonging to the Bridgehouse was a nuisance to his own; the cost was to be borne by 'hym in whom the defaute shalbe founde' and the viewers to report their findings to the Mayor and Aldermen. Apparently since both houses were in need of repairs the parties split the fee owing to the common clerk.

165. [B.160] 21 March 1542.
Parish of All Hallows the Great in Thames Street. Variance between the parson and churchwardens of St. Michael in Crooked Lane, pls., and the parson and churchwarden of All Hallows, defs., concerning a certain annuity and quit-rent of 26s. 8d. sterling by year which pls. claim of defs. and which defs.' predecessors have paid long and many years past of the gift and legacy and bequest of Thomas Attelegh, citizen and stockfish-monger, out of and for a certain cellar and void place above the same which sometime belonged to Thomas and Helen, his wife, deceased. The viewers say that as it appears by a deed, made by Thomas Attelegh and Helen, his wife, and enrolled in the Hustings of London, the cellar and void place over it lay on the S part of the said church of 'All Saints' and was 18 ft. 6 in. in length on the N side from the SE corner of the chancel of the church stretching westward under the wall of the chancel to a tenement of Sir Nicholas de Lonergue,[1] knight, on the W; it was 14 ft. in breadth on the E from the SE corner of the chancel stretching southward to the SE corner of the cellar and void place. It was 18 ft. in length on the S side from the SE corner stretching westward to the tenement of Sir Nicholas and it was 14 ft. 9 in. in breadth on the W from the SW corner of the cellar stretching northward to the chancel. By all the viewers can find or perceive, the predecessors of defs. have built and made the S aisle of their church and charnel house over and upon the cellar and void place. And the Church of All Saints from the NE corner of its steeple stretching eastward and all the E end, that is to say the chancel or quire, and all the S aisle of the church, has been new made and built a long time since (sithen) the making and enrolling of the deed. By reason whereof the cellar and void place lie under the E end of the S aisle, chancel, and charnel house of the church. All which the viewers suppose and affirm to be true in manner and form aforerehearsed without *etc.*[2]

Endorsed: 26.8 a[nno]33 . . . iste . . . co[mmun]is cler[ici] . . .

1. Probably Loveigne.
2. The dispute between the two parishes came before the Mayor and Aldermen; a note in Rep 10, f. 254b, indicates that it was respited 'for a season' because of the absence of Dr Day, parson of All Hallows.

166. [B.161] 30 March 1542.
Parish of St. Matthew in Friday Street. Variance between the master and wardens of the Goldsmiths, pls., and John Olyff, barbersurgeon, and his tenant, defs., concerning a certain tenement with the tewel (towell) of a withdraught. The viewers find by an old deed containing the measure of the tenement that in old time the tenement was divided by its owner; that is, the nether part and foundation which is now a vault for a withdraught belongs to pls. by all the length, breadth, and depth thereof, as appears by the deed. And the warehouse and solar over and above it belongs to defs. by all the length and breadth thereof. Over the solar and warehouse there is another solar with other edifications upright over and above it which belongs to pls., as appears by the deed. The tewel of the withdraught belonging to pls. ought to be repaired or new made and set within the frame, plate, and room that the old tewel now stands at costs and charges of pls. without any let, interruption, or contradiction of defs. at any time hereinafter, when need shall be. Since both pls. and defs. have stools of easement with towells into the vault and withdraught, the vault and withdraught ought to be purged and cleansed as often as need be at equal cost of both. All which premises *etc.*, without *etc.*

167. [B.162] 20 May 1542.
Parish of St. Andrew Undershaft. Variance between the master and wardens of the Fishmongers, pls., and the master and wardens of the Carpenters, defs., concerning a certain piece of garden ground with a pale thereon. The viewers say that the ground is 10 ft. in breadth in the N part from the SE corner of a stone house of pls. stretching eastward to the [E end] of the pale. [The ground is] 9 ft. 3 in. from the NW corner of a brick wall standing on the S side of the garden ground stretching eastward to the E side of the pale. (The brick wall stands 10 in. northward on the ground of pls.) The ground is 61 ft. in length N and S between the said SE corner post of the stone house and the said NW corner of the brick wall. The garden ground in all length and breadth, line right and plumb between the limits, 'the iiii viewers say in the judgement and sight of a man's ie belongeth to the said plaintifes' and the pale ought to be removed and set line right and plumb between the two corners of the stone house and brick wall. Without *etc.*

168. [B.163] 19 June 1542.
Parish of St. Botolph nigh Billingsgate. Variance between Edward Hall, pl., and Nicholas Howe, def., concerning a certain rasen and entertise [*sic*] of an old house. The viewers say that the rasen is 41 ft. 8 in. in length from the SE corner post that bears it at the S end stretching northward to the NE corner post that bears it at the N end; the rasen and entertise belong wholly to pl. Whereas three beams and nine single rafters

belonging to def. rest upon part of the rasen, the viewers say that def. a his own costs and charges ought of right to withdraw them and also the joists as much as they rest on the rasen and entertise. Without *etc.*

169. [B.164] 26 June 1542.
Parish of St. Botolph without Aldgate. Variance between William Myles [blank], pl., and Andrew Morys, grocer, def., concerning a certain ground for a new brick wall to be made and set up. The viewers say that the ground is 54 ft. 2 in. in length from the NW corner of the brick wall of pl. stretching northward to the NE corner of a post of a house there of def The new brick wall ought of right to be set on grounds of def.; that is, to wit, on the W side of a line to be set between the said two limits and corners, line right and plumb, at costs and charge of def., without *etc.*
Endorsed: 28.8 A[nno Henrici 8] 34
11.10 copia deliberat[a] fuit ux[ori] querentis infrascript[i]

170. [B.165] 15 July 1542.
Parish of St. Dionis. Variance between Henry Dolfyn, draper, and John Dymok, draper, concerning a certain noisome withdraught, 'which withdraught the said iiii viewers by all their discrecions have not oonly viewed and seen by thassent and agreement of bothe the said parties but also Mr. Thomas Bowyer, beyng the Aldermans deputie there, and the said viewers togethere have called afore theym the said parties, the whiche have graunted and promysed bothe to abyde and stand to the jugement of the said viewers aswell concernyng the breakyng up and clensyng of the withdraught as also the makyng up of the same ageyn'. The viewers say that the withdraught is partible. Dolfyn has but one stool, which serves only his own chamber. Dymok has three stools: one for his own chamber, another for his maidens' chamber, and the third for his menservants' chamber. Nevertheless, the viewers have caused the wall of the withdraught to be broken within the warehouse of Dolfyn 'and so to be clensed and conveyed through his house, the which was to hym and all his house a great noysaunce beyng no lesse then xxx tonne, as a reaport ys made thereof to the said viewers, which perceive well and se that the said withdraught ys made clene for many yeres to come. Wherefore, and in consideration that the said Dymok as is aforesaid hath iii stoles and the said Dolfyn but one, and Dolfyn hath had all the noyaunce and trouble about the makyng clene thereof and the said Dymok none at all, the said iiii viewers in their consciences thynk indifferent and do judge that the said Dymok shall pay and bere all the charges aswell of the clensyng and caryng awey of the withdraught as also of makyng up the wall ageyn where it was broken, at his own coste and charge. Whiche will coste in all things in the estimation of the said viewers l*vis.*, viii*d.*'

171. [B.166][1] 18 August 1542.
Ward of Farringdon ex[tra] in the suburbs of London. Variance between Thomas Babyngton, Esq., warden or keeper of the king's gaol of the Fleet, pl., and William Collyns, carpenter, Thomas Cosyn, butcher, and diverse other inhabitants or dwellers nigh adjoining the wall of the Fleet,

defs., concerning nuisances, hurts, and detriments. The viewers find a garden ground to the E [of the Fleet] belonging to Collyns which is so high raised and enhanced that not only may he, his wife, and his servants stand in his garden and look over the coping of the Fleet wall (the coping of the brick of which has been broken in diverse places), but also a great release (relees) of a brick water table above the foundation of the wall is drowned and buried under the earth of the garden, to the great hurt of the wall. The viewers say Colyns ought of right to take away all the earth that lies on the water table and not to lay nor set anything on any part of the wall. He ought to amend the coping of the wall where it is broken and not to set nor make any manner of building near the wall. Moreover, he has a brick cistern for a withdraught adjoining close to the Fleet wall without any wall between the withdraught and the Fleet wall to 'defend' the ordure of the withdraught. It is unlawfully done and ought not to be suffered. Also the viewers find in the ground belonging to 'the Bel Savage', now in tenure of Thomas Cosyn, [?a withdraught] and gutter of lead which he built so near the Fleet wall that the water of the gutter and withdraught issues through ... to the great nuisance of the garden of the Fleet and all the king's subjects resorting to it; he ought to withdraw all clean away from the wall. The ground of Cosyn is raised and enhanced with dung, which not only lies over and upon the release and water table of brick of the wall, to its great hurt and decay, 'but also the coping of the wall is broken with lokyng over into the Flete gardyn'. Cosyn ought to make repairs and to remove and take away the earth. Nothing is to be laid or set upon the release or water table, for it belongs wholly to the Fleet wall. Furthermore ... built and set adjoining to the Fleet wall over and upon the release and brick water table, and diverse holes are broken into the same. [They shall be repaired] and no man shall build so nigh the wall. All which premises *etc.*, without *etc.*

1. The certificate is in poor condition, with the right portion illegible in many places.

172. [B.167] 18 August 1542.
Parish of All Hallows in Honey Lane. Variance between Master Andrew Judde, Alderman, and John Garwey, mercer, executors of the testament of Master John Fayry, deceased, and the owner or landlord of a tenement in Westcheap, pls., and John Butler, tenant of the same by lease, def., concerning certain 'selyngs of waynescot, shelfes and warebourdes' in the shop, warehouse, and kitchen of the tenement, to determine whether the ceilings, shelves, and wareboards or any part of them may be removed and taken away without the assent and will of the landlord. The viewers say that the ceiling is set and made in the hall of the tenement and in two chambers over it, containing in all 89 yards square or thereabout. 'And that asmoche of the said selynges, shelfes, warebourdes and other necessaryes as have ben made in tyme past withyn the said tenement by tenantes of the same for their own ease whiche is not fastened nor nayled unto any part of the frame of the said tenement with any manner of nayles or pynnes of iron or tymber may be lawfully taken awey. And all suche of the premisses as be fastened or nayled with any nayle or pyn as is aforesaid may not be removed nor taken awey without speciall licence of

the said landlord. Except there be any covenant or promise made to the contrary.'

173. [B.168] 18 September 1542.
Parish of St. Olave in Silver Street. Variance between John Twyford, vintner, pl., and George Isotson, butcher, def., which two parties have and hold certain tenements by lease of the master and brethren of St. Bartholomew's Hospital in West Smithfield of London, concerning a certain little alley ground. The viewers say that the alley is 5 ft. in wideness at its W end against Mugwell Street at the door of the alley. At the E end, against the tenements of def., it is 5 ft. 8 in. in wideness. It is 25 ft. 8 in. in length between the limits. In all its length and breadth the viewers say by all their discretion the alley belongs of right to pl. Without *etc.*

174. [B.169] 18 September 1542.
Parish of St. Martin in the Vintry. [No variance stated]. The viewers have been charged to view and oversee a certain new frame for a house which one Robert Swayne, cooper, is setting up, to determine whether it is set on any part of the common ground of the City. The viewers say that the frame is 11 ft. 11 in. in wideness from its SW corner post stretching northwards to a stone wall and it is 23 ft. $4\frac{1}{2}$ in. in length from the SW corner post stretching eastward. It is 11 ft. $9\frac{1}{2}$ in. in wideness at the E end. It is encroached and set westward on the common ground of the lane there; it ought of right to be withdrawn eastward 1 in. Furthermore, there is a little lane on the S side of the new frame which has ever been a common way between two lanes leading down from the Vintry toward the Thames; the little lane ought to continue and be common hereafter as it has been before. Without *etc.*

175. [B.170] 24 September 1542.
Parish of St. James in Garlickhithe. Variance between the parson and churchwardens of the parish, pls., and Thomas Don and Thomas Smyth, his tenant by lease, defs., concerning a certain little new house lately built and set up within the Lord Marquis Dorsett's place, upon the W side of it, by Thomas Don. The viewers say that the new house contains 18 ft. 6 in. in length N and S. It is set adjoining the side of an old stone wall and a house thereon built of old time called 'the Preests Comons of saint Jamys', belonging to pls. Def. that built the house has broken the stone wall in five places to put in the ends of two lengths of timber for the floor over the cellar of the new house, and the ends of three somers of timber for the floor of the chamber of the house, to the great hurt, weakening, and decay of the stone wall. Def. ought to take out the ends of timber and make the wall whole again and make frames of timber on his own [ground] to bear up the ends of the somers, with nothing to rest within nor upon the said wall. Moreover, def. ripped and took away the side of the old house to make a gutter between it and the new house at its building, and he has not amended it nor made it up again but has let it lie open and untiled, by reason whereof the . . . and timber work of the old house is

rotten and sore decayed and in peril of falling. Wherefore said def. ought of right to make again substantially the old house and wall at his own proper costs and charges. Without *etc.*

176. [B.171] 24 September 1542.
Parish of St. Sepulchre without Newgate. Variance between Thomas Lane, waxchandler, pl., and the parson and churchwardens of the parish church of St. Sepulchre, defs., concerning the making of a gutter between a house belonging to defs. and a new house which pl. has built adjoining the E side of the same defs.' house, which new house is 16 ft. 4 in. in wideness N to S. The viewers say that pl., at the setting up of his new house, broke down the rafter feet and tiles of the E side of defs.' house. Pl. shall make a new gutter of timber and lead between the two houses for the defence of both houses and shall amend the tiling of the old house that was broken by setting up his own house; the work shall be done at equal costs and charges of both parties since defs. ever before have had their water falling eastward upon a paved stone gutter made by them. And def. shall keep . . . reparations of the said gutter hereafter as often and when need shall be and also shall pay . . . [?5 shillings] . . . charges of this view. All which premises *etc.* without *etc.*
Endorsed: 14.12 . . . recordum . . . Curia . . . quer . . . fcod . . .
A° 33 . . . 23 . . .
9 10 11 12 13 14
15 16 17 18 19 20

177. [B.175] 26 September 1542.
Parishes of St. John in Walbrook and St. Mary Bothaw. Variance between Ralph Robynson, draper, pl., and Agnes Partriche, widow, def., both parties being tenants to the dean and chapter of the cathedral church of St. Paul's by leases for terms of years in two tenements set adjoining together in Candlewick Street, one being in the parish of St. John in Walbrook and the other in the parish of St. Mary Bothaw. The viewers say that pl. has a chamber in the upper part of his house toward the N part, under which chamber def. has a chamber and under that a house for wood and coal and a withdraught at the ground. The chamber and woodhouse was divided as it is now many years before the making of the leases and so has continued. Either of the parties ought of right to have, hold, and enjoy his own house with the appurtenances according to the purport, tenor, and effect of the said leases. Without *etc.*
Endorsed: . . . 10 34 Hen[rici] 8

178. [B.174] 21 November 1542.
Parish of St. John Zachary. Variance between the master and wardens of the Goldsmiths and the master and wardens of the Haberdashers, concerning certain nuisances of buildings. The view is with assent and consent of both parties. The viewers say that the NE corner principal post of the house there belonging to the Goldsmiths overhangs $4\frac{1}{2}$ in. eastward against a new counting house lately set up by the tenant of the Haberdashers; it ought to be withdrawn and set upright. From the said

NE corner post southward to the W side of a NW corner principal post of the first storey of the Haberdashers' house, [the Goldsmiths' house] is in length 11 ft. 6½ in; it ought to be line right and plumb between the two principal posts. So being line right, the end of the binding joist (bynding juest) of the counting house, which is hung (hanged) with a stirrup of iron against the principal post that stands upon the jetty of the Haberdashers' house, overhangs the rasen of the Goldsmiths' house at the S end by 2 in. and ought of right to be withdrawn eastward. All which nuisances *etc.*, without *etc.*

179. [B.173] 30 April 1543.
[No parish given]. Variance between Stephen Nott, fishmonger, pl., and William Revell, carpenter, def., concerning a certain brick wall which def. has lately caused to be made and set against the E side of Paul's Wharf, 'which wall the said iiii viewers by all their discretions have not only viewed, serched and seen but also have herd, examined and well considered the depositions, evidence and testymony of iiii old inhabitantes and dwellers thereby, that is to say, Robert Kytchyn, dyer; John Edsall, Richard Fetford, and Arthure Purseys, watermen, being sworne as afore a judge to give true evidence unto the said viewers in that behalf.' The viewers say that the brick wall is set and standing upon the old foundation of certain old houses lately belonging to the late dissolved monastery of St. Bartholomew in West Smithfield of London and that the wall is not encroached upon Paul's Wharf save only a little buttress of brick which stands without the wall westward on the ground of the wharf and which ought to be taken away by def. And a door made in the wall for a withdraught ought to be stopped and closed up by def. Furthermore, pl. ought to have 22 ft. 3 in. upon the wharf, as appears by his lease from the dean and chapter of [St.] Paul's, from the water of Thames against the S stretching northward by the W side of the brick wall to a strike made upon the wall by the viewers. All which premises *etc.*. without *etc.*

180. [B.172] 15 July 1543.
Parish of St. Sepulchre in the suburbs of London. Variance between the parson and churchwardens of the parish church of St. Alban in Wood Street, pls., and William Collyns, carpenter, def., concerning certain ground for a wall or defence to be made and set within the tenement called 'the George'. The viewers say that [the ground goes] from the king's highway leading from Holborn Cross to Holborn Bridge against the S, stretching northward 24 ft. 5 in. to the NE corner of a principal post of pls. there; and from the same post stretching more northward 12 ft. 9½ in. to the NE corner of another principal post of pls. line right and plumb; and from the latter principal post stretching more northward 46 ft. 9 in. to another NE corner principal post of pls., line right and plumb; and from the last NE corner post stretching more northward 23 ft. to the SE corner principal post of a house or stable. The same house or stable is 12 ft. 8 in. in wideness from the said S principal post thereof, stretching northward against the garden ground belonging to def. line right and plumb as aforelimited. Without *etc.*

181. [B.176] 17 October 1543.
Parish of St. Martin Orgar. Variance between John Gardener, fish-monger, pl., and the parson and churchwardens of St. James Garlick-hithe, defs., concerning a nuisance of the side of an old house. The viewers say that the SW corner principal post of the old house, which belongs to defs., overhangs the ground of pl. 6¾ in. southward. Stretching from the same post 17 ft. 6 in. to a SE corner principal post of the old house, there the SE corner post overhangs the ground of pl. 6¼ in. southward. Defs. ought of right at their costs and charges to set the two posts and all the wall [between them] upright, line right and plumb from post to post all the length. Furthermore, if defs. will not set their house upright in form aforesaid, then it shall be lawful to pl. to cut down as much of the said old house as overhangs his ground. Which nuisance *etc.*, without *etc.*

182. [B.177] 12 March 1544.
Parish of St. Margaret in Bridge Street. Variance between Roger Welles and Richard Medilton, churchwardens of the church, and the par-ishioners of the same church, pls., and Sir Richard Archer, clerk, parson of the said church, def., concerning a certain gutter of lead with certain timberwork and other charges thereto belonging. The viewers say that the gutter is partible between the parties from the rood-loft of the church stretching eastward 39 ft. 9 in. to the E end of the quire of the church. The gutter, with the assent of the parson, was but lately new made at the sole charge of the parishioners. Wherefore the parson ought of right to recompense them for one-half of the same charge. And the parson ought to bear one-half of the charges of repairing or renewing the leads of the vestry there, as far as the water of the gutter falls upon the leads and as often as need shall require. Furthermore, all the procession way and the ground between that way and the churchyard ought of right to belong to the churchyard as parcel of the same, for burials, reserving only a right of way for the parson to and from his parsonage and mansion there, being over the said procession way. All which premises *etc.*, without *etc.*
Endorsed: 18 March A[nno] 35 H[enrici] 8 insert[ur] iste visus quo die sol[utum] feod[um] co[mmun]is cl[er]ici

183. [B.178] 20 March 1544.
Parish of St. John Zachary. Variance between the parson and church-wardens of the church, pls., and the master and wardens of the Waxchan-dlers, defs., concerning a certain nuisance. The view is by assent and consent and also at the request of both parties. The viewers find a certain void ground, now 17 ft. 8 in. in length and which was 7 ft. 3 in. in breadth or wideness, which void ground by force of a view [?6] made in the first year of the reign of our same sovereign lord the king that now is, was reserved and kept unbuilt for saving of lights on the E part of the houses and tenements of both parties. Notwithstanding, defs. since that time have built and made a brick wall from the ground up under the jetty of pls.' tenement and have stopped the lights of the said tenement contrary to the force and effect of the former view. The wall ought of right to be

taken down and made open as it was before, according to the tenor of the said view. Furthermore, defs. have encroached and made certain ovens to their kitchen upon the ground and vault of a withdraught belonging to pls., from the kitchen against the N stretching southward 6 ft. 11 in., which ovens and encroachments ought of right to be taken away as well as the said brick wall, and ought not to stand and remain there without the assent, will, and agreement of pls.

Endorsed: 20 Marcii A[nno] h[enrici] 8 debet feod[um] v s. infert[ur] iste visus

184. [B.179] 22 March 1544.

Parish of St. Mildred in the Poultry. Variance between William Wyat, grocer, pl., and Robert Austen, grocer, def., concerning a certain cellar. The viewers find that the cellar lies under the tenement of pl. where Thomas Bolt, grocer, now dwells as tenant to pl. The cellar is 13 ft. in breadth or wideness within the walls at its E end against the lane called Coneyhope Lane. Stretching from the lane westward 13 ft. 6 in., it is 8 ft. in wideness within the walls. The cellar has a door and stairs out of the said lane to go into the cellar, which in time past were used and occupied, as plainly appears. 'And by all that the said viewers can fynde or perceyve by all the Inquisition and serche that they can make in that behalf they saye upon their consciences that aswell the said Celer by all the lenght and brede thereof aforesaid with the thykness of the walles of the same, as also the said tenement thereupon now standing, ys all within the said parishe of Saint Mildrede and belongeth hooly unto the said playntif.' Without *etc.*

Endorsed: A[nno] 35 Joh[ann]es Hamond impor . . . visu 28.5 copia deliber . . . infranominat[o] Thome Bolt, qui soluit feod[um] co[mmun]is clerici quod . . . videlicet ultimo d[i]cti mens[is] recepit

185. [B.180][1] 28 April 1544.

[Parish illegible. ?St. Clement Eastcheap; see **98**]. Variance between Edward Cornwalys, gentleman, and Alice his wife, pls., and John Glascok, def., concerning two tenements which John Turpyn, carpenter, and Elizabeth his wife, late wife and executrix of the testament and last will of [Thomas Sympson], do hold by virtue of two several leases under the convent seal of the late dissolved monastery of Stratford Langthorne in [the county of Essex] . . . of the said tenements called 'Abbotts Inne' for the term of life of the said Thomas and Elizabeth and the longer liver of them, and the . . . which two tenements and their appurtenances the said parties lately have severally purchased in fee simple to them and their heirs of the king's [majesty] . . . [the said def. having purchased] the said tenement called 'Abbotts Inn' and the said pl. the other tenement thereto adjoining, which tenements the said [iiii viewers have seen,] searched, measured, separated and indifferently divided between the parties, to either of them his own right of and in the same. And thereupon they say that pls.' tenement stands by the king's highway of St. Clement's Lane afore[said] . . . going into the other tenement called 'Abbotts Inne' and is 21 ft. 10 in. in breadth by the lane against the W from the middle of the . . .

upon the S . . . gate toward the N stretching southward. And it is 11 ft. 9½ in. in breadth above and over the said gate from . . . S stretching northward. And it is 55 ft. 2 in. in length over the gate and entry from the [?]lane eastward to the] SE corner principal post standing there from the ground upward. The which length . . . is built with solars and chambers over the gate and entry and is parcel of pls.' tenement. And the same [tenement] . . . is in length from the said lane stretching eastward to the E part of an old stone wall there belonging to the said tenement of the foresaid . . . stretching more eastward on the S side of the said solars and chambers to the said SE corner principal post . . . ought of right so to stand and continue to the said tenement of pls. as they were first built and set up . . . where the said Thomas Sympson in his lifetime after the taking of the lease did break the wall at the . . . making a door going [out] of a stair there belonging to the tenement called 'Abbottes Inne' has taken in [?a chamber of the tenement] . . . called 'Abbottes Inne'. The same chamber belongs to the said tenementof the said [?def.] . . . [Thomas Sympson] also in his life made out a little gallery at the end of the said old stone wall a 'stole' room to . . . the ground belonging to the said tenement of the foresaid pls.

Endorsed: . . . 23 John Hamond protulit . . . a[nno] pred[?icto] copia . . . quer[entibus] . . . sol[utum] feod[um] co[mmun]is clerici . . .

1. Much of the certificate is illegible.

186. [B.181] 28 April 1544.
Parish of All Hallows the Little in Thames Street. Variance between the Rt. Rev. Father in God Cuthbert [Tunstal], Bishop of Durham, and Master William Latymer, clerk, parson of All Hallows the Little, concerning an old vault of stone under the quire of the church. The view is by assent and agreement of both parties. The viewers say that the vault and foundation of the quire is 26 ft. in length from the king's highway of Thames Street stretching southward and 19 ft. 6 in. in breadth from the gate going into the great place of the Bishop there called Coldharborow stretching eastward. The vault and foundation, as well the walls as the roof, is so greatly in ruin and decay that it must all be taken down and new made all the length and breadth, at the cost of the Bishop and his successors as owners of the tenement under the quire. And the parson and his successors must bear all the charges of reparations of the quire from the roof of the vault upwards from time to time as need shall require.

187. [B.182] 6 May 1544.
Parish of St. Botolph without Bishopsgate. Variance between William Parker, pl., and John Stryngfelowe, def., concerning a certain brick wall. The viewers say that the brick wall at the W end against the king's highway of Bishopsgate Street is set and made under the house or tenement of pl. on pl.'s ground. Stretching eastward from the street, the wall is 153 ft. 7 in. in length and 13½ in. in thickness above the water table. The brick wall, by all its length and thickness, stands on grounds of pl. except the water table, which stands southward 2 in. on the ground of def. The 2 in. ought to be withdrawn by pl. and not to stand and continue

without the assent and will of def. The brick wall by all its length and breadth belongs to pl. and ought to be made, repaired, and kept from time to time as need requires at his cost and charges. Without *etc*. *Endorsement faded and illegible.*

188. [B.183] 18 September 1544.
Parish of St. Margaret in Bridge Street. Variance between John Core, grocer, pl., and the master and fellows of Pembroke Hall in Cambridge, defs., concerning a certain old stone wall, parcel of the great messuage or tenement called 'the Blak Bell'; the wall stands on the S side of the tenement and belongs to def. The viewers say that the stone wall is 36 ft. 9 in. in length from the SE corner stretching westward to the SW corner of a wall which, stretching from the W end thereof eastward, is 14 ft. There the [stone] wall overhangs the ground of pl. southward 11 in. from the upper part of the wall to the nether part. The wall so overhanging and likely to fall to the great damage and peril of men's lives ought of right to be taken down and made line right and plumb from end to end, E to W, by all the length aforesaid at cost and charges of def. Without *etc*.

189. [B.184] 9 December 1544.
Parish of St. Gabriel Fenchurch. Variance between William Wever, mercer, pl., and Margaret Williamson, widow, late wife of Thomas Williamson, carpenter, deceased, def., concerning reparations needful to be done and made upon certain tenements with their appurtenances. The late Thomas Williamson in his lifetime held all the said tenements with their appurtenances of the king's majesty by indenture for a term of a years with the obligation to repair the same, as appears by the indenture. Pl. has lately purchased the tenements with appurtenances of the king's majesty. The viewers say that, first, they find that the tenements that William Somerland, grocer, and Miles Skynner, cordwainer, dwell in need to be ripped because the roofs are sunken and it rains in at every time of rain. Also [?in] the gable end of the house over the entry going into Williamson's house and [?in] his house there within the entry a girder of timber is broken and a chimney sore decayed and ready to fall down. Also, from that to St. Margaret Pattens Lane, and within the lane in Robert Walter's house, there is a withdraught broken into the cellar and diverse joists of the cellar and of the kitchen floor are rotten and falling down. And the alley called Poppinjay Alley lacks tiling and daubing. And all the tenements need tiling and to be ripped and the broken and sunken roofs to be new framed and new rafters to be laid in. So there lacks carpentry work, brickwork, tiling, daubing and lead gutters (which are broken) on and upon all the tenements to be substantially repaired in all things where needed. It will cost all manner of charges by the estimation of the viewers ... the sum of 80 pounds sterling.
Endorsed: ... 5 February a[nno] regis henrici 8 xxxvi ... visus ... feod[um] co[mmun]is clerici pro ...

190. [B.185] 10 January 1545.
Parish of St. Dunstan in the West. Variance between William Jamys, pl.,

and Henry Lee, def., concerning certain houses and tenements with appurtenances which the said two parties lately severally purchased and bought of the king's majesty. The viewers say that the tenement where pl. dwells is built and set on the little gate leading down toward the late Whitefriars Church and adjoins eastward on the tenement of def. The E part of pl.'s house stands on a stone wall which bears it and belongs to pl. down to the foundation, line right and plumb. In the wall, there come down two tewels (towells) of two withdraughts which serve the two houses of easement for the houses of both pl. and def. which ought of right so to continue as has been divided and used of long time past and ought to be repaired and cleansed as needed at the costs and charges of both parties. Also, from the NE corner of the stone wall and also from the NE corner of the principal post of pl.'s tenement stretching westward against the king's highway of Fleet Street to the tenement there of St. James Garlickhithe is 43 ft., which belongs wholly to pl., reserving always the way of the said little gate leading to the said late friars' church. The tenement of pl. is 5 score 13 ft. 6 in. in length from the king's highway of Fleet Street against the N stretching southward on the W side of the little gate to a house or chamber there belonging to Serjeants Inn. Furthermore, pl. ought of right to have the easement, commodities, and profits of the ground within the little gate on the E side of the way adjoining to the tenement of def., reserving always the said way as far as the tenement is built over the gate and way. All which premises *etc.* without *etc.*

191. [B.186] 30 January 1545.
Parish of St. Dunstan in the West. Variance between the parson and churchwardens of the parish church of St. Christopher of London, pls., and John Croke, gentleman, def., concerning certain ground and houses. The viewers say that the ground and houses there belonging to pls. [together] are 13 yds. or 39 ft. and $7\frac{1}{2}$ in. in breadth against the king's highway of Fleet Street toward the S from E to W. And [they are] 39 yds. or 5 score 17 ft. in length from Fleet Street stretching northward to the garden ground of def. against the N. And there the ground and building of pl. is 12 yds. or 36 ft. in breadth from E to W. Also, def. ought of right to turn the water of his gutters that falls on ground of pls., to their great annoyance, and either party to bear their own water to fall into their own ground. Without *etc.*

192. [B.187][1] 26 June 1545.
John Hilmer, William Walker, Henry Pesemede, and John Russell, freemasons and carpenters, viewers.
Parish of St. Giles without Cripplegate. Variance between the masters and brethren of the brotherhood of Our Lady and St. Giles and Richard Cull, grocer, of the same parish, concerning a certain pale or lawful fence. The view is by consent of both parties. The viewers say that from the SE corner post of a soaphouse belonging to Richard Cull stretching eastward to the NW corner post of a house of the parson and churchwardens of St. Giles is [?70] ft. 6 in. in length. The pale or fence ought to be made line

right and plumb between those limits or corner posts at the sole costs and charges of Richard Cull. It shall be lawful for Richard Cull, his executors and assigns, at all times to have and enjoy the brick sluice for conveying water as it now goes; he shall have authority and licence of the masters of the brotherhood of St. Giles to break [and] dig within their grounds at all times when need shall be for repairing the sluice belonging to him. Without *etc.*

Endorsed: 4 Julii a[nno] 37 H[enrici] 8 . . . inser . . . iste visus et sol[?utum] feod[um] . . . clerici

1. The handwriting of this certificate differs from that of preceding certificates.

193. [B.187A] 18 September 1545.
Parish of St. Bottalles without Aldgate. [No variance stated]. The viewers have been charged to view and oversee a little parcel or plot of garden ground lying on the N part of the yard, or back side, of an inn called 'the III Nones' without Aldgate, which inn one John Fyrmynger has lately bought with a great garden ground lying upon the back side toward the N and with appurtenances thereto belonging. The little plot of ground is now in tenure of one John Margetson. The viewers have measured it; they say it is 10 ft. in breadth from the N side of an old pale stretching northward. The ground has been staked out by the viewers from W to E. They say by all their discretions as it appears in an old indenture that the ground is parcel and part of the appurtenances of the purchase and ought of right to belong to John Fyrmynger. Without *etc.*

Endorsed: 29.12 a[nno] 37 henr[ici] 8 infert[ur] iste visus per . . . feod[um] co[mmun]i[s] clerici . . . 2 s

194. [B.188] 18 September 1545.
Parish of St. Giles without Cripplegate. Variance between the wardens of the Brotherhood of the [Parish] Clerks within London and John Core, grocer, def., concerning the making of a pale or lawful fence between the garden ground there belonging to pls. against the E and the garden ground belonging to def. against the W. The viewers say that from the S side of a little house or jakes of def. against the N stretching southward to a brick wall there against the S, the fence between the parties is 87 ft. 10 in. in length. It ought of right to be made and repaired at equal charges and expenses of both parties indifferently between them. Without *etc.*

Subscribed: . . . Octobrii A[nn]o 37 h[enrici] 8 rec[eptum] hunc vis[um] et sol[utum] feod[um] inde etc.

195. [B.189] 3 January 1546.
Parish of St. Dunstan in the West. Variance between John Hornebye, pl., and Henry Taylor, def., concerning certain reparations which def. ought of right to do in a tenement called 'the Sygne of the Dolfyn', 'in Fletestrete before the Temple Barre'. The viewers say there is much need of repairs as in plating in sundry places and boarding of floors, rasens, posts, and quarters of timber, which are decayed. Also, the tenement needs to be ripped and newly lathed and tiled throughout. Because it needs mending of chimneys and hearths, underpinning of plates with brick, and lathing and daubing of walls, the house is now in decay.

Endorsed: feod[um] co[mmun]is clerici [?6 Maii] a[nno] 38 H[enrici] 8

196. [B.190] 29 January 1546.
Parish of St. Mildred in the Poultry. Variance between John Myller, pl., and David Wylkynson, def., concerning a principal partition set between pl. on the E and def. on the W. The viewers say that the partition is partible and pl. ought of right to have for his part 2 in. eastward of the principal post of the partition, which 2 in. ought of right to belong to pl.'s house or tenement from the king's highway of the Poultry against the N stretching southward by all the breadth of the tenement, that is, from the upper part of the door and entry that leads the way into the dwelling house where William Brothers dwells, up to the upper part of the rasen belonging to pl.[1] Without *etc.*
Endorsed: 20 May A[nno] h[enrici] 8

1. The certificate lacks the formula statement that the viewers have viewed and seen etc.

197. [B.191] 8 March 1546.
Parish of St. Giles without Cripplegate. Variance between John Tyller and Nicholas Lasye, pls., and the parson and churchwardens of All Hallows Bridge [*sic*] Street, concerning a pale or lawful fence and cleansing the common sewer betwen them. The viewers say that [the pale] ought of right to be made from the S side of a brick sluice against the E stretching W to the S side of a stake set by the viewers and from the stake more westward to a brick sluice which is the head of the sewer from Moor Lane; it ought to be made line right and plumb at costs and charges of defs. 'And furthermore they saye that the playntif shall not reyer the Erthe whereby the partie defendant shall be hurte bye. And thus to be used or continued' without *etc.*[1]

1. The formula varies throughout this certificate and there are errors in syntax.

198. [B.192] 4 May 1546.
To the right honorable lorde Maire of the Citie of london and his right Worshipfull Brethern thaldermen of the same.
Shewen unto your good lordship and discrete Wisedoms the iiii[th] day of Maye in the xxxviii[th] yere of the reign of our soveraign lorde Kinge Henry the Eight John Hylmer, Willm Walker, John Russell, and Gilbert Burffame, the iiii maisters of Fremasons and Carpenters, Viewers indifferent sworne to the said Citie, that where as thei were late charged by your honorable commaundement to viewe and oversee a variaunce in the parishe of the Holy Trynytye [the Less] Betwene Robert Kynge, fysshemonger, plaintif, of the one partie and the parson and churche wardeins of the churche, defendauntes, of the other partie, Whiche variaunce is for an olde stone wall whiche stondethe upon the West side of the grounde belonginge to the partie playntif, the whiche grounde is in bredthe there againste the kinges highe waye called Knight Ryder strete againste the southe from a southwest principall post there of a house belonginge to the Chamber of london againste the Est stretchynge westwarde xxvii foote ii ynches of assise to the southest corner of an olde stone wall belonginge to the said defendant and stretchynge fro the said

81

southest corner of the stone wall fro the kinges highe waye stretchynge northwarde xxii foote x ynches of assise. And the grounde there belonging to the partie plaintif is in Bredthe betwene the West side of the house there belonginge to the chamber aforesaid & the stonewall there belonginge to the tenement belonginge to the trynytye churche aforesaid xxvii foote & v ynches of assise. And the said grounde of the partie playntif stretchynge more Northwarde fro the said xxii foote x ynches to the hole lenght of the grounde belonginge to the partie plaintif lix foote vii ynches of assise. The whiche foresaid grounde belonginge to the partie playntif oweth of right to be lyne right & plombe betwene the lemettes aforesaid, without there be any evydence to shewe the contrarye.[1]

1. The certificate lacks the formula statement that the viewers have viewed and seen etc.

199. [B.193] 14 May 1546.
Parish of St. Bottalls without Bishopsgate. Variance between Lady Katharine Adams and Christopher Campyon concerning the making of a lawful pale. The view is by assent of both parties. The viewers say that the pale shall be made of timber and board like the pale that Campyon has made on his ground on the N side of the way there. It shall be set upon the garden ground of Lady Adams stretching eastward to the common way, being 9 ft. broad and . . . score and 8 ft. in length. Campyon shall new make and set up the pale at his own proper costs and charges before the feast of St. James the Apostle next coming [July 25], and shall set the posts and rails with nails' point toward the ground of Lady Adams. Lady Adams, her heirs, and successors shall make and repair the said pale forevermore after the making as aforesaid. Without *etc.*
Endorsed: 20 May A[nno] 38 . . . iste visus et sol[utum] feod[um] co[mmunis] clerici

200. [B.194] 5 July 1546.
Parish of St. Faith in Paul's Churchyard. Variance between Miles Partrich, gentleman, pl., and Stephen Mason, vintner, def., concerning a cellar. The viewers say that pl. ought of right to have the cellar there now, which is on the ground of the 'Great Stepell' [of St. Paul's]. And def. has and must have a little yard with a stair going up to his house, which he holds by lease of the dean and chapter of St. Paul's. Also, there is a lead gutter that must be made on the house of def. Pl. shall lay the lead, with pipes down to the ground, which belong to the gutter, at his cost and charges. Def. shall find all other charges belonging to tiling and carpentry, upon recompense of the carriage of the old lead away by pl. Without *etc.*[1]
Endorsed: . . . fuit istud Recordum et . . . co[mmun]is clerici 5 s.

1. The certificate lacks the formula statement that the viewers have viewed and seen etc.

201. [B.195] 15 July 1546.
Parish of St. Toulles [Olave] in Hart Street beside the Crossed Friars. Variance between Edmund Smyth, pl., and Thomas Pyke, def., concerning bearing of waters between the parties. The viewers say that pl. ought of right to make a fillet gutter to bear the water that falls from the S side of

certain houses and tenements belonging to him, that is, from the brewhouse called 'the Cock' against the E stretching westward 70 ft., at his own proper costs and charges. One half of the lead there now, together with the tiles that belonged to pl., is to be delivered by def. [to pl.]. Furthermore, there is the N side of a house of def. stretching from Sydon Lane[1] against the W stretching eastward 15 ft.; [def.] ought of right to bear the water of the said house with a fillet gutter of lead all its length at his own proper costs and charges. Without *etc.*[2]

1. Seething Lane.
2. The certificate lacks the formula statement that the viewers have viewed and seen etc.

202. [B.196][1] 1 September 1546.
Parish of St. Peter the Poor 'besyde the late Freyers Augustynes of London'. Variance between Thomas Carmardon, pl., and George [?Asshe], def., concerning two jakes or withdraughts adjoining and set together between the parties. The viewers say that from the king's highway there against the S stretching northward to the NE corner post and plate of pl.'s old house there [the distance] is 39 ft. 6 in. Against the E side of pl.'s ... there are two jakes adjoining together, one of pl. [and one of def.], which jakes have an old stone wall between them ... falling down. The old wall ought of right [to be] new made 2 ft. thick and set in the same place that it now stands in ... at costs and charges of both parties ... and that the parties ... cleanse and carry away the ordure or dung that is within his ground ... may be made for the easement of both parties. Without *etc.*
Endorsed: ... Septembrii A[nn]o 38 Hen[rici] 8 infert[ur] his visus v s.

1. The certificate is in very poor condition, particularly toward the bottom. It lacks the formula statement that the viewers have viewed and seen etc.

203. [B.197]
[The entire certificate is illegible; no visible endorsement.]

204. [B.198] 14 September 1546.
Parish of St. Michael in Cornhill. Variance between Richard Tate, Esquire, pl., and Edward ... def., concerning the repair of a great tenement brewhouse called 'the Skomer' in Birchin Lane, and two small tenements with appurtenances, which repairs the viewers have seen and say that there lacks a ... plate at the street door within the said house ... repaired. Also there is a groundsill of the same decayed ... in the malt loft and in other places ... decayed, with dauplyng [*sic*] of the walls of the same in diverse places. Also, there is a rafter foot decayed and the gutter of lead and the ... the same gutter within the said tenement .... further tenement the floor of the upper garret ... with pointing, tiling, and daubing of the same. Which reparations aforesaid within the said house, to be sufficiently done before the Feast of St. Michael the Archangel [September 29] next coming, will cost £6 8*s.* 4*d.* as estimated ... reparations the said def. ought to do according to his lease.

See also **281** below.

205. [B.199] 16 October 1546.
Parish of St. Martin in the Vintry.
[The plaintiff is John Maw . . . ; apart from his name and some common-
form, the certificate and endorsement are illegible.]

CORPORATION OF LONDON
RECORDS OFFICE MISC. MSS.
BOX 91 [C]
(Loose Certificates Filed *Temp.* Edward VI and Mary)

206. [C.1] 25 February 1547.
To the right honorable lorde the Mayre of the Citie of London and his
ryght worshipfull Brethern thaldermen of the same.
Shewen unto your good Lordship and discrete Wisedoms the xxv[th] daye
of Februarye in the fyrste yere of the reign of our soveraign Lorde King
Edward the Sixthe John Hylmer, Wyllm Walker, John Russell, and
Gylbert Burffaine, the iiii maisters of Fremasons and Carpenters, viewers
indifferent sworne to the said Citie, that where as they were late charged
by your honorable commaundement to viewe and oversee a variance in
the parishe of Crystes Churche within Newgate of London betwene John
Vandernott, Phisicyon, playntif, of the one partye And Thomas Eyre,
defendaunt, of the other partie, Whiche variance is for the Reparying of
the Ten[emen]t where the said Thomas Eyre dwelleth and holdethe by
lease. Thereupon the said viewers say the said John Vandernott beinge
Owner and Landlorde owethe of right to make newe the plates of the said
house agaynste the Este partie therof, the whiche be sore dekeayed and
sonken and by reason thereof there is a Chymney in the ketchyn whiche is
sore dekeyed and sonken whiche owethe of right to be reparyd by the said
John Vandernott. And the forsaid Thomas Eyre owethe of right to
repayre the walles with quarters, Lathe, Lome and Nayles after the newe
playtynge of the said house. Also with other thinges as wyndowes and
walles above in the Seconde Story that be dekeyed. Also there is a jakes
whiche is a Noysaunce to the said tenement whiche is partable betwene
the said partie defendaunt and one Maister Norres, Gentilman usher, and
oweth of righte to be clensed and repayred at the costes and Charges of
bothe the said parties. Also the Southesyde of the tenement is to be
repayred with tilynge and owethe to be done by the said Thomas Eyre.
Also the said Thomas Eyre hathe ii other tenementes by lease wherein
there is a ... whiche ys paved with brycke sore dekeyed for Lak of
pavynge with stone and rottethe the [?front] of the house. And also the
sayd house hathe nede of tylynge and daubynge and mendynge of the S
... and pype of lede with other reparacions nedefull. Also there is
reparacion to be done in the tenement there belonginge to John
Vandernott nowe in tenure of Wyllm Hasyllwood by lease, the whiche
reparacion for the pryncypalles owethe of right to be done by the said
John Vandernott with newe plates under a shed of a Woodhouse
towardes the West of the same house and the reparynge of certayn
Chymneys where nede requireth. And the said Wyllm ought to repayre

the same houses as well with quarters of tymber, Pentyses, Lathe, Nayles daubyng, tyles and tylynge, As with all manner of workmanship appertayninge to his lease. Whiche is much dekeyed. Also there is an open galarye paved with stone whiche is sore dekeyed bothe tymber stone, and lede and lyke to fall Whiche oweth of right to be repayred at the costes [and charges of] the said Wyllm Hasylwoode, all savynge the princypall.

See also **244** below.

207. [C.2] 1 April 1547.
Parish of St. Benet Gracechurch. Variance between Richard Ivatt, grocer, pl., and Patrick Cornysshe, fruiterer, def., concerning the repairing of the great tenement or inn called 'the Taberd' in Gracechurch Street (Graceyoustrete) with appurtenances belonging to it. The view is at the desire of pl. The viewers say that pl., lord and owner of the tenement, is bound to repair and maintain all principals of the tenement with appurtenances at his costs and charges when need requires. Def., tenant, is bound to all other reparations, that is to say stone walls, bricks, or tiling, where needed: stone, bricks, tile, lathe, nails, and workmanship. Def. is also responsible for carpentry work: timber, boards for floors, quarter-boards, and quarters for pentices which are broken, planks for the stable's doors or windows, and workmanship. Also for daubing the walls, lathe, for nails, loam, and quarters where the walls are broken, both stuff and workmanship. Also for gutters of lead where needed, and glass windows. Also for cleaning the sieges and withdraughts and for maintaining the tenement with appurtenances from wind and rain, wind tight and water tight. The viewers say that the repairs to make the tenement tenantable will cost £13 6*s*. Def. shall and ought to do all the aforesaid reparations before [the Feast] of St. Bartholomew the Apostle [24 August] next coming without any further [?delay].

208. [C.3] 18 April 1547.
Parish of St. Lawrence in the Jewry. Variance between Richard Rede, salter, and Mistress Margaret Parke, widow, concerning an old stone wall and other edifications or buildings there between the parties. The view is by assent of both parties. The viewers say that there are two tenements with appurtenances belonging to Master Rede, 25 ft. in breadth against the N and against the king's highway now called Cateaton (Catton) Street, from the NW corner post of the house adjoining the little alley there stretching eastward to the NE corner post of the house of Rede. From the NE corner post, they stretch southward 16 ft. 4 in. There the houses and ground belonging to Rede are 24 ft. 6 in. in breadth from the said alley against the W stretching eastward. Stretching further southward from the 16 ft. 4 in., which is [?a total of] 34 ft. 8 in., the houses and grounds belonging to Rede are in breadth 24 ft. 5 in. from the alley against the W stretching eastward. They ought of right to be line right and plumb from place to place and limit to limit as aforesaid and according to the evidence or deed of Rede. Without *etc.*
Endorsed: . . . visus . . .

86

(*in a later hand*): Visus anno primo 2° et tertio E[dwardi] 6

209. [C.4] 18 April 1547.
Parish of St. Ellen without Bishopsgate. Variance between Jane Hawt, gentlewoman and widow, and James Josken, gentleman, concerning the repairing and cleansing of a withdraught or jakes partible between them. The view is by assent of both parties. The viewers say that Mistress Hawt ought of right to have a space 7 ft. in length and 4 ft. in breadth at the ground over the withdraught or jakes, plumb upright to the floor of the first storey. The jakes is partible between the parties. The jakes and its floor are fallen and broken and ought to be repaired and cleansed. Mistress Hawt has but one stool of easement to fall into the cistern of the jakes and Mr. Josskyn has three; the viewers say he ought of right to pay for three parts of the charges for the cleansing of the cistern and jakes and she ought of right to pay and bear one part. Moreover, he ought of right to bear and pay all the charges and costs for timber, boards, and workmanship of the floor that has fallen down, for as much as is within his own ground. Without *etc.*

210. [C.5] 13 August 1547.
Parish of All Hallows in Honey Lane. Variance between John Butler, pl., and John Atkynson, def., concerning the setting up of a little frame of timber. The viewers say that def. has set up the little frame, 18 ft. long and 7 ft. high, upon his own ground. It stands on the frame of the house of def. The viewers say that every owner may lawfully build upon his own ground line right and plumb. The lead gutter there between the parties is a partible gutter, for conveyance of the water of both their houses, and so ought of right to continue hereafter for easement of both parties.
Endorsed: 4/12/a[nn]° primo E[dwardi] 6

211. [C.6]¹ 10 October 1547.
Parish of St. Peters beside the late Austin Friars. Variance between Mr. Chalenger, gentleman, pl., and John A'Borowe, def., concerning the [?despoiling] and taking away timber of the house wherein def. now dwells. The viewers say that def. has spoiled and taken down . . . W side of the old hall of the house, which was 27 ft. in length and 6 ft. [?in breadth] and 8 ft. in height to the rasen. The principal posts of the old hall . . . the W side 5 in. thereof is cut away. There are taken away from the hall [?certain] brases of old timber, which is a great decay to the hall. There was a timber porch 7 ft. square before the hall door, which has been taken away. Def. has taken away a large bay window of timber, and glazed, that appertains . . . schedule annexed to certain indentures thereof made. As more at length is [?set out] in the said indentures.

1. The certificate is badly blurred, with passages illegible even under ultraviolet light.

212. [C.7] 11 October 1547.
Parish of St. Leonard's in Eastcheap. Variance between Thomas Kendall, pl., and William Kynge, butcher, def., concerning a principal post of the entry of pl. on the W side coming into the entry of the

tenement [?called] 'the Smyte', Eastcheap, which post is 9 in. of size and is partible between the parties. It bears one leaf of the door of the entry of 'the Smyte'. There is also a door of def., coming out of his shop into the entry of pl., which ought of right to be stopped up and to have no recourse or way into the entry of pl. nor to diminish (mynysshe) the entry. And def. ought to enjoy all he has above the entry. There is also a variance between pl. and Anthony Cowley, grocer, def., for the bearing of the water of the side of a house of def. [Cowley] which is 11 ft. 10 in. in length. The water falls into the gutter of pl. and ought of right to be borne with a fillet gutter of def. Or else def. to agree with pl. for bearing the water. 'All which foresaid variance oweth of right to be reformed as is aforesaid without there be any evidence or specialty to shew the contrary.'

213. [C.8] 12 October 1547.
Parish of St. Botolph without Aldrichgate. Variance between William Carter, barbersurgeon, pl., and the wardens of the Trinity Brotherhood within the parish of St. Botolph, defs., concerning the making of a pale or lawful fence between the gardens or grounds of the parties lying in the parish. The ground where the pale or fence should stand is 52 ft. in length from Pylkyngton's place against the S stretching northward to the tenement called 'the Wollsacke'. It ought of right to be made line right and plumb between two stakes there set indifferently between the said grounds by the viewers, whereas there is now no indifferent fence. The pale or fence ought of right to be made at costs and charges of pl. against the W part toward the ground of defs. that is called 'the Wollsacke'. The rails and points of the nails ought to be turned to pl. Without *etc.*

214. [C.9] 14 October 1547.
Parish of St. Gabriel Fenchurch. Variance between Iwold Docwraye, pl., and John Haynes, def. The viewers say that of late times past def. or his predecessors have encroached eastward beyond the frame of def. within the ground of pl. and made a room for a privy or jakes. The encroachment is 11 ft. 6 in. in length from N to S and is 5 ft. in breadth within the walls. The encroachment, they say by all their discretion, ought of right to be withdrawn by def. so that pl. may have and enjoy his own ground as aforemeasured. Without *etc.* Also, the viewers have viewed and seen at ... desire of pl. the reparation which is needed to be done in and upon the ... tenement there in the tenure and holding, by lease, of Evered Shepperd; the tenant is bound by lease to all manner of reparations. They say there is needed a ... plate of timber 10 ft. in length at the N end of the kitchen and another plate 7 ft. long at the ... side of the kitchen. And there is a principal post at the S ... post of the kitchen which is sore decayed and perished by water falling from a [?gutter]. The corve of the well needs to be repaired. Also, the house that is ... needs repairing, both carpentry and tiling.

215. [C.10] 18 October 1547.
Parish of St. Michael in Cornhill. Variance between Bryan Calverley, pl., and John Camewe, Thomas Sentalbye, John Goodolphyn, and one Mr.

Camewes, defs., concerning a house stretching 16 ft. 6 in. in length northward from a house of defs. and 10 ft. 10 in. in width from the W of the house of defs. and stretching E abutting the house where Thomas Baker now dwells. The viewers say that of right pl. ought to have the whole house and frame of 16 ft. 6 in. in length and 10 ft. 10 in. in width, because it is all one frame. 'Except there may be any evidence or specialty to shew the contrary.'

Subscribed: Sol[utum] Feod[um]

216. [C.11][1] 21 October 1547.
Parish of St. Martins Outwich. Variance between John Rypleye, pl., and George . . . , def., concerning an old stone wall between the properties and certain buildings and housing made and set up on the wall. The viewers have viewed and searched and seen the variances together with other variances between the parties as hereafter follows. They say that from a SW post of a house belonging to pl. standing upon the old stone wall and stretching E 15 ft. 4 in., the wall is partible between the parties. Twelve inches of the thickness of the wall by all that length belongs of right to pl. Stretching more eastward 6 ft. 4 in., there is a brick wall 11 ft. 4 in. in length, which by all its length and thickness belongs to def. At the E end of the said 11 ft. 4 in. there is another wall stretching eastward, 23 ft. 5 in. in length, which is partible in all its length. Four in. of the thickness belongs to pl. Stretching more eastward 19 ft. to an old shed of pl. where of late time a frame of new timber was built and set up, the wall is partible. Pl. ought to have 9 in. of the thickness all the length, line right and plumb from place to place as limited. Without *etc.*

1. The certificate is in poor condition, with many words illegible from dampstaining. The upper right corner is missing.

217. [C.12] 22 December 1547.
Parish of St. Mary Hill. Variance between Christopher Draper, ironmonger, and Thomas Lucas, fishmonger. The view is by assent of both parties. The viewers say there is a great gate coming out of the street there against the E end of the church of St. Mary Hill, which leads into a great yard or void ground with other edifications and houses within the gate held by lease of Lucas. Draper has and holds by lease within the great gate upon the W part of the yard a great cellar or warehouse by the ground and a stair going up to certain houses above and over the cellar, with a great jetty jetting eastward over the yard. The viewers say by all their discretions and by the words and grants of the leases of both parties that Lucas ought of right to have all the yard by all the length and breadth both E and W to the wall of the cellar, as well under the jetty as without, to lay his wares or merchandises, so long as he stops no light of the cellar windows. Furthermore it shall be lawful for Draper to have his recourse with horses and carts and all manner of carriages and recarriages in at the said great gate and yard to his cellar and the edifications over the cellar at all times, without let or disturbance of Lucas or any of his assigns. Without *etc.*

Endorsed: A Vewe between Draper and Lucas.

(*in a later hand*): Supplications . . . Visus de temporibus H8 E6 et P&M.

218. [C.13] 12 January 1548.
Parish of St. Katharine Coleman. Variance between the Master and Wardens of the Fishmongers and John Busshe, goldsmith, concerning the new making of a brick cellar by Busshe. The view is by assent of both parties. The viewers say that the W end of the cellar is encroached and set upon and within the ground of the Master and Wardens from the N part of the cellar stretching southward 14 ft. 4 in. By all the said length the cellar and brick wall is set westward 13½ in. within the ground of the Master and Wardens. It shall be lawful (leifull) for the Master and Wardens and their successors at all times to build upon and take the 13½ in. by all the said length as their own proper ground and wall. [The land is also theirs] stretching more southward from the said 14 ft. 4 in. to the NE principal corner post of the house of the Master and Wardens along by their pale, which ought to be line right and plumb from place to place. Without *etc.*
Endorsed: 21 Januarii A[nn]° R[egni] R[egis] E[dwardi] 6 primo illat[us] fuit visus [?iste] in Cur[iam]. Feod[um] non sol[utum] etc.

219. [C.14] [?12] January 1548.
Parish of St. Mary Colechurch in the Old Jewry. Variance between William Wyatt, pl., and William Pery and Martin Pery, his son, defs., concerning an old garret which has been used for a hay loft belonging to a brew house called 'the Rose'in the Old Jewry, which brewhouse defs. hold by a lease for many years yet to come. The viewers say that the garret or hay loft is 34 ft. 6 in. in length N and S and is 14 ft. 6 in. in wideness E and W. The nether part of the floor of the garret is under the upper part of the rasen of the said garret 9 in. The garret is in peril of falling and is set over and above certain tenements there belonging to pl. 'And people dwellinge in the said Tenementes, yf it [*the garret*] fall, it will distroye them that dwell [*there*].' Therefore, the viewers say, it is so decayed, the joists, the rasens, and the rafter being broken and in peril of falling, that it cannot be repaired but must be taken down, with the tenements under it, to the ground, and must be newly built, all the nether part at costs and charges of pl. The garret and hayloft are to be taken down and new made at costs and charges of defs. Because the said parties def. are bound by their lease to all manner of reparations.
Endorsed: 31 Januarii A[nn]o primo E[dwardi] 6 illatus erat iste visus in Cur[iam] et feod[um] communis clerici solu[tum].

220. [C.15] 6 February 1548.
Parish of St. Alphaes within Cripplegate. Variance between Robert Harrys, gentleman, pl., and Sir Ralph Rowlett, knight, def., concerning a little void ground. The viewers say that the ground is 5 ft. 4 in. in breadth or wideness at the N end against the brick wall belonging to the Curriers' (Coryers') garden, between an old brick wall belonging to pl. on the E and a new brick wall on the W towards the garden of def. The ground is 14 ft. 4 in. in length stretching southward to the gable end of a house belonging to pl., where it is 4 ft. in breadth between the foresaid old brick

wall against the E and the new brick wall against the W. The void ground
belongs to pl. by all the length and breadth. And 4 in. of the new brick
wall on the W of the little void ground belongs to pl. for all its length.
Without *etc.*

221. [C.16][1] 2 March 1548.
Parish of St. Dunstan in the East. Variance between the masters and
wardens of the Mercers and Thomas Cuttull, tallowchandler, concerning
an old stone wall. The view is by assent of both parties. The viewers say
the old stone wall is 52 ft. 4 in. in length from the king's highway of
Thames Street against the S, stretching northward to the NW corner post
there belonging to the Mercers. Of the stone wall, 2 ft. of the thickness
belongs to Cuttull. Stretching more northward from the corner post to a
new brick wall of a house belonging to Cuttull, the wall is 23 ft. 1 in. in
length and 2 ft. of the thickness belongs to Cuttull. And all the thickness
of the rest of the wall eastward belongs to the Mercers for the entire
length. Without *etc.*

> 1. This certificate is copied in Mercers' Company, Register of Benefactors' Wills, vol. I,
> f. cxx; in the margin of that folio is written 'A viewe of an olde stone wall in St. Dunstan
> in the Est'.

222. [C.17] 13 March 1548.
Parish of Our Lady in Aldermanbury. Variance between the master and
wardens of the Brewers, pls., and Lewes Stockkett, def., concerning a
little ground in the parish. The viewers say that def. holds certain
tenements with a little ground lying and being under the E end of the
Brewers' hall by lease of the dean and chapter of the Cathedral Church of
St. Paul. The ground is 21 ft. 4½ in. in length from the SE corner post there
belonging to the Brewers' hall stretching northward. It is 3 ft. 10½ in. in
breadth from the old stone wall there belonging to the Brewers' hall
stretching eastward to the outside of the principal post of the hall. The
viewers say that the little ground has of old time belonged to def. Def.
ought of right to maintain and uphold all the principal posts that stand
there within the said little ground up to the floor of the Brewers' hall at his
own proper costs and charges as often and when need shall be. Pls. ought
of right to have and enjoy all manner of lights belonging to them as they
now are and have been used of old custom. Without any disturbance of
def. Unless there can be any evidence or specialty *etc.*

223. [C.18] 23 April 1548.
Parish of Our Lady called Colechurch. Variance between William
Hamond, pl., and Mr. William Locke, alderman, def., concerning six
tenements that pl. holds by lease for years yet to come. The viewers say
that the six tenements are 106 ft. 1 in. in length from the SW corner
principal post stretching eastward by the king's highway called Bucklersbury. They are 22 ft. 2 in. in breadth or wideness from N to S,
stretching from the foresaid SW corner principal post northward to the
NW corner principal post of the tenements. They are 18 ft. from the NW
corner principal post stretching eastward by the king's highway called the

Poultry. All the houses and tenements are well and sufficiently repaired according to the words of the [lease] that pl. holds of def. Without *etc.*
Endorsed: ... Maii A[nn]o ... iste visus sed feod[um] ... sol[utum]

224. [C.19] 11 May 1548.
[No variance stated]. The viewers have been charged to view a little ground lately parcel of the churchyard of St. Nicholas Shambles, which the wardens of the Butchers of London desire to have by lease with the parsonage for certain years to come. The little ground is 10 ft. in breadth from the E side of the parsonage stretching eastward and it is 26 ft. in length from the N side of the church stretching northward to the outside of the stone wall of the churchyard. The viewers say that it is necessary for the Company and shall be no manner of hurt or prejudice to any part of the lights of any part or parcel of the same church.

225. [C.20][1] 10 July 1548.
Parish of St. Michael in Bassishaw. Variance between John Grymes, pl., and Edward Boner, def., concerning three tenements and certain ground in Horsehed Alley, of which houses and ground def. has a lease and which was void ground at the taking of the lease. The viewers say there is a gutter between pl. and Henry Modye, mercer, which ought of right to be partible between the houses. Except there be any evidence *etc.*

    1. Tear at top, with salutation and part of the first five lines of the certificate missing.

226. [C.21] 10 July 1548.
Parish of Christ Church within Newgate. Variance between Robert Traps, William Southwood, Fabyon Wythers, and Simon Palmer, wardens of the Goldsmiths, pls., and Thomas Blage, haberdasher, and John Shorton, skinner, executors of Jane Jewett, widow, defs., concerning certain implements and standards belonging to the great house or tenement called the sign of 'the White Horsehed' which belongs to pls.: certain seats, benches, doors, locks and keys, glass, lattice, and windows that are there fixed and fastened. The viewers say that they ought of right to remain there as implements and standards of the said house according to the ancient custom of the city of London. Without *etc.*
Endorsed: 19 Julii A[nn]o 2do E[dwardi] 6 infer[tur] iste visus et feod[um] sol[utum] etc.

227. [C.22] 18 July 1548.
Parish of St. Mary Woolchurch. Variance between Steven Cobbe, pl., and George Whetnoll and Alice, his wife, and William Bynynge, defs., concerning a lease of two tenements belonging to pl. and for a chamber over one of the tenements. The viewers say that the chamber stands within the tenement of pl. and he ought of right to have it. Except the words of the lease be to the contrary or any other evidence be shewed to the contrary.
Endorsed: 19 Julii A[nn]o 2do E[dwardi] 6 infer[tur] iste visus et feod[um] sol[utum] etc.

228. [C.23][1] 27 . . . ?1548.

To the right honorable Lorde the Mayre of the Citie of London And his Worshipfull Brethern thaldermen of the same.

Shewen unto your good Lordship and Discrete Wysedoms the xxvii[th] day of . . . Second yere of the reign of our Soveraign Lorde Kynge Edward the Syxth [John Hilmer], Wylliam Walker, John Russell, and Gilbert Burffame, the iiii maysters of the Fremas[ons and carpenters], viewers Indifferent Sworne to the said Citie, that where as they were [late charged by your] honorable commaundement to viewe and oversee a variaunce in the parish of [St. Dunstan in] the West of London betwene Robert Fletewood, gent., playntif of the one partie, [and Edmond] Walter, gent., defendaunt of the other partie, Where as the said iiii viewers were desyr[?ed to] oversee parcell of the tenement there belongynge to the said Robert Fletewood . . . intendeth to take downe parte of the olde house and to newe buylde the same . . . thei say that the grounde and olde house now standynge whiche is to be . . . in Lenght fro the North syde of a princypall post of a house of the sayd Robert . . . made agaynst the Southe stretchynge Northwarde xxxiiii feet ix ynches . . . sayd olde house whiche ys to be newe buylded ys in Bredthe at the South . . . x ynches of assyse. And yt ys in Bredthe at the Northe ende thereof xx foote . . . Further the sayd viewers saye that for bearyng of the water of the said Tenements . . . sayde . . . that yt oweth of ryght to be conveyed and borne as yt was when the sayd Tenements . . . all one [?parcel]. Except the partyes otherwyse do agree. Moreover, as touchynge the makynge of the pales or fences [?between the] Gardeyns of the sayd partyes, the sayd viewers saye that the sayd Robert Fletewode oweth of right to make the pale beynge upon the right hande of his grounde with the postes and Rayles toward his owne grounde. And the foresayd Edmond oweth of right to make the pale upon the . . . hand of hys grounde with the posts and Rayles towarde hys grounde, lyneright and plomb, [from] place to place and from Lemett to Lemett, Without there be any other evydence or comp . . . be shewed to the contrarye.

Endorsed: A vew between Fletewood and Walter

> 1. The certificate is torn so that the right end is missing.

229. [C.24] 24 October 1548.

William Walker, John Russell, Gilbert Burffame, and Nicholas Ellis, freemasons and carpenters, viewers.

Parish of St. Margaret in Friday Street. Variance between the master and wardens of the Cordwainers, pls., and John Thatcher, merchant taylor, def., concerning a stone wall there belonging to the Cordwainers. The viewers say that the wall is 22 ft. in length from the SE corner post of an old house stretching northward. Def. has taken away 10 in. of the wall all the length, whereby it is likely to fall down. 'Except there be Spedye Remedye for the same, contrary to right and consciens.'

Endorsed: 25 Octobrii A[nn]o 2[do] E[dwardi] 6 infert[ur] iste visus sol[utum] feod[um].

230. [C.25] 12 December 1548.

Parish of St. Faith's in Paul's church yard. [No variance stated]. The viewers have viewed a house and great stone wall in the parish, which Thomas Dewexsell, pl., owns and occupies by deed of gift. They say that on the S it abuts on Paul's churchyard for 18 ft. 4 in. along the ground, from the dwelling house of one James Holiland on the E stretching W to the dwelling house of one Henry Tabbes. Stretching N from Paul's churchyard to the tenement belonging to the Bridge House, the house and stone wall are 14 ft. 11 in. in breadth from E to W. There is a gutter to convey water which ought to run from Tabbes' house through Dewexsell's house as of ancient custom it has been used. And Holiland has a jetty of 2 ft. 1 in. all the length of his house, which ought of right still to stand, except *etc.*

231. [C.26] 15 January 1549.
Parish of St. Mary Abchurch in Candlewick Street. Variance between John Broke, executor to George Monox, draper, and Francis Pope, tenant by lease, pls., and Robert Decroft, grocer, def., concerning a warehouse and loft. The viewers say that def. has a warehouse and loft over pls.' kitchen all under one roof, which ought of right to belong to pls. 'Except the partie defendant had the seid warehouse and lofte at the tyme of a certeyn decree made in my lorde Cardenall's tyme when he was Lorde Chancelor of England, onless there be any other evidence or specialtye to the contrarye to be shewed.'

232. [C.27] 21 January 1549.
Parish of St. Foysters in Foster Lane. Variance between Thomas Holland, haberdasher, and Thomas Rede, goldsmith, churchwardens of the parish, pls., and Thomas Dewye, goldsmith, def., concerning a house belonging to the parish church. The viewers say that there is an old stone wall on the N side of the house of pls. From that wall stretching southward there is a house 13 ft. 9 in. in breadth; it contains 13 ft. 3 in. from a gable end of def. at the W stretching E. From the lower side of the plate to the upper side of the floor (flower) is 8 ft. 2 in. Def. ought to have the house. It is lawful to pls. to build over it and set up their house on it. Pls. are to have 9 in. of the stone wall on the N and to build a floor over the little house, at their own costs. They are not to move the floor of the house of def. Pls. occupy two little lofts over the entry with a jakes between the parties; they ought to do and have so 'except there be any man that can shewe any writing, evidence, or specialty to the contrary.'

233. [C.28] 22 January 1549.
[West Smithfield]. Variance between Edward Basshe, pl., and Richard Daye, def., concerning two houses. One is a house which belonged to the abbot and convent of Burton upon Trent, which pl. purchased of the king's grace. The other is a house belonging to Little St. Bartholomew in West Smithfield, in which def. dwells. The viewers say, by seeing of the parties and other ancient men, that there was a lane or highway that went from Smithfield to the Town Ditch. Pl. has built a brick wall by his gate; one end of his wall stands $19\frac{1}{2}$ in. upon the lane. He also has a door opening upon the lane, which he ought to have, and a gallery standing

upon the lane 4 ft. 11 in. On the other side, def. has built his house beyond
the wall standing upon the lane, which the viewers say ought not to be
except there be any writing, evidence, or specialty or covenants to the
contrary.[1]

1. Because of the wording of the certificate, it is difficult to know whether the words
'which viewers say ought not to be' refer only to def.'s house or to the building by both
pl. and def.

234. [C.29] 4 February 1549.
Parish of Christ Church. Variance between Richard Bradbery, citizen
and saddler, pl., and George Tadlowe, citizen and haberdasher, def.,
concerning a piece of ground that sometime was a parish church called
Saint Ewyins [Audoen] within Newgate of London, which ground abuts
part of a tenement or inn called 'the Bell' wherein pl. dwells and a former
church ground which def. holds by lease. The variance is for a porch or
way adjoining the late church. The viewers say that there is a way or porch
abutting the house or inn of pl. From a principal corner post of the NW
side of pl.'s house or inn stretching northward to an angle of a wall [the
ground is] 5 ft. 2 in. in breadth. From that angle stretching E to a quoin or
corner of a stone wall [the ground is] $6\frac{1}{2}$ ft. All the ground within this said
square of the ground so measured is parcel of the king's highway street
there. Except there be any man that can shew any writing or evidence to
the contrary.

235. [C.30] 27 February 1549.
Parish of St. Botolph without Bishopsgate. Variance between John
Strilley, vintner, pl., and John Gates, clothworker, dwelling at the sign of
'the White Harte' without Bishopsgate, def., concerning a brick wall and
fence belonging to pl. by lease. The viewers say that the brick wall on the
N side of the ground belongs to pl. Twenty-five feet of the fence and wall
have fallen down from W to E, which pl. ought to make up at his own cost.
The SW corner of a stable or house of def. stands 6 in. on the wall of pl.; it
stretches 8 ft. eastward. At the E end it does not stand upon the wall. It
ought not of right to stand upon the wall, for all the wall belongs to pl. all
its length. Except *etc.*

236. [C.31] 11 March 1549.
Parish of All Hallows in Lombard Street. Variance between the master
and wardens of the Fishmongers, pls., and Master Thomas Curtes,
pewterer, def., concerning certain houses and gutters. The viewers say
that there is a certain gutter of pls. on the W side of their houses and on
the N side of the house of def. From the high street stretching S there is a
lead gutter which contains 18 ft. between their houses, which pls. ought to
repair at their own cost and charges. Further S at the end of that gutter
there is another gutter of 31 ft. 6 in. It is a party gutter; each party ought to
bear their own water there through their own grounds. There is another
gutter at the end of the party gutter which belongs to pls. Def. has taken
away some of the lead of that gutter and has taken up the tiles of pls.'
houses. Def. ought to re-lay the gutter and to tile pls.' houses at def.'s

cost and charges. Either party to bear his [*sic*] own water in their own ground after the manner and custom of the City of London. Except *etc.*

237. [C.32] 13 March 1549.
Parish of St. Lawrence in the Old Jewry. [Variance between] Nicholas Bacon, mercer, pl., and Roger Andrewes, innholder of 'the Mayden Hed' there, def., concerning a house and appurtenances in Catling Street alias Cat Street,[1] belonging to pl. The viewers say that there is a yard on the E side of the house of pl. From the king's highway it stretches N 44 ft. 6 in. to a corner post of the house of pl. and from that post E 14 ft. 9 in. to another principal post. From that house it stretches S 24 ft. 3 in. toward the gatehouse of def. Each of the parties ought to bear his own water according to the custom of London. Also, there is a house at the N side of pl.'s that belongs to 'the Sarson's Hed' and that has a gutter from which water falls to the ground of pl., which ought not of right to be; every man ought to bear his own water after the manner and custom of London. Except *etc.*

1. Cateaton Street.

238. [C.33] 22 March 1549.
Parish of St. Bride's in Shoe Lane. Variance between Peter Newes, pl., and Thomas Cole, dwelling in the parish of St. Andrews in Holborn, def., concerning certain houses with a garden held of pl. The viewers say that there is a fence on the N side of pl.'s house and garden and the S side of def.'s. The fence stretches line right W from the NW side of a corner post of the house of pl. to a little elm which is pl.'s; it contains 96 ft. From that elm it stretches further W 9 ft. to a hedge abutting westward toward the ground of the Goldsmiths of London. The fence is pl.'s and he ought to make a sufficient fence. From the post of the house beforenamed stretching E to the king's highway is pl.'s. Both parties ought to bear their own water according to the custom of London, except *etc.*
Endorsed: 29/5 A[nn]o iii E[dwardi] 6 infert[ur] iste vi[sus] B stat . . . [?sol] feod[um]

239. [C.34] 5 April 1549.
To the right honorable Lorde Mayre of the Cytie of London and to his Worshipfull bretheren the Aldermen of the same.
Shewen unto your good Lordships and discrete wysdomes the vth day of Aprill in the thyrd yere of the Reign of our soveraign lord Kyng Edward the VIth Willm Walker, John Russell, Gylbert Burfane, and Nicholas Ellys, the iiii masters of Freemasons and Carpenters, viewers indifferent sworn to the said Cytie, that where as they were late charged by your honorable Commaundement to viewe and oversee a house and the Cellers, Solers, and Buyldings therof in Bowe Lane in the parish of Aldermary of London in the Warde of Cordwaner strete of London, sett & being on the southside of the parishe churche of Aldermary aforsaid, belonging to one John Apsley, Citizen and merchanttaillor of London, plaintif of thone partie, and Jefferey Hamlyn, also Cytizen and merchant-taillor of the same Cytie, defendant on the other partie, All whiche

96

houses & buyldinges therof being in variance betwene the said parties, the said iiii viewers have seen and viewed And therupon they say that the partie plaintif hath bought thre ten[*emen*]tes there together with Cellers, Solers, Chambers, Loftes, and all other theire Apperteining therunto belonging, appertayning, or being parcell of one [blank] Overton, who bought the same of the Kinges Majestie in as ample manner and forme as the same and every parte therof to our said soveraign lorde the kinge dyd come and belonge by Acte of Parliament. As by his writings and conveyances therof to the said partie plaintif made more playnly appereth. And further the said iiii viewers say that the said house that the said partie plaintif dwelleth in and the ii other his ten[*emen*]tes therunto adioyning be all under one hole and entier Frame, And that the partie plaintif ought of right to have all the Cellers and other Appurtenances under the same frame by all the lenght and bredeth therof lyne right and plombe by vertue of his said purchase, except a certen entrie or way whiche is there going inwards to the house of the partie defendante from the said strete of Bowlane through and underneath the frame of the house of the partie plaintif. The whiche hath bene used of a custome for a way to goo into the house of the said partie defendant, And they say that the entrie conteyneth from the said Lane Eastward xii fote of assise and in breadth north and south five fote iii Inches of assise. Whiche we say the said partie defendant ought to have. Except there be any writing, evidence, or specialtie to the contrary to be shewed.
Endorsed: 8 May A[nn]o 3 E[dwardi] 6 infert[ur] iste vis[us] et sol[utum] feod[um] etc.

240. [C.35] 5 April 1549.
Duplicate of **239**, but in a different hand; no endorsement visible.

241. [C.36] 27 April 1549.
Parish of St. Margaret Pattens. Variance between Sir John [?Kidson], parson of the same ... of the one part and Edward Rewe and Robert Duckett, churchwardens of the same, of the other part, concerning a little house beside the parsonage there. The viewers say that the church-wardens ought of right to have the little house, which was at some time a store house, to their proper use and to repair it at their cost and charges and to set it there away from the parsonage so that it does not rest upon the parsonage house. The parson is to have the course into the church-yard to come and go as he has had ... of a long custom.
Except *etc.*
Endorsed: 29 A[nn]o 3 E[dwardi] 6 infert[ur] iste vis[us] etc. feod[um] [?nondum] so[utum]

242. [C.37] 14 May 1549.
Parish of St. Stephens in Coleman Street. Variance between Hugh Davy, currier, pl., and Edward Cloxton, mercer, def., concerning a garden place and the fences of the same. The viewers say that pl. should have the garden with egress and regress into, through, and from the same at all times needful and convenient by the alley there called Swan (Swane)

Alley, which alley ought to be 4 ft. 6 in. in breadth, and by all other alleys and ways to and from the same as of old time has been used and accustomed, as by deed it more plainly appears. Also, def. ought to make the fence between Swan Alley and his own garden at his cost and charges. In def.'s garden there stands a little house. From the NE corner post of that house stretching E all the length of the garden to the common sewer, there is a fence which ought to be made by pl. at his cost and charges by Lammas Day [August 1] next coming. Also there is another fence to be made on the N side of the garden of pl.; a house stands there, and from its SE corner post stretching E to the common sewer, the fence ought to be made by one Mistress Jekyll, widow, at her cost, by Lammas Day. Except *etc.*

Endorsed: 8/7/A[nn]o iii E[dwardi] VI infert[ur] iste vis[us] et sol[utum] feod[um]

243. [C.38][1] 26 May 1549.
Parish of St. Dunstan in the West. Variance between William Blage, tailor, pl., and Richard Wheler, tailor, def., concerning a foundation of a wall for a house to be set up. The viewers say that pl. ought of right to have 9 in. of the thickness of the wall by all the length thereof to have his plates upon, and so to raise his frame from the same line right and plumb. Except *etc.*

Endorsed: 5/8/A[nn]o iii E[dwardi] VI infert[ur] iste vis[us] et sol[utum] feod[um]

1. The certificate has no salutation and no space has been left for one.

244. [C.39] 27 May 1549.
Parish of Christ Church. Variance between Hugh Losse, squire, pl., and John Vandernott, physician, def., concerning various tenements. The viewers say that there is a house, in which one John Hilton now dwells, which is tenantable, if repaired, for any honest man to dwell in. And there is a wood house that the viewers found in decay in the first view[1] that they made. [Repairs] have not been done and amended according to that view; 'for John Vandernott hathe doone the principalls and the partie defendant ought to quarter and daubbe it with all other reparacions thereto belonging and yt is yet undone.'

Endorsed: 1/8/A[nn]o iii E[dwardi] 6 infert[ur] iste vis[us] sed nondum sol[utum] feod[um] etc.

1. The 'first view' referred to is dated 25 February 1 Edward VI; see **206** above. In this certificate, the status of the parties is somewhat confusing; John Vandernott is referred to as defendant, but the statement that he has done the principals and that the defendant ought to do further work suggests that perhaps he should have been identified as plaintiff. In any event, it is unclear whether he is to be responsible for the further repairs needed.

245. [C.40] 28 May 1549.
Parish of St. Botolph's without Bishopsgate. Variance between John Lowen, draper, pl., and Robert Dunkyn, tailor, [def.], concerning a way to certain gardens which have been purchased of the king's grace and which before belonged to a chantry in Paul's. The viewers say that from

the king's highway on the E side of def.'s tenement, there is an entry 18 ft. long and 4 ft. 6 in. broad going into certain gardens of both parties. At the end of the 18 ft., there is a way to the gardens of both. Both parties and tenements ought to have their course to and from by and through the entry and way at all times convenient, and both ought to maintain the door with both posts of the door of the entry and to pave the king's high street the breadth of the entry, at costs of both. Except *etc.*

Endorsed: 6 Junii A[nn]o 3 E[dwardi] 6 infert[ur] ist[e] vis[us] et sol[utum] feod[um].

See also **297** below.

246. [C.41] 28 May 1549.
Parish of St. Pulcres without Newgate. Variance between George Alyn, skinner, pl., and the Lady Pecok, def., concerning a foundation in an alley called the George Alley in Seacoal (Cecole) Lane. The viewers say that it is 28 ft. 3 in. from the brick wall SE of pl. stretching E of a house now being built. From that corner post all the length of pl.'s grounds to an old pale post on the S side of his grounds, pl. ought to have [?the land] line right and plumb. It is 7 ft. from the old pale post to the S corner post of a tenement or shed of pl. Also, in the alley at the S side there is a brick wall. Pl. ought to have 6 in. of that wall. From the end of the brick wall stretching W to the little tenement or shed of pl., there ought to be a lawful fence or pale made at def.'s cost. Except *etc.*

247. [C.42] 29 May 1549.
Parish of Abchurch in Candlewick Street. Variance between Walter Williams, draper, pl., and John Mynors, draper, def., concerning a wall. The viewers say that the wall stretches S 19 ft. 9½ in. from the SE corner post of pl. to a house of def. At the N end of the wall, it encroaches 16 in. on the lane called Bell Alley and at the S end, [it encroaches] 2 ft. It ought not of right so to do. Except *etc.*

Endorsed: 6 Junii A[nn]o E[dwardi] 6 infert[ur] iste visus sed feod[um] non sol[utum] etc.

248. [C.43] 30 May 1549.
Parish of St. Benet Graschurche. Variance between John Starky, the king's fletcher, and Leonard Richeman, armorer, concerning a brick wall. The view is a party view. The viewers say that from the brick wall on the N side of the ground of Starky and from the W end of that wall stretching S to the N corner post of a house of one Ralph Clarves, grocer, Starky ought to have the wall line right and plumb from limit to limit all the length of the wall. Except *etc.*

249. [C.44] 2 June 1549.
Parish of St. Sepulchre without Newgate. Variance between My Lady Pecok., pl., and George Alyn, [def.], concerning tenements and grounds in an alley called Pecok Alley. The viewers say that there is a little house on the NW side of pl.'s ground which contains 20 ft. 3 in. from W to E to a corner post; it contains 4 ft. 1 in. from the corner post more N to the wall

of def. Def. ought of right to have the house and grounds by all the length and breadth aforesaid. Also, there is a door coming into pl.'s grounds in the alley from the Clothworkers' grounds there adjoining, which ought not of right so to be. And either of the parties ought to bear his own water after the manner and custom of the City of London. Except *etc.*

250. [C.45] 2 June 1549.
Duplicate of **249**; no endorsement visible.

251. [C.46] 3 June 1549.
Parish of St. Botolph Aldrichgate. Variance between the Chamber of London, pl., and William Harvie, otherwise called Somersett,[1] def., concerning a piece of ground without Aldersgate. The viewers say that the ground on the E side of the gate, from the town wall to the def.'s wall, ought of right to belong to pl. And because there was at some time a way there, def. ought to have his lights into the said grounds. Except *etc.*

    1. William Harvey became Somerset Herald in 1545–6.

252. [C.47] 22 June 1549.
Parish of St. Saviour in Southwark. Variance between Thomas Hedgson, pl., and [blank] Kightley, widow, concerning a piece of ground. The viewers say that there is a pale from a stone wall on the S side of the church yard stretching northward 23 ft. 6 in. to a corner post; from that post, it stretches E to a house of pl. containing 25 ft. 6 in. The ground is the lord's waste ground and the pale ought to be taken away.[1] Except *etc.*

    1. From the facts given, it is not possible to know the exact nature of the underlying dispute, nor to know who 'the lord' is. Perhaps the reference is to the Saviour, whose namesake church is involved, or the lord of the [Guildable] manor in Southwark.

253. [C.48] 8 July 1549.
Parish of St. James in Garlickhithe. Variance between Miles Byre, pl., and George Colsell of the parish of St. Martin in the Vintry, def., concerning a house belonging to pl. The viewers say that there is a stone wall between pl. and def. on the NE side of pl.'s house; it is 27 ft. 2 in. in length from a lane called [blank] lane and now commonly called the Church Lane, stretching S to a party [?wall] of both parties. The viewers say that the wall is pl.'s all its length from the [?upper] side of the floor of the cellar upward; in the cellar, def. ought to have 13 in. of the wall between the parties. Also, pl. must keep and bear up the somers that stand in the walls at his cost and charges; afterwards, def. shall maintain them at his cost continually forever. Either party is to bear his own water at his own cost and charge, according to the [custom] of the City of London. Except *etc.*
Endorsed: 15 July A[nn]o 3 E[dwardi] 6 infert[ur] his vis[us] feo[dum] inde sol[utum]

254. [C.49] 15 July 1549.
Parish of St. Faith within Paul's Church. Variance between Robert Toye, pl., and Sir Richard Smyth, one of the Petty Canons of Paul's, def.,

concerning a house on the W side of Paul's churchyard leased by pl. from the bishop of London. Def.'s house belongs to the Petty Canons. The viewers say that pl. ought of right to have all his house or tenement by the ground as it now stands on the W side of Paul's churchyard and abuts (butts) onto a wall of def. Def. has on the a wall a jetty that sails over pl.'s ground, which he ought to have to its outer part. Beyond the jetty, pl. may build hard by and upright at his pleasure and either party is to bear his own water. Except *etc.*

255. [C.50] 28 July 1549.
Parish of St. Michael in Bassishaw. Variance between Faith Patenson, widow, at the sign of 'the Bell' there, pl., and John Martyn, baker, def., concerning a brick wall at the S end of pl.'s ground. The viewers say that def. has broken and put down the wall with the laying and setting up of his wood against the same. The wall is 30 ft. 3 in. in length and 4 ft. 6 in. in height beside the coping thereof. The viewers say that def. ought of right to make the wall of the same thickness, length, and height with the coping as it was before the breaking, substantially and workmanly, before Christmas now coming at his own cost and charges. He is to have the old bricks remaining from the wall toward the making of the new wall. Also, there was of late a jakes of pl.'s house which def. has taken away contrary to right, and which he ought to build up again at his cost because the jakes was there when pl. purchased the house. Either party is to bear his own water of his own house after the custom of the city. Except *etc.*

256. [C.51] 30 July 1549.
Parish of St. Lawrence in the Old Jewry. Variance between Roger Andrewes, innholder, dwelling at the sign of 'the Maydenhed' in Cateaton Street (Catlyng Street, alias Catte Street), and Nicholas Bacon, mercer, def., concerning a gutter and the bearing of its water. The viewers say that either of the parties ought to bear the water of his own house upon his own ground. Also, there is a brick wall on the N end of the court of def. The water by half the coping of the wall falls onto pl.'s house, which it ought not of right to do. Def. ought to bear his own water and not annoy his neighbor thereby. Except *etc.*

See also **237** above.

257. [C.52] 14 August 1549.
Parish of St. Katharine Coleman. Variance between Mistress Beatrice Bodley, pl., and John Rauf, def., concerning a way to certain gardens, pales, and garden ground and fences thereof. The viewers say that pl. ought of right to have her way to her garden or gardens quietly, without any let or stop at any time. Also, there is a wall or fence at the N side of pl.'s garden abutting on the ground called the Lord of Northumberland's place, in the tenure of one Chapman. Chapman ought to repair and make the fence of the yard at his costs and charges. Also, there is a pale or fence of pl. on the W side of her ground which she ought to make up line right and plumb. 'Also there ys a dore of the partie defendaunt's house that

101

goeth into the Aley there by the gardeyn of the partie plaintiff, the which dore we cannot denie hym, But we thinke that there may evyll inconveniences growe by yt if that dore do stonde there. Unto all this we the said viewers ar agreed.' Except *etc.*

258. [C.53] 16 August 1549.
Parish of St. Augustine in Watling Street. Variance between Christopher Nycolson, pl., and John Thatcher, def., concerning a way and certain lights and buildings. The viewers say that pl. took his dwelling house by lease, with free passing to and fro at all times without let of any person or persons. Def. has built a house before the door of pl. and has stopped the light of a window of pl. Further, def. has made an entry 3 ft. 6 in. broad for pl. to go into his house. Pl. ought of right to have the entry upright and all the lights of the entry. Def. is to make pl.'s house as he found it, so that he [?pl.] may have his eaves dropping upon his own ground as it was before, when he took his lease. Except *etc.*

259. [C.54] 16 August 1549.
Duplicate of **258**, but pl.'s name is spelled 'Nicolson'.
Endorsed: 30 Augusti Anno 3 E[dwardi] 6 infert[ur] iste visus.

260. [C.55] 2 September 1549.
Parish of St. Pulcres. Variance between Peter Grene, pl., and William Lambkyn, def., concerning windows in a street called Suterhill Street. The viewers say that def. has three windows [looking] into pl.'s grounds 'and there were somtyme bordes against theym after tronk [trunk] light[s], whiche the partie defendant hath broken downe and we say that the partie defendant shall take the same bordes and set theym up agayn in manner and forme as herafter foloweth: firste to the lower wyndow the borde for to be nayled close at the lower parte of the wyndowe and at the higher parte of that wyndowe, to be fro the wall xvi inches, and to cutt the vywe all the lenght of the lyght. And to have the more light. Also the ii higher wyndowes lykewise for to be nayled close at the lower parte of theym windowes and xviii inches fro the wall at the higher parte of the wyndowes.' Pl. may build upright by the wall at any time at his pleasure so long as 'it be not done in no poynt of malice', except *etc.*
Endorsed: 7 September A[nn]o 3 E[dwardi] 6 infert[ur] iste vis[us].

See also **282** and **345** below.

261. [C.56] 19 September 1549.
Parish of St. Michael in Cornhill. Variance between Edward Perye, draper, pl., and Stephen Cobb, haberdasher, def., concerning certain gutters in Finch (Fynkes) Lane. The viewers say that pl. had a gutter running from his kitchen with a lead pipe, which def. has lately taken away; def. ought to set the pipe in the place where it was before, at his own proper costs and charges. Pl. has a gutter of lead on the W side of his house which ought to fall into def.'s yard. There is also another lead gutter on the E side of pl.'s house which is a party gutter and ought to be repaired from time to time at both parties' cost. Further, all the water of

the gutters ought to fall into the yard of def., because it was one lord's ground before it came into the king's hands. Therefore the viewers say that def. ought to bear the water, except *etc.*

Endorsed: 25/11 A[nn]o 3 E[dwardi] VI infert[ur] iste vis[us] et no[n] solut[um] feod[um].

262. [C.57] 10 October 1549.
Parish of St. Christopher's in Cornhill. Variance between Thomas Banaster, pl., and John Jakes, dwelling on the side of pl., def., concerning the fence of both their houses. The viewers say there is a double wall, on which each party ought of right to make the fence of his own wall. Also, there is a house on the W side of pl. which belongs to the Drapers and pl. is now building up a new house on the N side of the Drapers' house; he may build it line right and plumb as the foundation is now standing. Also, there is a house on the N side of pl. belonging to one Thomas Lawrence, and pl. has the lower part of the house and Lawrence has the upper. Pl. must keep up and maintain the lower part and Lawrence must tile and cover the upper part and keep it windtight and watertight. Pl. will build up a house on the E side of that house and Lawrence ought to have the walls of the new house, pl. to build upright by the wall of the said house. Each man shall bear his own water according to the custom of the City of London, except *etc.*

263. [C.58][1] 21 November 1549.
Parish of St. Mary Woolchurch. Variance between ... parish of St. Stephen in Walbrook, pl., and ... [St.] Nicholas Olive, Bread Street, def., concerning two vaults or falls of certain jakes which pl. has cleansed at his proper cost ... that as many falls as be to the said vaults ought of right ... cleansing to the cleansing of the said vaults and ... the pl. ... has taken down a little coal [?house] ... second storey of $3\frac{1}{2}$ ft. of size in breadth and ... pl. ought of right to make ... as many tunnels or jakes as there was at the ... and height as there were then at his proper costs ... Except ...

1. The certificate is badly faded and torn in half.

264. [C.59] 22 November 1549.
Parish of St. Bartholomew the Little [?West Smithfield].
Variance between Thomas Ormeston, pl., and the master and wardens of the Merchant Taylors, defs., concerning a fence and garden. The viewers say that pl.'s garden at its N end contains 37 ft. 6 in. in breadth from a brick wall on the W side stretching E. From the SW end stretching E to a pale and plumb draft in the brick wall, it contains 27 ft. Pl. ought of right to have all the ground as measured and to make all pales at his cost and charges, line right and plumb from limit to limit. Except *etc.*

265. [C.60] 6 December 1549.
Parish of St. Mildred in Bread Street. Variance between Adam Chatterton, pl., and Richard Humfrey of the same parish, def., concerning a stone wall on the W side of pl.'s house. The viewers say pl. ought of right to have the whole wall. Except *etc.*

266. [C.61] 9 December 1549.
Parish of St Leonard in Eastcheap. Variance between Robert Southwyk, pl., and William Alen and Anthony Cowley, churchwardens of the said parish, concerning the vestry of the church, which is under pl.'s house. It contains 11 ft. 8 in. from W to E and from the church wall N, 9 ft. 8 in. Pl. ought to have his house over the vestry as it was and as he had it at time of his purchase and no more nor otherwise. Except *etc.*

267. [C.62] 3 February 1550.
Parish of St. Gregory's at Paul's Chain. Variance between Christopher Basse, grocer, and Robert Davyson, merchant taylor, and Hugh Pope, haberdasher, concerning a jakes between Basse and Davyson in Knightrider Street. The view is a party view, by assent of all parties. The viewers say that Basse and Davyson ought to make, repair, and cleanse the jakes at both their costs and charges. There is also a variance between the said two parties for a pentice over the shop of Basse; it belongs to him and he ought to make and repair it at his cost and charges and he may make it large and high enough for his ease and commodity, so long as he does not annoy or stop any part of the light of Davyson's windows. Also, there is a jakes that falls into the house of Hugh Pope, dwelling at the figure of 'the Kinges Hed' there; it has three tunnels and it ought to be made clean by all three lessees thereof at their costs and charges. Also, Pope has a shop built upon the king's highway, 4 ft. broad and 12 ft. long; it ought not of right to stand there and the Chamberlain of London ought to pull it down. Except *etc.*

268. [C.63] 18 February 1550.
Parish of St. Botolph without Bishopsgate. Variance between the master and wardens of the Skinners, pls., and John Rowseley, who has the fee simple of the ground there that lately belonged to St. Mary Spittal, and George Holland, who has the lease of the same ground, concerning a ditch. The viewers say that the ditch is at the N side of pls.' grounds and contains 6 ft. in breadth, more at the upper side thereof. It ought to be from E to W all the length of the grounds of pls. to a common sewer there and as parcel of the common sewer, as it has been used of old custom. Except *etc.*
Endorsed: feod[um] no[n]du[m] solut[um].

269. [C.64] 25 February 1550.
Parish of St. Martin Outwich in the Ward of Broad Street. Variance between Rowland Staper, pl., and William Sell, def., concerning a little house with a jakes on the W side of the house of def. lying toward the house of pl. The house belonged to def.'s house long before the parties purchased their houses. It ought of right still so to continue. Also, pl. has a brick wall on the W side of his garden, on his own ground. He must maintain it at his own costs and charges; if he will, he may build upon the wall. Also, on the E side of the garden of pl. there is a pale, which pale and fence ought to be made at the costs and charges of pl. It must stand from the E corner post of the house of pl. stretching [?N] to a corner post

standing in a brick wall of a house there. Pl. ought of right to make it line right and plumb from limit to limit. Except *etc.*

270. [C.65] 11 March 1550.
To the right honorable lorde maire of the Cytie of London and to his worshipfull brethern thaldermen of the same Cytie.
Shewen unto your goode lordship and masterships the xi[th] daye of Marche in the iiii[th] yere of the Reigne of our soveraign lorde king Edwarde the VIth, Willm Walker, John Russell, Gylbert Burfame, and Nicholas Ellys, the iiii masters of Fremasons and Carpenters, viewers indifferent sworn to the said Cytie, that where as they were late charged by your lordships commaundment the xx[th] day of Novembre in the thirde yere of the Reign of our soveraigne lorde the Kinge that nowe ys to viewe and oversee certen variances in the parishe of Saint Mary Woolchurche in Walbroke of London, Betwene Willm Lane, grocer, of one partie, and Myles Ayer, vyntner, of the other partie, whiche variaunce was for a littell Cole house in the ground storry of the house of the said Willm Lane and two tonnelles of Jakes with a Cestern or vawte thereunto belongyng, whiche variance we then viewed and declared our myndes therin, As by the recorde thereof [?appeareth],[1] and nowe eftsones at your lordships commaundement the day of date herof, we the said viewers have viewed and overseen the same variance betwene the said parties and we fynd & say that the said littell house and two Tonnelles of Jakes with all other things concerning that variance aforesaid, to be . . . newe buylded and made by the said Lane according to right and Justice and according to our former viewe taken in that byhalf, ys allredy done by the said Lane. And as for the Cestern vawte, a Celler whiche was clensed and newe builded and parted asonder by the said Lane with a brik wall, we the said viewers have viewed and seen the same and therupon we say that the same is well and justely done by the said Lane in all poyntes according to the customs and lawes of the Cytie of London, and the said Mylys by the said buylding, As it is now made, ys nothing wronged. Except the parties have any writing or evidence to the contrary to be shewed.
Endorsed: 18 Martis A[nn]o 4[to] E[dwardi] 6 infert[ur] iste vis[us] et sol[utum] feod[um] etc.

1. There is no extant certificate dated 20 November 3 Edward VI. Certificate **263**, dated 21 November 3 Edward VI, may refer to the same variance.

271. [C.66][1] 11 March 1550.
Parish of St. Katharine Coleman. Variance between John [Hyde] . . . and John Defalles, merchant, concerning the fence of a garden. The viewers say that from a corner post of a little shed in the ground of the said Hyde . . . corner of that shed stretching northward to a corner post of a pale belonging to the garden of the said . . . that the said Hyde ought there to make a lawful fence, line right and plumb from limit to limit the said length. Except *etc.*

1. The right margin and part of the certificate are lost through tears and dampstaining.

272. [C.67] 14 March 1550.
Parish of St. Clement in Eastcheap. Variance between Bennett Jackson, butcher, pl., and George Smyth, butcher, def. The viewers say that there is a post on the E side of pl.'s house and from the middle of the post stretching W to the middle of a post standing between pl. and def. on Eastcheap, [pl.'s land] contains 30 ft. 11 in. Also, pl. has a house behind his shop and def. has a chamber over it. The floor under the chamber is decayed; def. ought to repair the floor that bears his chamber and to tile it and keep it dry at his own proper cost and charges and not annoy pl. under it. Pl. ought to maintain the walls and foundations under the chamber of def. Each ought to have the course of their waters and highways and lights as it has been in long time past before their purchases. Also, each ought to bear like part to every partition, as the posts and gutters be parted, and to cleanse their jakes according to their falls by even portion, according to the custom of the city of London. Except *etc.*
Endorsed: 17 Martii A[nn]o 4to E[dwardi] 6 sol[utum] feod[um]

273. [C.68] 25 April 1550.
Parish of Abchurch in Candlewick Street. Variance between Richard Cooke, draper, and Margaret Asshelyn, widow. The view is a party view. The viewers say that Cooke has a stone wall on the W side of his house bearing his house between Margaret Asshelyn and himself; he ought of right to have it to his own use and to take it down and build it at his pleasure, from the street there southward all the length of his house and ground. Also, there is a paper wall in the W side of his yard; it belongs to him and he must maintain the wall and fence at his proper costs and charges. Except *etc.*

274. [C.69] 3 May 1550.
Parish of St. Martin Orgar in Thames Street. Variance between Robert Meryk, fishmonger, pl., and William Brown, fishmonger, def., concerning a house of pl. in Thames Street. The viewers say that they have viewed the house and variance and also have seen the lease of pl.; it declares that pl. should have his house 92 ft. in length from S to N. Also, there was a view made upon the same house on the second day of October in the 22nd year of the reign of King Henry the VII [1506], and it declares that the house should have 92 ft. in length from S to N. 'And we have met the said house and it hath not nowe his lenght as the afforsaid lenght [*sic: rectius* lease] dothe declare it shuld have and therfore we say that the partie plaintif ought for to have the hole lenght of his house as it is before rehersed.' Except *etc.*

275. [C.70] 8 May 1550.
Parish of St. Botolph without Aldgate. Variance between William Grene and James Adlington, alias Alyngton. The view is a party view by assent of both parties. The viewers say that Grene has taken down a house in his own back side there, which house of late abutted on the E side of Alyngton's house and stable. Both those houses, Adlyngton's and Grene's, before their purchase belonged to Our Lord. Alington ought to have the paper wall that bears the E side of his little stable as he had it in

106

the time of his purchase, he to keep and maintain it at his own proper costs and charges. Also, there is a fence on the E side of Alington's garden and Grene of right ought to make a sufficient fence there between him and Adlington at his proper costs and charges line right and plumb from limit to limit. Except *etc.*

Endorsed: 12 Maii A[nn]o 4to E[dwardi] 6 infert[ur] iste visus et feod[um] sol[utum]

276. [C.71] 13 May 1550.
Parish of St. Sepulchre. Variance there and in West Smithfield between Christopher Jakson, glasier, pl., and Edward Barbour, scrivener, def., concerning a fence between the parties. The viewers say that pl. has a little house that ranges by the end of his main house. From the SW corner post of that little house stretching more W to a post standing in the fence of my lord the Bishop of York, def. ought to make a sufficient fence line right and plumb from limit to limit at his costs and charges. And either party ought to bear his own water. Except *etc.*

277. [C.72] 13 May 1550.
To the Right honorable Lorde Mayre of the Cytie of Lon[*don*] and to his Worshipfull Brethren thaldermen of the [same] Cyttie. Shewen unto your good lordshipe and maistershipps the xiiith day of Maye and the iiith yere of the Reigne of our soveraign lorde kinge Edwarde the Syxt Wyllm Walker, John Russell, Gylbert Burfane [and Nicholas] Ellys, the iiii Maysters of Fremasons and Carpenters, vyewers Indefferent Sworne to the said Cytie, [that] whereas thei were of late charged by your Lordships comaundement to vyewe and oversee a [?variance between] the wardens of the company of Salters, plaintyfes, of the one partye, and one Robt Melysshe, Merchaunte Taylor, defendante, of the other partye, in the parisshe of Alhallowes in Bredstrete in London, Which varyaunce is concernynge ii houses in Watlynge strete, at the syne of the Woolsacke and the syne of the Catt And the Fyddle, whiche houses we have vyewed and Seen and we the sayd vyewers saye that the partye deffendaunt hath leases of Both those houses for terme of vi yeres and above yet to come and we saye that the partye deffendaunt ought for to have both those houses All the tyme of his terme of his leases. And then when the leases of the partye deffendaunte are Expyred, yt may be lawfull for the parties plaintyfe, whiche are the lordes of both those houses, for to lett and sett the houses at theyr pleasures And for to make devysyon of the Rowmes at theyr pleasures. And not Els. Except there be any wrytyng, evydence, or Especialtye to the contrarye to be shewed.

278. [C.73] 1550.
Parish of St. Michael at Queenhithe. Variance between Thomas Kery, salter, pl., and Elisabeth Lonsdale, widow, def.[1] The view is a party view. The viewers say that either of the parties ought to have the commodities that either had in the time of their purchase of their houses, with lights and jakes and other commodities as at that time to the same did belong. Also, def. has taken down a little entry that goes into a jakes of pl.; it

107

contains 21 in. in breadth and 10 ft. 10 in. in length and def. ought to build it up again at her costs and charges. And pl. ought to have so many lights as he had in the time of his purchase and no more. Except *etc.*

Endorsed: 22 Maii A[nn]o 4[to] E[dwardi] 6 infert[ur] iste vis[us] et sol[utum] feod[um] co[mmun]is clerici

1. This is one of very few certificates in which the parties to a party view are nevertheless identified as plaintiff and defendant

279. [C.74] 12 June 1550.
Parish of St. Matthew in Friday Street. Variance between Thomas Metcalfe, goldsmith, pl., and Thomas Cage, salter, def., concerning lights and conveyance of the water and jakes of pl. The viewers say that forasmuch as pl. bought the fee simple of his house of the king's majesty with all the commodities to it belonging in as ample and large manner as it was before the time of his purchase, he ought to have any and all lights belonging to the same at the time of his purchase, and also to have the course of his water as it was before the time of his purchase, by and with a party gutter and sink there between the parties, together with the conveyance of both their jakes there falling into the vault between them as it was before the time of their purchase. Also, def. ought to have on the street side called Friday Street half of the principal posts in every side of his house. 'All this we say ought for to be had except' *etc.*
Endorsed: Con[fectum] pro Cage 28.8.1550 per Xpoffer

280. [C.75] 10 July 1550.
Parish of Our Lady in Aldermans Bery. Variance between Thomas Atkyns, Esquire, pl., and the dean and chapter of the Cathedral Church of St. Paul's, defs. The viewers say that there is a fence on the N side of pl.'s ground which pl. ought to have and maintain at his costs and charges, either party to bear their own water. Except *etc.*
Endorsed: 14/9 A[nn]o iiii E[dwardi] VI non sol[utum] feod[um]

281. [C.76][1] 30 August 1550.
William Walker, John Russell, Nicholas Ellys, and John Cowper, the iiii masters of freemasons, carpenters, and tilers, viewers.
Parish of St. Michael Cornhill. Variance between Thomas Bales, pl., and William Assheler, def., concerning a brick wall between the said parties on the N side of a [?house] there called the sign of 'the Scomer' in Birchin Lane. The viewers say that pl. ought of right . . . assise in thickness to the said wall by all the length thereof, that is to say from the inside of the principal post of . . . Pl. [*sic*] has broken down a piece of the wall according to right and . . . which . . . wall by him broken he ought of right to make and build up again at his own [proper costs and charges], so much as is broken. Also, there is a variance between pl. and one William Turner, gentleman, def. . . . on the S side of the . . . water there of def. The viewers say that it ought of right to fall . . . the house now called 'the Scomer'. Except *etc.*

1. The top left corner of the certificate is torn away and the entire certificate is blackened and creased.

See also **204** above.

282. [C.77]¹ [15 September 1550].
Parish of St. Sepulchre without Newgate. Variance between [Peter Grene], yeoman, pl., and Thomas Hylton, [merchant taylor, def.] . . . concerning a certain wall whereof the . . . from E to W 1 ft. of assise and . . . which of right he ought not to do. And . . . an entry with a door opening into the lane called [Fleet Lane] . . . which yard ought to be . . . and both the said parties to make a lawful fence in . . . them both at their several costs and charges and . . . according to the ancient custom of the City of London . . . Except *etc.*
Endorsed: 18 September A[nn]o 4ᵗᵒ E[dwardi] VI infert[ur] iste vis[us] et sol[utum] feod[um] etc.

> 1. Half the certificate is missing; only one viewer's name remains, William Walker. This certificate is reproduced in full in **345** below, which deals with a later stage in the dispute. The words here added in brackets have been taken from **345**, as has the date.

283. [C.78]¹ 18 September 1550.
[*Parish missing*]. Variance between the master of . . . pls., and John Wy . . . concerning certain buildings in the parish . . . church of London . . . The view is a party view. The viewers say that the party . . . gate called St. Austen's gate upri[ght] . . . that from the NW corner post of . . . def. has encroached . . . to the W 18 in. of as[sise] . . . either of the said . . . according to the ancient custom . . . to be, Except . . .
Endorsed: 18 September A[nn]o 4 E[dwardi] 6 infert[ur] iste vis[us] et sol[utum] feod[um]

> 1. More than half the certificate is missing; it can be dated only from the endorsement. The names of the viewers are missing.

284. [C.79] 23 October 1550.
[*Viewers as in* **281**]. Parish of St. Mary Abchurch in Candlewick Street. Variance between John Mynors, draper, and Richard Cooke, draper, concerning a brick wall now in making by Mynors in Candlewick Street. The view is a party view. The viewers say that from a new brick wall on the S side of the grounds of the parties, there is a plumb draught drawn with certain nails, from which nails, and stretching N to the W side of a corner post of Mynors, [the wall] ought to go line right and plumb from limit to limit all the length. Either party ought to bear his own water according to the ancient custom of the City of London. 'All this of right we say ought to be, except' *etc.*

285. [C.80] 3 November 1550.
Parish of All Hallows Barking near the Tower of London. Variance between Julian Knight, otherwise called Julian Jennynges, pl., and Thomas Pyke, skinner, def., concerning a certain house and wharf, stable, planks, two chimneys, tiling and guttering, and other certain decay there in the house wherein one Randall Haward, tenant at will of pl., now dwells. The viewers say that def. has built on the W side of his own house, by reason of which he has broken down the tops of two chimneys, broken tiles, spoiled the gutters, and decayed the walls of pl., which of right he ought to repair and make again at his own proper costs

and charges. There are floors, stables, walls, and a wharf at the water side, containing 25 ft. in length, decaying there. The lord of the house of right ought to repair and amend them at his or their own proper costs and charges. Every man to bear his own water according to the ancient custom of the City of London. Except *etc.*

286. [C.81] 18 November 1550.
Parish of St. Olave in Hart Street. Variance between Philip van Wylder, gentleman, pl., and Agnes Newton, gentlewoman, widow, def., concerning certain lights, walls, windows, and conveyances of water between the parties. The viewers say that pl. ought to have his lights and water-courses as they were at the time of his purchase. Further, there was a certain bay window on the E side of pl.'s house, glazed and framed, which def. has taken away contrary to all right and which window and glass def. ought of right to restore again. 'All this of right we say ought to be done. Except' *etc.*
Endorsed: 29/1/A[nn]o 4to E[dwardi] 6 infert[ur] iste visus et sol[utum] feod[um]
(*in a later hand*): Viewes temporum H8 E6 P&M & Eliz.
(*in a later hand, crossed out*): Supplicaciones

287. [C.82][1] [18 ?November 1550].
... in the parish of St. Mary Magdalen in Old Fish Street between Henry [Pemerton], barbersurgeon, and John ... being the ... of the Inn called 'the Kynges Hed' on the other party, being a party view ... said parties which view is of and for certain casualty of fire and burning (brennynge) of certain houses between the said parties, and which houses and variance thereof ... the same fire the said iiii sworn viewers have viewed and seen according to ... to [them] given and have ... examined diverse and many witnesses of and upon the same. 'And thereupon we say by our consciences and as far as we can perceive as well by our viewing of the houses as by the witnesses, that the said fire first began in the hayloft belonging to the same Inn called the Kyngs Hed. And that by our consciences it must needs so be, forasmuch as the Roof of the same house is clene brent ... and the said Pemerton's house lytle or nothing perished with the said fire. And this we find to be true in our conscience that the fire first began in the said hayloft belonging to the said Inn called the Kings Hed and not otherwise. Except there be any evidence or record they have not had.'
Endorsed: 20 November A[nn]o 4to E[dwardi] 6 infert[ur] hic visus et feod[um] sol[utum]

1. The certificate is badly damaged by water and decay. The date appears to be 18 November, but most of the salutation is gone. The viewers appear to be the same as in the immediately preceding certificates.

288. [C.83] 25 November 1550.
Parish of St. Mary Magdalen in the street called Knightrider Street in Old Fish Street of London. Variance between Thomas Ellys, merchant taylor, and William Hollingworth alias Snowden, fishmonger, concerning a certain jakes and water courses. The view is a party view. The viewers say that Ellys has taken down a tunnel of boards for a jakes which went

110

through his kitchen, having fall down into a cistern in the ground there. He ought of right to make it up again at his own proper costs and charges; and when need requires, the cistern shall be made clean by every man having his jakes falling into the same vault in the house of William Hollingworth, otherwise called Snowden. There is a party gutter all the length of the said house which of right ought to be repinned indifferently between the parties at their several costs and charges. And there are certain other gutters belonging to Ellys which have their course into the said long gutter, which of right they ought to have. Also, there is on the W side of the shop of Hollingworth a door and entry which he lately purchased of our Sovereign Lord the King, which door and entry one Roger Lewe, skinner, annoys with a certain table laid there by him, which he ought not of right to do. 'All these premises we say ought of right to be observed and kept. Except' *etc.*

289. [C.84] 23 December 1550.
Parish of St. Gabriel Fenchurch. Variance between Thomas Curtes of London, pewterer,[1] and Thomas Rydgeway and Alice, his wife, pls. [*sic*], concerning the making and letting of the lease of a house called 'the Ball' by Curtes to one William Gates and Elizabeth his wife, late deceased, which lease is now in the hands of pls. The viewers say that the variance is for repairs to be done to a roof of a chamber over the parlour, 22 ft. in length and 19 ft. in breadth. The roof is ready to fall down. The chamber over the hall next to the street side is in decay. All which things [*sic*] ought to be done and made tenantable at costs and charges of Curtes, as appears by the indenture and obligation thereof. 'All which premises we say ought to be done except' *etc.*

1. The irregular form of the certificate suggests clerical confusion which resulted in failure to identify Curtes as defendant.

290. [C.85] 31 December 1550.
Parish of St. Pulchres without Newgate in the suburbs of London. Variance between the Right Worshipful Sir Thomas Challennor, knight, and my lady his wife, pls., and Richard Hyll, tiler, def. concerning a messuage and certain tenements which are decayed. The viewers say that there is one plate, 26 ft. long, that must be new laid in, and the N end of the house lifted up and a new one made there. There is a party well in decay, which the two tenements ought to repair and mend. There is tiling, daubing, a party gutter, and other things which def. ought to repair at his costs and charges as he is bound to do by a lease which he holds upon the premises. The charges, by estimate, amount to £7. 'All this of right we say ought to be, except' *etc.*

291. [C.86] 19 January 1551.
Parish of St. Giles without Cripplegate. Variance between John Murfyn, cook, pl., and William Harper, merchant taylor, def., concerning a garden platt. The viewers say that def. holds the garden by lease, taken from the Brotherhood of St. Giles before it [the land] came into the king's hands. Therefore, def. ought to keep it. He also ought to make a lawful

fence on the S side of the garden. Pl. may build upon the E side of his garden all the length of his ground to a great elm tree, which he may fell. Except *etc.*

292. [C.87] 30 January 1551.
Parish of St. Oluf in Southwark. Variance between the Rt. Worshipful Sir Anthony Cooke, knight, pl., and Hugh Spencer, vintner, def., concerning a lease of a messuage and certain tenements at the sign of 'the Beare' at the Bridge foot of London. The viewers have seen the lease and variance and they say that pl. made a lease of the premises to one Ralph Willett, deceased, which lease yet endures and is now in the hands of one Master Middleton, draper. The house is not tenantable as it ought to be, 'for we say accordyng to the tenor of the lease which gevethe a quarter of a yeris warnyng yt may be made tenantable. And yf it be not made tennantable within the said terme after warnyng geven, that then the same lease is voyd.' Except *etc.*
Endorsed: 8 Februarii A[nn]o v° E[dwardi] 6 infert[ur] iste vis[us] feod[um]

293. [C.88] 9 March 1551.
Parish of All Hallows Barking. Variance between Thomas Blunte, citizen and mercer, pl., and Richard Smythe of the same city, mercer, def., concerning conveyance of diverse waters through the houses of def., one issuing through his chamber and another through his stable and yard. The viewers say that pl. ought to have his water courses through the said places because it was so used at the time of the purchase of his house. Furthermore, pl. ought of right to maintain the lead gutter through the chamber of def. as often as need shall require and not annoy def. with any manner of corrupt water or another thing going through it. Def. ought to suffer and maintain the water course through the stable and yard, as it was at the time of his purchase. Pl. ought to have all the houses [*sic*] with all other appurtenances as it was at the time of his purchase. Except *etc.*

294. [C.89] 9 March 1551.
Parish of St. Saviour in Southwark. Variance between Henry Helmer, draper, pl., and Randall Smyth, yeoman, def., concerning a fence of a pale [*sic*] between the parties. The viewers say that def. ought of right to make up the pale at his cost and charges, line right and plumb from the S corner of a little house on the W side of def.'s fence stretching E all the length of their grounds to a post there. Def. shall make the fence between this and St. Mark's Day next coming [25 April]; 'all this of right we say ought to be, except' *etc.*

295. [C.90] 13 March 1551.
Parish of St. Swithin. Variance in St. Swithin's Lane near Lombard Street between John Tocke, skinner, pl., and William Seeman, def., concerning a house with appurtenances which pl. purchased of def., which extends

20 ft. 7 in. along the king's highway of St. Swithin's Lane near Lombard Street. The viewers say that pl. has a kitchen over a certain party jakes. The viewers say that pl. may build upright over the jakes so long as he does not annoy or interrupt the [use] of the jakes by def. Either party to cleanse the jakes at their equal costs, according to the tenor of indentures made between them. Except *etc.*

Endorsed: 18 Mar[tii] A[nn]o 5 E[dwardi] 6 infert[ur] iste visus et sol[utum] feod[um]

296. [C.91] 14 April 1551.
Parish of St. Margaret in Friday Street. Variance between John Scot, salter, pl., and Humphrey Feylde, salter, def., concerning a principal partition on the N side of pl. from a post standing on the street side. The post leans 11 in. in breadth and is a party post; the partition ought to go indifferently in all things, stretching W to a jakes standing there. The viewers say that above the same jakes, the party [*sic*] ought to have 8 ft. 8 in. E and W and 2 ft. N and S for the fall of his jakes in a vault lying there between the parties as it was at the time of his purchase. There is a party gutter lying between the parties upon the same partition; it ought so to do. On the W end of the house of pl., abutting upon the house of the Earl of Bath, there stands a wall within which pl. may set his principals and build upright and plumb all the length of his ground. Pl.'s [land] abuts on the S toward the house of the Earl of Bath, which stands upon a stone wall; pl. ought to have 9 in. of that wall. Every man to bear his own water and their waters to be suffered to have their courses, also to have the fall of their jakes as it was at the time of their purchases. All which premises *etc.* Except *etc.*

Endorsed: 17 April A[nn]o v E[dwardi] 6 infert[ur] ist[e] vis[us] et sol[utum] feod[um] etc.

297. [C.92] 17 April 1551.
Parish of St. Botolph without Bishopsgate. Variance between Robert Donkyn, merchant taylor, pl., and John Lowyn, def., concerning an encroachment of the common way called Bell Alley. The viewers say that the alley is 6 ft. 6 in. in breadth at the W end; it stretches E 167 ft. from that end by the ground, line right and plumb by the side of the alley. It is and ought to be 6 ft. in breadth all that length. From an angle turning of the way there to a corner post, [the alley] ought to be 15 ft. in length and there, at that corner post, the alley is 3 ft. in breadth. From that corner post stretching E along by a pale [the alley] is 37 ft. in length; by all that length it is 7 ft. in breadth. Further, there is a garden platt of one Richard Mayne, draper, which contains 36 ft. in length along by the alley. At the SW corner of the garden there is an encroachment on the alley of 3 ft. At the E corner of the garden, there is an encroachment on the alley of 6 in. There the alley is 6 ft. in breadth. [The alley runs] more E to a corner house standing in the S side of the alley, which is there 5 ft. in breadth 'all which lengthes alonge by the same alley ought to goo lyne right and plumbe from lymytt to lymmytt.' Except *etc.*

Endorsed: 27 Aprilis A[nn]o 5 E[dwardi] 6 infert[ur] iste vis[us] et no[ndum] sol[utum] feod[um] etc.

See also **245** above.

298. [C.93] 21 April 1551.
Parish of Little All Hallows in Thames Street. Variance between John Mylnes, brewer, pl., and 'certeyne My Maysters thaldermen and others beyng maysters and roulers of the Hospytall of Saynt Bartholmewes in Smythfeild of London', defs., concerning a new house defs. are building. The viewers say that the nether storey of the house is 22 ft. in length from the W to the E along by the king's highway, to the middle of a party principal post there, 9 in. in breadth. The second storey is 21 ft. 7 in. in length W to E to a principal post 10 in. in breadth, also a party post. From the party post stretching N to another party post there stands a party partition. From that NE post stretching W measures 19 ft. 7 in. Defs. ought of right to build their house by the same measures. And every man ought to bear his own water according to the custom of the city of London. Except *etc.*
Endorsed: 22 Aprilis A[nn]o 5to E[dwardi] 6 infert[ur] iste visus et feod[um] sol[utum] etc.

299. [C.94] 28 April 1551.
Parish of St. Nicholas Coldabbey. Variance between Edward Hall, fishmonger, pl., and Thomas Wolfe, fishmonger, def., concerning a new frame set and being in the middle of Old Fish Street. The viewers say that there is upon the SE corner of the frame a post of the upper storey sailing over the middle of the kennel, which it ought not of right to do. Further, pl. ought of right to bear his own water from his own house and convey it to his own ground. Def. ought to bear his own water according to the custom of the city of London. 'All this of right we say ought to be except' *etc.*

300. [C.95] 4 May 1551.
Parish of All Hallows Barking. Variance between John Wylkockes, mariner, pl., and Thomas Dale, mariner, def., concerning a little back yard 13 ft. in length E and W and 6 ft. 11 in. in breadth N and S. The viewers say that pl. ought of right to have and occupy the yard by all its length and breadth as his lease, which he holds, licences him to do. Except *etc.*

301. [C.96] 26 May 1551.
Parish of St. Pulchres. Variance between Christopher Jackson, glazier, pl., and Stephen Gybson, cooper, def., concerning a house called the sign of '[the] Lambe'. The viewers say that def. has a lease of the house dated 32 Henry VIII [1540–1], of the grant and demise of the vicar and wardens of the Brotherhood of Our Lady and St. Stephen within the Church of St. Pulchres. The viewers have seen and read the lease and it appears that the lords having the fee simple of the house are bound to repair the same, as well against wind and rain as all other repairs, and to maintain the same

as often as need shall be. Further, there are two pieces of two pipes of lead lacking in the house, which were cut and taken away; one of the pipes is 8 ft. in length and the other 9 ft. For lack of the pipes the house is decayed by falling of the water there. It seems to the viewers that the pipes were conveyed away by the tenants of the house and def. ought of right to repair and restore them. All this of right *etc.*, except *etc.*

Endorsed: 28 Maii A[nn]o E[dwardi] 6 infert[ur] iste vis[us] et sol[utum] feod[um] mag[ist]ro

302. [C.97] 29 May 1551.
Parish of St. George in the Borough of Southwark, county of Surrey. Variance between George Thomson, carpenter, pl., and Humphrey Collet, bowyer, def., concerning the falling of water down off the house of pl. and a quick hedge at the S side of the ground of pl., stretching westward. The viewers say that pl. ought to have 16 in. on the S side, all the length of his house, for the fall of his water. The fence ought to be maintained and made sufficient by def. as it now is, and if any tree or bough hangs over into the ground of pl. more than of right it ought to do, pl. may lawfully brush and cut it plumb with his said grounds. Pl. may at all times hereafter build and join his house and building upright with the fence, so long as he bears his own water. All which things *etc.*, except *etc.*

303. [C.98] 29 May 1551.
Parish of St. Helen Bishopsgate. Variance between the master and wardens of the Leathersellers, pls., and Robert Kyrke, citizen and saddler, def., concerning a chamber in the second storey of a tenement of pl.'s house, which contains 11 ft. 2 in. E and W and 10 ft. N and S. The viewers say that def. ought of right to have the chamber 'because yt was in his tenure at the tyme of his purchase thereof'. Except *etc.*

304. [C.99] 13 June 1551.
Parish of St. Pulchres without Newgate. Variance between Richard Alleyne, haberdasher, pl., and John Holmes, weaver, def., concerning a common way or ground going into certain tenements in Seacoal Lane, in an alley there called Bear (Bere) Alley. The viewers say that def. has encroached on the common way 12 in. on the N side of the house he is building. On the W side of his house, from the corner of a wall and door there now stretching S to a house of his, def. has encroached 2 ft. on the common way or ground. All which of right he ought not to do. Except *etc.*

305. [C.100] 22 June 1551.
Parish of St. Mildred in Bread Street. Variance in a lane called Basing Lane between Davy Gyttons, vintner, pl., and Richard Wyther, salter, def., concerning a party stone wall between the houses of the parties, 3 ft. in thickness and 18 in. in length N and S. The wall bore and conveyed certain chimneys and other commodities at the time that both parties purchased their houses. The viewers say that both parties may build chimneys and other commodities in and upon the wall all its length at their several costs and charges, as has been done beforetime, so long as one does not annoy the other. All this of right *etc.* Except *etc.*

306. [C.101] 3 September 1551.
Parish of Holy Trinity [the Less]. Variance in a street called Knightrider Street between Sir John Darrell, clerk, parson of the parish church of the said Holy Trinity, and Simon Wall, cordwainer, and George Harryson, clothworker, churchwardens of the said church, pls., and Gervys Warter, cooper, def., concerning a procession way or lane 6 ft. in breadth at the E end of the church. The viewers say the way belongs to the parson and churchwardens and furthermore def. ought of right to have all the commodities, profits, and easements in the said land in as large and ample a manner as his lease, which he now holds, licenses him to have. Except *etc.*

307. [C.102] 17 September 1551.
Parish of St. Ethelburga within Bishopsgate. Variance between the master and wardens of the Tallowchandlers, pls., and Robert Chester, esquire, def., concerning a stone and brick wall lying between pls. and def. on the N side of pls.' grounds, containing 22 ft. 6 in. in length E and W. The viewers say that pls. may build and set up his [*sic*] frame that he [*sic*] is now building line right and plumb to the carpentry of the old house of def. Either party to bear their own water within their own grounds according to the ancient custom of the city of London. Except *etc.*

308. [C.103] 3 October 1551.
Parish of St. Stephen in Coleman Street. Variance between the master and wardens of the Merchant Taylors, pls., and Humfrey Berskerdfeld,[1] def., concerning a fence between the parties. The viewers say that pls. ought of right to make the fence E and W line right and plumb by all the length of def.'s ground at their costs and charges. Except *etc.*

    1. Baskerfeld or Baskervile.

309. [C.104] 3 October 1551.
Parish of St. Saviour's in Southwark in the County of Surrey. Variance between the master and wardens of the Fishmongers and John Maynforde, butcher, 'beynge a partie vyew of and for a variaunce betwene the said parties betwene the Crowne Key and the Black Bull'. The viewers say that the variance is for a fence lying between the parties. From a principal post of the house of Maynforde stretching E to a ditch where a certain plum tree stands, Maynforde ought of right to make the fence line right and plumb from limit to limit at their [*sic*] costs and charges. Except *etc.*
Endorsed: 7 Octobrii A[nn]o 5to E[dwardi] 6 infert[ur] iste visus

310. [C.105] 7 October 1551.
Parish of St. Olave in Southwark in the County of Surrey. Variance between Rychard Westram, brewer, pl., and William Broke, salter, def., concerning the repairing and upholding of all and singular reparations except principals belonging to the house where def. now dwells. The viewers say that def. ought of right as well to lathe, daub, and tile roundabout and upon his house, and all other rooms and his part of the

116

party gutters belonging to the same house, which are now in decay. He shall sufficiently defend the same house, with appurtenances, against wind and rain, and also pave the street side before his house and the entries within the same, which are also in decay, as often as need shall require. Furthermore, def. ought of right to make and do all repairs before expressed, tenantable and sufficiently, before the 25th day of March next coming, without further delay. Except *etc.*

311. [C.106] 14 October 1551.
Parish of St. Mary Woolnorth alias Wolnothe. Variance between George Cholmeley, waterbearer, pl., and Agnes Postelatte, widow, and William Wall, clothmaker, defs., concerning a jakes belonging to the tenement of pl. in a lane called Sherborne, which tenement George Postelatte, late husband of Agnes, sold to pl. as more plainly appears by his deed. The viewers say that pl. ought of right to have and occupy the jakes as it was at the time of his purchase. Furthermore, there is an entry on the N side of the house of pl. 18 ft. in length E and W and 3 ft. 10 in. in breadth N and S, which entry Wall withholds from pl. The entry belongs of right to the house of pl., as more plainly appears by a deed thereof made to him. Except *etc.*
Endorsed: 25/12 A[nn]o V° E[dwardi] VI sol[utum] feod[um]

312. [C.107] 27 October 1551.
Parish of St. Mary Woolchurch in Lumberstreet. Variance between Thomas Betenham and William Draper, gentleman, pls. in the right of their two wives, daughters and heirs of Seth Bothe, late of London, gentleman, deceased, and [*blank*] Pynchester of London, widow and late wife of Roger Pynchester, citizen and draper, deceased, def., concerning a certain parcel of ground or garden plat in the S part of pls.' tenements. The viewers say that pls. ought of right to have 19 ells[1] and 1 ft. of the ground E and W and 9 ft. in breadth N and S from their said tenements by all the said length as by deed to pls. by their ancestors more plainly appears; the deed is dated 21 Edward IV [*1481–2*]. All this of right *etc.* except *etc.*

1. The standard ell in measurement of land in London was 36 inches.

313. [C.108] 27 October 1551.
Duplicate of **312**.

314. [C.109][1] 9 November 1551.
Parish of St. Michael in Cornhill. Variance in Birchin Lane between Sir John Gresham, Sir Rowland Hill, knights and aldermen of said City; George Barnes, alderman of the same City; and William Blackwell, gentleman, common clerk of the said City, pls., and Thomas Bates, draper, def. The viewers say that the houses in Birchin Lane, with the breadth of the door or entry into the alley called St. Thomas Alley, are and of right ought to be 38 ft. 7 in. from the SW corner post stretching N along by the . . . and lane there called Birchin Lane. Further, there is a jetty on the N side [of the] house of pls., which is 22 ft. 3 in. in length from

E to W and 19 ft. in breadth by all that length. The jetty is 10 [ft. from] the ground and sails over into the shop or entry of def. by all the jetty's length and breadth, as it ought of right to do. From the jetty [stretching] more E all the length of pls.' houses, being parcel of the said [Alley] . . . contains 40 ft. 5½ in. in length. The [said] parties ought of right at their equal costs and charges to make a lead party gutter . . . their said houses from the E end of def.'s house now new [built to] the jetty. And the parties at their equal costs and charges ought to make a lead pipe [to convey] the rain water falling into the gutters to the ground. And so to have [issue and course] . . . the said jetty and through the shop of def. to the lane called . . . Moreover, whereas def. has broken tiles, bared [timber] and hurt pls.' houses by means of his building there, def. ought of right at his costs and charges to repair and amend the same. All which *etc.* except *etc.*

Endorsed: ix November a[nn]o 5 E[dwardi] 6 infert[ur] iste visus

1. Most of the right hand margin of the certificate has been torn away. The following certificate is a duplicate of this one; it has been torn roughly in half. The bracketed words above are taken from the duplicate certificate.

315. [C.110] 9 November 1551.
Duplicate, torn approximately in half, of **314**.

316. [C.111] 14 December 1551.
Parish of St. Botolph without Bishopsgate. Variance between John Brycket and Katharine, his wife, pls., and Robert Dounkyn, citizen and merchant taylor, def., concerning a gate and gatehouse. The viewers say that the gate and gatehouse, on the N side of pls.' gate and gatehouse, is 9 ft. 5 in. along by the king's highway. Through the gate there is a way into certain tenements of def. called Boe Alley, which def. lately purchased of the king's majesty and which belonged to St. Michael's church in Cornhill. Pls. also purchased two tenements there of one Robert Rypley, brewer, which, with all appurtenances, lately belonged to the hospital called St. Mary Spital. The viewers say that the gate and gatehouse are under the same roof as pls.' two tenements, and are parcel of them. Also, Rypley ought to make a lawful fence from a NW corner post of his house stretching W 20 ft. 8 in. line right and plumb by all the said length. Pls. ought to suffer Rypley's water to fall off his house into his [*sic*] yard there and his chimney to stand in such place as it did at the time of pls.' purchase. All this of right *etc.* except *etc.*

317. [C.112] 14 March 1552.
Parish of St. Benet Fink. Variance between Sir William Sydney, knight, pl., and Martin Caltrope, citizen and haberdasher, def., concerning a certain brick wall set at the E end of the church called St. Anthony's[1] between the grounds of the parties. The viewers say that pl. may have the release of the [?thickness] of the wall[2] there and may of right build up or upon it. Furthermore, def. and other inhabitants there ought of right every man to bear his own water, according to the ancient custom of the city of London, and so convey the same into his own ground at his own proper cost and charges. Pl. may build upright and plumb through his own ground in front of any light there. All this of right *etc.*, except *etc.*

1. The hospital of St. Anthony of Vienne.
2. Meaning uncertain. The word is clearly 'release' (rellesse) although 'relief', meaning 'remainder', would seem more appropriate.

318. [C.113] 17 May 1552.
Parish of St. Pulchres without Newgate. Variance between John Danbye, citizen and merchant taylor, pl., and Emmanuel Lucar of the same city, merchant taylor, def. The viewers say that the variance is for certain grounds and houses, which are contained in a certain old lease or grant indented, which pl. ought of right to have and hold of the College of Eton for certain years yet to come. Whereas def. withholds from pl. certain ground and a house specified in the lease, the viewers say pl. ought of right to have and enjoy the said house and ground and all other things in as large and ample a manner as contained and specified in the lease. Except *etc.*

319. [C.114] 17 May 1552.
Parish of St. Swithin. Variance in St. Swithin's Lane between Richard Hastynges, waxchandler, pl., and the Rt. Hon. John, Earl of Oxford, def. The viewers say that the variance is for a fence or brick wall lying between the tenements or houses of the parties. Pl. ought of right to have 9 in. all the length of the brick wall. Either party to bear his own water according to the ancient custom of the city of London, except that the parties may agree to make a party gutter between their houses at their equal costs and charges. Either party may build upon his own ground, upright and plumb. Except *etc.*

320. [C.115] 22 June 1552.
Parish of St. Nicholas Olave. Variance in Bread Street of London between James Leonard, fruiterer, pl., and Thomas Lytton, salter, def. The viewers say that the variance is for the falling of a jakes, or tunnel, belonging to the new house of pl., stretching W 3 ft. toward the house of def. The tunnel of the jakes is 21 in. in breadth N and S at the ground. It ought of right to be made and built up again at def.'s costs and charges to the use of pl. in every point and as good and in like fashion as it was at pl.'s purchase of it. Also, the parties ought of right to clean the cistern of the jakes as often as need shall require at equal costs and charges. Def., who is now building his house, ought of right at his costs and charges to bear his own water according to the ancient custom of the city of London. Except *etc.*
Endorsed: 16/9 A[nn]o 6 E[dwardi] 6 sol[utum] feod[um] co[mmun]is clerici

321. [C.116]¹ 26 [June 1552].
Parish of St. Michael in Cornhill. Variance between . . . , grocer, pl., and the [master and wardens of the] Grocers, defs. The viewers say that the variance is for a . . . chamber with their appurtenances which pl. now holds of . . . by indenture. There is a certain covenant which lately . . . Meryfeld, and after him it was demised by lease by . . . to one Robert Saunders, carpenter, for certain years yet to come . . . and plaintiff now

119

has and holds during the years [?demised to] Saunders. 'And we say that the sayd plaintyf ought of right to have and enjoye the said tenement wyth appurtenances as it was at the tyme of the ataynyng of the said lease and then as parcell of thappurtenance of the sayd Robert Sanders lease.' All this of right *etc.*, except *etc.*
Endorsed: [. . . ?8] A[nn]o 6[dwardi] vi visus . . .

   1. The right third of the certificate is missing down to the last four lines of writing.

322. [C.117] 16 July 1552.
Parish of St. Pancras. Variance between John Bull, mercer, pl., and William Cheke, grocer, def. The viewers say that pl. ought of right to have his frame rise upright and plumb, according to a deed he showed the viewers. Either party ought to bear his own water according to the ancient custom of the city of London. Except *etc.*

323. [C.118] 1 September 1552.
Parish of St. Nicholas Acon. Variance between John Swygo, merchant of Milan, pl., and Elizabeth Bowrne, widow, late wife of Baptyst Bowrne, merchant stranger of Milan, def. The viewers say that the variance is for a new house all under one frame of pl., which is set on the S side of the house of def. and abuts eastward on the churchyard of St. Nicholas Acon and westward on the king's highway called Abchurch Lane. Pl., who has purchased and holds the same, may build, convert, alter and use all the building contained within the frame at his pleasure. The parties ought to make clean their cistern or jakes there when need shall require in manner and form following: that is to say, the party with more tunnels or stools falling into the same to bear charges after that rate indifferently. Either party to bear his own water, according to the ancient and laudable custom of the city of London. All this of right *etc.* except *etc.*

324. [C.119] 2 September 1552.
Parish of St. Magnus of London Bridge. Variance between Sir Roger Cholmeley, knight, Lord Chief Justice of England, pl., and Mr. Brydges, Master Monoux, Mr. Broke, Mr. Alford, and Richard Vaughan, executors of the testament and last will of George Monoux, late Alderman of London, deceased, defs. The viewers say that the variance is for certain houses and cellars lying in the said parish. Pl. ought of right to have and hold as much therein as he had at the time of his purchase thereof of the king's majesty, paying all such quit-rents as ought of right to be paid for the same tenements, which quit-rents must be paid to the Masters of the Bridgehouse, as it appears to the viewers. Further, defs., having the cellars in their tenure, ought of right to uphold, maintain, and keep up all the said tenements of pl.; pl. to uphold and save harmless defs. above in his buildings. Except *etc.*
Endorsed in two places: iiii die Septembrii A[nn]o R[egno] R[egis] E[dwardi] sexto sol[utum] feod[um]
3 Septembrii A[nn]o 6 E[dwardi] 6 infert[ur] iste vis[us] et sol[utum] feod[um] co[mmun]is cl[er]ici etc.

325. [C.120] 19 September 1552.

Parish of St. Olave in Hart Street. Variance between Gregory Jaye, pl., and Francis Barney, def., concerning a jakes between the parties. The viewers say that def. ought of right to have the jakes 4 ft. 6 in. one way and 6 ft. the other way and at his costs and charges to bring up the said jakes with brick work to the floor of pl. Pl. ought of right to have his water fall there upon the ground of def. as it was at the time of his purchase. The parties ought of right to bear every one his part at the making clean of the jakes, as often as need shall require. And when it is clean they may divide it if they will so agree. Except *etc.*

326. [C.121] 28 September 1552.
Parish of St. Pulchres. Variance in West Smithfield between William Averay, innholder, pl., and Roger Wade, yeoman, def. The viewers say that the variance is for the fall of certain waters from the house of def., which stretches NW 20 ft. from a stone wall belonging to the Chamber of London. Def. ought of right to have his water fall between the houses of the parties by all that length, unless pl. will at his costs and charges make a gutter to convey the same water otherwise, because before this time a mud wall stood upon the ground that is now between the houses. Further, pl. may build upright and plumb on his own ground. Either party to bear his own water in all other places, according to the ancient custom of the City of London. Except *etc.*

327. [C.122] 8 October 1552.
Parish of St. Anthelaine. Variance between the Right Worshipful Sir Ralph Warren, knight and alderman of the city of London, pl., and Thomas Myddleton, skinner, def. The viewers say that the variance is for an entry 6 ft. in breadth leading to and from a house called 'the Barge' in Bucklersbury, going into a street there called Budge Row. Pl. ought of right to have free ingress and regress to and from the house called 'the Barge' through the same entry, as all other men have had before this time. Def. ought not to have any door or way into the entry, nor more course of water than there is now going. His stalls ought not to extend further upon the ground of the entry than the breadth of the principals of his own house. Pl. ought to pave the entry and the street to the kennel thereof, all the breadth of his jetty, at his own costs and charges. His gate ought to be hung in the same place as it was hung in times past. All this we say of right *etc.* Except *etc.*
Endorsed: 13 Octobrii A[nn]o 6 E[dwardi] 6 infert[ur] iste visus

328. [C.123] 13 October 1552.
Parish of St. Leonard's in St. Martins Lane le Grand. Variance between Garret Williamson and Agnes Peterson, widow. The view is a party view. The viewers say that there is an entry going into an alley called St. John's Alley, which ought to be of right 4 ft. 7 in. in breadth all the length of the entry. At the W corner of the entry there stands a post; the viewers say that the party that builds there, either the carpenter or the party [himself], ought of right to set the post 4 in. more W than it now stands and bring it up line right and plumb at his own proper costs and charges all

the length of the frame. All other things of both parties, such as ingress and regress, ought of right to be observed and kept according to the tenor of their leases. Except *etc.*

329. [C.124] 15 October 1552.
Parish of St. Benet near Paul's Wharf. Variance between Robert Shurlock, woodmonger, pl., and William Edwards, cook, def. The viewers say that the variance is for a roof of a house which was lately within the ground of def. beside a well there; it was taken down by pl. and in its place pl. has built a shed. Pl. ought of right at his own proper costs and charges to make a roof there again, as it was at the time of the making of the lease to def., it to be made as large in length and breadth as it was at that time. Furthermore, def. ought of right at his own proper costs and charges to repair and amend all such walls and other hurts as he or any of his shall break or do within his house or other places adjoining it during his years [as lessee]. Either party to perform, fulfil, and keep all such covenants as are contained within a pair of indentures made between them concerning the grant of the same house. All this of right *etc.*, except *etc.*

330. [C.125] 30 October 1552.
Parish of St. Marie Buttolphe [Bothaw]. Variance between William Tailor, clerk, parson of the said parish; Henry Walker and George Goodder, wardens and keepers of the goods, lands, works, rents, tenements, hereditaments, and ornaments of the said parish church, pls., and Richard Staples, draper, def. The viewers say that the variance is for a shed and the ground thereto belonging, set, lying, and being at the SE corner of the church. The ground and shed contain 6 ft. 4 in. in length and 3 ft. 10 in. in breadth and belong of right to the parson and churchwardens and their successors forever. Further, there is a party gutter between the church and the house of def. which ought of right to be repaired, maintained, and upheld at equal costs and charges of both parties. Neither def. nor any other ought to have a way or passage through the ground or shed at any time without special licence of the parson and churchwardens. Except *etc.*

331. [C.126] 22 November 1552.
Parish of All Saints in Honey Lane. Variance between the master, wardens, and company of Mercers, pls., and Thomas Pannell, parson of the said parish church, and the churchwardens and parishioners of the parish, defs. The viewers say that the variance is for a certain vault or cellar under the church. The vault or cellar belongs and of right ought to appertain and belong to and is the freehold of the parson and church-wardens forever. Except *etc.*
Endorsed: 29 Novembris A[nn]o 6 E[dwardi] 6 infert[ur] iste visus et sol[utum] feod[um]

332. [C.127] 28 November 1552.
Parish of St. Bartholomews of London. Variance between Thomas

Armestronge, clothworker, pl., and John Owtynge, carpenter, def. The viewers say that the variance is for the bearing of certain waters between houses of the parties and for the breaking of certain tiles of the house of def. Pl. ought of right at his own costs and charges to amend and make up again so many of the tiles and other things of the house of def. as he has broken down by reason of his building there. Pl. ought to take the fillet gutter that lies on the house of def. and make thereof a perfect gutter at his cost and charges, for the safeguard of both houses; the gutter to contain 31 ft. in length between their houses and [pl.] so to convey the water that shall there descend into the gutter into his yard. The gutter, to be made by pl., shall be upheld and repaired ever after at def.'s costs. All this of right *etc.* except *etc.*

Endorsed: 13 Decembrii A[nn]o 6 E[dwardi] 6 infert[ur] iste visus feodu[m] . . . co[mmun]is cl[er]ici non[dum] solut[um]

333. [C.128] 14 December 1552.
Parish of St. Faith under St. Paul's. Variance between Thomas Petit, pl., and Mr. Doctor Gybbyns, doctor of the law, def., for a jakes and certain conveyances of waters by gutters and a pipe. The viewers say that the falls of both the jakes and the gutters with the pipe for the jakes ought of right to have their course as they did at the time of the parties' purchase [of their houses] and as it is now. Either party to bear like and equal charges toward the scouring of jakes, gutter, and pipes when need shall require. Except *etc.*

334. [C.129] 19 December 1552.
Parish of St. Olave in Hart Street. Variance between John Wyseman, Esquire, pl., and Mr. Worseley, gentleman, def. The viewers say that the variance is for a certain fence or pale now being built by pl. between the grounds of the parties. The pale or fence ought to be set line right and plumb from the SW corner post of a house of pl. stretching W to a corner post set on the NE side of a house of def. Further, pl. may cut away or dig up all such roots, boughs, or trees or any other thing that shall let (lett)[1] him to set his pale line right and plumb from limit to limit as aforesaid. Either of the parties to make their own fence so far as their own buildings go. Also, either to bear their own water, according to the ancient custom of the city of London. Except *etc.*

1. It is unclear whether 'lett' in the phrase 'or any other thing that shall lett him to set his pale' should be understood in the modern sense of the word, giving the meaning 'that shall allow him to set his pale' or in the older sense, thus meaning 'that shall hinder him from setting his pale.'

335. [C.130] 16 May 1553.
William Walker, John Russell, Thomas Ellys [*sic*] and John Cowper, 'the iiii masters of fremasons and carpenters', viewers. Parish of St. Botolph without Aldrichgate. Variance between the worshipful Sir William Peter, knight, secretary to the King's most excellent majesty, pl., and Robert Cattelyn, one of the Sergeants of the Law of our said sovereign Lord the King and [*blank*] his wife, late wife of Sir [*blank*] Burgon, deceased, defs. The viewers say that the variance is for a brick wall set N and S upon the

W side of the grounds of pl., of which wall as it is now set pl. ought of right to have half the thickness all its length. At the S end of the wall there stands an end of a stable; there pl. may build upright and plumb upon the foundation as it is now built there. Either of the parties to bear their own water according to the ancient custom of the city of London.[1]

> 1. 'Thomas' is a mistake for 'Nicholas' Ellys, and John Cowper was a tiler. The salutation of the certificate differs from all others in the collection for Edward VI; it is addressed to 'your discreet and sad wisdoms' rather than 'your good lordship and masterships', and there is no saving clause. The clue to the explanation probably lies in the fact that the certificate is in a hand different from that of others of the period: someone unfamiliar with the viewers and with their procedure wrote or recopied it, possibly using a much older certificate as his model.

336. [C.131][1] 4 April [1551 x 1553][2]
Parish of . . . Variance between . . . Peert, gentleman, pl., and Anne . . . concerning the S side of the ground in . . . The viewers say that the variance is for certain lights there cast out into a party [?wall] . . . a great glazed window there set forth which ought of right . . . a clerestory right with the same house, 6 ft. from the . . . set up to the soil of the same window and also . . . cast forth on that side of the house of the said party . . . the air after the ancient custom of London . . . charges of def. And further . . . part of the house on the W side of . . . annoy the pl. . . .

> 1. This certificate and the four following it are fragmentary.
> 2. The fragment cannot be dated exactly, but since the viewers' names still legible are 'Ellys' and John Cowper, the certificate must date from after 10 July 4 Edward VI, the date of the last extant certificate which lists Gilbert Burffame, whom John Cowper had replaced as a viewer by 30 August 4 Edward VI. Both Nicholas Ellis and John Cowper continued as viewers until the end of the reign.

337. [C.132] [No date or endorsement visible][1]
. . . John Cowper . . . variance in the parish of . . . there . . . party and . . . the other party which . . . hereafter ensuring . . . In primis ii pieces of timber and workmen . . . and in other tyme lyk thefore . . . and vessells set out in the great . . . the same bringing up the . . . of every side finding to the . . . tymes. Item, for certain . . . pavement before the same . . . to be [numbered] to . . . the chambre . . .

> 1. The certificate cannot be dated precisely, but it must date from after 10 July 4 Edward VI; see note to certificate **336** above.

338. [C.133] [10 July 1550 x 22 September 1553][1]
William . . . carpenters and tylers, viewers . . . lordships commandment to view and oversee a variance . . . between Edward Herenden, mercer, pl. . . . which is for a certain garden platt there . . . unto the party pl. which gardens . . . we say that from the NE corner . . . towards the mud wall of the bargayne . . . stretching W there lacks 6 in. of size . . . to a stick there driven is 40 and 14 ft. . . . there lacks one foot of size . . . the whole breadth according . . . to be. Except there be any . . .

> 1. The first legible word in the certificate is 'William', presumably referring to William Walker, and the reference is to 'carpenters and tylers', so the certificate must date from after the appointment of John Cowper as a viewer – that is, after 10 July 4 Edward VI – and before 22 September 1 Mary, when Walker had already been replaced by Thomas Peacock.

339. [C.134] 18 May . . . [temp. Edward VI]
. . in the Poultry . . . def. of . . . variance the . . . there is a . . . against the
:ing . . . to say five inches . . . Also there is a not . . . the king's highway . . .
lef. . . . is in wideness . . . 6 ft. . . . stretching . . .
Endorsed: 18 Maii A[nn]o . . . illat[us] fuit hic vis[us] Cur[iam] etc. sed
1on[dum] sol[utum] feod[um]

340. [C.135] 22 September 1553.
To the Right honorable lorde Maire of the Cytie of London and to his
worshipfull brethren the Aldermen of the same Cytie.
Shewen unto your good lordships & masterships the xxii[th] day of
September in the firste yere of the Reign of our soveraign Lady Quene
Mary, John Russell, Nicolas Ellys, John Cowper, and Thomas Pecok, the
iiii masters of Fremasons, Carpenters, & Tylers, viewers Indifferent
sworne to the said Cytie, that where as they were of late charged by your
lordships comaundment to viewe and oversee a variance in the parishe of
Sainte Lawrens Pulteney of London betwene Thomas Fisher and
Edmond Hasilparte, churche wardeyns of the goodes, rentes, and
ornamentes of the said parishe churche, playntifes on the one partie, and
Robt Browne, goldsmyth, defendant on the other partie, Whiche thinge
and variance therof we the said iiii viewers have viewed, serched & seen
and therupon we say that the said variance ys of & for a certain Celler and
newe building of the partie defendante sett on the Northside of the said
churche there. And we say that by reason of making of the said Celler and
setting up of the said building and frame, the churche ys decayed and the
building therof ys hurte & anoyed, whiche decay and hurtes we say that
the said partie defendant ought to repaire, builde, and make up agayn at
his proper costes and charges. Except there be any writing or evydence to
the contrary to be shewed.
Endorsed: 27 11 A[nn]o i d[omi]ne Marie Regine & infert[ur] istud
Record & Et sol[utum] etc.

341. [C.136] 25 October 1553.
Parish of St. Bride in Fleet Street. Variance between John Pursell, citizen
and skinner, pl., and Anthony Skynner, gentleman, def. The viewers say
that the variance is for a certain brick wall set on the N side of a house of
pl. and abutting on a garden of def. 'Whiche brycke wall we the said foure
viewers saie ought of right (as farre as we see by experyence and have
lerned by profe of certen wrytyngs), to belonge and to be and is parcell of
the lytle yarde of the sayd partie plaintyf and dothe of right belonge unto
him as his fee simple.' Except *etc.*
Endorsed: xxvi die Octobrii A[nn]o i° Marie Regine infert[ur] iste visus
Et sol[utum] feod[um] etc.

342. [C.137] 25 October 1553.
Parish of All Hallows Barking. Variance between William Armorer,
gentleman, pl., and [blank] Sydley, gentleman, def. The viewers say that
the variance is for the dividing of a certain tenement of pl. from one of
def. The tenement of pl. ought to be abutted and contain in length and

breadth as follows: from the SE corner post of the dwelling house of pl
stretching E 18 ft. 2 in. along by the Tower Street to the middle of a part
post there. On the N side of the tenement of pl., from a stone wall of pl
stretching E 18 ft. 11 in. along by the ground of def. to the middle of a
party post. Further, pl. ought of right or may at his pleasure build there
upright and plumb in length and breadth as his tenement is now set
keeping the measures above limited. Except *etc.*

343. [C.138] 25 November 1553.
Parish of St. Olave in the Borough of Southwark. Variance between
William Lambe, joiner, pl., and Richard Roberts, plumber, def. The
viewers say that the variance is for a certain chamber over a tenement in
tenure of pl. and a house over the gate of def. The chamber and house
over the gate belong to and are appurtenances of the two tenements now
in tenure of pl. He of right ought to have and enjoy the same during his
lease of the two tenements. Except *etc.*
Endorsed: xxviii November A[nn]o primo Regine Marie infert[ur] istud
[*sic*] visus

344. [C.139] 20 December 1553.
Parish of St. Giles without Cripplegate. Variance between John Ryge-
way, goldsmith, pl., and John Garrett, salter, def. The viewers say that
the variance is for reparations of a tenement and certain houses and
buildings set on the back side of the same, set, lying, and being in Red
Cross Street, now in tenure of def. by virtue of a lease which he holds. The
tenements, buildings and houses ought to be repaired, upheld, and
maintained in manner and form following: a whole house on the back side
of the tenements, which is now a stable; a house on the back side of the
tenement which was lately a mill (mylne) house; and a shed over a well,
ought all to be newly ripped, tiled, raftered, plated, daubed, and set
upright and tenantable, with such breadth and compass as they now have.
The tenement, both in hall and parlour, with the buildings joined to it
ought to be repaired in carpentry, tiling, daubing, and plumbery of the
gutters. The reparations of all the houses will stand in and cost def., by
estimation, to make the same tenantable the sum of £23. 13*s*. 4*d*. of lawful
money of England. The reparations ought to be done and repaired within
such time as is limited to def. by his lease or else, at the farthest, before
the feast of St. James next coming [25 July].
Endorsed: xv° Januarii A[nn]o primo Regine Marie infert[ur] iste visus &
sol[utum] feod[um]

345. [C.140] 8 January 1554.
To the right honorable lorde maire of the Cytie of London and to his
worshipfull brethren thaldermen of the same.
Shewen unto your good lordship and maisterships the viii[th] day of
Januarie in the fyrst yere of the reigne of our soveraigne ladye Quene
Marie, John Russell, Nicholas Ellys, John Cowper, and Thomas Pea-
cocke, the fowre maisters of Fremasons, Carpenters, and Tylers, vyewers
Indyfferent sworne to the said Cytie, That whereas they were of late

charged by your lordships comaundement to view and oversee a varyance in the parishe of Saint Sepulcre withoute Newgate of London betwene William Collins of London, Carpenter, plaintyf on the one partie, and Peter Grene, yoman, defendante on the other partie, which thinge and varyance therof we the said foure viewers have viewed, serched, and sene and thereuppon we saye that there was presented unto Sir Rowland Hill, knight, late Maire of London, a certen view in these wordes following, that is to saie:[1]

To the right honorable lord Maire of the Cytie of London and to his Worshipfull brethren thaldermen of the same Cytie, Shewen unto your good lordshipe and worships the xvth daye of September in the fourth yere of the reigne of our soveraigne lorde kinge Edwarde the Syxt Willm Walker, John Russell, Nicholas Ellys, and John Cowper, the iiii maysters of Fremasons, carpenters, and Tylers, viewers Indyfferent sworne to the said Citye, That whereas they were of late charged by your lordships Comaundement to view and oversee a varyance in the parishe of St. Sepulcre withoute Newgate in the Olde Baylie of London Betwene Peter Grene, yoman, plaintyf, on the one partie, and Thomas Hilton, merchaunttailor, defendante, on the other partie, which varyance is of, for, and [concerning] a certen wall whereof the partie defendaunte hath cut awaye and taken down from the east to the west one fote of assyse and from the north to the south Seven Foote of assyse, which of right he ought not to doo, And further we saie that the partie plaintyf hath an entrie with a doore openynge into the layne called Flete Lane and goynge to a yarde there, which yarde we saye ought to be viii Foote brode by all the length of the said Tenement, and bothe the said parties to make a lawfull fence in the said yarde indifferently betwene them bothe att their severall proper Costes and charges and either of them to bere their owne water according to the ancyent Custome of the Cytie of London. And this of right we saie ought to be except therebe any wryttinge, evidence, or other specyaltie to the contrarie to be shewed.

And at the makinge of the said view there was shewed forth unto us a certen lease by the said Peter Grene dated the xxxiiiith yere of the raign of our late soveraign lorde of worthie memorie Kinge Henrie theight and made by the Maister and Chaplaynes of the House of Savoye. By the whiche and a certen platt indented annexed to the sayd lease it appeared that the said Peter Grene was intytuled to an entrie and a dore openinge into the Flete Lane. And also a certen house on the West syde of the said entrie wherein one William Browne, waterbearer, now dwelleth. And for that the said William Collins, carpenter, hath now shewed forth unto us, the said viewers, a leese made unto hym by the said Maister and Chaplayns of the Savoye dated the xxviith yere of Kinge Henrie Theight with certen platt indented and annexed unto the same lease, and for that the said lease is dated afore the lease of the said Peter Grene, and that thereby it appereth that the said William Collyns is entytuled to the said entrie, house, and dore by reason of his said lease, Therefore we doo saie that the said William Collyns ought of right now to enioye and have the said house, dore, and entrie wherein the said Brown now dwelleth with theire appurtenances accordinge to his said lease, except a Celler under the said house which of right belongeth to the said Peter Grene. Except there be any wryttynge Evydence or other Especialtie to the contrary to be shewed.

Endorsed: ... istud script[um] infert[ur] [?iste] visus & sol[utum] feod[um]

1. A fragment of the original certificate has survived; see **282** above.

346. [C.141][1] 12 January 1554.

Parish of St. Mary at Hill, ward of Billingsgate. Variance between Thomas Blanke, haberdasher, pl., and the parson and churchwardens of the parish church of St. Mary at Hill, defs. The viewers say that the variance is for a stone wall set on the S side of the churchyard and on the N side of pl.'s ground, of which wall pl. ought of right to have 11 in. [thickness], provided always that a certain [?chimney] for ... same wall ought to remain as it is now. Defs. to bear their own water according to [the ancient custom of] the city of London. Except *etc.*

1. The certificate is in poor condition, with the writing badly faded and indecipherable even under ultraviolet light.

347. [C.142] 19 January 1554,

Parish of St. Faith in Warwick Lane. Variance between Roger Maskall, brewer, pl., and Edward Mundes, def. The viewers say that the variance is for a window going into a gutter of pl. The window ought of right to be stopped up at cost and charges of def. Also, def. ought of right to bear the water of his own house. Except *etc.*

348. [C.143][1] 14 March 1554.

Parish of St. Mary Somerset. Variance at Broken Wharf of London between John Sturgyon, Chamberlain of the City of London in the right of the same City, pl., and the master and wardens of the Fishmongers and Clement Kyllingworth, citizen and pewterer, defs. The viewers say that the variance is for a certain plat of ground stretching S from the street called [blank] down to the river of Thames, which has in time past been a common way there, set, lying, and being between the houses and [?grounds] now belonging to the said master and wardens on the E and the ground now in the tenure of the said Kyllingworth on the W. Which common way or ... [?plat] of ground ought to be open, and lie and be as in time past it was: that is to say, between the principals of the houses belonging to the master and wardens and Kyllingworth. Except *etc.*

Endorsed: 29/6 A[nn]o primo Marie Regine infert[ur] iste visus non[dum] sol[utum] feod[um] quia pro Camerar[io] etc.

1. The right side of the certificate is torn away, affecting the last word in each line.

349. [C.144][1] 8 May 1554.

Parish of St. Giles without Cripplegate. Variance between William Pryce, draper, pl., and Gregory Nicholas [blank], def. The viewers say that the variance is for a certain fence or pale set between the grounds of the parties, which contains in length 29 ft. and stretches northward from the mansion house of pl. to a NW corner post of an alley house of pl. From the NW corner post [it runs] 13 in. more W. The fence ought to be set and made there as the viewers have marked, that is, 4 ft. from W to E from the mansion house of pl. Also, forasmuch as the fence is a headland, the parties ought to make it indifferently at their several costs and charges by all the said length on both sides of the mansion house in the garden there. Except *etc.*

1. The certificate is closely written in a careless hand different from the preceding certificates.

350. [C.145][1] 8 May 1554.
Parish of St. George in Southwark. Variance between William Smyth, currier, pl., and William Bastley, esquire, def. The viewers say that the variance is for a certain fence and ground about the fence lying between the parties' grounds. Upon the viewing of the same and for the appeasing and quieting of the said parties of and for the same variance, they say pl. ought to set his pale or fence eastward from his house 1 ft. all its length for the dripping and fall of his water from his house. Also, pl. ought to have all the trees growing between the grounds of the parties and ought to make a sufficient fence upright as the trees stand and grow, all the length of his ground. Except *etc.*
Endorsed: 2/8 A[nn]o primo Marie Regine

1. The certificate is in the same hand as **349**

351. [C.146] 17 June 1554.
Parish of St. Sepulchre. Variance between Thomas Whytelocke, merchant taylor, pl., and Richard Dytcher, alias Massie, lorimer, def. The viewers say that the variance is for certain water courses falling both into the ground and yard on the back side of the houses of both parties and into a party gutter between the houses. The water courses have of long time issued and had their course through the kitchen now in tenure of one John Awdrye, weaver, and through the shop of def. They ought of right so to continue and not be stopped up by the parties, as they are now. Further, def. has a door out of his house into the party gutter; by water from the door, the gutter is filled and the house annoyed with filth and the water course there stopped, 'and therefore we saie and adiuge it to be equytie and right that the said partie defendaunte shall stoppe uppe his said Doore and make there a window. And that the said party plaintyf ought at all tymes hereafter to make there the said Gutter.' Def. alleges that pl. has, since the time of his purchase, built certain houses within his grounds, by reason of which the water course is greater and more annoys the def. than it did before the building. Therefore, pl. ought of right to bear and convey all the water descending from the buildings which he has built since his purchase, excepting only rain water, without the hurt, annoyance, or damage of def. Except *etc.*
Endorsed: 27 Junii anno primo Marie Regine infert[ur] iste visus

352. [C.147] 17 June 1554.
Parish of St. Olave in the Borough of Southwark. Variance in Bermondsey Street between Richard Westram, brewer, pl., and William Tow,

mariner, def. The viewers say that the variance is for $9\frac{1}{2}$ in. of ground from a NW corner post of the house of def. to the common sewer at the W end of the garden of def. The $9\frac{1}{2}$ in. was in time past a piece of ground for the water falling off the house of pl. to fall upon. It is the ground of pl. and he may and ought of right to have and build upon it if he will. Furthermore, either party ought to bear their own water according to the ancient custom of the city of London. Except *etc.*

Endorsed: 27 Junii anno primo Marie Regine infert[ur] iste visus

353. [C.148] 21 June 1554.

To the right honorable lord maire of the Cytie of London and to his worshipfull brethren the Aldermen of the same

Shewen unto your good lordship and maistershisp the xxi[th] June in the fyrst yere of the Reigne of Our Soveraigne lady Marie, by the grace of god Quene of England, Fraunce and Irelande, defender of the Fayth and on earth of the Churche of England and also of Ireland the Supreame Head,[1] John Russell, Nycholas Ellys, John Cowper, and Thomas Peacock, the iiii maysters of Fremasons, carpenters, and Tylers, vyewers Indyfferent Sworne to the said Cytie, that whereas they were of late charged by your lordships comaundement to view and oversee a varyaunce in the parishe of Seint Gabriel Fanchurche of London betwene John Demmock, Draper, playntyf on the one partie, and Frauncys Carcidonii, merchaunte stranger, defendaunt on the other partie, which thinge and varyance thereof we the said iiii sworne viewers have viewed, serched, and sene and thereuppon we saie that the said varyance is of and for a certen platt of grounde lying on the South and bacsyde of the house of the said partie defendante and which platt of grounde Mr. Thomas Curtys, Alderman, hath demysed unto the said partie defendante as appurtenance of his said house by a certen Indenture of lease of certen yeres yet to come. Which platt of grounde we saie the partie defendante ought of right to enioye accordinge to the tenor of his said Lease. And further we saie that the said partie defendante ought to bere all the buyldinges belongyng to his house without the damage of the said partie plaintyf. And that the said partie plaintyf ought to bere the water descendyng from his owne houses according to the ancyent Custome of the Cytie of London. Except therebe any wrytyng, Evydence, or other especialtie to the contrarie to be shewed.

Endorsed: 4/9 A[nn]o primo Marie Regine etc. infertur iste visus

1. This certificate, although it introduces a new form of reference to the sovereign, is in the same hand as the two certificates immediately preceding it. The elaborate recitation of titles is not repeated in the following certificates.

354. [C.149] 25 July 1554.[1]

Parish of St. Peter le Poor in Bread Street. Variance between Margaret Johnson, widow, pl., and William Powy, embroiderer (broderer), def. The viewers say that the variance is for a certain brick wall set between grounds of the parties and on the N side of pl.'s grounds, which is the wall of def. Pl. ought not of right to build upon any of the wall. Furthermore, def. ought to bear the water [now] falling from his own house into the ground of pl. according to the ancient custom of the city of London. Except *etc.*

1. Technically, 25 July 1554 was the first day of the joint reign of Philip and Mary, but neither this certificate nor **355**, dated 28 July 1554, makes any mention of Philip.

355. [C.150][1] 28 July 1554.

To the right honorable lorde maire of the Cytie of London and to his worshipfull Brethren Thaldermen of the same

Shewen unto your good lordship and maysterships the xxviii[th] day of Julie in the seconde yere of the Reigne [of our sovereign] lady Quene Marie, John Russell, Nycholas Ellys, Jown Cowper, and Thomas Peacok, [the iiii masters] of Fremasons, Carpenters, and Tylers, vyewers Indyfferent sworne to the said Cytie, [that whereas they] were of late charged by your lordships comaundement to viewe and oversee a varyaunce in the parish [of Saint] Gregorie and Saint Fayth at Saint Austen's Gate wythin the Cytie of London, Betwene the Wardens . . . of the Mystery of Mercers of the said Cytie, plaintyfs on the one partie, and John Wilkinson, merchant [?taylor, defendant] on the other partie, Whiche thing and varyance thereof we the said fowre sworne viewers have [viewed and] . . . measured. And thereuppon we saie that the said partie defendaunte ought of right to build . . . the said Gate in Bredeth fower foote and ten ynches of assyse from the east to the west Betwene . . . belongynge to the Bridgehouse of London on the easte parte and the Tenement belongynge to the said [?Mercers] on the West partie, upright and plumbe, by all the said Bredeth of vii foote and x ynches. And further . . . that the said partie defendaunte may buylde over the said Gate toward the north from his . . . up close to the house of the said parties plaintyfes as before this tyme his said house was buylded [and] lymytted. Also we saie that the said parties playntyfs ought of right to have a stone wall . . . betwene the said Ten[emen]ts belongynge to the Bridgehouse and their owne Tenement wyth all the . . . belongynge to the same wall. And that every of the parties ought to bere their own water [according to the] Ancyent Custome of the Cytie of London. Except there be any wryting, Evydence [or other especialty] to the contrarie to be shewed.

1. The certificate is torn at the right margin, with resultant loss of several words at the end of each line.

356. [C.151] 9 March 1555.

To the right honorable lorde maire of the Cytie of London and to his worshipfull brethren thaldermen of the same

Shewen unto your good lordship and masterships the ix[th] day of Marche in the first and seconde yeres of the reignes of our soveraigne lorde and lady Philippe and Marie, by the grace of god Kinge and Quene of England etc., John Russell, Nicholas Ellys, Thomas Peacock, and Water Cowper, the foure maysters of Fremasons, Carpenters and Tilers, viewers Indifferent sworne to the said Citie, That whereas they were of late Charged by your lordships Commaundement to viewe and oversee a varyaunce in the parishe of Saint Peter at Pouleswharf betwene Thomas Blakethelder, [*Blake the elder*], haberdasher, plaintyf on thone partie, and Sir Richard

131

Sackfeld, knight, defendaunte on the other partie, which thynge and variance therof we the said foure sworne viewers have viewed, serched, sene, and measured and thereuppon we saye that the said variance is of & for a Brickwall betwene the grounds of the said parties on the southsyde of the grounde of the said partie plaintyf, which wall we saye ought of right to go lyne right and plome on the south syde of bothe the postes of the house of the said partie plaintyf and further we saie that the yarde of the said partie plaintyf there conteyneth in lengthe xxii foote ix ynches of assyse from the east to the west. Except there be any wrytyng, evidens, or especialtie to the contrarie to be shewed.

357. [C.152] 8 August 1555.
To the right honorable lorde Maire of the Citie of London and to his worshipfull brethren thaldermen of the Same
Shewen unto your good lordship and masterships the viii[th] day of August [in the second] and thirde yeres of the Reignes of our sovereigne lorde and lady [Philip and] Marie by the grace of God Kinge and Quene of England, France, Neapells, Jerusalem, and Ireland, Defendours of the Fayth, Princes of Spayne and Sicilie, Archdukes of Austria, Dukes of Myllayne, Burgoyne, and Brabant, Countes of Haspurge, Flanders, and Tirolle, John Russell, Nicholas Ellys, Thomas Peacok and Water Cowper, the four maisters of Fremasons, Carpenters, and Tilers, viewers Indyfferent sworne to the said Cytie, That whereas they were of late charged by your lordships commaundement to view and oversee a varyaunce in the parishe of Saint Bennet at Pouleswharfe of London Betwene Anthony Hill, mercer, plaintyf on the one partie, and William Bonner, carpenter, defendaunte on the other partie, Whiche thinge and varyaunce thereof we the said foure sworne viewers have viewed, serched, and sene and thereuppon we say that the sayd varyaunce is of and for and aboute the upholding of a syde of a house of the said partie defendaunte. And therefore we say there stondeth a stone wall on the east syde of the said party defendauntes groundes uppon which wall the said partie defendaunte ought of right to buylde uppe the syde of his house for the upholdinge of the same by all the length of the same wall, lyne right and plome. And that the said partie defendaunte ought to have no light hole or wyndow thorow the same wall and syde of his said house wythoute the lycense of the said partie plaintyff. And that the said partie defendaunte ought of right to amende such hurtes as he hath done to the house of the said partie defendaunte [*sic*]. And either of the said parties to bere their owne waters according to the ancyent custome of the Cytie of London. Except therebe any wrytting, Evydence or Especialtie to the contrarie to be shewed.

358. [C.153][1] 5 September 1555.
To the right honorable lorde Mare ... the Worshipfull brethren thaldermen ...
Shewen unto your good lordship and maystershps the Vth day of September in the seconde ... lorde and lady Philippe and Marie by the Grace of God King and Quene of England and Ireland, Defender of the fayth, Prince of Spayne and Sicilie ... Burgoyne and Brabant, Countes of

Haspurge, Flanders, and Tiroll, John Russell, Nicholas Ellys, [Thomas] Pecock, and Water Cowper, the foure maisters of Fremasons, Carpenters and Tilers . . . sworne to the said Cytie that whereas they were late charged by your lordship . . . and oversee a varyaunce in the parishe of St. Bryde in Fletestrete between [Johanna Robinson], widow, playntyf on the one partie and Stephen Harman, gyrdler, defendaunt on the other partie . . . and variance thereof we the said foure sworne viewers have viewed, serched . . . thereuppon we saye that the said variaunce is first of and for one gutter Betwene the houses . . . parties in length xii fote of assyse which gutter is the proper gutter of the said partie defendant . . . therefore we saie that the same partie defendaunte ought of right to repayr, uphold, mayntene and . . . his owne Water by and all the length of the same gutter at his proper costes and charges. And also we [say] that from the southe ende of the foresaid gutter stretching more south there is a gutter in length . . . . foote of assyse and yet further from the south ende of the same measure a gutter of xxxvi . . . is an other gutter stretching more south xii fote of assyse which gutters we saie the said . . . playntyf ought of right to uphold, make, and mayntayne at her proper costes and . . Also we saie that from the said gutter of the said partie defendaunt stretching south all the . . . of his houses, the same defendaunte ought to make a Fillet gutter to bere and convey the water falling from all his said houses ther by all the length of the same & so to convey the same into his own grounde at his owne proper costes and charges. Also we saie that the said . . . defendaunt ought of right to make a lawfull fence from the south syde of his house stretching more south to London Wall xx[ti] fote of assyse at his proper costes and charges. Fynally, we saye that there is one Thomas Ryley who ought to make a lawfull [?gutter] for the conveyance of his water. Also there is a pype of lead to convey the seid Ryley . . . which grate and pype we saie the said Ryley ought of right to make and maynteyn in such . . . he do not annoye the said Johanna Robinson now plaintyffe with his said water course. And that he the said [?Ryley] have the said water course as in tyme past he hath had. Except there be any writing, evidence or especyalty to the contrary to be shewed.

1. The right end of the certificate is blackened and torn.

359. [C.154] 10 September 1555.
Parish of St. Michael at Queenhithe. Variance near the street called Timberhithe (Tymberhythe) Street between Richard Berne, alias Barnes, mercer, pl., and Richard Scallande, grocer, def. The viewers say that the variance is of and for a parcel of ground under a tenement of def. containing $11\frac{1}{2}$ ft. from a stone wall at the N end of a hote [*sic*] house stretching S and 16 ft. from W to E. Of right pl. ought to have and enjoy the ground and def. ought to have all the building over the ground according to the length and breadth aforesaid, as the parties have purchased the same and as it was severally held before this time and appertained to the houses of religion and late monasteries of St. John[1] and the New Abbey on Tower Hill. Except *etc.*

1. Probably either the priory of St. John of Jerusalem at Clerkenwell or the priory of St.

John the Baptist (Halliwell Priory), Shoreditch, both of which had property in ths parish: Keene and Harding, 88, 90.

360. [C.155] 25 September 1555.
Parish of St. Stephen in Coleman Street. Variance between Thomas Barnes, currier, pl., and John Leeke of Edmonton, esquire. The viewers say that the variance is of and for the building and setting up of a new house of def., which he ought of right to build and set up in manner and form following: close up to the E side of the NE corner post of pl., stretching S 14 ft. line right and plumb to a post which is pl.'s; then turning E 7 in. and from there stretching more S 12 ft. line right and plumb to a post of pl. Either of the parties ought of right to bear their own water falling from their houses according to the ancient custom of the city of London. Def. ought of right to repair and amend all such hurts and harms as he has done or shall do to pl. by reason of his building there. Def. ought of right to have his way and commodity to the well there between the parties as he has had in times past. Either of the parties to enjoy and have all other easements and commodities belonging to either of their houses as the same had and enjoyed in times past. Except *etc.*
Endorsed: 27 September annis 2do & 3 etc. in[f]ert[ur] iste vis[us] etc.

361. [C.156] 2 October 1555.
Parish of St. Martin in Bowyers Row. Variance between Robert Hicks, ironmonger, pl., and John Settill, haberdasher, and Lewis Tedders, merchant taylor, defs. The viewers say that the variance is of and for two posts, one on the E side and the other on the W side of the door or entry of pl. Pl. ought of right to have the post set on the E side of the entry which his door hangs upon, which post contains 12 in. in breadth. He ought of right to have 8 in. of the post set on the W side of the door and he ought of right to have his entry with all the breadth that he now has and enjoys and he ought to have the breadth and commodity in the street down to the kennel from the said posts by all the breadth aforelimited. Finally, Tedders ought of right to bear his own water falling from his houses according to the custom of the city of London and he ought not to annoy pl. with any filth cast forth at his windows and other places. Except *etc.*

362. [C.157][1] 9 November 1555.
Parish of St. Martin Bowyer[s Row] ... Variance between William Mortymer, carpenter, pl., and ... gentleman, tenant by lease of the demise of John Mastall, ... brewer, def. The viewers say that the variance is of and for ... upper rooms or lofts over the ground of pl., which lofts and rooms def. ought of right to have, hold, occupy and enjoy according as let to him by a certain lease and as he now holds and occupies the same. Further, def. ought of right to repair all such buildings as he occupies over pl.'s ground so that he does not annoy pl. through his default for non-repair of them. Pl. ought of right to maintain his house from the ground up to the loft that he does not annoy def. Either party to bear his own water according to the ancient custom of the city of London. Except *etc.*
Endorsed: Garrard M[aior] 9/1/A[nn]o s[e]c[un]do & 3° Phi[lippi] Regis et Marie Regine infert[ur] iste visus etc.

1. The top portion of the certificate is blackened and torn; much of the salutation is missing or illegible. The only viewer's name legible is the last, Walter Cowper.

363. [C.158][1] 14 February 1556.
Parish of St. [Olave], borough of Southwark. Variance between William Shakylton, grocer, pl., and . . . Johnsby, haberdasher, def. The viewers say that the variance is of and for a little house of def. set at the W end of the house of pl.; it stands N and S over a water course there and of right so ought to continue as it is now built and has continued of old time. Pl. has there an entry lying N and S which ought of right to be and contain in breadth 10 ft. 2 in. E and W. Except *etc.*
Endorsed: [14]/4 A[nn]is 2&3° etc. infert[ur] istud Recordum etc.

> 1. The top portion of the certificate is rotten and torn; much of the salutation is missing or illegible. Only the last two viewers' names are legible.

364. [C.159] 9 March 1556.
Parish of St. Botolph without Aldrichgate in the suburbs of the city of London. Variance between Cuthbert Hoop, yeoman of the Queen's larder, and Margaret his wife, pls., and Richard Standfeld of London, skinner, def. The viewers say that the variance is for the making of a certain fence on the S side of the garden of pls. Pls. ought of right to make it line right and plumb from their dwelling place stretching E line right and plumb to a stake set by the viewers. Also, def. ought of right to make the fence on the N side of pls.' garden line right and plumb from the SE corner post of def.'s house stretching E to a stake there also set by the viewers, and from that stake with a splay stretching N to a corner post of a jakes, to a nail there driven by the viewers. Further, the viewers say that the ground or garden of pls. contains 10 yards and a half in breadth from the N of the E end to the S [of the E end]. Finally, the viewers find that pls. have there a piece of a jakes containing 4 ft. in breadth and 9 ft. in length N and S, which pls. ought to have and enjoy as now he [*sic*] occupies and enjoys the same, as more plainly appears by a certain deed showed to the viewers. Either of the parties to have their commodities as they had at the time of their purchase of their grounds and from henceforth to bear their own water according to the ancient and laudable custom of the city of London. Except *etc.*

365. [C.160][1] 15 April 1556.
Parish of St. [Olave], Southwark. Variance between Henri Leke, alias Hocke, pl., and Richard Meriote, clothworker, def. The viewers say that the variance is for a fence where a pale now stands which ought of right to . . . N and S line right and plumb between two brick walls and between the grounds of . . . which pale or fence is pl.'s; after he has made a brick wall where the . . . he may build upon it, so long as he does not sail over the same towards def. . . . Except *etc.*

> 1. The certificate is rotten and torn, with the right third illegible.

366. [C.161][1] 16 April 1556.
Parish of Christ Church within Newgate. Variance between John Hill,

ironmonger, pl., and John Marten, haberdasher, def. The viewers say that def. has built a new frame on the W side of pl.'s house, which is set and stands upright as of right it ought to be, and def. has taken away a lead gutter between the houses of the parties, which he ought of right to cause to be new cast and laid again, to convey water there descending in the houses of the parties. After that the gutter is to be upheld, repaired, and maintained at equal costs and charges of the parties. Except *etc.*

1. The upper right corner of the certificate is decayed; only one viewer's name, John Russell, is legible.

367. [C.162] [16] April 1556.
Duplicate of certificate **366**, in bad condition, with many words and endorsement illegible.

368. [C.163] 2 May 1556.
Parish of St. Michael in Wood Street. Variance between John Pettytt, draper, pl., and William Austen and John Casie, saddler[?s], defs. The viewers say that pl. ought of right to have all lights, entries, and rooms with free ingress and egress, as he purchased the same. Also, there is a little gallery S of the house of Austen that sails over into the ground of pl.; it ought of right to be and remain as it is now built there. Pl. ought to uphold the same below and Austen to keep it tight and dry above. The gallery is to be built no higher, broader, or longer than it now is. Further, there is a privy or jakes at the E end of the gallery which serves the house of Austen as well as pl. They ought to cleanse the jakes as often as need shall be at their equal costs and charges and, the same [so cleansed, they] may sever the vault of the jakes if they can so agree, so [long as] pl. and his house are not withall annoyed by Austen. Except *etc.*

369. [C.164][1] 9 May 1556.
Parish of St. Olave in the borough of Southwark. Variance between John Dawes, grocer, pl., and William Shakilton, grocer, def. The viewers say that the variance is of and for a certain way or entry stretching from the king's highway there N into the tenements of pl. Pl. ought of right to have it as it was granted by King Henry VIII: 3 ft. in breadth all the length of the entry, with ingress and egress to and from the same to his land and tenements there. Pl. ought of right to make a lawful fence or pale on the W side of the entry, line right and plumb from the corner post of the house of pl. to a corner post of the house of def. Finally, at the N end of the house of pl., abutting the dyehouse of def., pl. ought of right to have $6\frac{1}{2}$ ft. stretching N toward the dyehouse, and 15 ft. E and W. Either party to have and enjoy all other commodities in their ground as they are expressed in their several leases of the same. Except *etc.*

1. The certificate is in bad condition, with much of the salutation illegible.

370. [C.165] 11 June 1556.
Parish of St. Stephen in Walbrook. Variance between Thomas Alsoppe, citizen and grocer, pl., and the Right Worshipful Lady Dame Johanne Warren, def. The viewers say that the variance is of and for a certain

cellar or warehouse directly under a house of pl., which cellar or warehouse as well as the houses of both parties at one time belonged to the College of Acon of the said City of London. At the time of pl.'s purchase, the cellar or warehouse was in tenure of def. or her predecessors. Because it appears by an old door going from the house of def. that the said cellar was long occupied as parcel of def.'s house, and from diverse other plain and probable things seen by the viewers, they say that the cellar belongs to def. and is and ought to be taken as parcel of the same house and def. ought of right to uphold and maintain the cellar or warehouse below and pl. ought of right to keep it tight above. Except *etc.*

371. [C.166] 10 [?July] 1556.
Parish of St. Bride in Fleet Street. Variance between Edmund Bragg, haberdasher, pl., and John Gilman, gentleman, def. The viewers say that the variance is of and for a certain garden plat and buildings in the same set on the N side of the house of def., which plat and all the buildings standing within the same up close to and with the plate and frame of the house of def. belong of right to pl. and is [*sic*] his proper ground and building. Further, a chimney and certain shed set on the N side of the house of def. stand within the ground of pl., which of right they ought not to do, as more plainly appears by certain deeds of pl. Except *etc.*

372. [C.167][1] 14 July 1556.
Parish of St. Leonard in [the precinct of] St. Martins le Grand within the city of London. Variance between John Mody, citizen and grocer, pl., and John Roper, merchant taylor; Robert Stuard, saddler; Richard Harding, leatherseller; and Thomas Butler, haberdasher, also citizens of London, defs. The viewers have viewed, searched, seen and adjudged that pl. has pulled down a certain room of Roper's; of right he ought to make it again in as large and ample manner and form with the same commodities as it was when he plucked it down. Pl. shall bear two (twice) parts of the charges toward the building of it and defs. the third part. Defs., every one of them, shall have and enjoy all their said rooms in as large and ample manner as they have now of the tenure of the Bishop of London, without any let, trouble, vexation, or hinderance by pl. Pl. shall have and enjoy all that he now has of his tenure of the Dean and Chapter of Westminster, without any let, trouble, vexation, or hindrance of defs. Except *etc.*
Endorsed: Gerrard M[aior] 18/9 Annis s[e]c[un]do & quarto Phi[lippi] & Marie Regis et Regine etc. infert[ur] hoc Record[um]
Subscribed: a Thomas

1. The salutation is in part illegible and the top right corner of the certificate is missing.

373. [C.168][1] 17 November 1556.
To the right honorable Lord Maire of the cytie of London and to his worshipfull brethren thaldermen of the same
Shewen unto your good lordshipp and maysterships the xvii[th] day of november in the thirde and fourth [yeres of the] Reignes of our soveraigne lorde and Lady Phillippe and Mary, John Russell, Thomas

Pecock, and [Walter] Cowper, the three[2] maysters of Fremasons, Carpenters, and Tylers, viewers indyfferente sworne to the said cytie, That whereas they were of late charged by your lordships commaundement to view and oversee a varyaunce in the parishe of Saint Marten in Bowyer Row of London betwene John Warren, Barbersurgeon, and George Warre[n], goldsmith, citizens of London, plaintyffes, on the one partie and the worshipfull mayster Willm Armested, Doctor in Divinitie and one of the maysters of the chauncery of our soveraigne Lord and lady the kynge and quene's majesty, defendaunte, on the other partie. Whiche thing and varyaunce thereof we the said three sworne viewers have viewed, serched, and sene and thereuppon we saye that there is a great Brick and stone wall sett betwene a great capytall mesuage belonging to the Deane and Chappyter of the Cathedrall churche of Sainte Paule within the citie of London and now in the tenure and occupacion of the said mayster Armested and [in] the precinct of the late dyssolved Black Fryers wythyn the said Citie. Which wall we say is belonging and parcell of the said Capytall Mesuage and that the said Deane and Chapyter for the tyme beynge or their assignes may buylde in and uppon the same at their pleasure. And that they ought of right to bere the water dyscending from their houses now there Buylded wythoute the hurte or annoyance of the said plaintyffes. And further we say that there are certen Butteries of Brick Joyned and sett unto the southsyde of the wall some of which Buttries the said parties plaintyffes have taken downe as they might lawfully Doo for that they stande uppon their owne grounde. And fynally we saye that the said parties plaintyffes may buyld close uppe unto the said wall soo that they sett no parte of their Buylding into or uppon the said wall. All which thinges we saye of right ought to be done, Except therebe any wryting, Evidence or Especialtie to the contrary to be shewed.

Endorsed: Offley [Maior] 21/12 A[nn]is 4 and 5 [*sic*] etc infert[ur] iste visus

1. The upper right portion of the certificate is missing.
2. This is the only certificate in the collection, and the only one for this period I have seen anywhere, in which there are three rather than four viewers. It may be significant that this view was apparently brought into court more than 11 months after it was made, on 21 October 1557.

374. [C.169][1] 3 February 1557.
John Russell, Thomas Peacock, Walter Cowper, and John Humfrey, viewers.
Parish of St. Michael at Queenhithe. Variance between Francis Goldsmyth, gentleman, and Henry Bartelett of Windsore, draper, pls., and Cristopher Skenington, gentleman, and Roger Pillesworth, cook, defs. The viewers say that pls. ought of right to have and enjoy the ground on the E side of the kennel passing through a lane there called Dibbles Lane, S down to the river of Thames and down to the said kennel so far as his [*sic*] ground goes along by the same land and kennel, according to a lease dated the 27th year of the reign of King Henry the Eighth [*1535–6*] and now in custody of Bartelett. Except *etc*.

1. The upper right corner of the certificate is decayed.

375. [C.170]¹ 11 February 1557.
Parish of St. Ethelburga in the Ward of Bishopsgate. Variance between the master and wardens of the Leathersellers, pls., and Sir Robert Chester, knight, def. The viewers say that the variance is of and for a brick wall whereupon the E side of the hall sometime occupied by the parish clerks of the City of London stood. The wall of right is the proper wall of def. Furthermore, if def. takes down the wall he ought to make a sufficient fence in place thereof. Finally, there is a wall on the S side of the ground of def. which wall is also def.'s; if he takes away the wall, he ought of right to make another sufficient fence there. Except *etc.*²

1. The upper right corner of the certificate is missing.
2. Stow says that the Parish Clerks' hall was granted to Sir Robert Chester at the time the Clerks' brotherhood was suppressed in the reign of Edward VI. Sir Robert did indeed take down the wall; see Stow, *Survey*, i. 170–1, who does not mention the Leathersellers.

376. [C.171]¹ 27 April [?1557]
Parish of St. Ethelburga in the Ward of Bishopsgate. Variance between Ellice Lewys, Robert Lewys, citizen and joiner of London, her son, pls., and Thomas Wygett, citizen and vintner of London, def. The viewers say that the variance is of and for a vault containing within its walls 15 ft. E and W and 16 ft. N and S. The vault is under a parcel of the house of pls. The variance is also of and for a water course descending from the houses of the parties and issuing by a pipe made of lead under the house of pls. The vault was appurtenant and belonging to the house of def. at the time of his purchase and ought of right so to remain to him, his heirs or assigns forever, according to the tenor of his purchase. Forasmuch as the water course at the time of purchase of both parties was current and commodious from and for both their houses and issued as it now does through and under the house of pls. and conveyed the water descending from both their houses, it ought of right so to continue and remain. Also the back of the kitchen chimney of def. rests and bears upon a plate of the house of pls., which of right it ought not to do, but ought to stand upright and plumb upon def.'s own ground forasmuch as it was so built since the time of def.'s purchase. Finally, pls. ought of right at their own proper costs and charges to make up and build a piece of wall in a door that they have broken into the vault, as good as it was at the time that they broke it down. Either of the said parties ought of right to have and enjoy all their own water courses, lights, and commodities as they occupied and enjoyed the same at the time of their purchases. Except *etc.*
Endorsed: Offley M[aiore] 15/7/Anno 1557 infert[ur] iste visus

1. The upper right corner of the certificate is missing.

377. [C.172]¹ 7 May [?1557].²
Parish of St. Peter in Westcheap. Variance between John Bell, goldsmith, pl., and Humphrey Jones, goldsmith, def. The viewers say that the variance is of and for a counting house now being built S of the house of def., which counting house contains 6 ft. 4 in. N and S and 7 ft. E

and W, which counting house def. now builds over the house and ground of pl., which he ought not to do. Except *etc.*

1. The upper right corner of the certificate is decayed.
2. The certificate cannot date from before May, 1557, because in May, 1556, John Humfrey had not yet replaced Nicholas Ellis as a viewer.

378. [C.173][1] 29 July 1557.
Parish of Aldermary. Variance between John Pettingar, clothworker, pl., and Richard Castelen, skinner, def. The viewers say that the variance is of and for a gutter lying between the houses of the parties, which is a party gutter and ought of right to be repaired at equal cost and charges of the parties. Except *etc.*

1. The handwriting in this certificate differs markedly from that of preceding ones.

379. [C.174][1] 29 July 1557.
Parish of All Hallows Barking. Variance between Thomas Pyk, skinner, and John Howlat, salter, citizens, 'being a partie view of the assents of bothe the said parties and for the satisfying, unitie and tranquilitie of both the said parties.' The viewers say that there is a stone wall or fence stretching E and W between the grounds of the parties which bears one side of the house of Howlat. The wall is very dangerous, ruinous, and in great decay; forasmuch as it is the wall and fence of Howlatt, he ought of right to new-build the wall or another sufficient fence where it is now set, from a house of Pyke on the E, line right and plumb, at his proper costs and charges. The sheds and buildings of Pyke ought not to rest upon the wall or fence. Either of the parties to bear their own waters according to the ancient custom of London. Except *etc.*

1. The lower right corner of the certificate is decayed.

380. [C.175] 17 September 1557.
To the ryght honorable lorde Maire of the Citie of London and to his worshipfull brethren thaldermen of the same
Shewen unto your good lordshipp & mastershipps the xvii[th] day of September in the iiii[th] and v[th] yeres of the reignes of our soveraigne lorde & lady Phillip and Mary, by the grace of god kinge and quene of England etc., John Russell, Thomas Peacock, Water Cowper, and John Humfrey, the foure masters of fremasons, carpenters and Tylers, viewers indifferent sworne to the said citie, that whereas they were of late charged by your lordships comaundement to viewe & overse a varyance in the parishe of saint Margaret in Pudding Lane within the Citie of London Betwene Roger Paddy, gent, and Margery, his wyfe, plaintiffes on thone partie and Willm Froke, haberdasher, defendant, on the other partie, which thing & varyance therof we the said Foure sworne viewers have viewed, serched, measured, and sene and thereuppon we saye That the said varyaunce is of & for the reparacions of a great Capitall mesuage of the said parties plaintyffes of the which house & reparacions therof we say that there is first in the hall defaced with taking down away of an entrie south of the same & a Doore towardes saint Margarettes churcheyard thorow a stonewall there. Also we saye That there was a stone wall in

thyknes ii fote and a half and in lengthe north and south xx^{ti} foote which wall the said partie defendant hath taken awaye and in place thereof hath set a slender [?skor . . .] of timber which of right he ought not to doo. And further we saye that there are dyvers Rofes of leade in sondry places within the said Capitall mesuage which are very ruynous & in great decay & ought not of right to be taken away but to be kept in reparacion & amended & remayne in lede Rofes as they nowe be. And also the same mesuage is ruynous and in decaye in timber worke in dyvers other thinges of reparacions as doth appere. And finally we say there is within the same Capitall mesuage dyvers selinges of waynscott, glasse, flores of bordes which of ryght the said partie Defendant ought not to take awaye by Custome of the citie of London and which Capitall mesuage by estymacion to be made Tenantable will coste forty markes as we now esteme. All which thinges we say of ryght out to be done.

381. [C.176] 20 September 1557.
Parish of St. Michael in Wood Street. Variance between Launcellot Yonge, clothworker, pl., and William Prior, latener, def. The viewers say that the variance is of and for the stopping up of a [?light] in a party gutter between the houses of the parties. Of right he ought not to do so, nor ought to meddle towards the house of pl. any further than the middle of the gutter. Further, the parties ought to have their waters falling from the houses into the said gutter, to have course and pass as they did at the time of the purchase of their houses, into a gallery there and so into the street. The said parties at their several costs and charges ought to repair, uphold, and maintain the gutter as often as need shall require. Except *etc.*

382. [C.177] 29 October 1557.
Parish of St. Ethelburga in the Ward of Bishopsgate. Variance between Thomas Wygat, vintner, pl., and Ellys Lewys, widow, and Robert Lewys, joiner, defs., 'which thing and variance thereof we the said four sworn viewers have viewed serched and sene and thereupon we say that the said . . .' [*end of certificate*].

See **375** above, involving the same parties, probably six months earlier.

383. [C.178] 2 December 1557.
Parishes of St. Michael's in Bassishaw and St. Lawrence in the Old Jewry. Variance in the street called Kettleng Street[1] between Richard Rammesey, cobbler, pl., and Thomas Kyne, blacksmith spurrier, def. The viewers say that the variance is for a jakes which stands within the ground of pl. It is the proper jakes of pl., which of right he ought to have and enjoy as he now has and holds it. Further, there is another jakes within the house of def. which he ought of right to cleanse from time to time as need shall require at his proper cost and charges and without disturbance or disturping [*sic*] pl. in the cleansing. Also def. ought there to make a stone wall upon his own frame within his own ground, whereby he ought not to hurt or impair the wall of pl. Either party ought of right to bear their own water according to the ancient and laudable custom of the city of London. Except *etc.*

Endorsed: 4 Decembris A[nn]is 4to & 5to etc. infert[ur] his visus feod[um] nondum solut[um]

1. Cateaton Street.

384. [C.179] 8 January 1558.
To the reight honorable Lorde Maire of the Cytie of London and to his reight worshipfull Brethren the Aldermen of the Same Shewen unto your good Lordship & mastershippes the viiith day of Januarie in the fourth and fyfte yeres of the reignes of our soveraigne Lorde & Ladye Phillip & Marie by the grace of god kinge & quene of England etc., John Russell, Thomas Peacock, Water Cowper, and John Humfrey, the foure masters of fremasons, Carpenters, and Tylers, viewers indifferently [*sic*] sworne to the said Cytie, That whereas they were of late charged by your Lordships comaundment to viewe & overse a variance Betwene the inhabitantes of the Warde of Cordwaynerstrete on thone partie and the inhabitants of the Ward of Chepe on thother partie, That is to say, Willm Parker, Edward Lee, Richard Castell, and other inhabitantes of the foresaid Warde of Cordwanerstreet, playntyfes, on thone partie and George Barnes, John Barnard, Willm Malborne and others, inhabitantes of the said Warde of Chepe, Defendauntes on thother partie. Which variance we the said foure sworne viewers have viewed, serched, and sene and there uppon we say that the saide variance is of & for the north ende of Bowlane sometyme called Hosier Lane entering into chepesyde, which we say is and ought of reight to be a parte & parcell of the warde of Cordwaynerstret. Excepte therbe any wryting, evidence or especialtie to the contrarie to be shewed in that behalf.
Endorsed: 7/3 A[nn]is 4to & 5to infert[ur] iste visus etc. sed feodum non[dum] solut[um]

385. [C.180]^{1} 13 January 1558.
Parish of St. Michael in Wood Street. Variance between John Pettyt, draper, pl., and . . ., haberdasher, def. The viewers say that the variance is of and for the alteration of a [?pair of stairs] altered by def. and the flooring (flowreng) of a piece of a chamber made by pl. . . . in tenure of def., which stairs, flooring, and chamber ought of right to be and remain as they are now occupied by the parties during the lease of def. Pl. ought of right to have his way to his chamber forth from Wood Street as he now has and occupies the same and in no other way, without any let or trouble of def. Except *etc.*
Endorsed: 17/3A[nn]is 4to & 5to etc. infert[ur] iste visus sed feod[um] non[dum] sol[utum]

1. The upper and lower right corners of the certificate are decayed.

386. [C.181] 20 January 1558.
To the Right honourable Lorde maior of the Cytie of London and to his worshipfull brethren thaldermen of the same
Shewen unto your good lordship and mastershippes the xxth day of Januarie in the ivth and vth yeres of the reignes of our soveraigne lorde and lady Phillipp and Mary, John Russell, Thomas Peacok, Water Cowper,

and John Humfrey, the foure maysters of Fremasons, Carpenters, and Tilers, viewers indyfferent sworne to the said Cytie, that whereas they were of late charged by your Lordships Comaundement to view in the parishe of saint Stephen in Walbrok within the Cytie of London of the groundes of Thomas Frank, gentilman, and Henry Mynge, grocer, on thone partie and John Howe, gentilman, on the other partie, Whiche specially was for the assignment of suche grounde and to certenly know how moche there belongeth to the said Henry Mynge. Whiche we the said foure sworne viewers have viewed, seerched, measured and sene and thereuppon we saye that the ground that ys most Doubtfull that belongeth to the said Henry Mynge ys and conteyneth as hereafter foloweth, That is to saye, From the kinge and quenes majesties strete called Bucklers bery and the plate of the house there on the northe partie stretchinge south to a mayne post there xxxiii^{ti} foote and a half of assyse, whiche post is in Thyknes xi ynches of assyse. And from that corner post stretchinge more southe alonge by a bryckwall there to the southwest corner of the same wall xiii foote vii ynches of assyse And from the southwest Corner of the same wall stretchinge east to a princypall post there ys and conteyneth xviii^{ti} foote and a halfe of assyse. And from that pryncypall post stretching south to an other princypall post there ys and conteyneth xxvi foote of assyse. And from that pryncypall post stretchinge west to an other princypall post there ys and conteyneth xvi foote and iii ynches of assyse. And fynally we saye that the said John How ought of right to have his Water Course as he hath and enioyeth the same there now. Except there be any wryttyng, evydence or specialtee to the contrary to be shewed.

Endorsed: Curtis M[aior] debet pro imposic[ione] huius vis[us] 25/3 Annis 4 & 5 etc. infert[ur] hoc Record[um]

387. [C.182] 25 January 1558.
Parish of St. Giles without Cripplegate. Variance beside the Barbican there between Ralph Broke, citizen and goldsmith, pl., and John Berdon, poulter, and Richard Borne, merchant taylor, defs. The viewers say that the variance is of and for a fence that is now a pale being broken down at the NW end of the garden ground of pl. The fence and pale is a party fence between the parties and ought of right to be made up again at their several and equal costs and charges and so to be upheld and kept as often as need shall require. Further there is another pale there that stretches from a corner post of the house of defs., which ought of right to be set line right and plumb all along the said pale from the said corner post as far as the said pale stretches, at the costs of defs. Except *etc.*

Endorsed: Curtes M[aior] 7/4A[nn]o 1557[1] infert[ur] iste visus

1. The months of the mayoral year were counted from November, while the calendar year began on 25 March: hence 7/4 [February] 1557.

388. [C.183] 29 January 1558.
Parish of St. Andrew in the Ward of Castle Baynard. Variance between Thomas Reynold, citizen and draper, pl., and Robert Shurlok, citizen and woodmonger, def. The viewers say that the variance is for a lawful

fence or pale between the parties from the SW corner post of the dwelling house of pl. stretching down to the Thames, to a principal post there standing which is the post of pl. Pl. ought to make the said fence line right and plumb from limit to limit at his own proper cost and charges. Finally, of right def. ought to deliver to pl. all such posts and boards as he has taken away there. Except *etc.*

389. [C.184] 7 February 1558.
Parish of St. Nicholas Coldabbey in Old Fish Street. Variance between the parson and churchwardens of the parish church of Cole Abbey, pls., and Edward Hall, citizen and fishmonger, def. The viewers say that the variance is for certain principals and principal posts in the house which def. now inhabits, that is to say, one principal plate that bears a kitchen above in the said house and two principal posts that bear a principal somer under the same kitchen. The principals and principal posts ought of right to be maintained and upheld at cost and charges of pls. as often as need shall be and require. Except *etc.*

390. [C.185] 5 March 1558.
Parish of St. Dionis Backchurch. Variance between John Lute, cloth-worker, pl., and Rowland Richardson, carpenter, def. The view is a party view. The viewers say that the variance is for a piece of ground between the parties containing 9 ft. in length N and S and 2 ft. 9 in. in breadth E and W. Pl. ought of right to have the ground to the first storey of def.'s house. From the said piece of ground beneath 9 ft. and 9 in. at the first floor, stretching S from the said piece of ground 9 ft. 9 in. [def.'s house] ought of right to jetty 2 ft. 9 in. over pl.'s yard by all the length of 19 ft. 1 in. Also, there is a water course that goes out of pl.'s ground and yard into the king's street there through def.'s house, which water course ought to pass from the [?wall] of pl. through the yard of def. into the street, and which water course pl. ought to maintain and keep, either in lead or hard stone of Kent, being hollow gutter stone; at the entry of the water course ought to be a sufficient iron grate so that nothing shall pass through except water. Moreover, def.'s house by the ground contains 28 ft. 10 in. in length N and S by the street called Philpot Lane to the middle of a party post between pl. and def. At the S of def.'s house, stretching E and W, it contains 17 ft. 2 in. Def.'s house ought to be and contain 19 ft. 8 in. in breadth at the N end thereof, E and W. Def. may build upon all his said ground, line right and plumb by all the length and breadth aforelimited. Except *etc.*
Endorsed: Curtes M[aior] 8 Marcii 1557 infert[ur] iste visus et sol[utum] feod[um]

391. [C.186]¹ 31 March 1558.
Parishes of St. Benet Sherehog and St. Stephen's in Walbrook. Variance between the Worshipful Lady Dame Johanna War[ren] . . . and Henry Mynge, grocer. The view is a party view. The viewers say that the variance is for certain walls between the parties. Henry Mynge shall '. . . have so muche as joineth upon his ground as ys made of ragged stone.

And so muche thereof as ys [?made of] bryck on the north syde of a cole house we say belongeth to the Lady Dame Johanna Warren. And . . . we say that the said Henrye Mynge ought not of right to deminyshe or ympayre any parte of the said [?wall] by reason of his buylding there. But that the frame thereuppon standing may stand upright and plumb . . . doth.' Except *etc.*

Endorsed: Curtes M[aior] 19/6 Annis 4 & 5to etc. infert[ur] iste visus

1. The writing at the right margin of the certificate is illegible.

392. [C.187]^1 22 April 1558.
Parish of St. [*word omitted: presumably* Martin] at Ludgate. Variance between Alexander . . . Gracely, haberdasher, def. The viewers say that the variance is for a shop or kitchen and a chamber and . . . said pl. with the kitchen, chamber, and room ought of right to be and remain . . . purchasers of the [?leases] of the parties. Either party ought of right to uphold . . . and building as are within the rooms in their several tenures during the years in the leases . . . ought of right to bear their own waters and maintain their gutters so that neither of them . . . [Except] *etc.*

Endorsed: Curtes M[aior] . . . 4&5to etc. infert[ur] . . . posit . . .

1. The certificate is in very bad condition and is in part illegible.

393. [C.188]^1 23 April 1558.
Parish[?es] of St. Bartholomew the Little and St. . . . [Variance between] . . . and governors of the Hospital of St. Bartholomew in West Smithfield within the suburbs of . . . Bocher, haberdasher, def. The viewers say that the variance is for a wall of stone and brick between the . . . [It is] a party wall and ought of right to be made and upheld at equal cost and charges of the parties . . . corner post of a house belonging to def. stretching more E to the . . . the def. Except *etc.*

Endorsed: Curtes M[aior] 5/ . . . & v^{to} infert[ur]. . .

1. The certificate is in very bad condition and is in part illegible.

394. [C.189] 3 May 1558.
Parish of St. Andrew in Holborn. Variance between Allen [Leverat], haberdasher, pl., and Richard Flower, haberdasher, def. The viewers say that the variance is for the repairing, upholding, waste, and maintaining of certain tenements there which def. holds for the term of the life of one Richard Stiverton, gentleman, late porter to King Henry the Eighth. The tenements are very ruinous and in great decay, so far that the most part of the same are ready to fall down and cannot be repaired unless they are newly built and edified.

Endorsed: Curtes M[aior] 5/7 Annis 4&5to etc. infert[ur] ist[e] visus vacat quia sol[utum] feod[um]
debet pro imposit[ione] huius visus [*crossed out*]

395. [C.190] 28 May 1558.
Parishes of St. Magnus and St. Michael in Crooked Lane, in the wards of Bridge Within and Candlewick Street of London. Variance between the Worshipful Lady Dame Mary Morgan, widow, tenant to Sir William

Garrard, knight and alderman of the city of London, pl., and William Alleyn, citizen and baker, def. The viewers say that def. ought of right to set up his foundation, to bear up his house, ground, and building there, 25 ft. 1 in. in length E and W, line right and plumb. And the same foundation to be brought up, also line right and plumb, at the E end even with the plate of the house of def. and at the W end even with an iron nail by the viewers driven into a lath there. Also, the parties ought of right to have all their watercourses as they now have them and have had in time past, and not otherwise. And close up to the said foundations the ground is the ground of Sir William Garrard and he or his assigns ought of right to make a fence of brick or stone there at their pleasure, close up to the said foundations of def. all the length thereof. Except *etc.*
Endorsed: Leie M[aior]
3/13 [*sic*] A[nn]is 5 & 6 etc. infert[ur] iste visus non[dum] sol[utum] feod[um]

396. [C.191] 25 June 1558.
Parish of St. Pancras. Variance between John Bull, citizen and mercer, pl., and John Grenell, waxchandler, def. The viewers say that the variance is for the sailing and hanging of def.'s house over the grounds of pl. where he is now about to build and set a new frame and house. For the pacifying of the variance, the viewers say that pl. may set his building close to the plate of the house of def., 15 ft. 7 in. of size N and S. He may build upright and plumb as high as he shall think good, at his pleasure. Either of the said parties ought of right to bear their own rain waters according to the laudable custom of the city of London. Except *etc.*
Endorsed: Curtes M[aior]
2[?6]/8/Annis 4&5 Philippi & Marie Regis et Regine etc. infert[ur] istud visu[m] sol[utum] feod[um]

397. [C.192] 27 July 1558.
Parish of St. Leonard in the precincts of St. Martin le Grand. Variance between the Reverend Father in God John, abbot of Westminster,[1] pl., and the Right Reverend Father Edmond, by the sufferance of God bishop of London,[2] def. The viewers say that the variance is for a certain ground lying in Bell Alley on the back side of a current and square frame of the houses belonging to def. For the appeasing of the variance, the viewers say that the ground and soil to the square frame there is privileged and sanctuary ground, and is parcel of Bell Alley, and of right belongs to pl. Further, at the NE corner post of a house of one Tho[mas] Butler there is a stone wall stretching more N in length 24 ft. The wall is the wall of pl. and the ground lying within the same is privileged and sanctuary ground and belongs to Bell Alley and is the ground of pl. Except *etc.*
Endorsed: Curtes M[aior]
8/12 A[nn]is 5&6 etc. infert[ur] ist[e] visus

1. Queen Mary refounded Westminster Abbey in 1555, at which time John Feckenham was installed as mitred abbot.
2. Edmund Bonner.

398. [C.193]¹ 2 August 1558.
To the right honorable lorde maire of the Cytie of London and to his worshipfull brethren thaldermen of the same
Shewen unto your good lordshippe and masterships the seconde day of August in the fyfte and Sixt yeres of the Reignes of our soveraigne lorde and lady Phillippe and Mary, by the grace of god king and quene of England, Spayne, Fraunce, both Ciciles, Jerusalem and Ireland, Defenders of the Fayth, Archdukes of Austridge, Dukes of Burgundy, Myllayne and Brabant, Counties of Hespurge, Flanders and Tyroll, John Russell, Thomas Peacok, Water Cowper, and John Humfrey, the foure maysters of Fremasons, Carpenters, and Tilers, viewers indifferent sworne to the said Citie, That whereas they were of late charged by your lordshippes Comaundement to view and oversee a varyance in the parishe of our blessed lady at Bowe in Hosyer lane wythin the Cytie of London Betwene Peter Baker, Citizen and Scriver, ... plaintyff, of the one partie and Sir Thomas Whyte, knight and Alderman of the same Cytie, Defendante, on the other partie, [which] thinge and varyance therof we the said foure sworne viewers have viewed, serched and sene and thereuppon we say [*that the*] said varyaunce is of and for a water Course issuing forth of a yarde in the tenure of the said partie plaintiff into and ... a yarde and entry of the said partie Defendant there next adioyning in the tenure of one Henry Adams, clothworker. And of ... certen Brykwalles inclosing the house and grounde now also in the tenure of the same partie plaintiff whiche water course we [*say ought*] of right to have free course and passage as it now hath and as tyme out of mynde it hath contynewed. And also we say that the [*partie*] plaintyff ought of right to have suche parte Comoditye, use, and occupacion of a well there Betwene the groundes of the said [*parties*] as he now hath. And that he, the said partie plaintyff, ought of right to have all the said house, grounds ... as they are nowe there sett and enclosed and are in his tenure. And fynally we say that the said partie plaintyff ought [*of right to*] clense and repayre aswell the one half of the said well as to repayre and amend all the said Brykwall. As they now ... Grounde. Except there be any better evydence or specialtie to the contrary to be shewed.
Endorsed: ... 8 August ...

1. The lower right portion of the certificate is missing.

399. [C.194]¹ [1553 × 1555].²
... Ellys, John Cowper & Thomas [Peacock] ... and tylers, viewers indyfferent ... charged by your lordshippes comand ... sett lying and beynge in the parish ... and Humfrey Collett of London, bo[wyer] ... of ... the said houses and buyldings there ... viewers saie that the said Humfrey ... St. Clements Lane from a bryckwall ... stretching North to a principall of the house ... and ix inches of assise. And further we ... Westward from the said St. Clements Lane ... ground and houses with suche length and bredeth ... buylde up right and plumbe and no more but ... there is a shed with a celler under the same betwene ... Southwest corner of his said houses which containeth ... syde of the same shed ix fete and eight ynches of assyse ... on the East syde of the same shed x fote & vi ynches of assyse ... and East of the yard now in tenure of Gyles

Bridges, Esq. . . . the said Humfrey Collett ought to bere all his waters discending . . . according to the ancyent custom of the Cytie of London . . . wryttinge, evidence or other specialtie to the contrary . . .

1. The right half of the certificate is missing, and the date is torn away. The viewers presumably are John Russell, whose name is missing, Nicholas Ellys, John Cowper, and Thomas Peacock.

2. William Walker was still acting as a viewer on 16 May 7 Edward VI, the date of the last extant certificate for Edward's reign. He had been replaced by Thomas Peacock by 22 September 1 Mary, four months later, in the first extant datable certificate from Mary's reign. This certificate, then, cannot date from earlier than the summer of 1553. John Cowper last appears in a certificate dated 28 July 2 Mary; by 9 March 1&2 Philip and Mary, chronologically the next extant certificate, he had been replaced by Walter Cowper. This certificate, then, cannot date from later than early March, 1555. So much of the parchment is missing that it is not possible to attempt more precise dating.

400. [C.195][1] 31 July [?1555].[2]
To the right honourable lorde maire of the Cytie . . . and to his worshipfull Brethren the . . .
Shewen unto your good lordshippe and masterships the last day of July . . . Reignes of our soveraigne lorde and lady Philippe and Mary [*by the grace of God King and Queen of*] England, France, Neapulles, Jerusalem and Ireland, Defendours of . . . Cycilie, Archdukes of Austrie, Dukes of Myllayne, Burgoyne, and Brabant, [Counts of Hapsburg] . . . Flanders and Tyroll, John Russell, Nicholas Ellys, Thomas Peacok and [Walter] Cowper, the foure maysters of Fremasons, Carpenters, and Tylers, viewers Indyfferent sworn to [the said city] that whereas they were of late charged by your lordships comaundement to view and oversee a variance in the parish of Seint Bryde in Fletestrete of London Betwene Frauncys Barker, Citizen and merchant taylor of London, plaintyff, on the one partie and Thomas Launce, citizen and Cutler of London, and Dorothie his wyfe, defendantes, on the other partie. Which thinge and varyance thereof we the said foure sworne viewers have viewed, serched, and sene and thereuppon we saie That the said varyaunce is of and for a certen Fence to be sett . . . a mudde wall is now sett north and southe Betwene the groundes of the said parties, And for the [tranquility], quyetness, and pacyfynge of the said varyaunce Betwene the said parties we saie that where the said [?mudwall] now standeth there ought of right to be made a lawfull and sufficient Fence at the equal costes and charges of bothe the said parties upright from the grounde in the garden of the said partie plaintyff, vi foote above the grounde of the said partie defendante. And the same Fence being so sufficientlie made we saye that the said partie defendante From thence forth ought to maynteyne, repayr, and upholde the same Fence of such height sufficientlie During his yeares yet to come. And also we saie that there is a Fence at the southende of the said muddewall which lyeth east and west, which Fence we saye the said partie defendante ought to uphold at his proper costes and charges, lyne right and plome. And that he ought not to buylde any thinge to sayle over the same Fence into the garden of the said partie playntyff. Except there be any wryttinge, Evidence or especialtie to the contrarie to be shewed.

1. The right end of the certificate is torn and stained.

2. The certificate must date from after 28 July [*sic*] 2 Mary, the date of the last extant certificate in which John Cowper appears as a viewer; he was succeeded by Walter Cowper by at least 9 March 1&2 Philip and Mary (see comments to preceding certificate). It is clear that the Cowper shown here is Walter, not John, because as was the custom he is named last, indicating that he was the newest viewer. The last extant certificate with the above set of viewers dates from 14 July 2&4 Philip and Mary but there were probably others since the next extant certificate, dated 17 November 3&4 Philip and Mary, indicates that Nicholas Ellys had recently died; it shows only three viewers, probably meaning that Ellys' replacement had not yet been appointed. This certificate, then, could date from 31 July 1&2 Philip and Mary, 31 July 2&3 Philip and Mary, or 31 July 3&4 Philip and Mary. The recital of all the titles of the king and queen suggests the middle date, because 2&3 Philip and Mary is when that form was most commonly used.

401. [C.196][1] [1553 × 1556].[2]
Shewen unto your good lord . . . of the Reignes of our . . . Russell, Nicholas E[*llys*] . . . of Fremasons, Carp[enters] . . . whereas they were of . . . varyance in the parish . . . Thomas Goodman, gentil . . . defendante on the other . . . sworne viewers have viewed . . . we saye that the said . . . woadhouse of the said partie . . . for a quiettinge of the said . . . of the sayd woadhouse wherein . . . the sayd parties and ought there . . . lyne right and plombe vii[xx] Foote . . . way there ought to be in Bredeth . . . the northe fence stretchinge east . . . stretche south in Bredeth xii foote of . . . hundredth foote of Assyse there the sayd . . . mudwall ten foote of Assyse and so the . . . as aforesaid from lymmytt to lymmytt . . . ot the sayd woadhouse stretchinge more . . . ought to be xxxvi foote of assyse and . . . woadhouse stretchinge southe . . . Sewer sometyme hath bene . . . defendante ought to make a lawfull fence . . . partie plaintyffes grounde. And fynally . . . make a Comon Sewer there as it . . . any wrytinge evydence or especialty . . .

1. Only a fragment of the certificate exists; the date is torn away and the salutation is missing.
2. The certificate must date from after 10 July 4 Edward VI; on certificates up to and including that date, Gilbert Burfame was listed following John Russell. The first extant certificate showing Russell's name followed immediately by Ellys' dates from 30 August 4 Edward VI. The spacing following their names suggests that they were the first two viewers mentioned; if so, the certificate must date from after 16 May 7 Edward VI, the last extant certificate which shows William Walker as the first viewer. Likewise, the presence of Ellys' name means that the certificate must date from before 17 November 3&4 Philip and Mary. See note to preceding certificate.

402. [C.197][1] [1554 × 1557].[2]
Shewen unto your good lordship . . . of our soveraign lorde and lady . . . Thomas Peacocke and Water . . . Indifferent sworne to the said . . . to view and oversee a varyaunce . . . of Surrey betwene John Swyng . . . Scryver, defendante on the other . . . viewed, serched, sene and examyned certen Tenement sett wythin the Ally . . . Ten[*emen*]ts late belonged to the churche of . . . said partie defendante and therefore we . . . the same in as large and ample . . . And after such sorte as when as . . . Overys. And furthermore we saie . . . Tenements are partie partitions Betwene the . . . there buylde may take half of bothe the . . . parties shall bere their owne water . . . of London. Except therebe any wrytting . . .

1. Only a fragment of the certificate exists; the right half is missing.
2. Since the viewers include Thomas Peacock and Walter Cowper, the certificate cannot

date from before 28 July 2 Mary (see note to preceding certificates). The first extant certificate listing both Peacock and Walter Cowper as viewers dates from 9 March 1&2 Philip and Mary. Likewise, the certificate must date from before 3 February 3&4 Philip and Mary, since a certificate of that date shows John Humfrey replacing Walter Cowper.

403. [C.198][1] [1555 × 1556].[2]
To the right . . . and to his
Shewen unto your good lord . . . reignes of our soveraigne lord . . . Peacok and Water Cowper the . . . sworne to the said Citie, That where . . . oversee a variaunce in the parish . . . Drapers, plaintyff, on thone partye . . . and varyaunce thereof we the said foure . . . we say that the said varyaunce is of . . . the sayd parties. Whereuppon we say . . . repayre all the upper partes . . . holdeth and occupyeth the same that . . . east xliiii[ti] foote of assyse. And further . . . the nether parte of the house there . . . foote & half one fote of assyse in Bredeth . . . above. And that the sayde partie plaintyff . . . & commodytes he hath purchased and as . . . the said partyes and every other lorde or . . . according to the ancyent and laudable . . . partyes ought of right to annoye the . . . Evidence or especialtie to the contrary.
Endorsed: Garrard M[aior]

1. Only a fragment of the certificate exists; the right half is missing.
2. Sir William Gerard was mayor from November 1555 until November 1556.

404. [C.199][1] [?1554 × 1558].[2]
Shewen unto your good lordshippe . . . of the Reignes of our soveraign . . . Quene of England etc. John . . . foure maysters of Fremasons . . . that whereas they were of . . . a varyaunce in the parishe of . . . plaintyff on the one partie . . . said Cytie, defendantes on the other . . . sworne viewers have viewed ser[ched] . . . [*variance*] is of and for certen worsted presses . . . now dwelleth which presses we say . . . playntyff. And that the same plaintiff . . . convert, transpose, and remove the same . . . wyth earth and make the place where the same . . . presses were there fyrst sett equall with . . . Evidence or especialtie to the contrarie.

1. Only a fragment of the certificate exists; the right half or more is missing.
2. The word 'reignes' indicates a date after 25 July 1554.

CORPORATION OF LONDON
RECORDS OFFICE MISC. MSS. BOX 91
(Envelope marked 'Viewers' Certificates circa 1554')

The envelope contains fragments of 11 separate certificates strung together. They are printed here in chronological order, so far as that can be ascertained: the letters [a] – [k] following the item number represent the file order. Salutations throughout are largely missing or illegible and have been omitted here.

405. [d] 16 February 1555.
. . . Russell, Nicholas Ellys, Thomas . . . Carpenters and Tilers, viewers . . . of late Charged by your lordships commaund[*ment*] . . . [*parish of St.*] Saviour in the Borow of Southwarke betwene . . . and Humfrey Collett, Bowyer, defendaunte . . . the said foure sworne viewers have . . . saye that the said varyance is of and . . . said parties which fence we say is the same . . . to be by him sufficiently made, upholden, . . . the Southeaste Corner post of the dwelling . . . east to the Comon Sewer and a nale by the upper . . . strycken into a bourde of the northe syde of a Jakes . . . the brinke of the said Comon Sewer. All these . . . be observed, kept and done and every man to bere . . . they have done. Except there be any wryttyng . . . to be shewed.
Endorsed: 16 Feb[ruary] A[nn]os [*sic*] 1 & 2 infert[ur] iste visus

406. [c] February 1555.
. . . and Mary, Kinge and Quene . . . & Tylers, viewers indifferent . . . in the parishe of Saint Saviour in the borough of Southwark . . . partie and William Giverson, Bowyer, defendant . . . serched & seen and thereupon we say . . . same to be devyded betwene the . . . whiche houses, tenementes and rentes we . . . tenements in tenure of Richard Pever in . . . tenements in the tenure of Thomas Pen . . . at xlvi s. viii d. Furthermore we say & app[*oint*] . . . tenement in the tenure of Thomas Forman . . . out of his iiii d. land and tenement in the tenure of . . . William Pynson who rented yerely at his iiii . . . We appoynte, Judge, and thinke in our consideration . . . therof ymmedyatly after the same is due . . . And to take distresse for the same so that yt . . . Clea[?n]sed to my Lord Maior and Aldermen . . . Also either of the said parties to bere their . . . London as they now be . . . devyded tenements so long as . . . writing, evidence or specialty . . .
Endorsed: . . . February Anno 1&2 infrascr[?iptorum] visus . . .

407. [e] 20 April 1555.
Shewen unto you . . . 20th daye of April in the first and second yeres of the Reignes of our soveraign . . . Philipp and Mary, by the grace of god Kinge

151

and Quene of England, France etc. John Russell, Nicholas Ellys, Thomas Peacock and Water Cowper, the foure Maysters of Fremasons, carpenters, and Tylers, viewers indyfferent sworne to the said Cytie That whereas they were of late charged by your Lordships comaundment to view and oversee a varyance in the parishe of Saint Sepulchre withoute Newgate of London betwene William Averell, Innholder, defendaunte on the other partie [*sic*] which varyance therof we the said foure sworne viewers have viewed, serched, & sene & theruppon we saye that the said varyance is of & for the bering of the waters fallinge from the houses of the parties. Which Waters we saye ought of right to be borne by either of the said parties accordyng to the anciente and laudable custome of the Cytie of London & furthermore we saie there is a variance betwene the said plaintiff & John Sturgion, Chamberlayne of the Cytie of London,[1] of & for a stone Walle on the east syde of the grounde of the said partie plaintyf whiche brykwalle [*sic*] is in length north and south xxix fotte di. of assise. Which walle overhangeth in the ground of the said partie plaintiff at the northe ende v ynches of assyse, Which walle ought to go lyne right and plome from the north to the south by all the length aforesaid. Except there be any wrytinge, Evidence, or especialtie to the contrarie to be shewed.

1. The Chamberlain may here be appearing in a private capacity.

408. [g] 17 or 27 May 1555.
Shewen unto your good . . . xvii^{th} day of May in the firste & seconde yeres of the Reignes of our . . . lorde & lady Philipp & Marie by the grace of god etc. John Russell, Nicholas Ellis, Thomas Peacock, and Walter Cowper the foure masters of Fremasons, Carpenters & Tylers viewers indifferent sworne to the said Cytie that whereas they were of late charged by your lordships comaundement to view and oversee a variance in the parishe of Holy Trinitie in the Warde of Bred Street of London betwene Robert Kyng, fishmonger, plaintyf on the one partie & Henry Mellyshe, merchanttailor, defendaunt on the other partie, which thinge and variance therof we the said iiii sworne viewers have viewed, serched & sene being for a gutter and water corse lying north and south betwene the said parties and there upon we say the gutter and water corse ought of right to be repaired, upholden, and mayntayned at the equall costes and charges of both the said parties as often as nede shall require & the water descendyng by the same gutter as it is now at this present tyme without interrupcion of ayther of the said parties. And further we saye that as concerning all other gutters and eavesdropping betwene the said parties & their houses that ayther of the said parties ought to bear the same water corse accordyng to the ancient & laudable custome of this Cytie. Except there be any evidence, writing, or especialty to the contrary to be shewed in that behalf.

409. [b] 10 July 1555.
. . . Reignes . . . England, France . . . Cowper the foure . . . sworne to the . . . Commaundement to . . . of Langbourne of London . . . one the one partie and . . . on the other partie which Thing . . . viewed serched and

sene . . . a certen stone wall sett Betwene . . . from the house of the said partie defen . . . hath encroached with his Buyldinge the . . . and at and over the south ende of the . . . not so to do. Except therebe any . . . shewed.

Endorsed: 10 July A[nn]is 1&3 Regis et Regine infrano[m]i[n]atorum infert[ur] iste vis[us]

410. [a] 20 July 1555.

Shewen unto your . . . and . . . Lady Philippe and Mary . . . Nicholas Ellys, Thomas Pecock . . . indifferent sworne to the said . . . and oversee a varyance in the . . . plaintyfe on the one partye . . . varyance therof we the same . . . uppon we say that the said . . . and south Betwene the ground . . . from the house now in the tenure of . . . Wall ought to lye lyne right and plome . . . stretching West to a Brickwall of the . . . uppe and uppon the same at his pleasure . . . to the contrarie to be shewed.

Endorsed: 20 July A[nn]is 1&3 Regis & Regine infrano[m]i[n]at[orum] etc. infert[ur] iste visus

411. [i] [1554 × 1555][1]

Shewen unto your good lordshipp . . . of the reignes of our soveraign . . . Ellys, John Cowper, and Tho[mas Peacock] . . . and Tylers viewers indyfferent . . . were of late charged by your . . . parishe of Christechurch . . . Edward Boyse, draper, plaintyf, on the byhalfe of the . . . Defendante on the other partie . . . have viewed, serched, and sene . . . of and for a lytle Tenement sett . . . Nicholas Chomells now in tenure and . . . lyttle Tenement we say is the freeh[*old*] . . . and doth of right belong to him . . . Especialtie to the contrary to be shewed.

1. Since the fragment speaks of 'reignes', the certificate cannot date from before 25 July 1554. The *terminus ad quem* is before 15 March 1555, because there is a certificate of that date showing Walter Cowper, who replaced John Cowper, as a viewer.

412. [f] April 1555.

Shewen unto your . . . day of Aprill the firste and [second] years . . . John Russell, Nicholas Ellys, Thomas Peacock and Walter [Cowper] the foure maysters of Fremasons, Carpenters, and Tylers . . . sworne to the said Cytie, That whereas they were of late charged by your lordships comaundement to view and oversee a varyaunce in the parishe of Saint Katerin Coleman of London betwene Richard Barnes, Gentilman, plaintyff on the one partie, and Thomas Heath, Baker, defendant on the other partie, which thing and varyaunce therof we the said sworne viewers have viewed, serched, measured and sene And thereuppon we saie that the said varyaunce is of and for a certain Pale or Fence sett on the west syde of the ground of the said partie plaintif Which fence we saie is a partie fence betwene the said parties and ought to be made uppe and mayntayned at the equall costes and charge of the said parties, lyne right and plombe from a naile by us the said foure sworne viewers beaten into a Brickwall on the southsyde of the grounde of the said partie plaintyf to a stake by us sett one foote West from a post sett in the west ende of a pale which pale is sett on the south syde of a garden of the said partie plaintyf now in tenure of one John de Saloys, alias Barbour, merchantestraunger. Except there be any wrytinge, Evidence or especialtie to the contrarie to be shewed.

413. [j] [25 July 1554 × 15 March 1555][1]
Shewen unto your good lordshippe . . . Reignes of our Sovereigne . . . lorde and . . . Thomas Peacock the foure mayst[*ers*] . . . sworne to the said Cytie That . . . to view and oversee a varyaunce . . . Xpofer Bumstede, mercer, plaintyf . . . the other partie whiche they . . . viewed, serched and sene And . . . certen Jakes and the annoyaunce of . . . defendante during his yeres. And ther . . . of right to clense and skowre the same . . . up right and plumbe uppon his . . . Annoye the said partie playntyff. And . . . the houses of the said parties which ought to . . . equall and severall costes and charges . . . wyth comyng into the said gutter. And further . . . ought of right to make a lawfull fence in his . . . and the grounde of the said partie defendante . . . postes that there now stande. All the prem . . . and kept. Except there be any wryttinge . . . to be shewed.
Endorsed: . . . Marie etc.

1. Thomas Peacock was viewer from before the beginning of the reigns of Philip and Mary (25 July 1554); from at least 15 March 1555, the most junior and therefore last-named viewer was Walter Cowper.

414. [k] [25 July 1554 × 15 March 1555].[1]
Shewen unto your good lordship . . . of the Reignes of our soveraign . . . Ellys, John Cowper and . . . and Tylers, viewers Ind[*ifferent*] . . . of late Charged by your lord[*ship*] . . . parishe of Saint Sepulchres . . . Governors of Saint Bartholomew . . . of the King and Quenes Chap[?*el*] . . . Betwene the parties whiche . . . Sworne viewers have viewed . . . the said varyaunce Betwene the said . . . said parties where an old pale nowe stands whiche Fence we saie . . . parties at their severall and equall . . . mayntayned From tyme to tyme . . . Evydence or esspycyaltie to the contrary . . .

1. John Cowper was viewer from before 25 July 1554; he had been replaced by Walter Cowper by 15 March 1555.

415. [h] [28 July 1554 × 10 November 1556][1]
Shewen unto . . . Reignes of our soveraigne lorde and lady . . . Russell, Nicholas Ellys, Thomas Peacock and . . . viewers Indyfferent sworne to the said . . . commaundement to view and oversee a varyance in the parishe of Saint Martens [Outwych of London] betwene Thomas Altam, clothworker, plaintyff on thone partie, and Robert Spencer, cloth-worker, defendant . . . and varyance therof we the said iiii sworne viewers . . . we say that the said varyance is of and for a brickwall . . . we say of right ought to stretche east from the southeast corner post of the . . . defendaunte to the grounde of the said partie plaintyf lyne right and plome xxxv foote . . . and further we saye that said partie plaintyf may buylde upon the same wall at his pleasure . . . save that the Brickwall at the east ende of the garden of the said partie defendante ought . . . dothe. And that no man may Buyld upon the same But onely the said partie defendaunte . . . each to bere their own waters accordinge to the Ancyent

and laudable custome of the Cytie . . . wryttinge, Evydence or Especialtie
to the contrarie to be Shewed.

1. The view must date from after 28 July 1554, the date of the last extant certificate of the previous set of viewers, and before 10 November 1556, when Nicolas Ellys' death is reported in Rep. 12 (2), f. 447.

CORPORATION OF LONDON
RECORDS OFFICE MISC. MSS. BOX 91
(Envelope marked 'Viewers' Report bet. 22 Oct. 4 E VI and 6 May 7 E
VI found among Mayor's Court Original Bills, Box No. 209A')

416. [1550 × 1553][1]
To the right honorable lorde Maire of the Cytie of London and to his
Worshipful Bretheren the Aldermen of the same Cytie. Shewen unto
your goode Lordship and discrete Wysdoms William Walker, John
Russell, Nicholas Ellys, & John Cowper, the iiii masters of Fremasons,
Carpenters and Tylers, viewers indifferent sworn to the said Citie, that
whereas they were late charged by your lordships comaundement to
viewe & oversee a variaunce in the parishe of Saint Botall without Algate
of London Betwene Jamys Adlington plaintif on the one partie, &
William Grene defendant on the other partie, Whiche variance we the
said viewers have viewed & seen And thereupon we say that the said
variance ys for the water course of the partie plaintif. And upon the
viewyng therof we say that the said water course ought to go through the
grounde or dyche of the partie defendant as yt dyd at the tyme when yt
belonged to the Menorys, unto a Comon Synke stonding there nowe in
the grounde of the partie defendant. Except there be any writing
evydence or specialtie to the contrary to be shewed.

1. The names of the viewers indicate that the certificate dates from between 22 October
1550 and 16 May 1553. See also **275** above.

JOURNALS, REPERTORIES, AND LETTER BOOKS

A small number of surviving certificates (**28**, **64**, **119**, **151**) were also copied into the City's Journals and Letter Books. One certificate and two memoranda of views or awards for the period covered in this volume, copied into the Journals and Letter Books, are not otherwise known (below). A document similar to a certificate, dated 17 July 1590, is copied into Repertory 22, f. 230v.[1] Both the Journals and the Letter Books also contain copies of certificates for the period before 1508, as do the Plea and Memoranda Rolls and several of the Miscellaneous Rolls in the Corporation's archive.

> 1. I am grateful to Anne Sutton, then assistant archivist at CLRO, for drawing this to my attention.

417. [Journal 11, f. 215v, and Letter Book M, f. 238v; ?April 1514.][1]
Memorandum that of late a variance was had between the Custos and the Brethren of the Guildhall Chapel and the Goldsmiths about a partible brick wall lately made by the Goldsmiths between their tenement in the parish of St. Vedast where one William Lowth dwells and the tenement called 'the Sarrasynes Hed' belonging to the Custos and Brethren wherein Richard Kene, goldsmith, now dwells. For the appeasing of the variance, Nicholas Mattock, chamberlain, John West, and Mighell Englysshe, mercers, and William Calley, draper, were appointed by the Mayor and Aldermen to view and see the wall. 'Whereuppon the said persons named and appoynted, callyng to theym oon [blank] Waterhouse, carpenter, and oon [*blank*: ?*John*] Elmer, fremason, went to the said tenements and with good deliberacion & diligence enviewed the same and therupon make Reporte to the said Mair and Aldermen in manner and form as hereafter followeth.' They say that the Goldsmiths have encroached between $2\frac{1}{2}$ and 4 in. and that 'the Sarysens Hed' bears the water of the Goldsmiths' new building on the W. The Goldsmiths and their successors shall allow the Custos and his successors and their tenants to have all such lights as they have or have had without interruption or stopping by the Goldsmiths or their successors forever and the Goldsmiths are to pay the Custos and Brethren and their successors yearly for the ground they have encroached and for a lead gutter they have made and laid on 'the Sarasynes Hede' until such time as the Custos edifies or builds on 'the Sarysens Hed'; then they are to lay their plates upon half the wall and hold it forever as their own grounds.[2]

> 1. The dating is approximate, based on the dates of entries before and after this one and on the note, not contained within the entry itself, that George Monoux was mayor of London at the time. Monoux was mayor from November 1513 to November 1514.

2. There is no statement that the City viewers were involved. Waterhouse was not sworn viewer at the time of the view; John Elmer, or Hilmer, was, but it is unclea whether he was acting in that capacity.

418. [Letter Book O, f. 202] 27 October 1530.

Theffect and tenure of thawarde of us, Thomas [*sic*] Hylmer, fremason Phillip Cosyn, carpenter, Thomas Newell, fremason, and Stephyn Pon cheon, carpenter, co[*mm*]en viewers of the Citie of London & arbitrator indifferently electe and chosen betwene M[*aster*] Richard Pace, Deane o the Cathedral Churche of Seint Paule of London on the oon partie anc Maister Christofer Ascue, Alderman of the said Citie, on the other partie by us made, yeven, and awarded for the fynall determynation anc pacyfieng of certeyn varyances dependyng betwene the said perties concernyng the buyldyng of a tenement of late newelye made by the saide M[*aster*] Askue in the parish of Seint John the Evangelist in Watlyngstre in London.

First where as we have right good knowlege and profe that hertofore the hath bene a cestern for withdraughts the whiche dyd serve aswell to the house of the said Deane and Chapitre now in the tenure of Ric Dobbes Skynner, in the said parishe of Seinte John the Evangelist As also to the house whiche the saide Maister Askue holdeth there of the same Deane and Chapitre, the whiche Cesterne and withdraught the said M[*aster*] Askue by reason of his buyldyng ther hath dampned up and also hath taken downe the waies to the same out of the house of the said Dobbys. And other Rowmes of Easment of the same house. Wherefore we awarde ordeyne and deme by these presents that the said Maister Askue at his propre Costes and charges shall in as short tyme as convenyently may bee done, cause to be made in this his newe house ther now in buylding a newe Cesterne with a vawte of Bryke or Stone in depeness viii foote of assise and in wydness from the North to the South vi foote of assise and in length from the Easte to the Weste x foote of assise or more, Soo that ther maye & shalbe two towells of Breke aryse from the same vawte where the plate of the saide newe frame now lieth to serve to the house of the saide Dobbys. And also that ther shalbe a Bryck walle made there arysing from the said vawte with the said Towells up to the friste [*sic*] flowre of the said newe house. The whiche walle the said Master Askue shall suffre to be made a breek of length within the Easte syde of the plate of the saide newe house. And the same Breyke wall and Towells shalbe made at the equalle charges of bothe the saide parties to the lenght of the said first flowre. And from thens upwardes the saide Towells to be made at the Charges of the said Deane and Chapitre. And that the saide M[*aster*] Askue shall also permytte and suffer asmoche tymber of the saide new frame to be cutt as shalbe nedefull and Requysite for the Roomes & goyng upp of the said Towells. Also we awarde and Iudge that the saide Cesterne and vawte shalbe clensed alwaies when nede shalbe through the said howse of Dobbys. Also we awarde Iuge & ordeyn that the saide Master Askue shall Reyse sett upp and fynyshe his saide newe house after such proporcion in length bredeth and height as it is nowe redy framed withoute any lett interupcion or contradicion of the saide Dean and Chapitre or of theyr Successoures or assignes at eny tyme. Also we awarde ordeyne & deme that the said Master Ascue shall Reserve & make an entre at the West syde of his said newe house upon the ii[de] floore of the same house when yt is borded & shall make a particion and walk from the same floore up to his garet flore in theste syde of the same entre the whiche entre shalbe in wydnes within the said newe frame fowre foote of assise and in lenght from the South end thereof stretching northward xx[ti] foote of assise, the which entre soo to be made shalbe appraprysed [*sic*] & appurtenant to the said house of Dobbys alwaies hereafter as parcell of the same house. Also we awarde adiuge and ordeyne that the said parties shall paye and bere equally betwexte theym all the charges concernyng the makyng devysynge and writtyng up of this our present awarde. In witness whereof we the saide Arbitratours to either syde of this our awarde Indented have putt our Seales. Yeven the xxvii day of October the xxii[th] yere of the Reigne of Kyng Henry the viii[th].

419. [Journal 14, f. 200] 22 April 1540.[1]
To the Right honorable lorde the Mayer of the Cytie of london and to his worshipfull brethern the Aldermen of the same
Shewen unto your good Lordeship & discrete wysdomes the xxii[th] daye of Aprill in the xxxi[th] yere of the Reign of our soveraign lorde Kyng Henry the eight John Hylmer, William Walker, John Kyng, and Henry Pesemede, the iiii maisters of fremasons & Carpenters, viewers indifferent sworne to the said Cytie, That where as they were late charged by your honorable commaundement to viewe and oversee a new foundacion of brykwork late bygon and made by one Cristofer Campyon, mercer, on the Est syde of the high waye nygh unto Seynt Mary Spyttell without Bisshoppesgate of London, The whiche foundacion the said iiii viewers by all their discrecyons have viewed and seen. And therupon they say that the said foundacion is encroched and sett into the comon grounde of the said high way withoute the olde stone wall that closed in the grounde there belongyng to the said Spyttell at the south ende of the said brykwork xvii fote of assise and at the North ende of the same xvi foote et di. of assise. And the said brykwork is in lenght all redy at this present daye North and south xxxv foote of assise. And it is purposed to be buylded and made of more lenght than it is yet. The whiche foundacion & brykwork by all the lenght and bredeth therof aforsaid the said iiii viewers saye that it standeth upon the common grounde of the kynges hygh wey and oweth not of right to be suffered without ther can be any other evydence showed to the contrarye.
Margin: 26 July a[nn]° 32 Henr[ici] 8 billa original' inde deliberat[a] fuit Georgio Medley Camerari[o] civit[atis] London in plena Cur[ia] in presenc[ia] W Pykering et W Dummer, clericorum et alii.

1. Pickering and Dummer were clerks of the Mayor's Court at the time. This appears to be one of the rare extant examples of a 'public' view; that is, there is no private plaintiff and the view was made on behalf of the City itself. A later (1546) dispute of Christopher Campyon, or Campion, evidently about property at the same location, is set out above at **199**.

LIVERY COMPANY RECORDS: THE DRAPERS AND THE MERCERS

Copies of two certificates in the Corporation of London Records Office collection (158–9) are bound into the Drapers' Company's first surviving minutes and records book, at Drapers' Hall. For the period covered by this volume, the Mercers' Company records contain copies of three known certificates (87, 117, 221), three more not found elsewhere (420, 422–3), and one which is related to but not an exact copy of a certificate in the CLRO collection (421; see 116). There are copies of certificates from the reign of Elizabeth, for which the Corporation of London has no originals, in the Mercers' Company Register of Writings, vol. II, ff. 196v, 198–199v, 200v–201 and the Register of Benefactors' Wills, vol. I, ff. cxx v, cxxi v. The Mercers' Company records are at Mercers' Hall.

420. [Mercers' Company Book of Ordinances, f. 221] 1500.
To the right honourabull Lorde the Maior and Aldremen of the Citie of London
Shewen unto your good Lordeship and Wysdomes Thomas Wade, John Burton, Robert Crosby, and Thomas Maunsey, the iiii maisters of Masons and Carpenters sworne unto the said Citie that where they late were charged by your honorable commaundement to oversee a noyance of a comon sewer beyng in the kyngs highway in the parish of Seynt Buttolphes without Byshoppesgate of London Now beyng in varyaunce betwene the Maister, Wardens and Feliship of the Craft or Mistier of the Mercers in the Citie of London and the Priour and covent of the hospitall of Our Lady Saynt Mary Virgine called Saynt Mary Spetyll withoute by Bisshopesgate of London aforenamed, Which noyance the same iiii maisters have seen, serched, and examyned by all their dyscressions, And thereupon they say that they fynd by the sight and due serche made of the olde arches and sluses ther nowe being that the said common sewer oweth to have his course estward into a comon lane ther called Barward Lane. Onlesse they ther can be shewed any other Evydence or specialtie unto the contrary. Sir John Sha thanne being Mayre. Anno xv c.[1]
Endorsed: Sir John Shaa . . . his testibus . . . et inherer . . . erth

> 1. Because this certificate, copied into one of the blank pages at the back of the Book of Ordinances, shows both the mayor's name and the names of the viewers, it is useful in dating 1 above, itself undated.

421. [Mercers' Company Register of Benefactors' Wills, vol. I, f. cxvii] 13 March 1536.
John Hylmer, Philip Cosyn, Thomas Newell, and William Walker, viewers.

Parish of St. Mary Colechurch. No variance stated. The view is a party view of ground and buildings belonging to the Master, Wardens, and Fellowship of the Mercers, made by assent, consent and agreement of the Mercers and the Master of St. Thomas of Acon. The viewers say that the chapel and new building of the Mercers in Westcheap is 32 ft. in wideness in the E end against 'the Myter' and 60 ft. in length from E to W. There the ground is 26 ft. 8 in. in wideness between the street and the SW corner of the church of St. Thomas. Stretching more W 39 ft. 10½ in. along Westcheap to the SW quoin and corner of the new building and from there more N 26 ft. 8 in., the ground is 40 ft. in wideness between the W end of the church and the E side of a tenement belonging to the Prior of Elsing. Stretching more N 62 ft., the ground is 40 ft. 2 in. in wideness between the NW quoin and corner of the church and a tenement of the Master of St. Thomas on the W. Stretching more northward 27 ft. 7 in. to the S side of a house of the Master of St. Thomas, now in tenure of Henry Fitzherbert, the ground belonging to the Mercers is 46 ft. 4½ in. in wideness between a tenement belonging to the Master of St. Thomas on the W and the NW corner post of a little house of the Master on the E. Stretching southward from that corner post of the little house, along the W side of the same house and the W end of a little chapel there 27 ft. to the NW corner of the church, there the ground is 45 ft. 6 in. in wideness between the W end of the chapel on the E and the tenement of the Master of St. Thomas on the W. And the ground of the Mercers is 25 ft. in breadth between a SE corner post of the house in tenure of Fitzherbert and the great tenement of the Master of St. Thomas now in tenure of Nicholas Wythers on the N. And from the NE corner post of Fitzherbert's house stretching eastward by the S side of Wythers' house to the W end of a stone wall bearing another house of the Master of St. Thomas, [it is] 40 ft. 4 in. in size. From the SE corner post of Wythers' tenement stretching southward to the N side of the little house of the Master of St. Thomas, the Mercers' ground is 25 ft. 4 in. in wideness. From the SW corner post of the stone wall of the Master on the E stretching westward to a SE principal post of Fitzherbert's house, the ground is 42 ft. 4 in. in length on its S side. Also, there is an entry coming out of Ironmonger Lane into the Mercers' ground, which is 6 ft. 4 in. in wideness at the E end and 6 ft. 2 in. in wideness at the W; it is 34 ft. 9 in. in length. All the ground belongs to the Mercers line right and plumb from place to place as limited, except the buttresses of the church as they now stand and the lights of the church always reserved as they now are. Without *etc.*

Heading at top of folio: Irr' in Rotuli Memorand' tempore Joh[ann]is Aleyn militis, maioris Civitatis London secunda vice anno RR Henrici Octavi xxvii quiquidem Rotuli sunt Annex' Rotuli memorand' Temporibus Joh[ann]is Rudston, Rad[ulf]i Dodmer, Thome Pergettor, Nich[ol]i Lambert, Steph[an]i Peco, Christoferi Ascue, Joh[ann]is Champeneys etc.

Margin: A view of ten[eme]nts & buyldyngs in West Chepe betwene the M[aste]r of St. Thomas of Acon & the Company of the Mercers for the Chappel benethe the buildings.

422. [Mercers' Company Register of Writings, vol. II, f. 197] 9 May 1558. John Russell, Thomas Pecock, Walter Cowper, and John Humfrey viewers.

Parishes of St. Peter and St. Michael in Cornhill. No variance stated. The wardens have been charged to view and oversee certain grounds and buildings between the Mercers and Sir Andrew Judd, knight and Alderman, so that they should by their discretions 'butte, bounde and measure' certain tenements belonging to the Mercers. The viewers say that the tenements are set, lying, butted and bounded as follows: From a brick wall of a house called 'the Helmet' at the NW corner of the ground of the Mercers stretching S 29 ft. 3 in. to an angle and NW corner post of a house of Judd; the angle there contains 15 ft. 6 in. in breadth E and W. From the N end of the angle and corner post stretching 55 ft. further S to a brick wall belonging to the parish church of St. Michael in Cornhill. From a brick wall belonging to St. Michael's on the W to the king's street called Gracechurch Street (Gracyoustrete) on the E. The ground and tenements of the Mercers contain 89 ft. 8 in. along the street, N and S. Further, Judd ought of right to have his lights and ground for his eaves' dropping according to an indenture of bargain and sale made to him before the Mercers had any interest in their ground. And Judd or his tenants ought not of right to annoy the Mercers or their tenants with laying of dung there. Except *etc.*

Margin: The vewe of the greate place in Saint Antonines parish which Mr. William Dauntsey, Alderman, dwelled and the ten[*emen*]ts within and on eyther seyde of the utter grate gate there. And also of the ten[*emen*]ts in gracious strete also.

423. [Mercers' Company Register of Writings, vol. II, f. 197v] 9 May 1558. John Russell, Thomas Peacocke, Walter Cowper, and John Humfrey, viewers.

Parishes of St. Antony and St. Thomas the Apostle. Variances between the Mercers, pls., and Thomas Lambart, citizen and mercer. The viewers have viewed, searched, seen, and measured and they say that the tenements of pls. contain 79 ft. 9 in. E to W along the street called Budge Row. There is a broad gate in the street, with two leaves leading into the house of def. within the same gate. Pls.' tenants ought at all times to have free ingress and egress through the utter gate without interruption of def. or his assigns. Pls. ought of right to maintain and uphold the gate as often as need requires and to pave the ground within it. Def. ought of right to have a key to pass in and out of the gate at his pleasure when it chances to be shut. Both parties ought of right to have all their lights, water courses, privies, rooms, and other commodities as they were held and occupied, upward and downward, at the time of the death of William Dauntesey, late citizen and Alderman. Finally, pls. have certain other tenements in the street called Turnebase Lane which contain 76 ft. E and W along the lane. Except *etc.*

Margin: A vewe of ten[*emen*]ts in St Athoines parish

GLOSSARY

Binding joist. A joist carrying other joists.
Brases. Braces, usually timber.
Cabin. A small room, a bedroom.
Campshed, campshide. Campshot: the facing of the bank of a river with planks.
Causey, cawsey. Causeway: a paved area, the paving of a street.
Coyne, *see* quoin.
Defence. A fence.
Dog(g). A clamp, a device for holding two things together.
Dormant, dormaund. Fixed or stationary; ?dormer.
Draught house. A privy.
Entertise, enterteyse. A horizontal beam which acts as a connection between two upright ones.
Fillet gutter. A sloping gutter with a raised rim.
Fled (out). Fluctuating, wavering.
Foreign, foreyn. Short for foreign chamber, a privy.
Frame. The wooden structure of a building, composed of various beams etc. fitted together.
Gable end. The upper end of the wall at each end of a pitched roof.
Garner, garnar. A storehouse for grain.
Groundsill. The timber foundation for a building, usually a wooden building; the lowest horizontal beam in the plate.
Headland. A boundary.
Implements. Equipment, as household equipment.
Jakes. A privy.
Jetty (jetie). An overhanging upper storey.
Kennel. The gutter of a street.
Kytt. Obsolete past tense of the verb *to cut*.
Latten, laten. A yellow metal; an alloy of base metals.
Lattener, latener. A worker in latten; ?a brassworker.
Loupe (lowpe) lights, loop lights. Long, narrow windows, usually widening inward.
Malengin, malengyne. Fraud, malice.
Marstones. Moorstones, pieces of a kind of granite.
Met. Obsolete past tense of the verb *to mete*; measured.
Pale. A stake, a stake fence.
Paper wall. ?A thin or insubstantial wall.
Pentice, penthouse. A lean-to building; sometimes an elevated passage.
Plate(s). A timber used longitudinally at the top or bottom of a frame.
Plat, platt. A plot (of ground).
Principal post. A main post or corner post in a wood frame.

163

Putgally, putgaley.   A device for lifting water from a well.

Quarter(s) (timber).   A timber, usually 4"x4", used in building as an upright in a wall.

Quoin, quoyne, coyne.   The dressed corner stones of a building.

Rasen, raisen, resyn, etc.   The timber laid on top of a stone wall, to which roof rafters are nailed.

Release, relees or relief.   Often used to mean the residue or remainder of a thing; a projection; more technically, the distance between the top of a parapet and the bottom of the ditch beside it.

Siege, sege.   A privy.

Skew (of a buttress).   Angle, or a line of coping, or a gutter-slate.

Solar.   An upstairs room, often used as a bedroom.

Somer, summer.   A horizontal bearing beam supporting the joists of a floor.

Spurs.   Struts, placed diagonally against an upright to support it.

Standard.   ?An upright timber, support; ?a large chest (*see* **226**).

Tewel, tonell, towell.   A shaft, a privy shaft.

Tresance, tresaunce.   A corridor.

Trestle, trestyll.   A support, a braced framework.

Trunk (window).   A tunnel or shaft made to let in light; here, designed to let in light while cutting the view.

Wainscot.   Panelling of wood, wood panels.

Wareboards.   Boards, often projecting towards the street from a shop, for the purpose of setting out merchandise; part of the fixtures of a shop.

Water table.   A horizontal ledge, along the side of a wall, to keep rain from the base of the wall.

Withdraught.   A privy.

INDEX OF PERSONS AND PLACES

For a note on indexing procedure, see p. lxv.

INDEX OF SUBJECTS

LONDON RECORD SOCIETY

The London Record Society was founded in December 1964 to publish transcripts, abstracts and lists of the primary sources for the history of London, and generally to stimulate interest in archives relating to London. Membership is open to any individual or institution; the annual subscription is £12 ($22) for individuals and £18 ($35) for institutions. Prospective members should apply to the Hon. Secretary, Miss Heather Creaton, c/o Institute of Historical Research, Senate House, London, WC1E 7HU.

The following volumes have already been published:

18. *Parish Fraternity Register: fraternity of the Holy Trinity and SS. Fabian and Sebastian in the parish of St Botolph without Aldersgate,* edited by Patricia Basing (1982)
19. *Trinity House of Deptford: Transactions, 1609–35,* edited by G. G. Harris (1983)
20. *Chamber Accounts of the sixteenth century,* edited by Betty R. Masters (1984)
21. *The Letters of John Paige, London merchant, 1648–58,* edited by George F. Steckley (1984)
22. *A Survey of Documentary Sources for Property Holding in London before the Great Fire,* by Derek Keene and Vanessa Harding (1985)
23. *The Commissions for Building Fifty New Churches,* edited by M. H. Port (1986)
24. *Richard Hutton's Complaints Book,* edited by Timothy V. Hitchcock (1987)
25. *Westminster Abbey Charters, 1066–c.1214,* edited by Emma Mason (1988)
26. *London Viewers and their Certificates, 1508–1558,* edited by Janet S. Loengard (1989)

Most volumes are still in print; apply to Hon. Secretary. Price to individual members £12 ($22) each, to non-members £20 ($38) each.